DRAW ANIMALS

DRAW ANIMALS

Edited by David and Brenda Herbert

Mr. H. Davidson,
Bryley House,
87 Burnmill Road,
MARKET HARBOROUGH,
Leics.
LE16 7JG

ADAM & CHARLES BLACK · LONDON

*Draw Animals** first published 1983
by A & C Black (Publishers) Ltd
35 Bedford Row, London WC1R 4JH

* This volume contains material already
published in
Draw Birds © 1979 David Brown
Draw Cats © 1979 David Brown
Draw Dogs © 1980 Pitman House Ltd.
Draw Farm Animals © 1980 Pitman House Ltd.
Draw Horses © 1980 Pitman House Ltd.

Draw animals.
1. Animal painting and illustration
I. Herbert, David II. Herbert, Brenda
743'.6 NC780

ISBN 0-7136-2379-9
ISBN 0-7136-2372-1 Pbk

ISBN 0-7136-2379-9

ISBN 0-7136-2372-1 Pbk

Printed in Great Britain
by Pitman Press Ltd, Bath

Contents

Introduction

Making a start

Learning to draw is largely a matter of practice and observation—so draw as much and as often as you can, and use your eyes all the time. Drawing teaches you to observe more fully, and observation helps you to draw—so the more you do of both the better.

Carry a sketchbook with you whenever possible, and don't be shy of using it in public. You can draw in trains, cafés, museums, farmyards—in fact anywhere you find yourself.

Good drawings can be done with poor equipment, but it helps enormously if your pencils are a good length and you have a sharpener or knife that works. Try to keep all your equipment in good condition and don't be afraid to use it freely. Experiment with different materials; for example, look for the biggest piece of paper and the boldest, softest piece of chalk or crayon you can find and fill the paper with lines, scribbles, funny faces, lettering—anything to get a feeling of freedom. Get to know your materials; they are yours to do exactly what you like with.

Be self-critical; if a drawing looks wrong, solve the problem or scrap it. A second, third or even fourth attempt will often be better than the first, because you are learning more about your subject all the time. An eraser can be useful but don't rely on it; piecemeal correction won't necessarily help. If a line is right the first time you draw it, leave it alone; heavier re-drawing leads to a dull mechanical look. The time you spend on a drawing is not important; a ten-minute sketch can say more than a painstaking drawing which takes many hours.

You can draw anywhere at any time—there is no need to wait till you can get outside. Look around you: chairs, tables, plants, pets, yourself in a mirror—everything is worth drawing. A lot can be learned from practice and from books but a teacher can be a great help. If you get a chance, don't hesitate to join a class; even one evening a week can do a lot of good.

Drawing animals needs enormous patience because, of course, they seldom stand still. While a beginner, choose those likely to remain at least fairly still: cows in their milking stalls, a cat asleep, a horse grazing.

Draw the basic shape quickly, and if the animal moves be prepared to move with it to keep much the same viewpoint as before.

Since everyone is unique, your approach to drawing will be different from everyone else's, and the results will be your own. You are really your own best critic, and judge, of what is right and wrong for you. Don't be restricted by other people's ideas and don't be afraid to enjoy yourself. If you worry you won't enjoy yourself, and if you aren't having fun you probably won't draw.

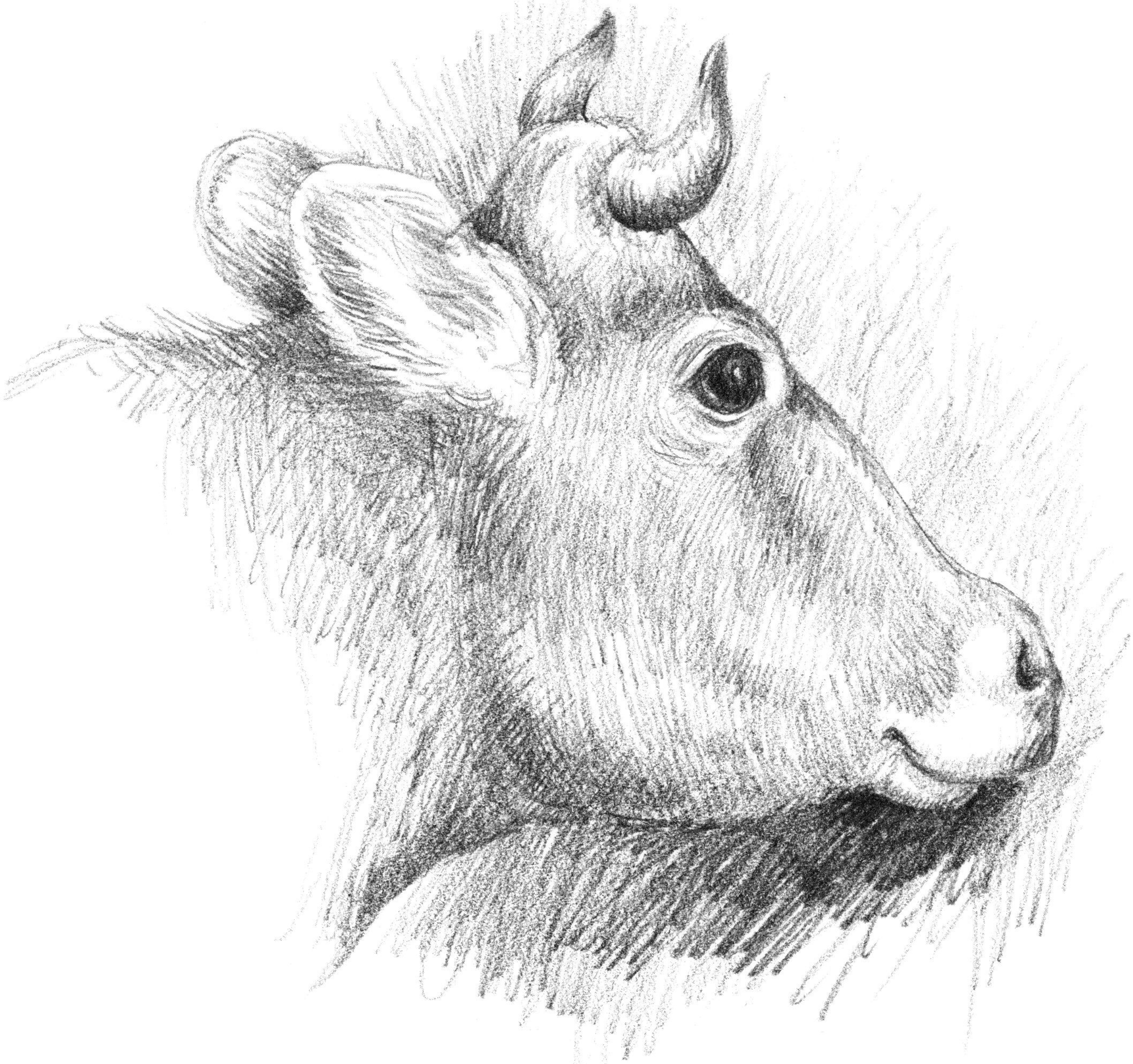

Jenny Holden

What to draw with

Pencils are graded according to hardness, from 6H (the hardest) through 5H, 4H, 3H, 2H to H; then HB; then B, through 1B, 2B, 3B, 4B, 5B up to 6B (the softest). For most purposes, a soft pencil (HB or softer) is best. If you keep it sharp, it will draw as fine a line as a hard pencil but with less pressure, which makes it easier to control.

Charcoal, which is very soft, is by nature useful for bold drawing, but with skill you can achieve a great subtlety with it. Charcoal pencils, such as the Royal Sovereign, are also very useful.

Wax crayons (also soft) are not easily smudged or erased. You can scrape a line away from a drawing on good quality paper, or partly scrape a drawing to get special effects.

Conté crayons, wood-cased or in solid sticks, are available in various degrees of hardness, and in three colours—black, red and white. The cased crayons are easy to sharpen, but the solid sticks are more fun—you can use the side of the stick for large areas of tone. Conté is harder than charcoal, but it is also easy to smudge. The black is very intense.

Pastels are very soft and available in a wide range of colours. Nevertheless many of the best drawings have been done with a very limited number of colours.

Pens vary as much as pencils or crayons. The Gillott 659 is a very popular crowquill pen. Ink has a quality of its own, but of course it cannot be erased. Mapping pens are only suitable for delicate detail and minute cross-hatching.

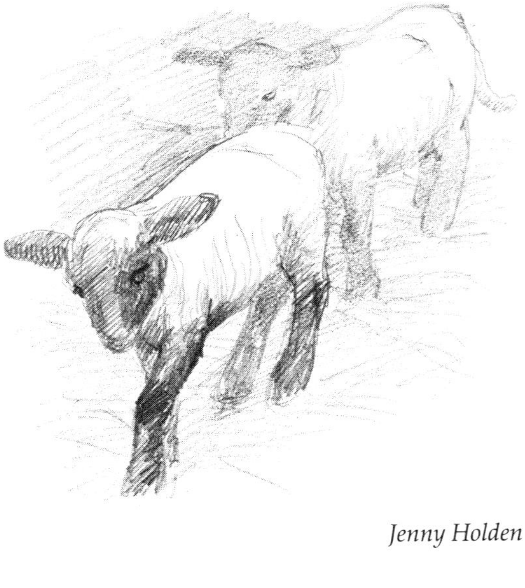

Jenny Holden

Special artists' pens, such as the Gillott 303 or Gillott 404 allow you a more varied line, according to the angle at which you hold them and the pressure you use.

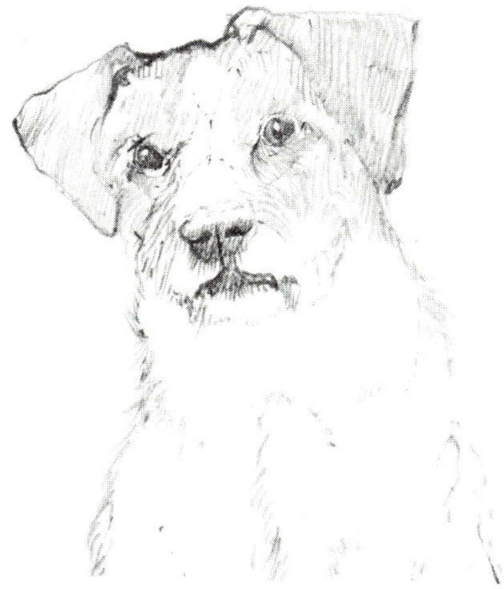

Jeremy Morgan

Reed, bamboo and quill pens are good for bold lines. You can make the nib end narrower or wider with the help of a sharp knife or razor blade. This kind of pen has to be dipped frequently into the ink.

Fountain pens are convenient for sketching, provided they make a fairly even line in any direction. Rapidograph and Rotring pens are not generally desirable. They are really for mechanical drawing.

Inks vary according to the manufacturer. Waterproof Indian ink is generally the most useful. If it is too thick and clogs the pen, water it down with distilled water or boiled water out of the kettle. It is very necessary to use a waterproof ink if you intend to combine line and wash.

Ball point pens make a drawing look a bit mechanical, but they are cheap and fool-proof and useful for quick notes and scribbles.

Fibre pens are only slightly better, and their points tend to wear down quickly.

FRENCH STICK – TIGHTLY ROLLED CARD

Felt pens are useful for quick notes and sketches, but are not good for more elaborate and finished drawings.

Brushes are most versatile drawing instruments and therefore very difficult to use. The Chinese and Japanese until recently have never used anything else, even for writing. The biggest sable brush has a fine point, and the smallest brush laid on its side provides a line broader than the broadest nib. Sables are very expensive but you can find cheaper brushes which are less springy but still good to use.

A wash of watercolour or ink may be used to extend a pen or pencil drawing. It should not be used for effect but to say something about the subject, such as the pattern of colour or the light and shade.

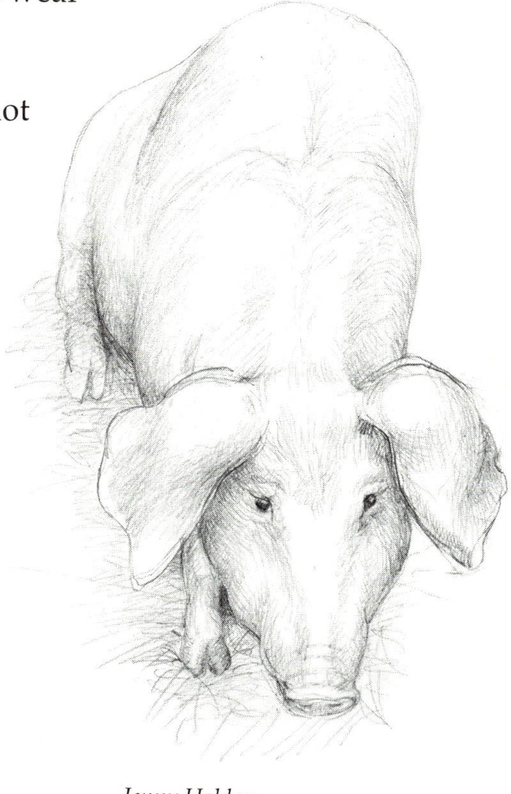

Jenny Holden

What to draw on

Try as many different surfaces as possible.

Ordinary, inexpensive paper is often as good as anything else: for example, brown and buff wrapping paper (Kraft paper) and lining for wallpaper have surfaces which are particularly suitable for charcoal and soft crayons. Some writing and duplicating papers are best for pen drawings. But there are many papers and brands made specially for the artist.

Bristol board is a smooth, hard white board designed for fine pen work.

Ledger Bond paper ('cartridge' in the UK), the most usual drawing paper, is available in a variety of surfaces—smooth, 'NOT surface' (semi-rough), rough.

Watercolour papers also come in various grades of smoothness. They are thick, high-quality papers, expensive but pleasant to use.

Ingres paper is mainly for pastel drawings. It has a soft, furry surface and is made in many light colours—grey, pink, blue, buff, etc.

Sketchbooks, made up from nearly all these papers, are available. Choose one with thin, smooth paper to begin with. Thin paper means more pages, and a smooth surface is best to record detail.

Lay-out pads make useful sketchbooks. Although their covers are not stiff, you can easily insert a stiff piece of card to act as firm backing to your drawing. The paper is semi-transparent, but this can be useful—almost as tracing paper—if you want to make a new, different version of your last drawing.

An improvised sketchbook can be just as good as a bought one—or better. Find two pieces of thick card, sandwich a stack of paper, which may be of different kinds, between them and clip together at either end.

Composition

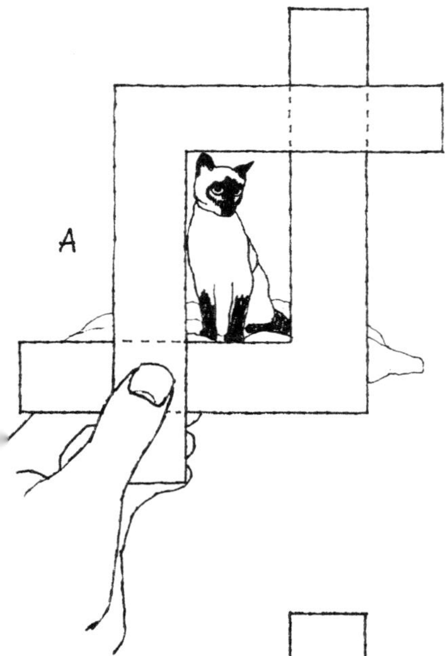

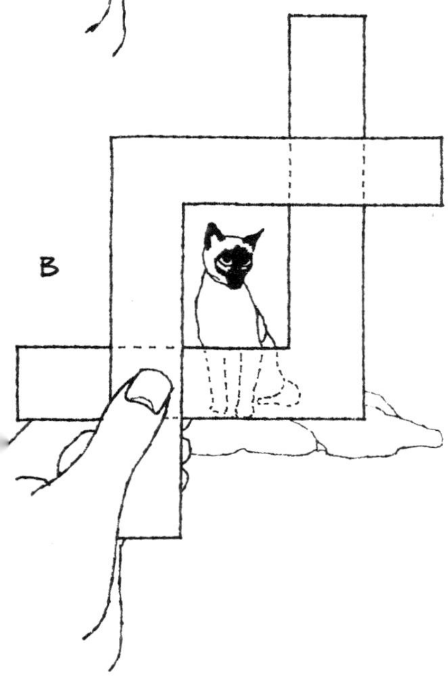

David Brown

This does not only apply to large, finished paintings. Deciding where to place even the smallest sketch or doodle on a scribbling pad involves composition. Your drawing will be greatly affected by its position on the paper.

When you are drawing more than one animal on a sheet of paper, the placing of each one is important. Try as many variations as possible.

Before you begin a drawing, think about how you will place it on the paper—even a few seconds' thought may save you having to start your drawing again. One of the most common mistakes is to start by putting the head in the centre of the paper, regardless of which way the body goes. Never distort your drawing in order to get it all in, or you will wonder why it looks wrong.

Cut out two pieces of card so that they form corners. Hold them up between you and your subject. Position them so that the inside edges touch the furthest points of the animal (A). This will show you the correct proportion of the area taken up by the subject, and will help you to position your drawing on the paper.

Another way to help you compose your drawing is to form the corners into a picture frame (B).

The alternative is to use a large sheet of paper so that you can leave plenty of space around your drawing. The paper can then be trimmed down to produce a pleasing composition.

Before starting an elaborate drawing, do a few very rough sketches of the main shapes to help you decide on the final composition. When you have decided which to use, rule a faint network of lines—diagonal, vertical and horizontal—over this preliminary sketch and on the piece of paper to be used for the finished drawing. (Take care that both pieces are the same proportion.) You will then have a number of reference points to enable you to transfer the composition to the final drawing.

Perspective

You can be an artist without knowing anything about perspective. Five hundred years ago, when some of the great masterpieces of all time were painted, the word did not even exist. But most beginners want to know something about it in order to make their drawings appear three-dimensional rather than flat, so here is a short guide.

The further away an object is, the smaller it looks.

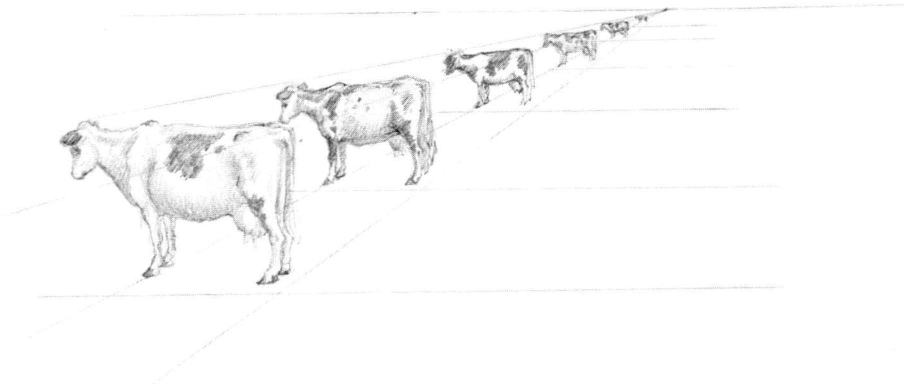

Jenny Holden

All parallel horizontal lines that are directly opposite you, at right-angles to your line of vision, remain parallel.

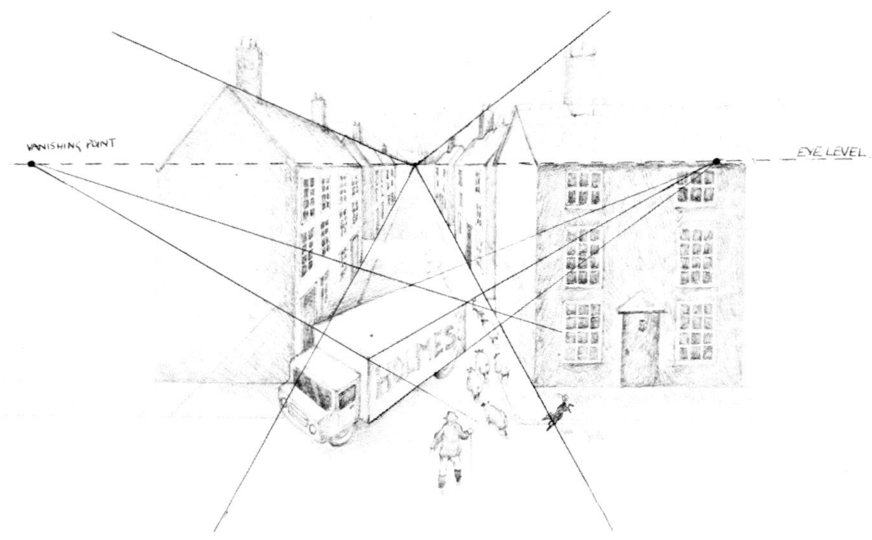

Jenny Holden

All horizontal lines that are in fact parallel but go away from you will appear to converge at eye-level at the same vanishing point on the horizon. Lines that are above your eye-level will seem to run downwards towards the vanishing point; lines that are below your eye-level will run upwards. You can check the angles of these lines against a pencil held horizontally at eye-level.

The larger and closer any object is, the bigger the front of it will seem to be in relation to the part furthest away, or to any other more distant object. Its actual shape will appear foreshortened or distorted.

If the side of an object is facing you, one vanishing point is enough, but if the corner is facing you, two vanishing points will be needed. To understand this fully, practice drawing simple objects such as boxes on a large sheet of paper, allowing yourself room to draw in the vanishing points.

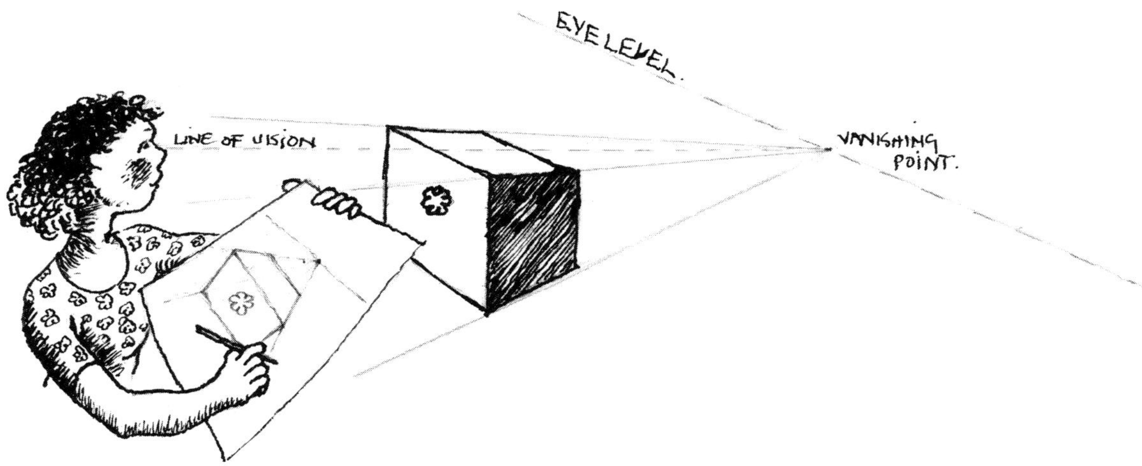

Jenny Holden

If you look at an animal from different angles, you will notice that its shape seems to change, depending on your viewpoint and the animal's position. It is important to draw the shape as it appears rather than as you know it actually is.

Once you have absorbed these basic perspective principles, you can, to all intents and purposes, forget about them. The knowledge you have absorbed will be used subconsciously, and your drawings will not have that over-stiff appearance which can result from adhering to the rules too painstakingly.

Farm Animals

Jenny Holden

Form and proportion

You can learn a lot from looking at a skeleton; if you know where the bones are, you can more readily understand what you see in a living animal.

Below, is the skeleton of a horse. Skeletons of pigs, sheep and cows differ in their proportions; but all these animals have similar bones which fulfil similar functions, and a knowledge of the bones of any one will help you to draw all of them. If possible, have a look at a real skeleton in the countryside or a reconstructed one in a museum, and walk round it to see the bones from every angle. This drawing only provides one viewpoint.

When drawing animals, remember all the time that the layers of skin and muscle in front of you cover a strong structure of bone. Every movement of the bones is reflected in the surface of the body.

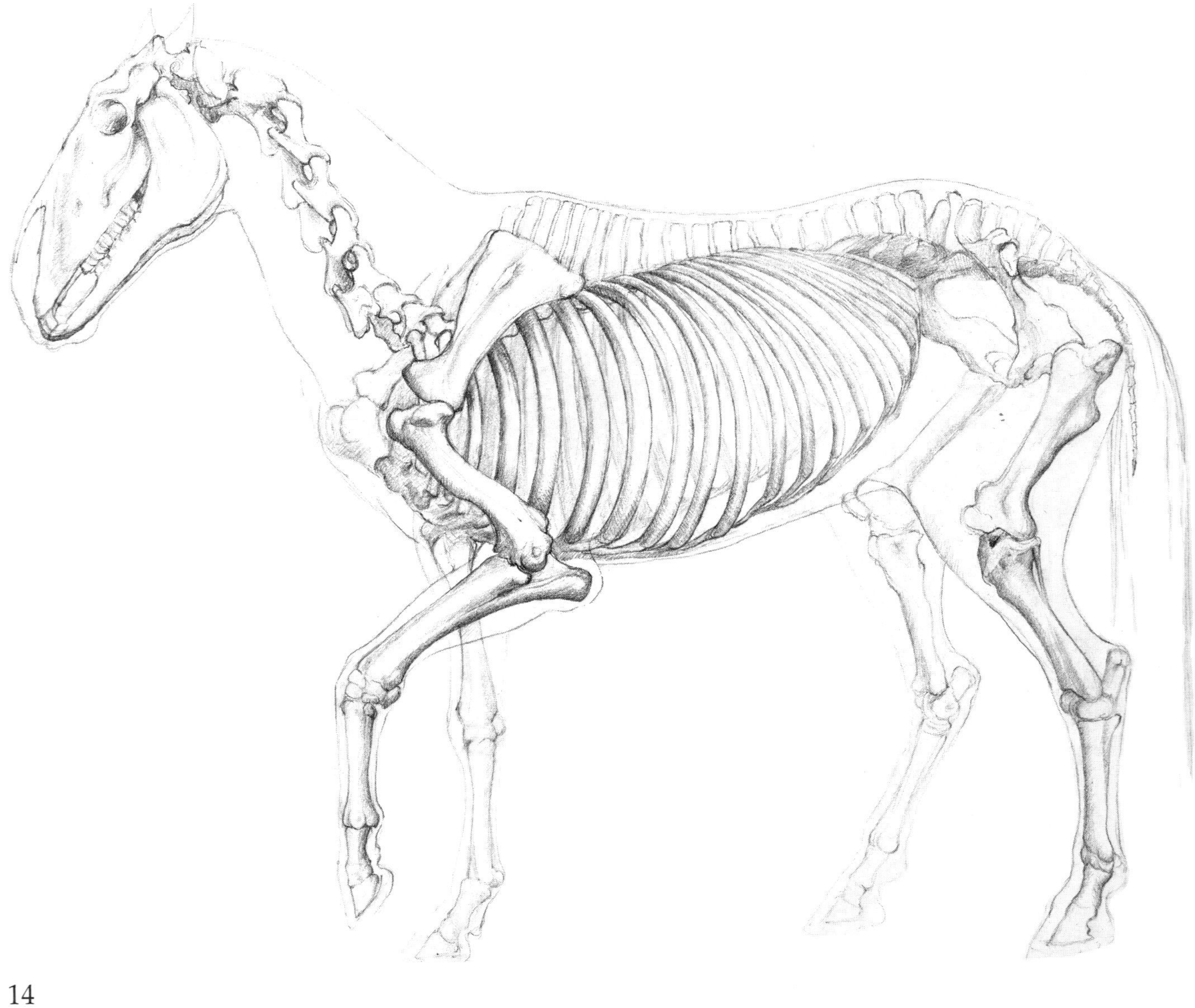

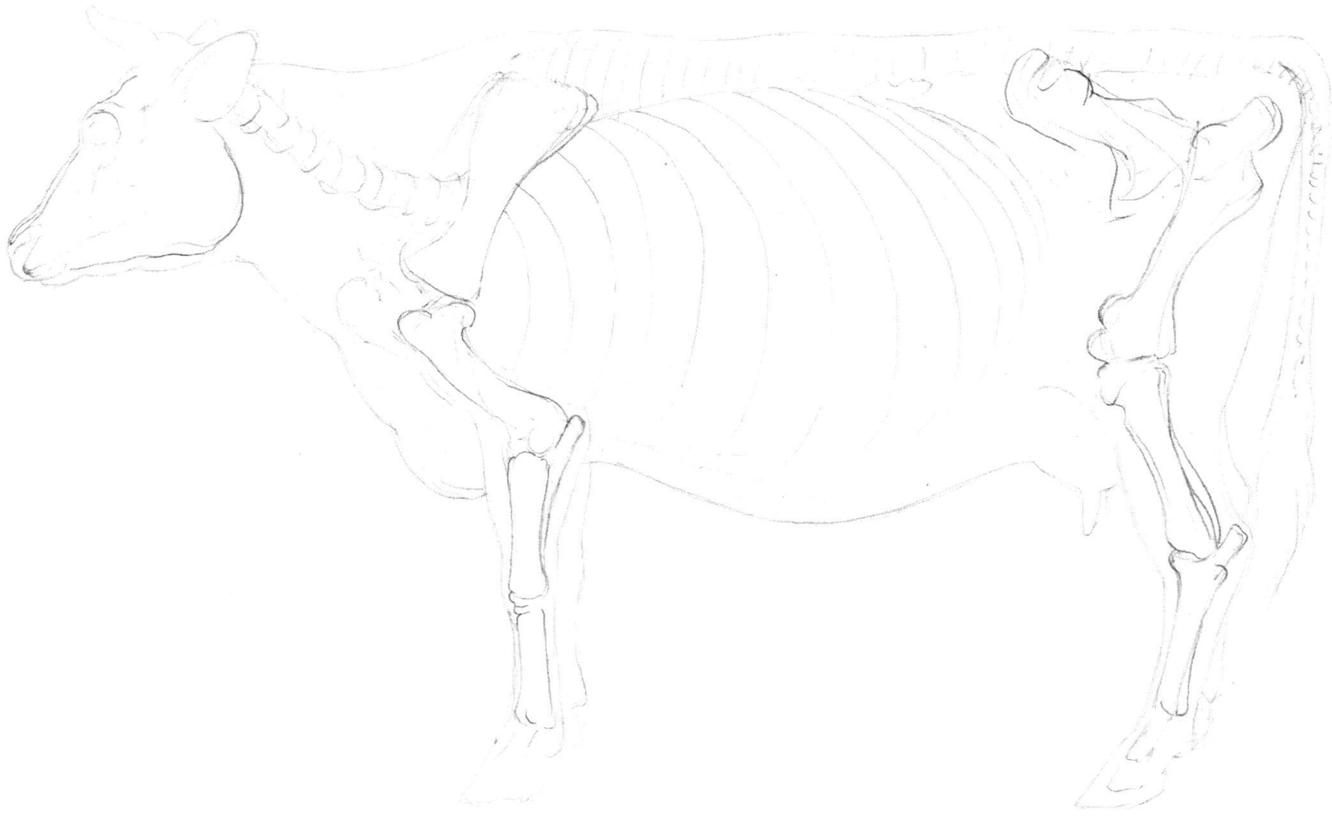

The cow is a particularly good example of this; it is a mass of bumps and bulges made by the muscles and bones under the surface. In the drawing below I have attempted to show all those bumps and bulges, and then to relate them to the position of the bones as demonstrated in the anatomical sketch above.

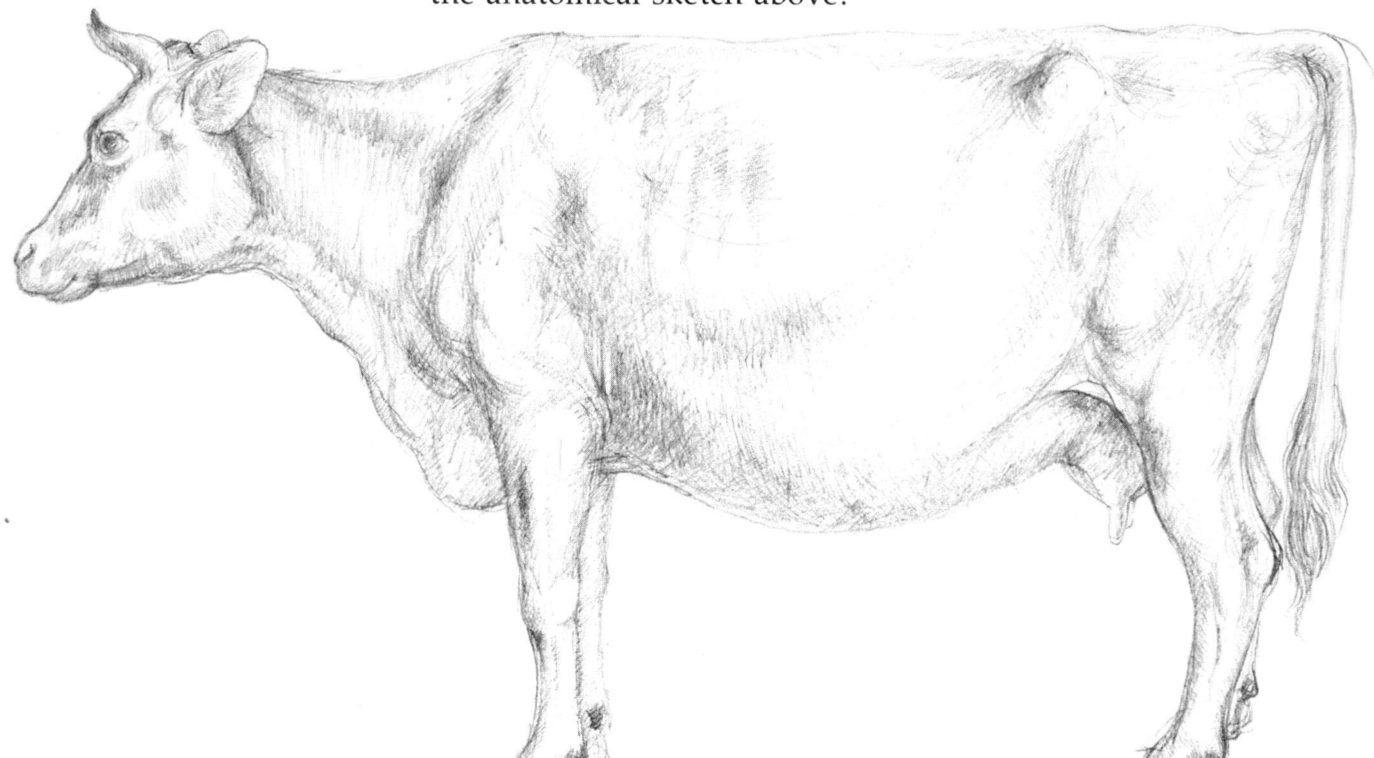

The rules of perspective outlined on pages 12–13 are not absolute, but they can help to clarify a complicated subject. By obeying these rules in a drawing, it is relatively easy to make the subject look like reality as we think we see it. However, there is no reason why you should choose to obey them rather than to follow your own instincts. I find perspective a useful notion to have at the back of my mind; it can be applied to animals as well as to objects made up of straight lines such as boxes, and may be helpful when dealing with problems such as foreshortening.

When an animal is facing you its shape will be foreshortened; and it will be more foreshortened if it is close to you. So the more you exaggerate the distortion, the closer the subject will appear to be. When you are trying to draw a foreshortened object—a head for example—you will be tempted to draw it as you know it best, rather than as it appears now in front of you—perhaps at a slightly unfamiliar angle. To help you resist this temptation and to get the proportions right, try holding a pencil at arm's length in front of the subject and measuring the distances between different features with your thumb.

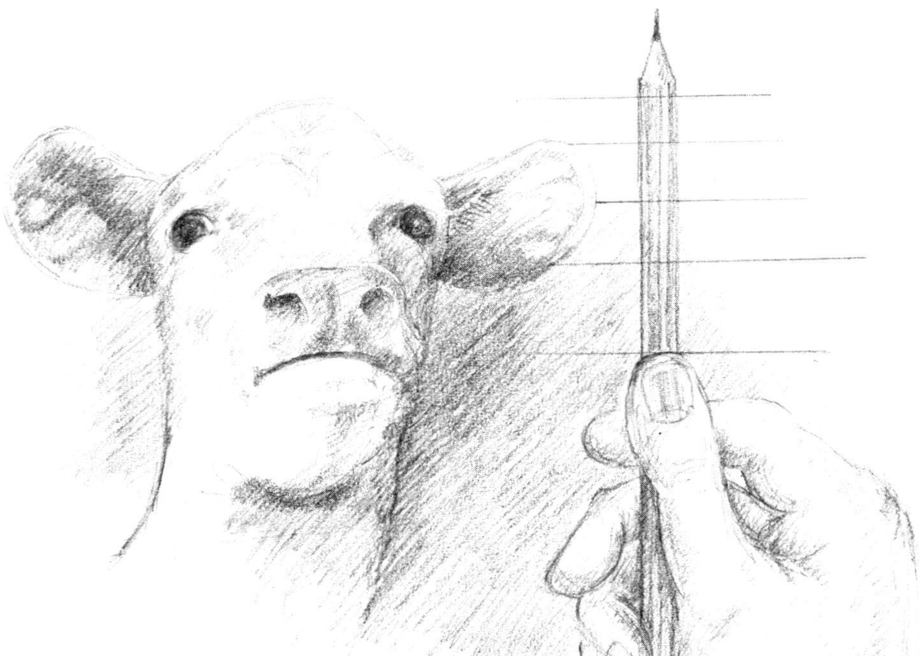

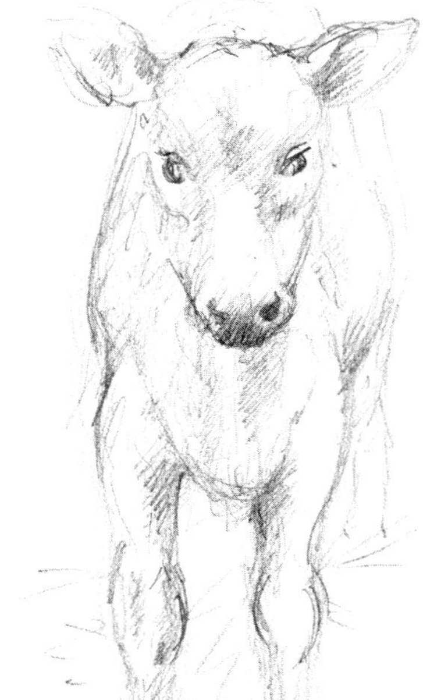

If your subject is moving around, this is not a very practical thing to do: in that case you can only rely on your eye to assess the distances between features. I make most of my assessments by eye.

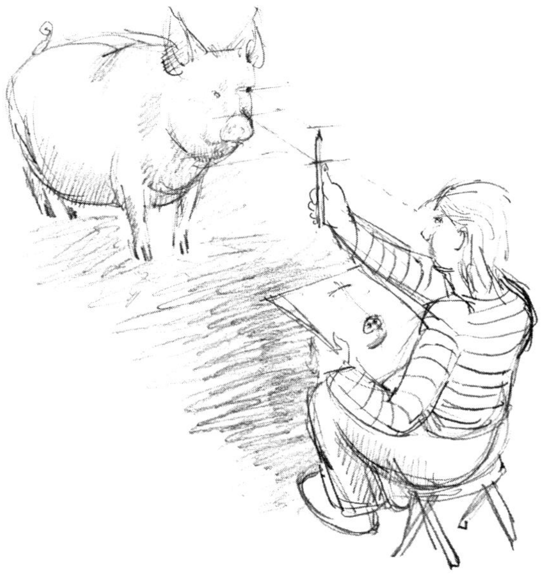

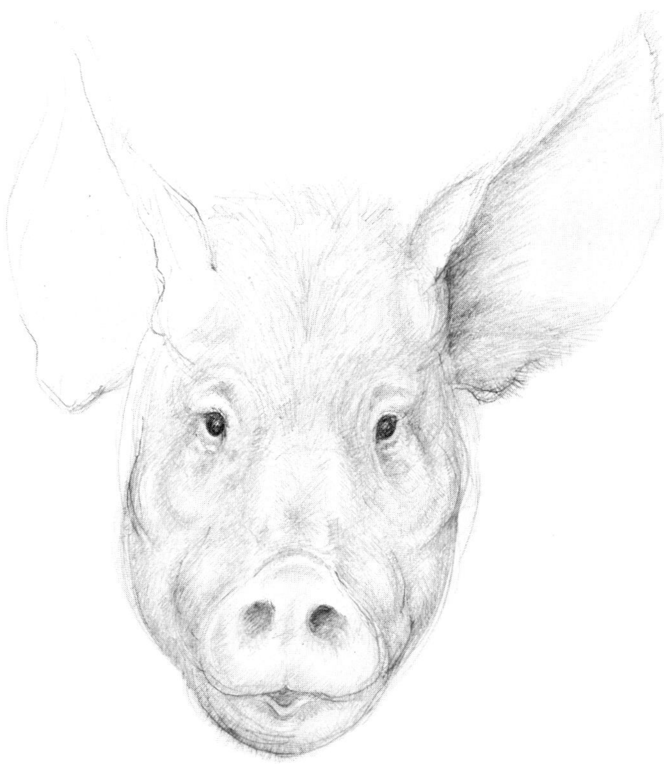

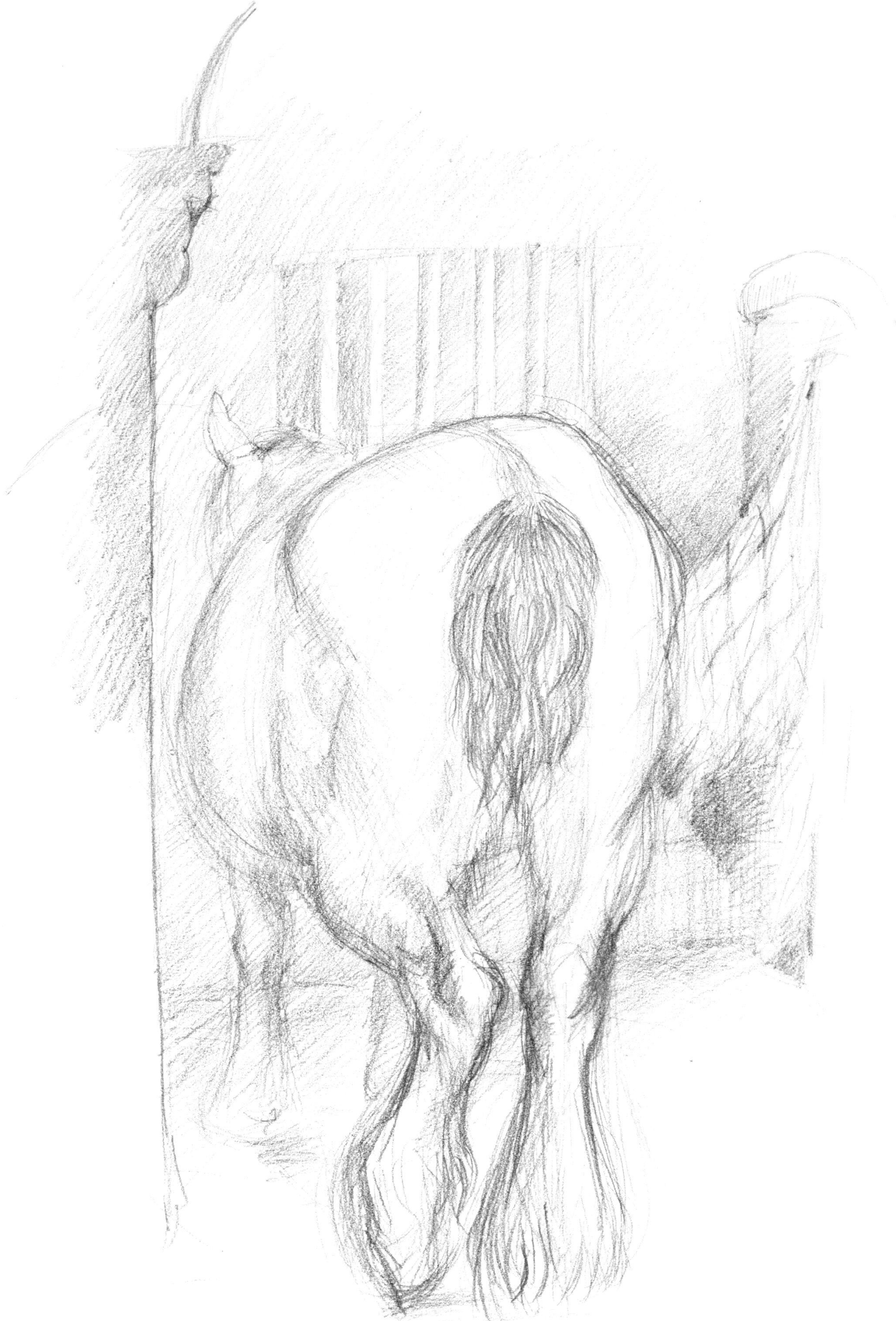

The relationship between the members of a group is just as important as the proportions of each individual. Try to draw the group as a whole before you get down to the details of any one animal.

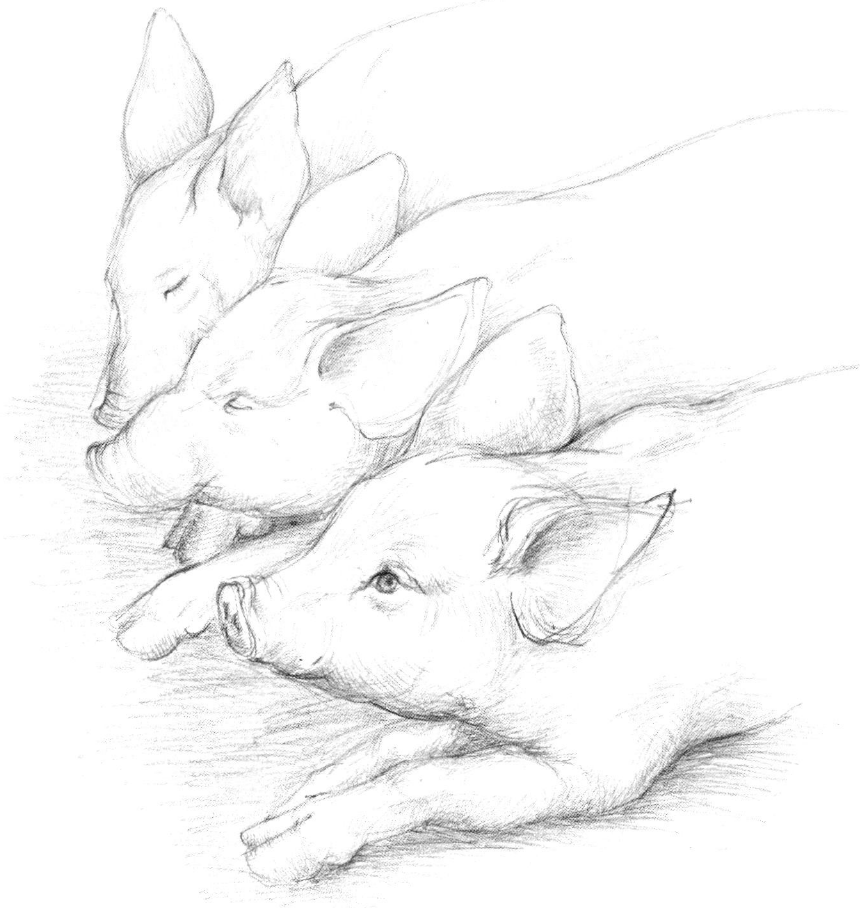

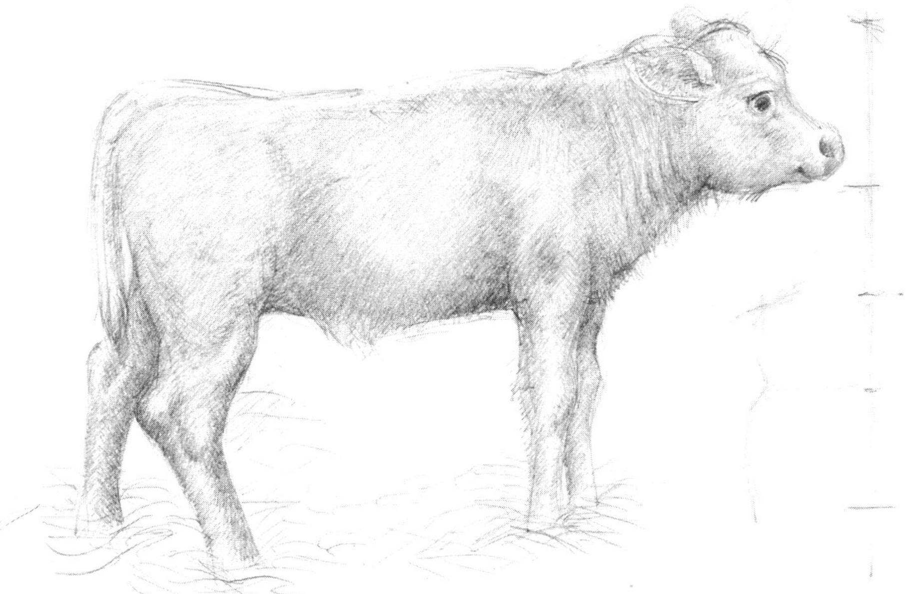

Composition

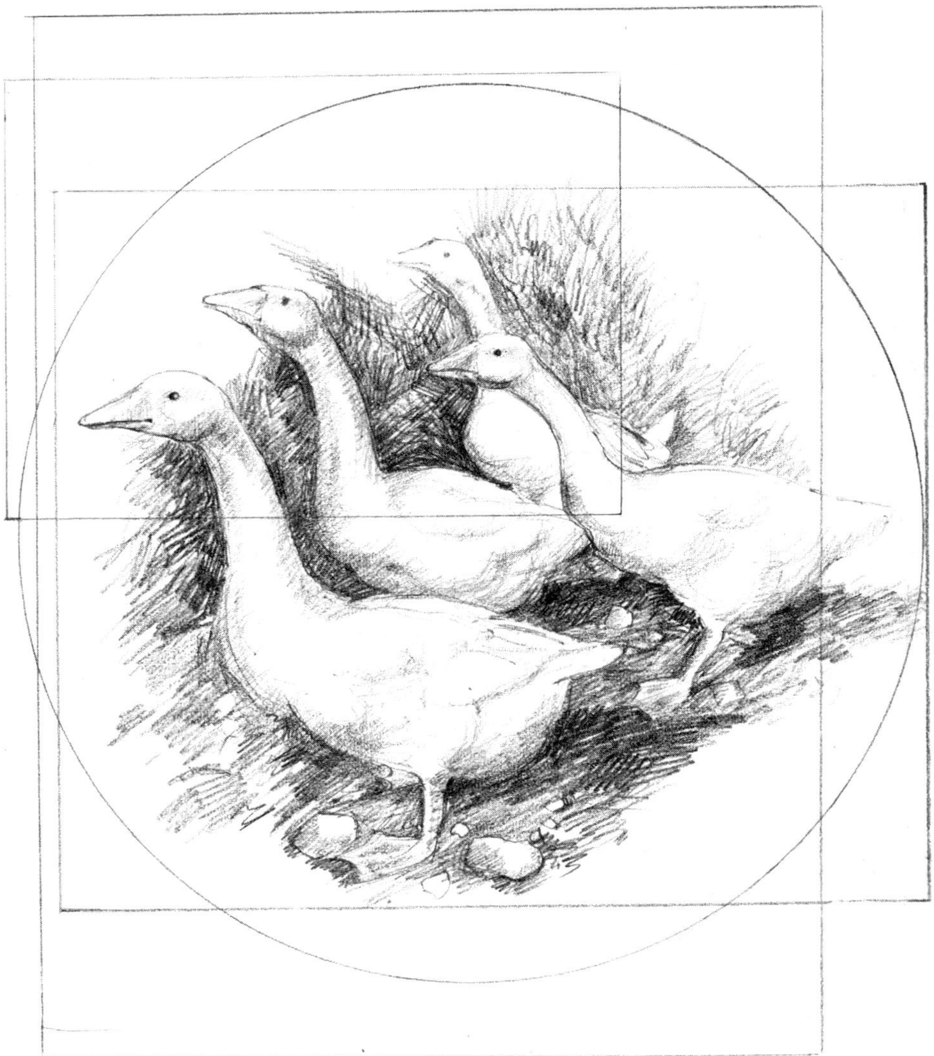

The sketches on these two pages illustrate the general advice on composition given more fully in the introduction to this book on page 11.

Where you place a drawing on the page, and how you arrange the elements in it, are very important to its success. Some of the questions to consider are: whether to include the whole of the subject in the drawing; whether to fill the whole of the paper with it, or only part; whether to place the drawing at top, bottom, or centre of the paper.

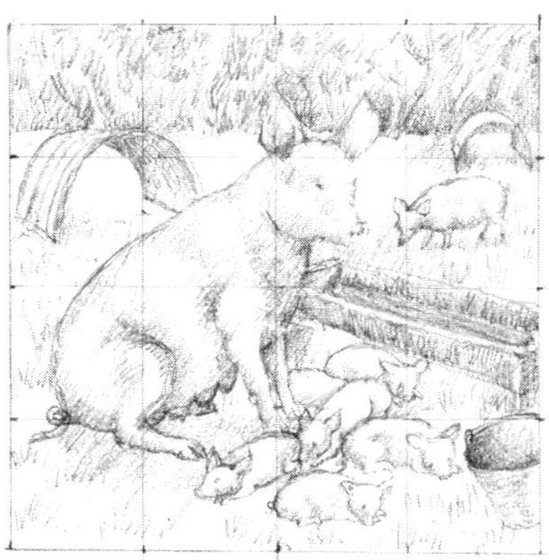

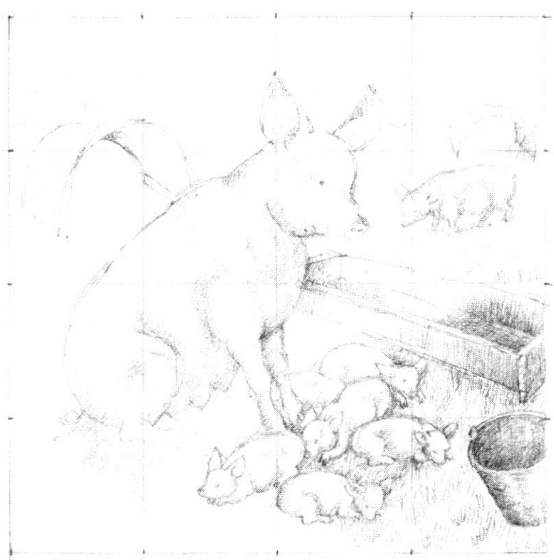

Once you have worked out a composition in a small preliminary sketch, take the trouble to scale it up accurately. Choose, for your finished drawing, a piece of paper with the same proportions as your sketch, but larger, and follow the suggestions given in the last paragraph of page 11, as illustrated here.

In general, the smaller the subject is in relation to its surroundings the further away it will appear to be. The drawing can vary from an overall view to an eye-to-eye confrontation, according to where the main subject is placed on the page and how much space there is round it.

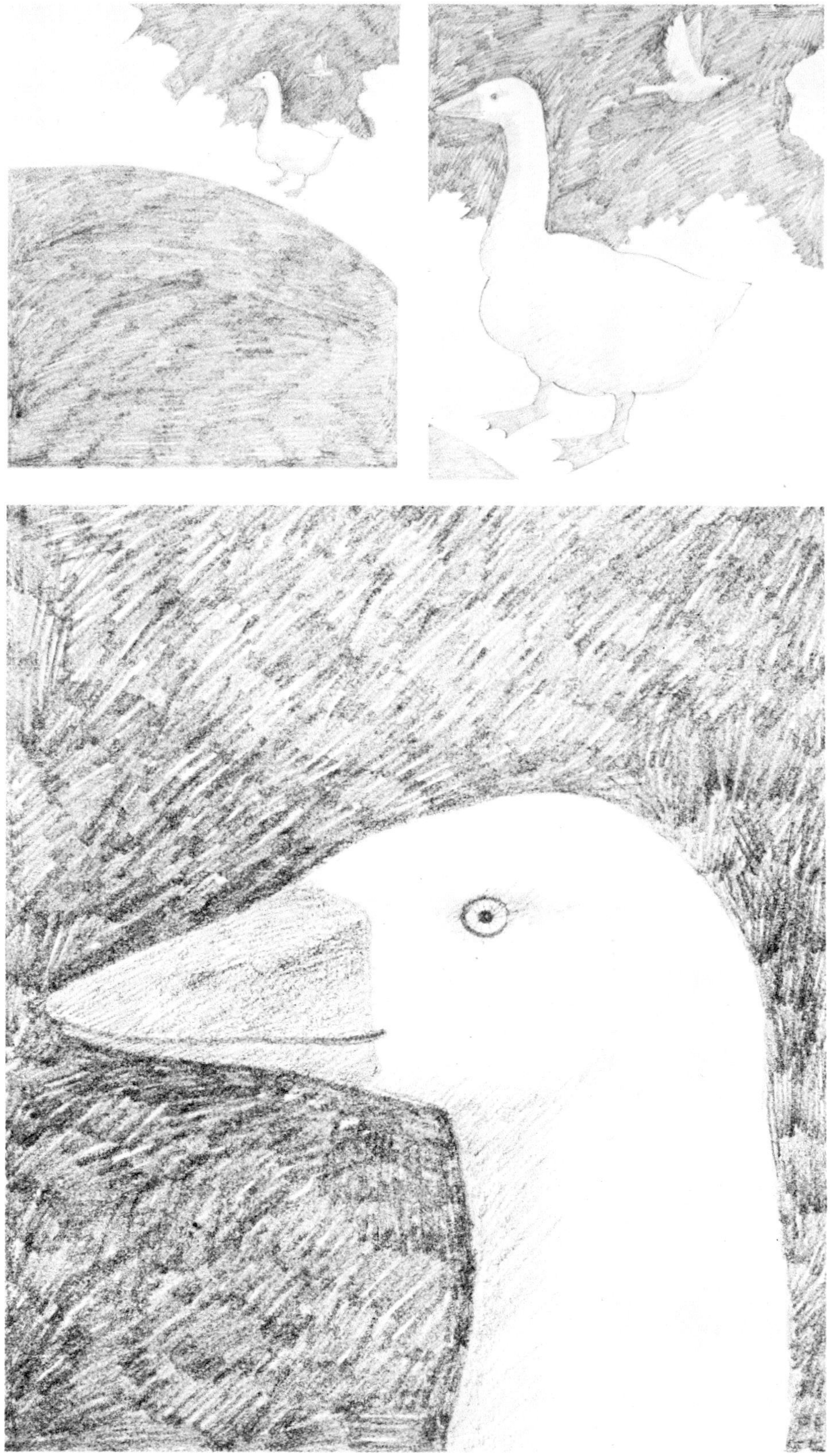

Tone and space

A pencil is a very versatile instrument, which will produce totally different results in different people's hands. The picture on the right is an experimental drawing which shows some of the techniques I use to build up texture and shape. The little drawings below illustrate a number of different effects that one 3B pencil can produce.

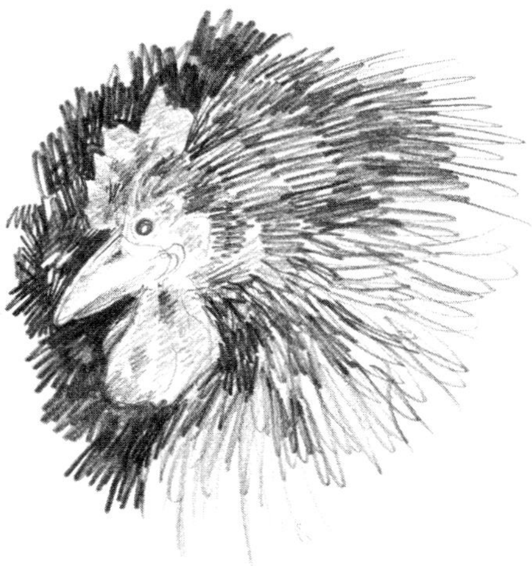

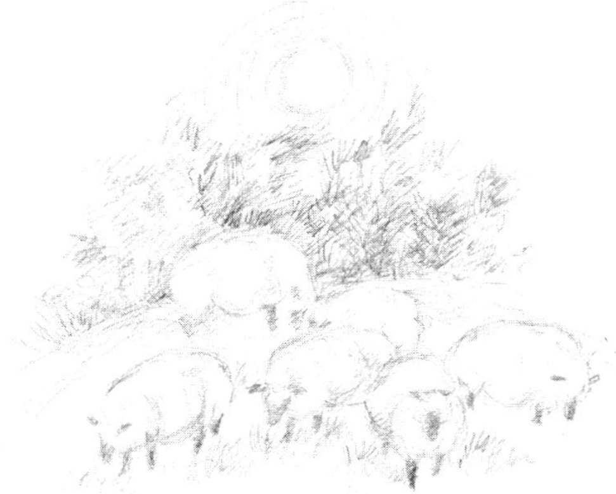

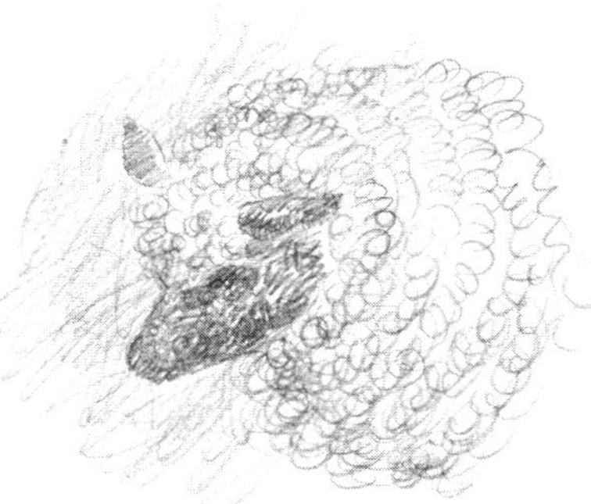

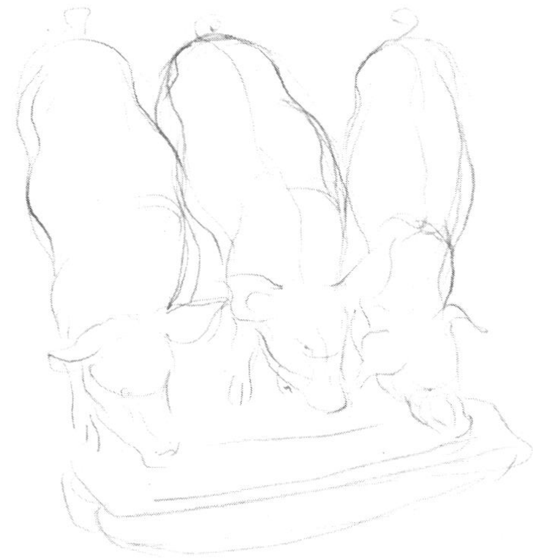

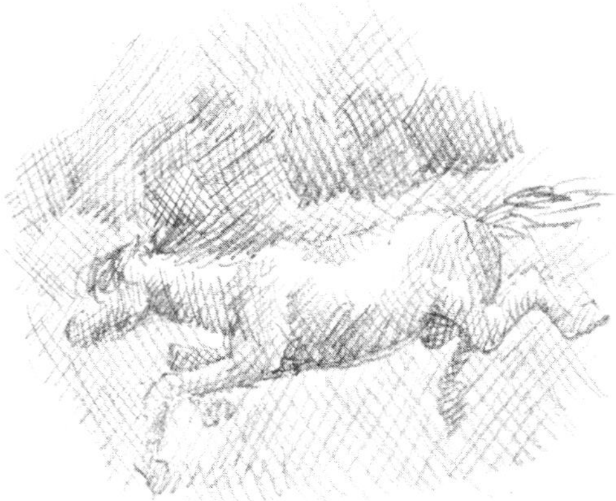

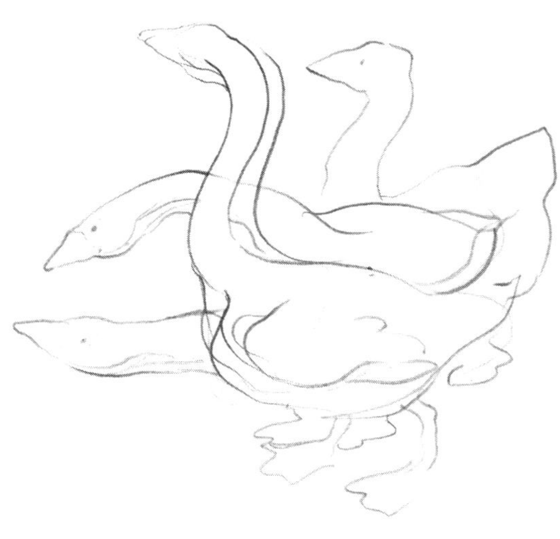

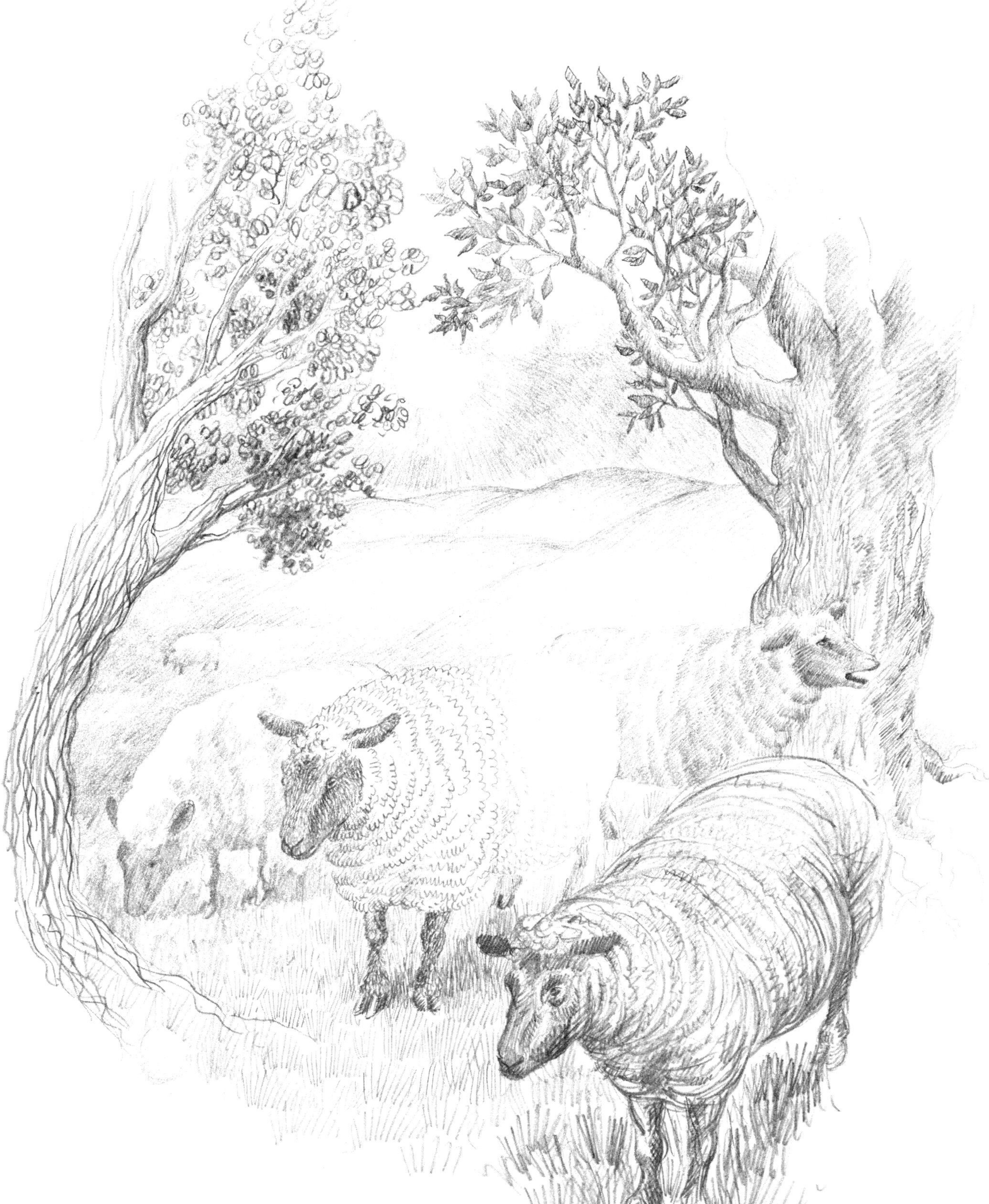

Your drawing is your interpretation of its subject, not a copy. You can manipulate the tones that are there to describe your subject in the way you want. In the drawing on this page, I have made the lamb and its mother's back half, softer and greyer than her head and front. As a result, they appear to move back towards the wall, while the sheep's front is brought forward by its greater contrast and detail. I have not, of course, drawn each individual straw as it was; I first studied the straw and then drew the impression it gave. But notice how the straw also changes as it moves back in space.

More contrast in the foreground than in the background gives an impression of space to your drawing. This is true whether the background is lighter or darker (see the sheep drawings opposite).

In the drawing of black and white cows (also opposite), tone has been used to describe colour changes as well as shape. When drawing a subject which involves strong colour, don't get so lost in colour that you forget shape. Notice how the pencil marks change as they move back in space towards the trees, and how the difference in tone of each cow helps to make it seem to be behind the one in front.

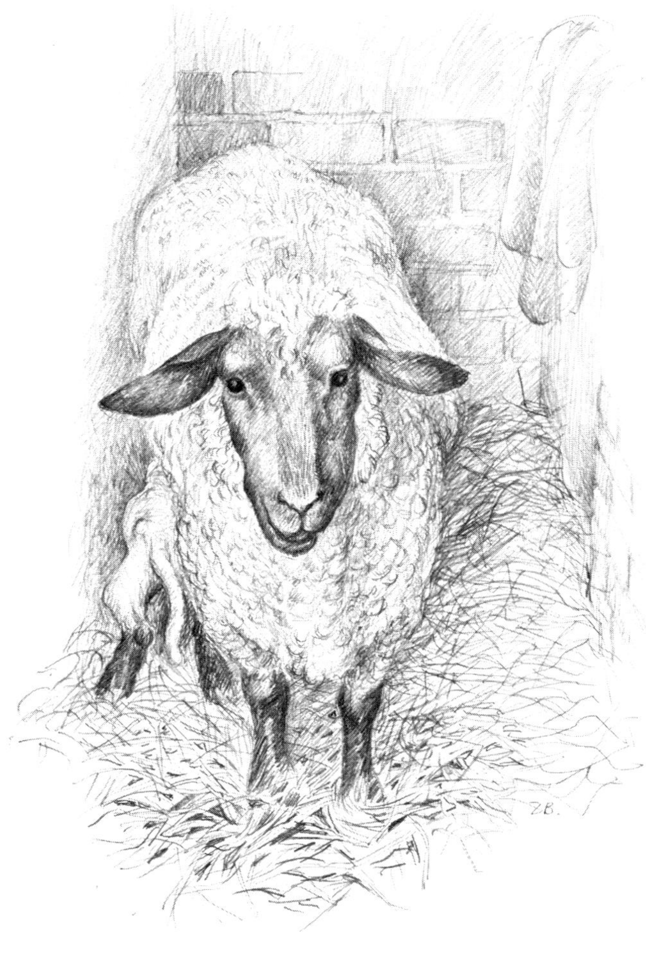

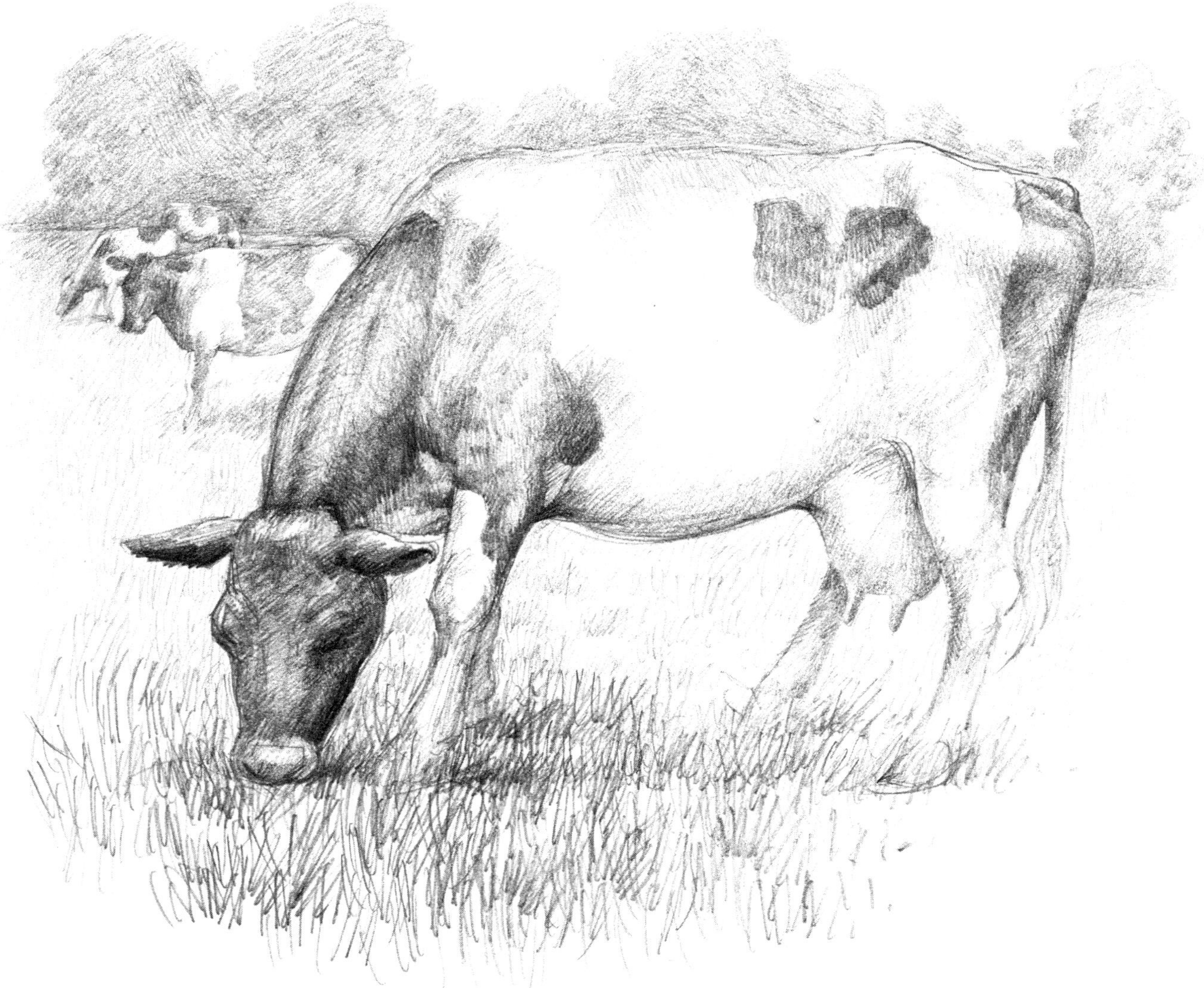

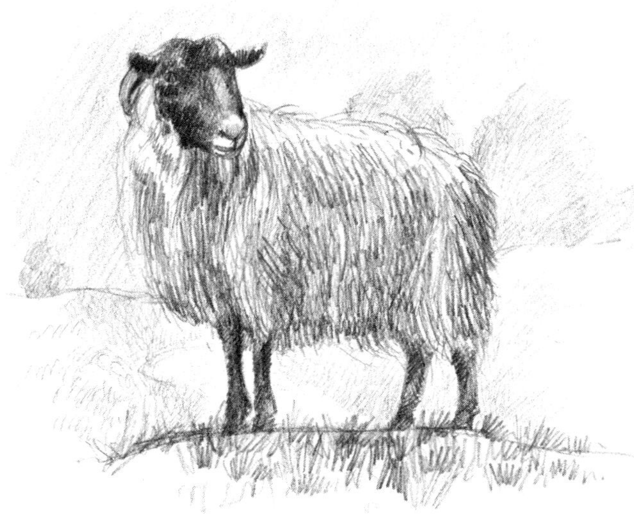

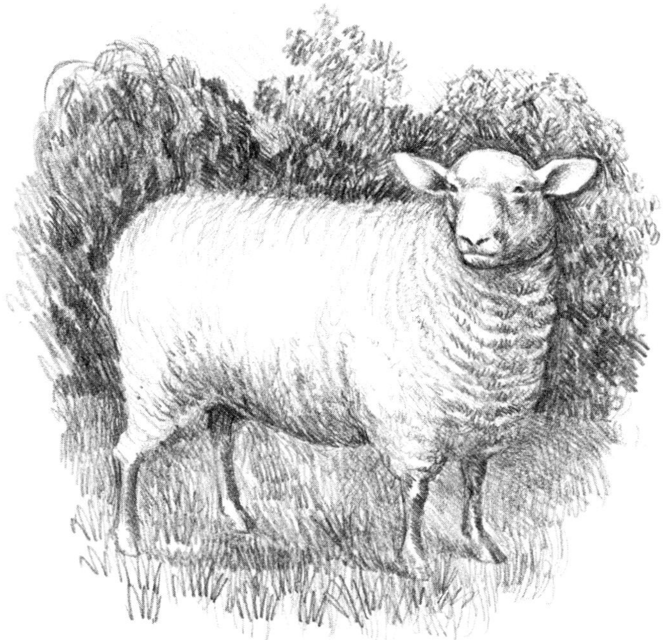

Sketching

When you go sketching the less you take with you the better. I recommend a soft pencil, pen and ink (or, preferably, a fountain pen) and/or charcoal. I always take a putty eraser, a sharpener or knife and, of course, a sketchbook. Dress warmly, because you lose heat quickly when sitting still except on the hottest days. Usually, it is easier to get close to animals in a farmyard than in a field where they have more room to wander off.

A good way to start is to make a number of small, quick studies of animals in different positions. Then, if you want to take one of them further than the others, go ahead, ignoring the other sketches on the page. If your subject moves away, look around in case there is another in a similar position which might help the drawing you are working on.

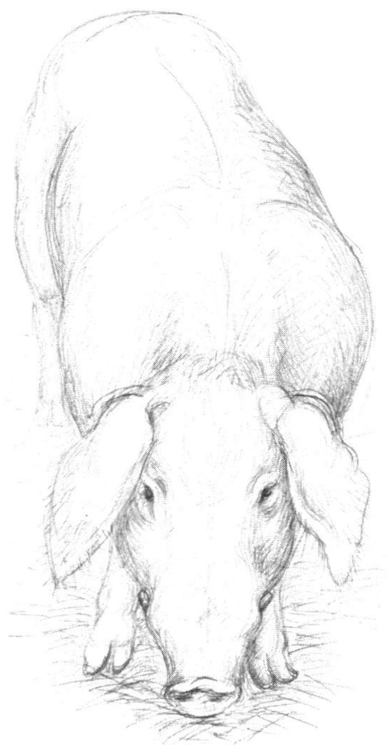

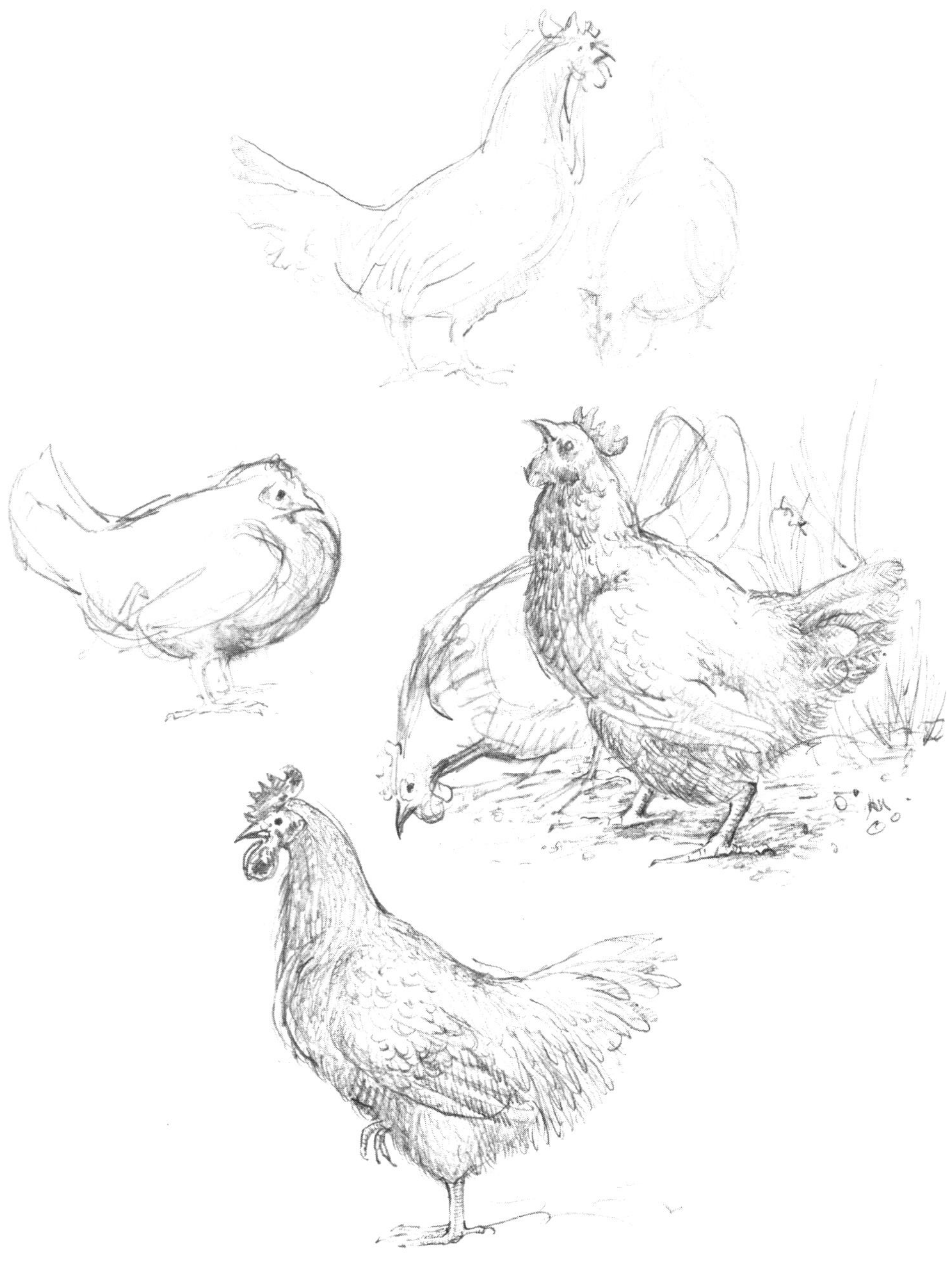

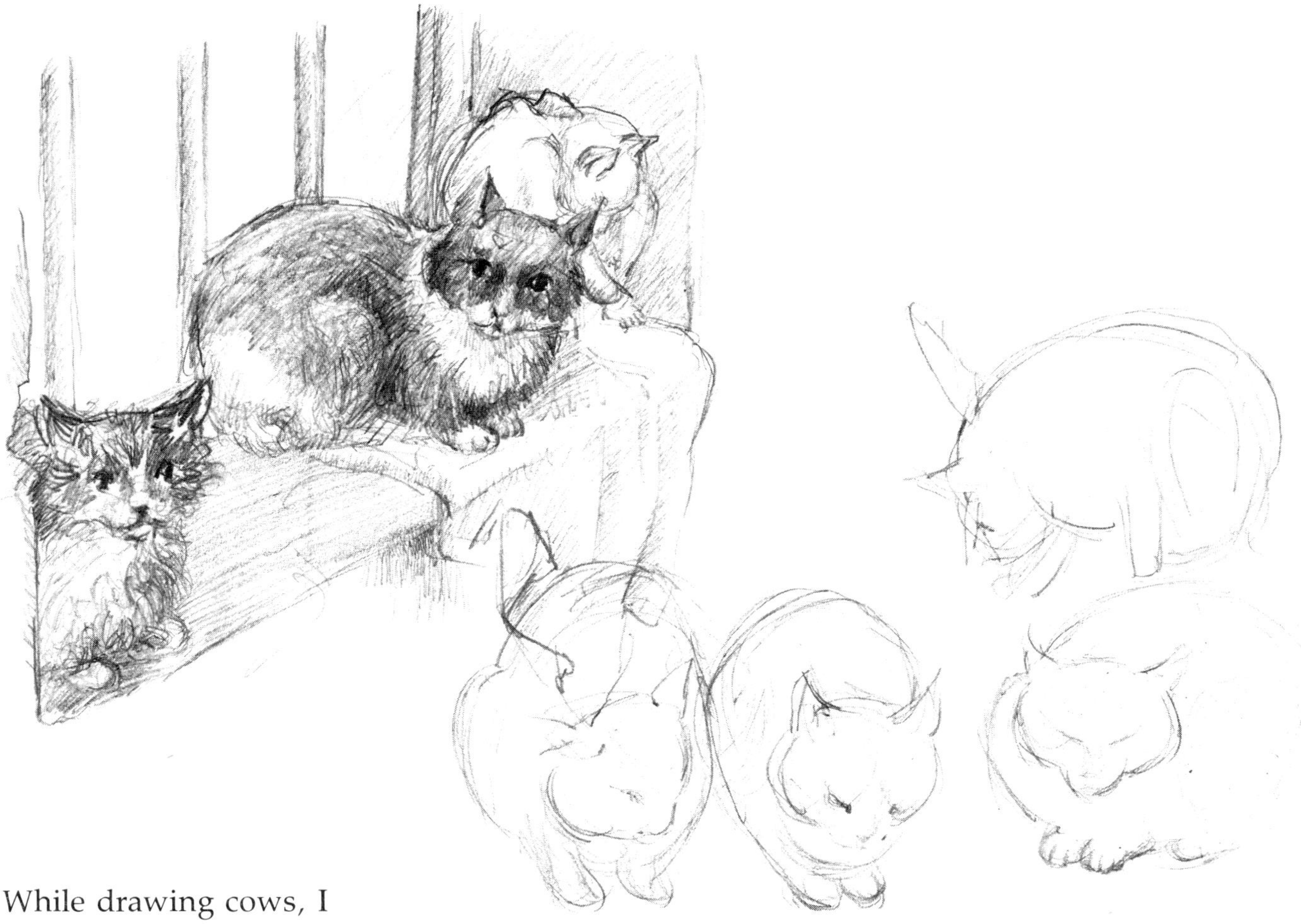

While drawing cows, I noticed these scruffy farm cats waiting to be fed and decided to draw them while I had the opportunity. I used pencil to indicate colour as well as shape in the two on the left: the other sketches are quick studies of some of the positions they got into.

It always pays to sketch the basic shape quickly. Once you have this on paper, it doesn't matter too much if the animal moves; you can follow him round and add to your drawing from new positions.

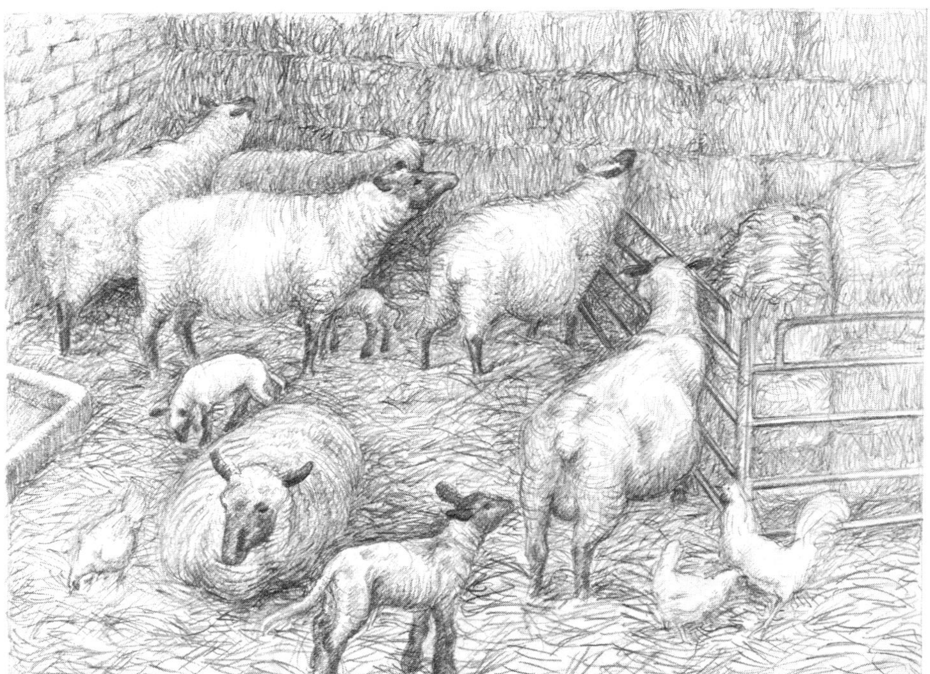

You may find that you come home with a mass of brief, unfinished sketches which you couldn't complete outside—because the animal moved too much, or you were uncomfortable or cold. In that case, select one sketch which you feel has enough basic information, and develop it further indoors. This old Welsh boar moved round and round his pen at an auction; he was in quite a state. I made a lot of quick sketches of him in different positions because he was very handsome. When I got home I worked on this one to produce a more finished drawing.

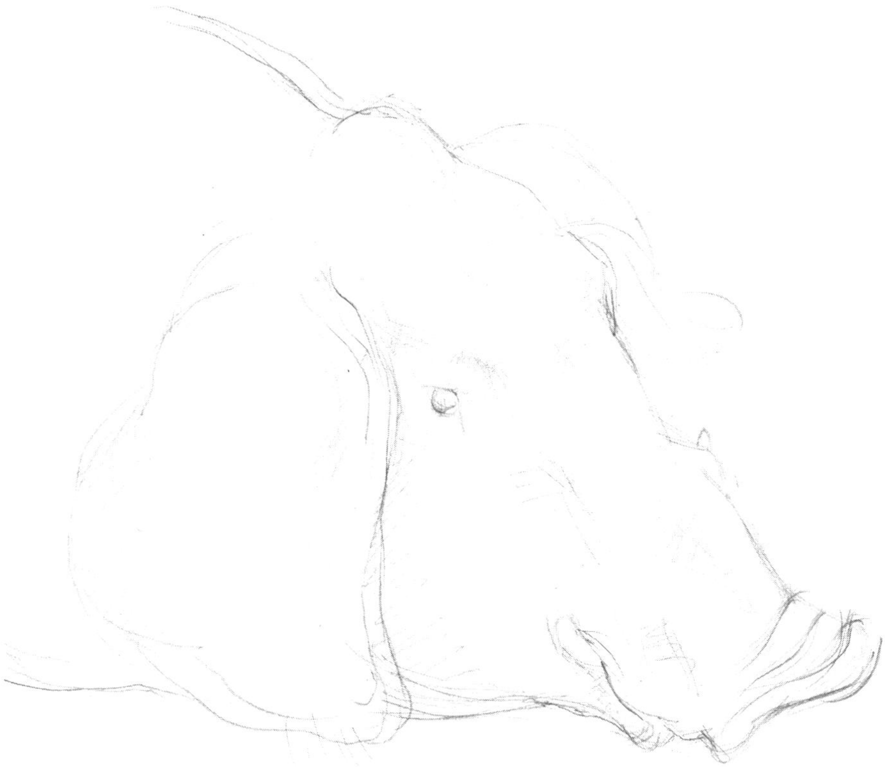

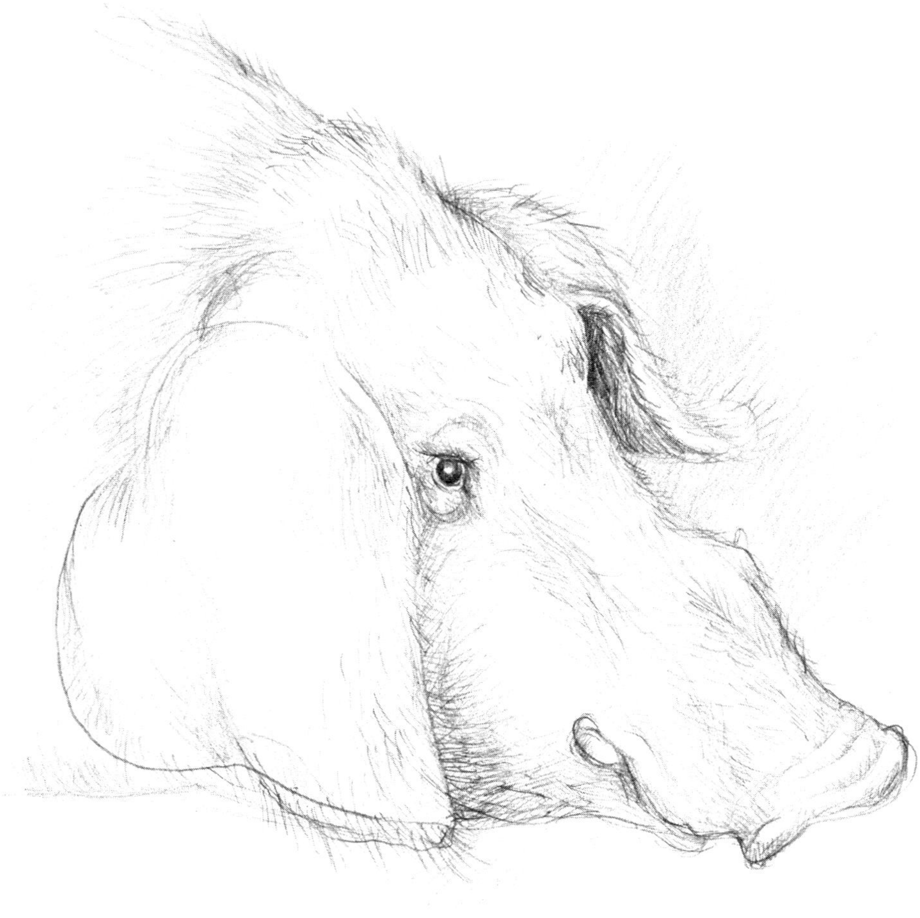

Quick sketches can be complete in themselves; many would be ruined by working on them at a different speed and intensity. I felt that the drawings on this page had caught the poses and characters of their subjects, and would be spoiled by further work.

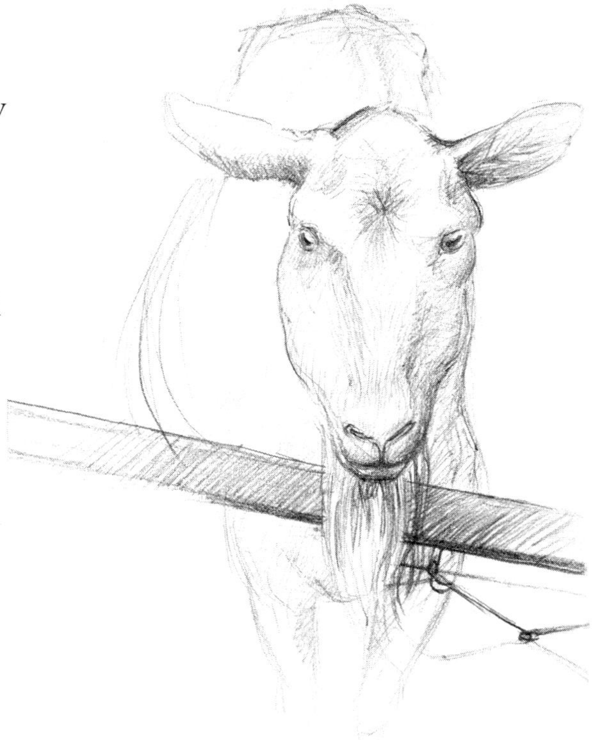

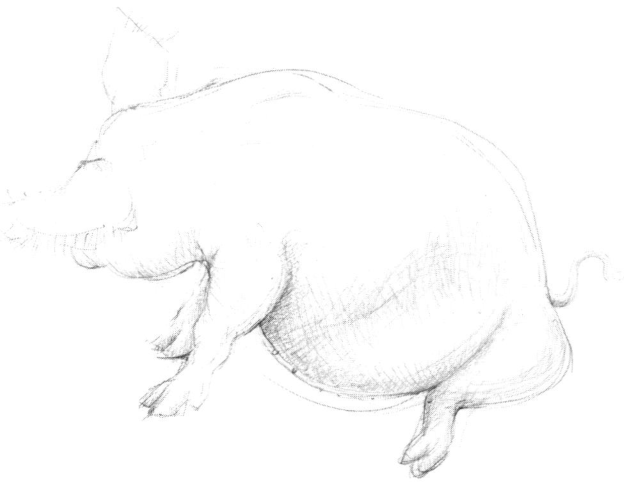

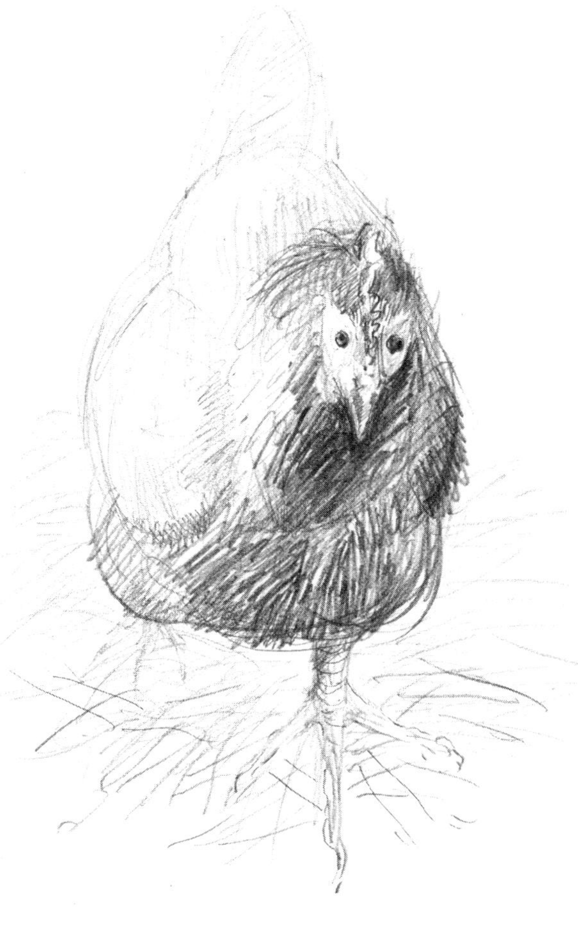

A drawing in stages

The sketches on these two pages are preliminary studies for the step-by-step drawing of a goat and cow that follow on pages 32–3. While I was making them, the animals were getting used to me and I was getting to know them. Afterwards I tried out a few compositions (page 31)—a kind of 'thinking on paper' to clarify the possibilities in my own mind. Once I had decided that I liked the last one best, with the goat peering through from the other side of the cow, I was ready to start the drawing.

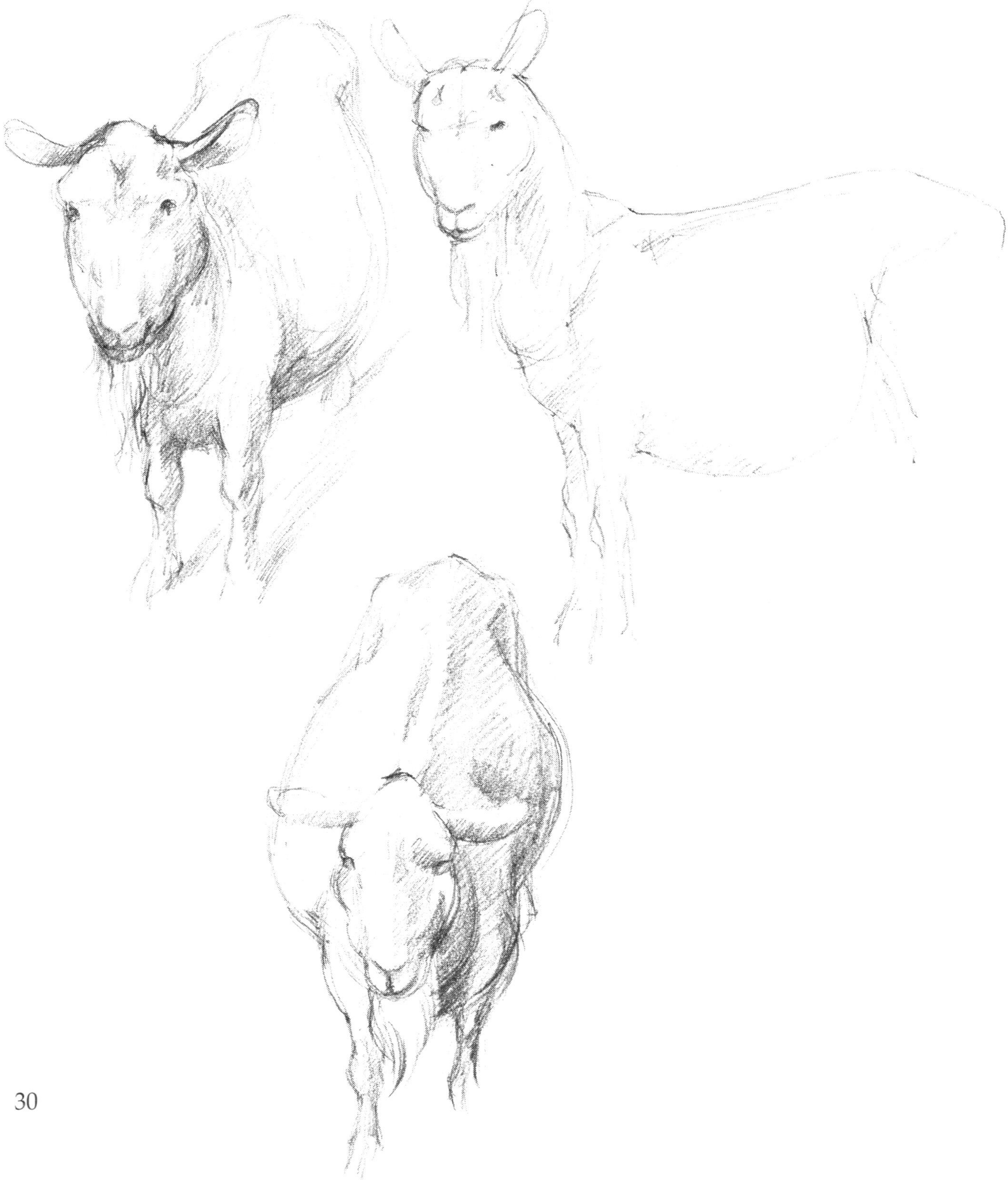

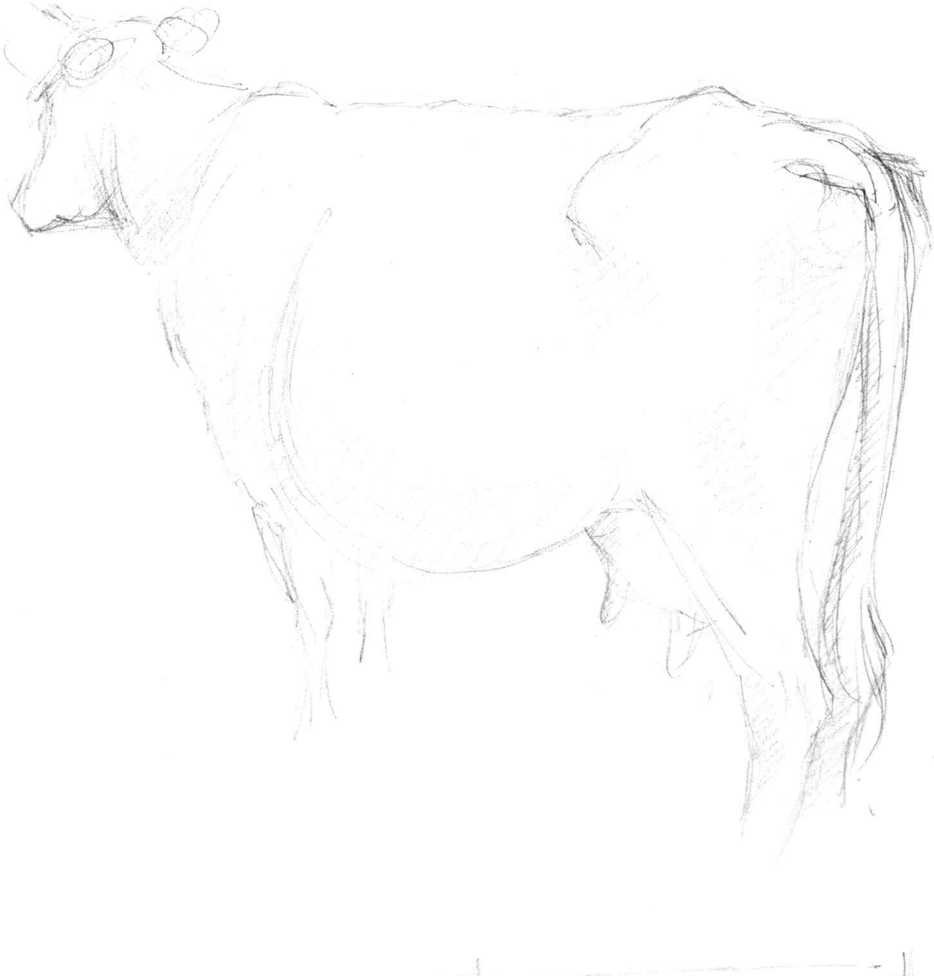

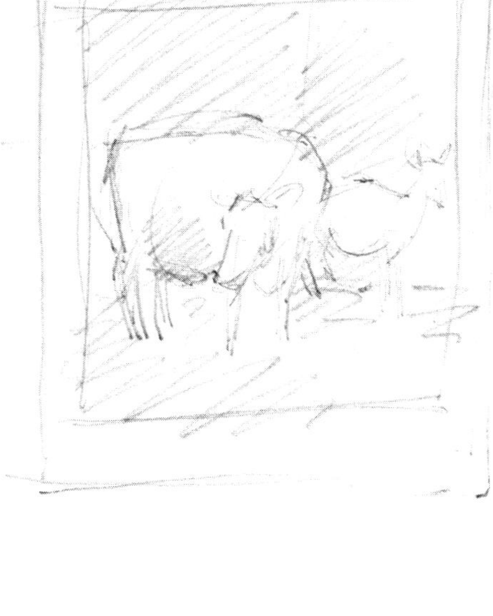

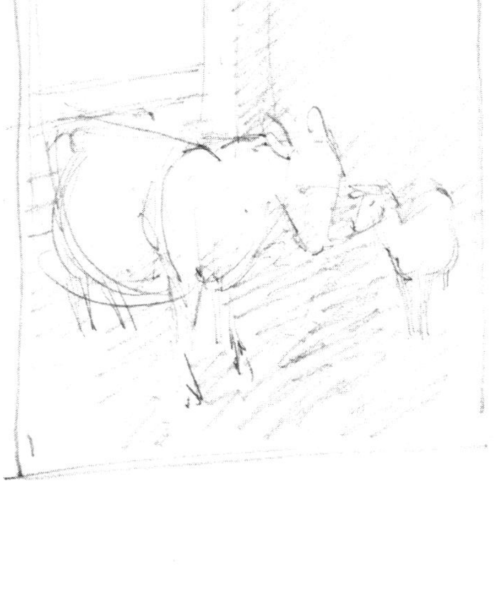

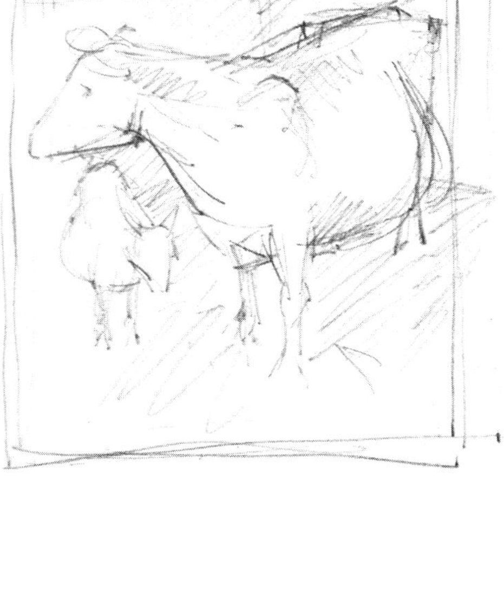

In the first stage below, I have lightly indicated where the subject is placed on the page, and concentrated on sorting out the proportions.

Stage two begins to find the lights and darks—which here reveal the muscles on the cow.

Stage three shows the background being pushed back with shading and greater detail emerging as I work into the drawing. There is more contrast between lights and darks, and gradually the animals are beginning to look three-dimensional.

At every stage, develop the drawing as a whole; don't take any one part faster than another. The subjects did not stand still all the time; I moved round and round the enclosure, getting first one and then the other in the right position for my drawing.

Notice how the pencil has been used loosely to describe the subject in a build-up of lines—indicating the bumps and bulges, the round parts and flat parts, near parts and far parts. In the finished drawing, the goat's hind quarters are very faint, which makes them look much further away than her head. The cow's head is drawn more strongly than the goat's, and this makes it look nearer still.

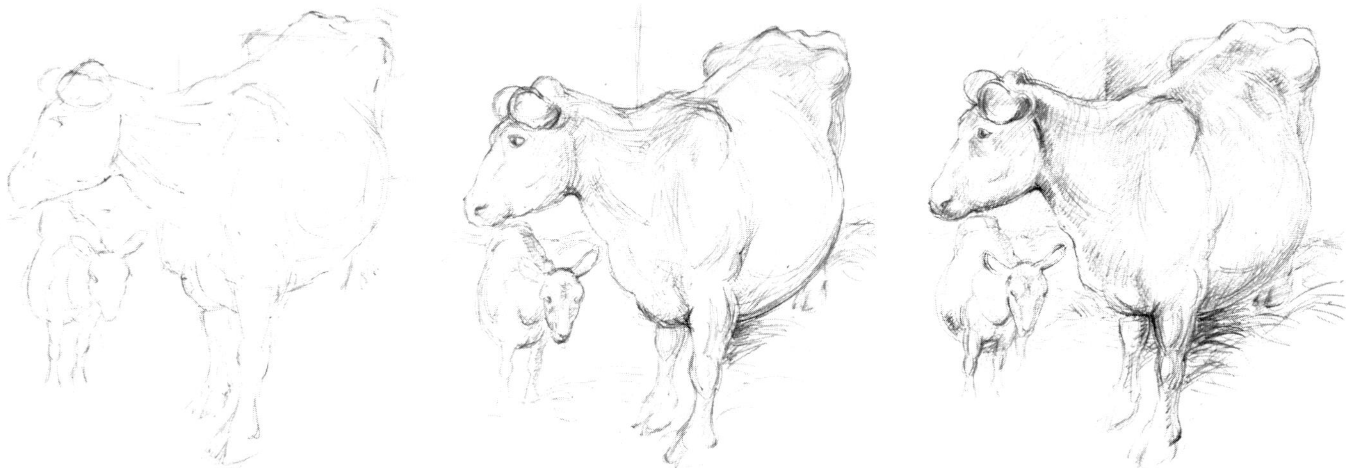

The drawing was made with a 6B pencil on smooth cartridge. It took me about three hours to complete, but everyone works at a different speed and your drawings may take less or more time.

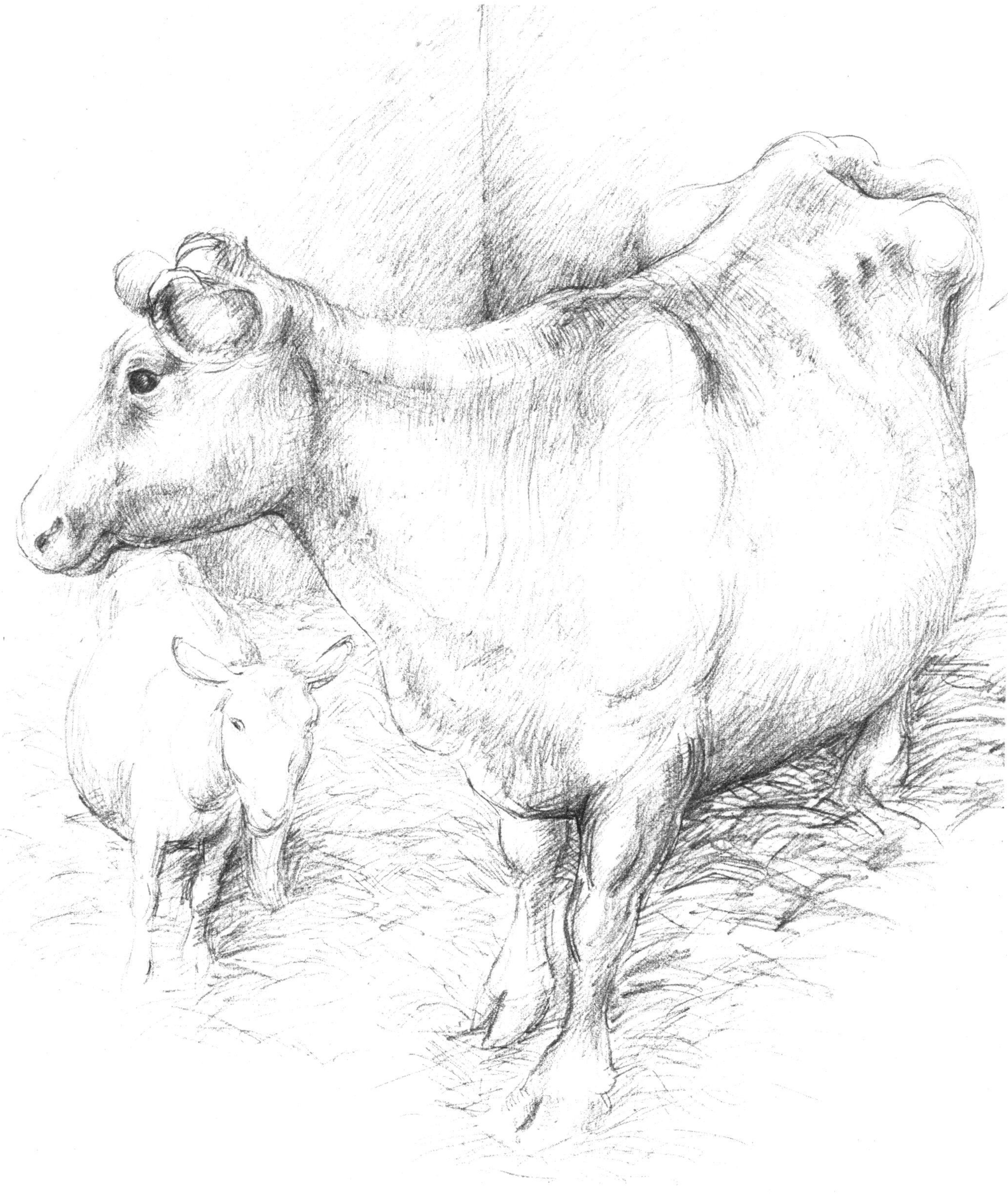

Drawing groups

It is not easy to make drawing sense of a continually moving sea of bodies. You need to think about what is going on and use your imagination all the time. I generally start by sketching the nearest creature and working back, using it as a key to the scale of those behind. In the first sketch here, I drew one hen with care, and then sketched in the others loosely, showing how the hens' shapes change as they get further away. The nearer hens are individuals, and drawn as such; the others are figures in a crowd, indicated rather than drawn. This is what I saw in the chicken house.

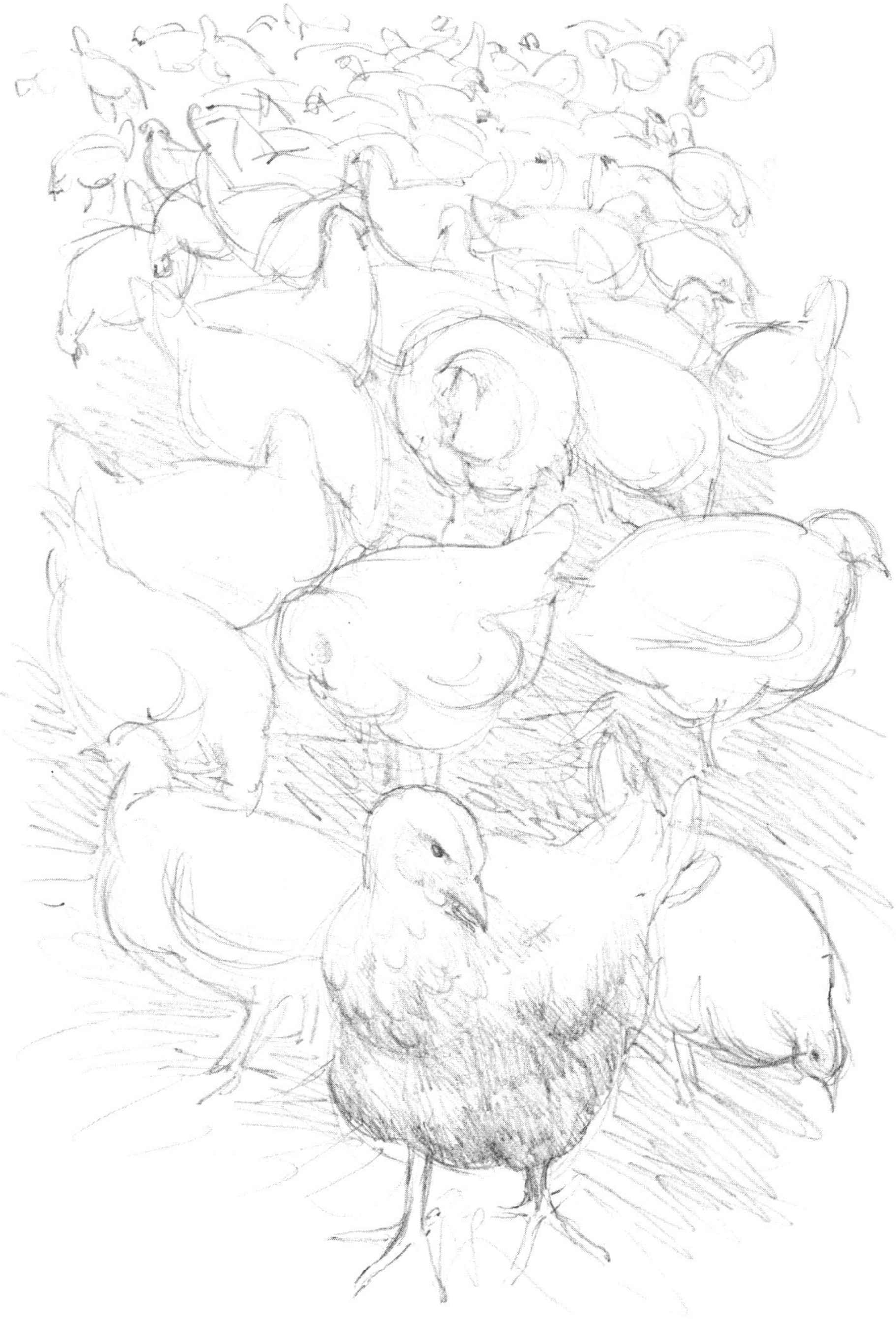

Don't expect a crowd of chickens to stand still; you have to make your own picture of a constantly changing group. I found the two feeders in the second drawing here helpful as a fairly stationary point of reference.

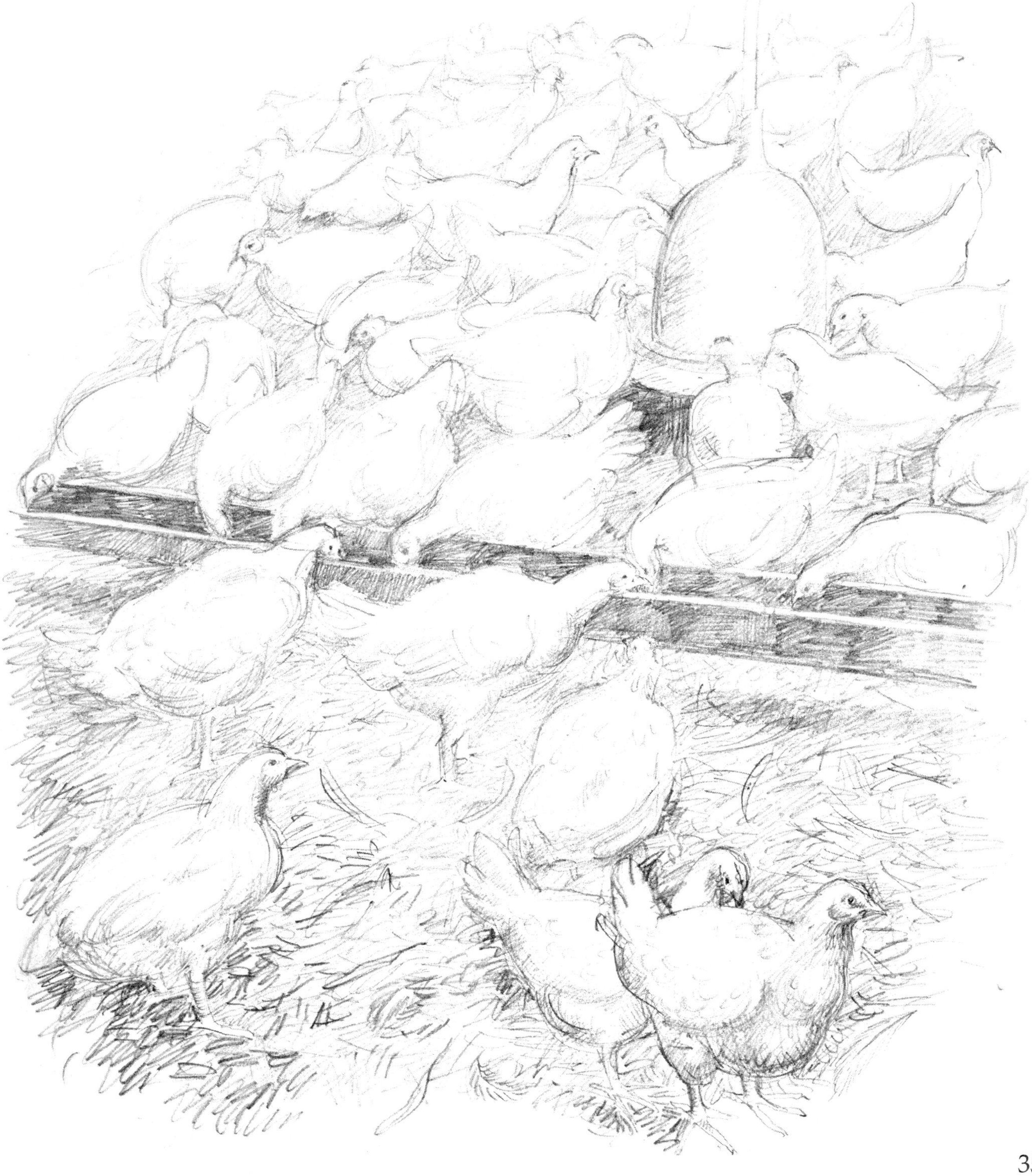

In smaller groups more animals can be clearly seen. It is important to get the scale right, and to relate each animal to its companions. Look for points of reference. At what point does one animal's shape overlap another? How big is the gap between one animal and another (a head's length, or a body's length)? Is the gap as wide as this or as narrow as that? Alter anything you have drawn if it looks wrong to you.

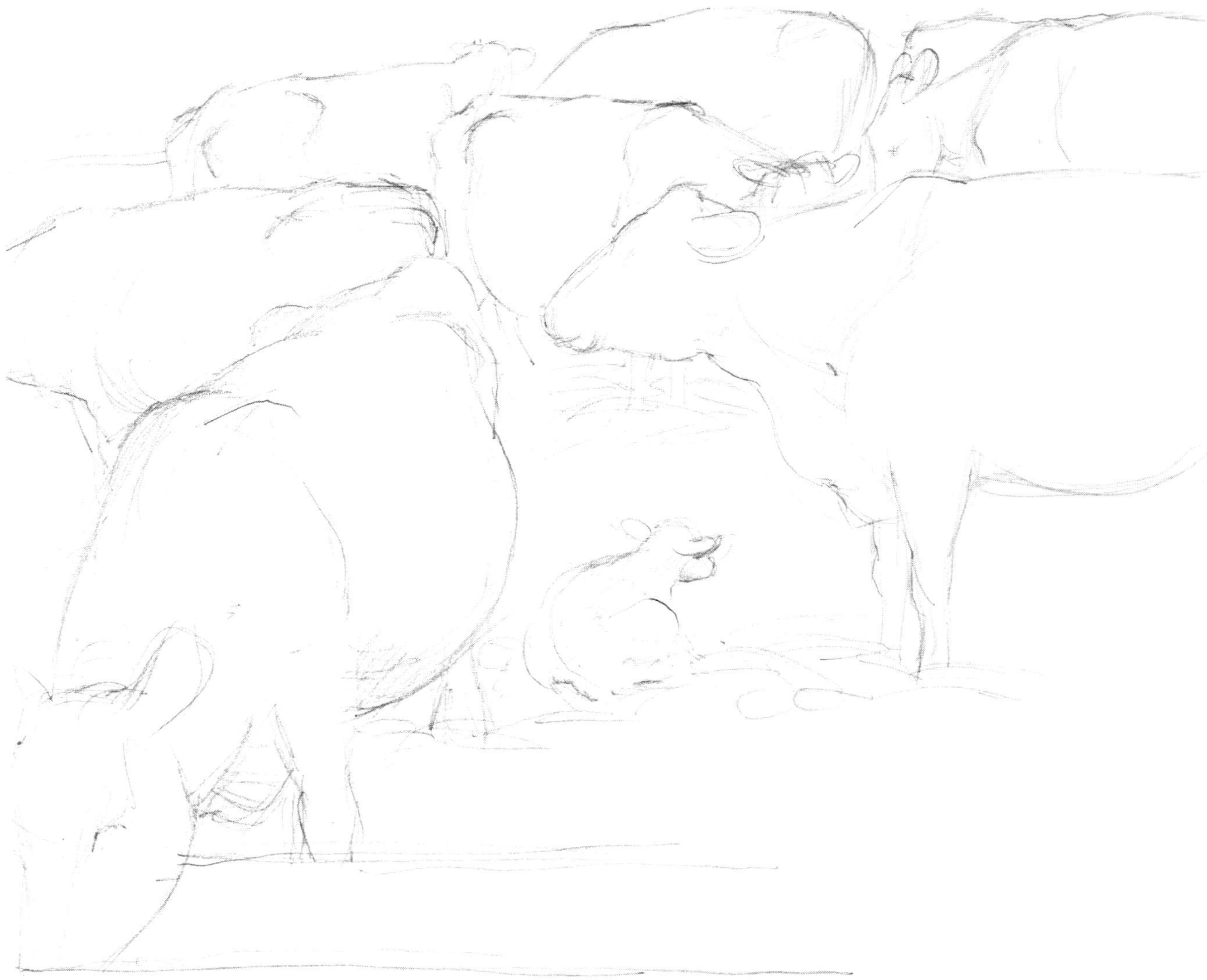

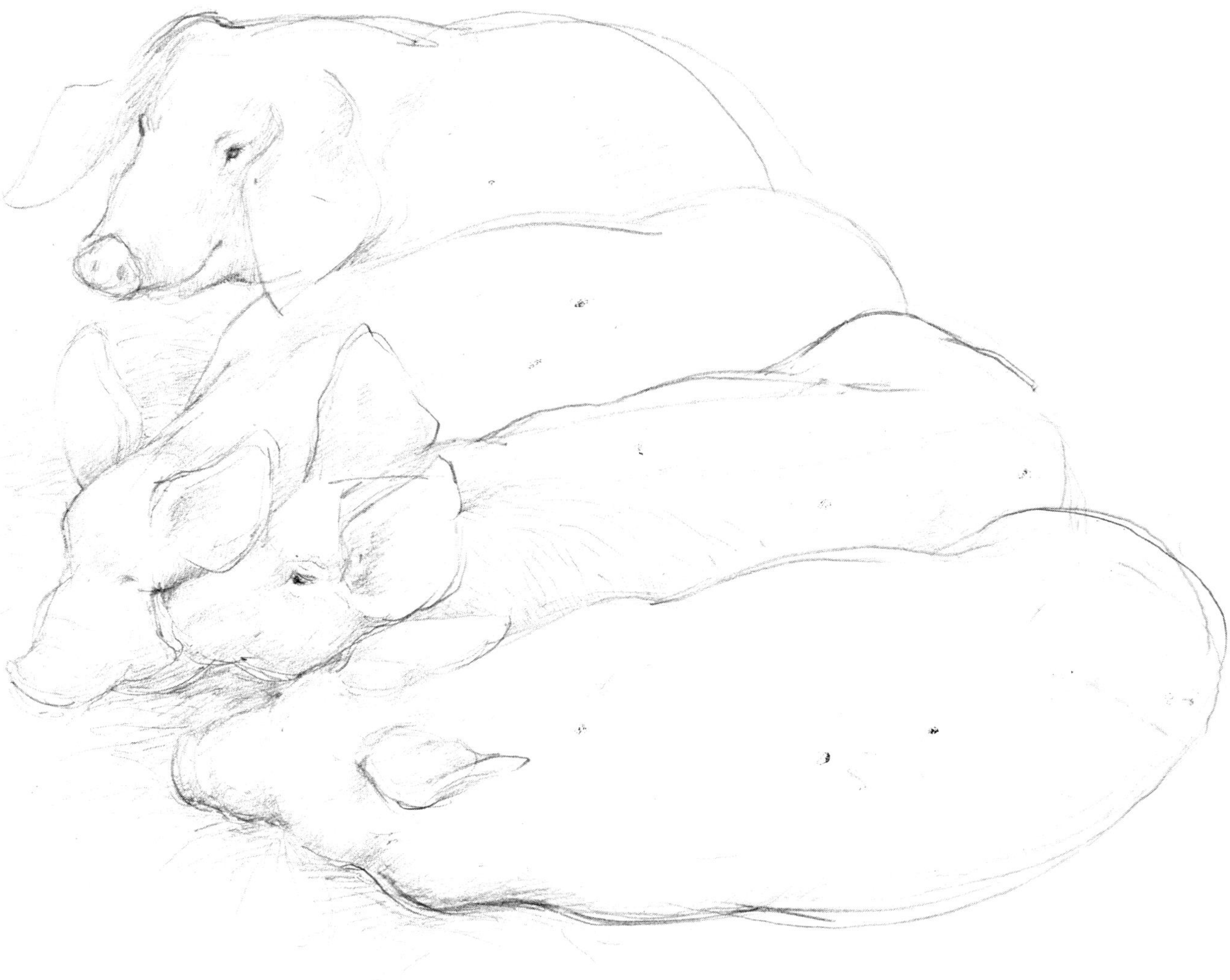

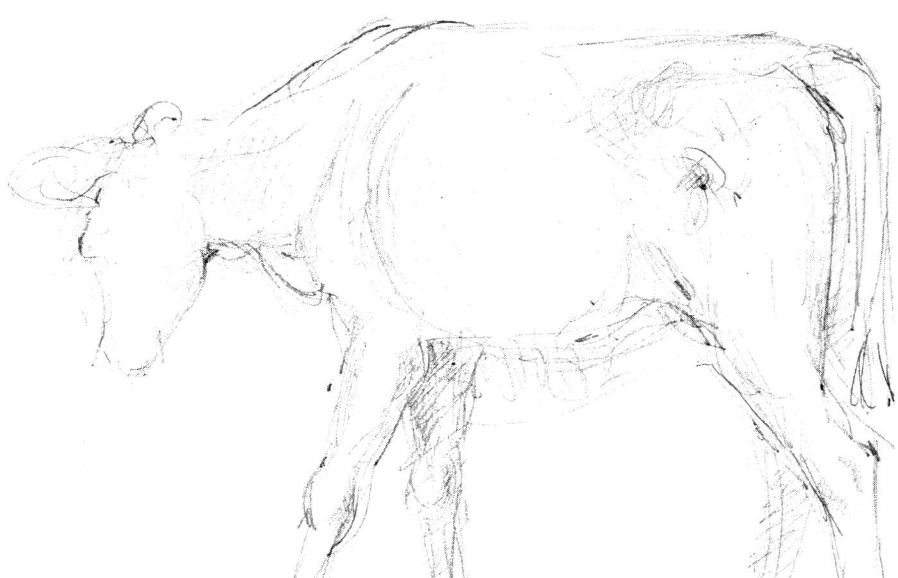

Animals in their surroundings

When drawing animals within their landscape or farmyard surroundings, take care to relate everything to everything else, constantly checking the distance between an animal and a tree, and the size of a near object against a far one, to ensure that all is to scale.

Remember that objects become smaller as they move back in space, and that there is less contrast and less detail in things far away than in things near at hand. Using this knowledge will help you create space within a drawing.

Don't feel tied to reality; be ready to alter and adjust what you see if you think it will improve your drawing (compare the two lower drawings opposite).

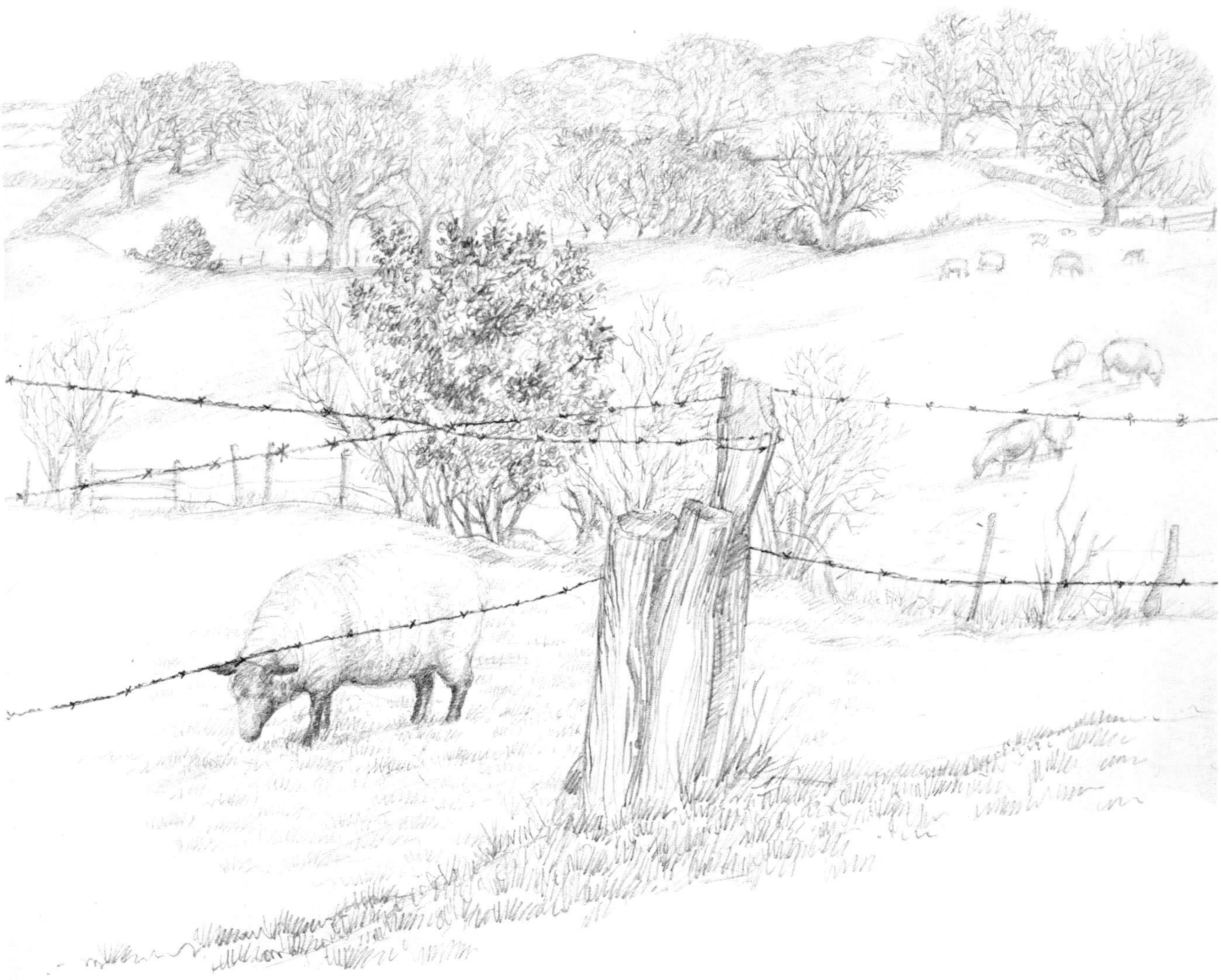

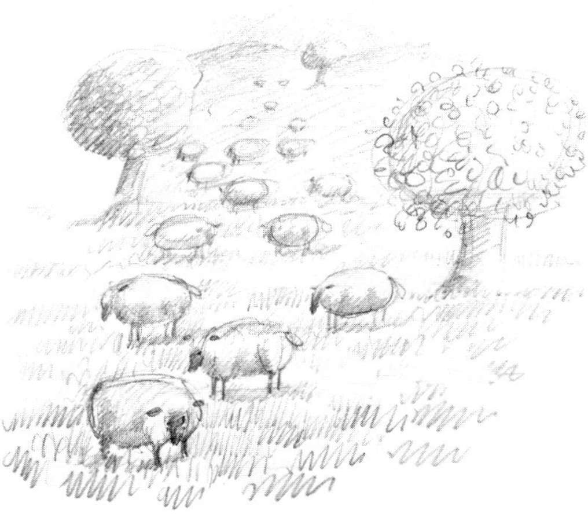

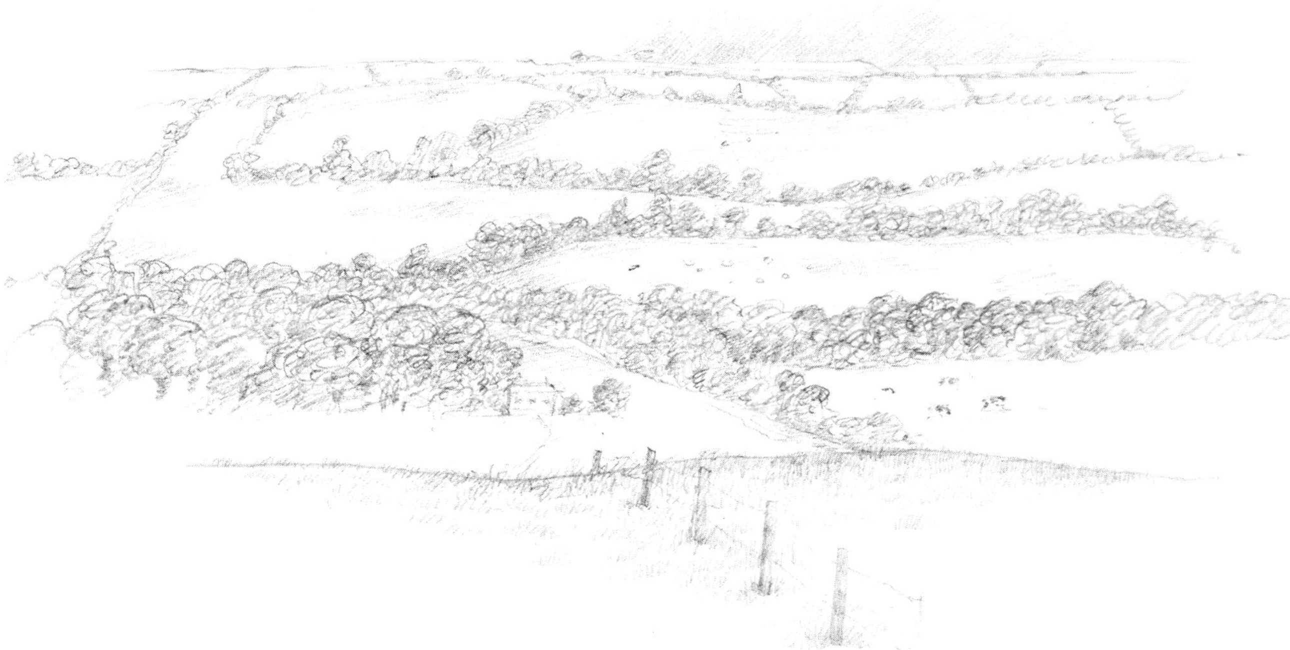

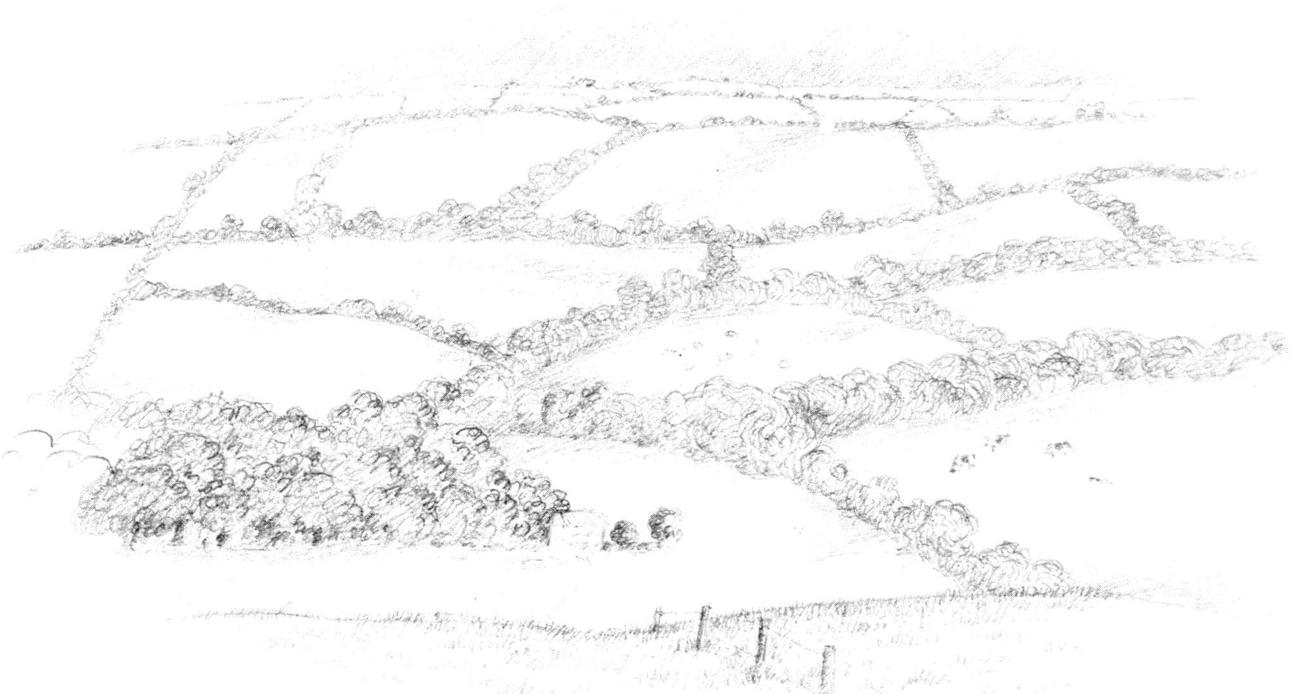

Here, the animals appear to move back in space, not only because of the way they are drawn but because each object is placed so that it overlaps another. Thus the objects themselves tell you something about their positions in space.

The drawing opposite reveals many different textures. Look closely at the pencil marks that bring these out. The bricks in the background, for example, are not so much drawn as built with lines.

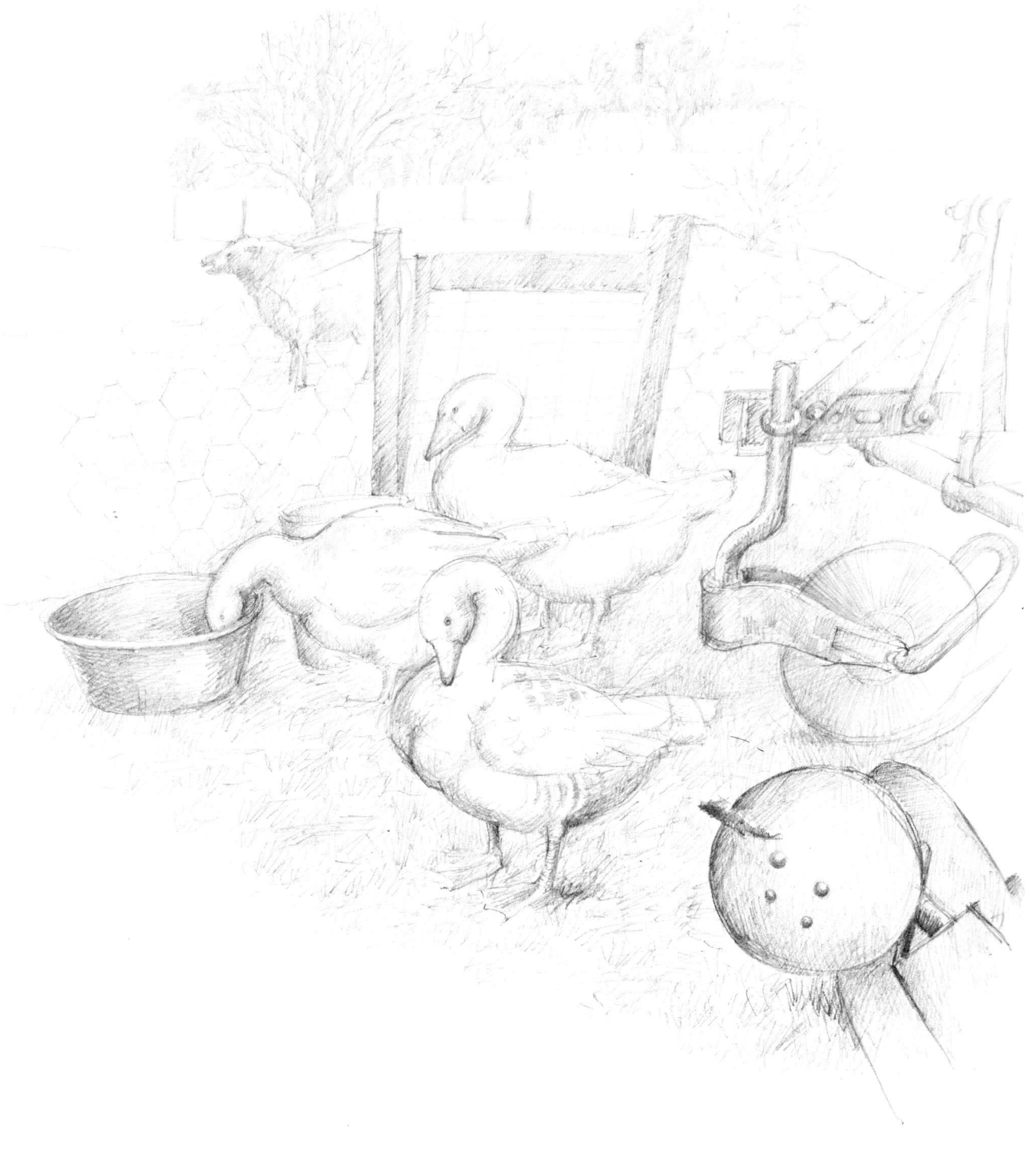

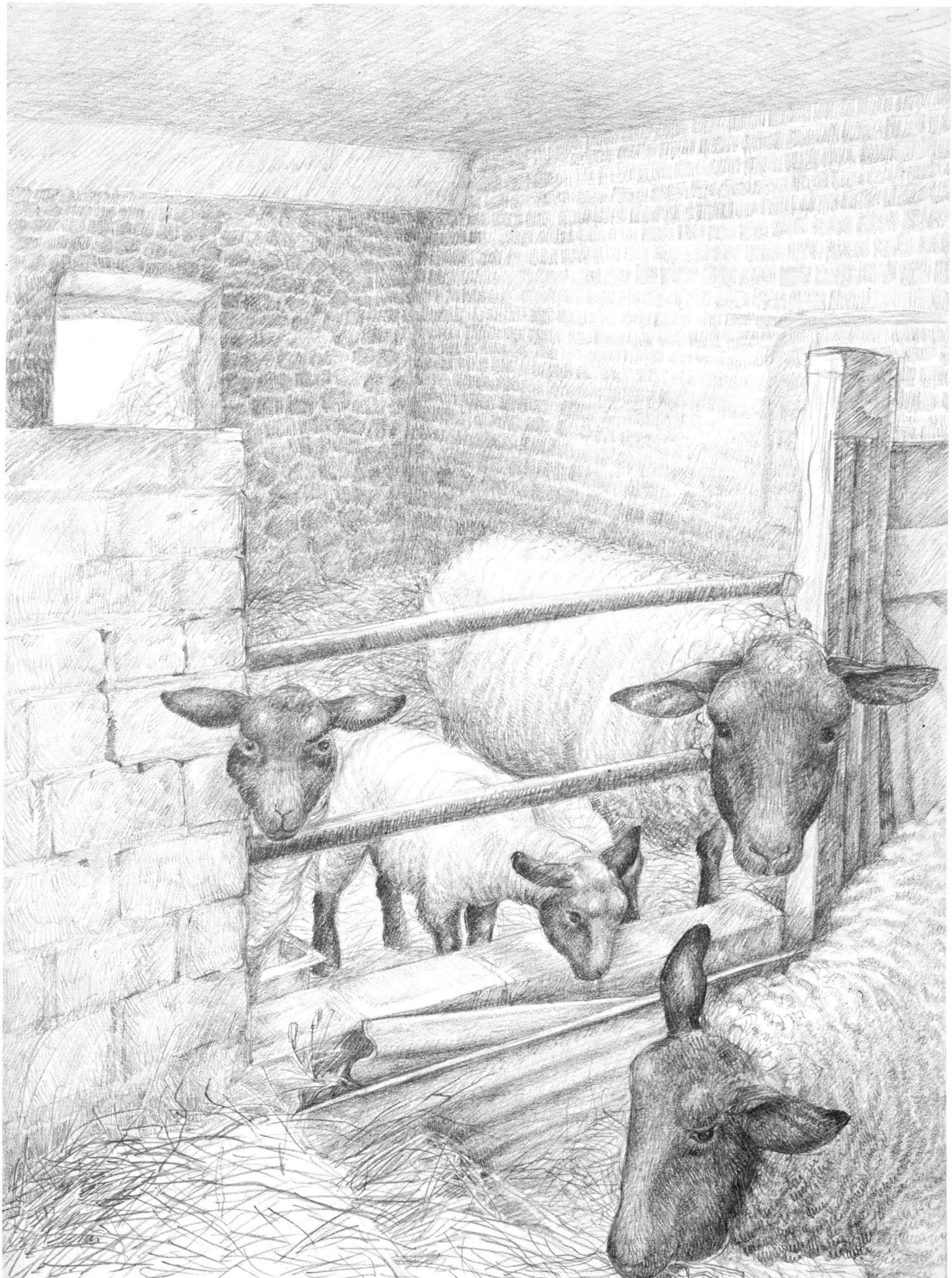

Young animals

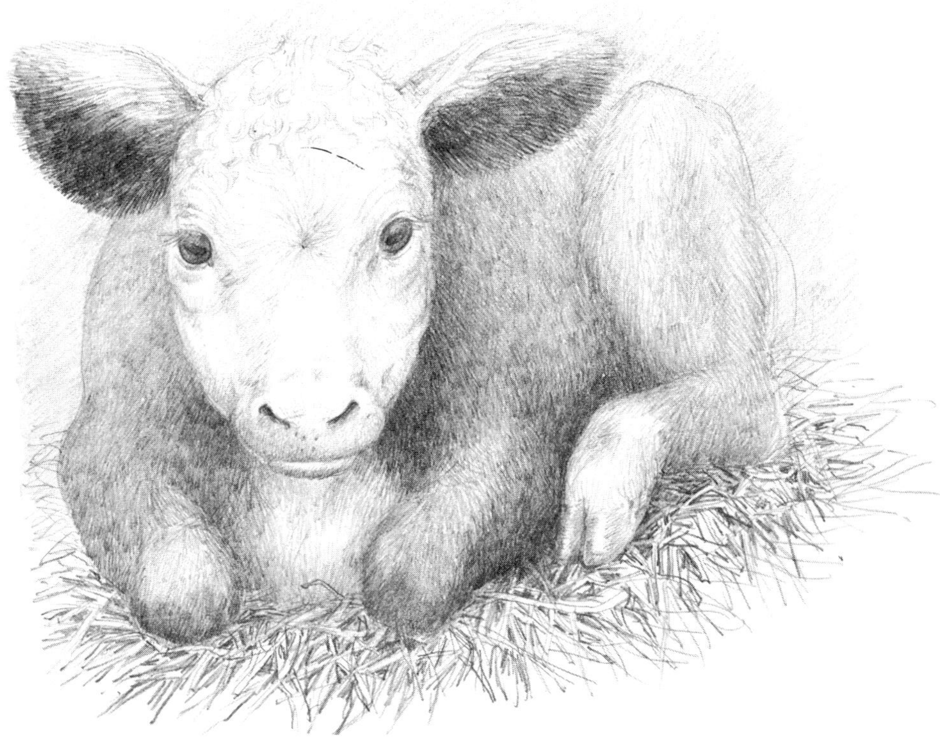

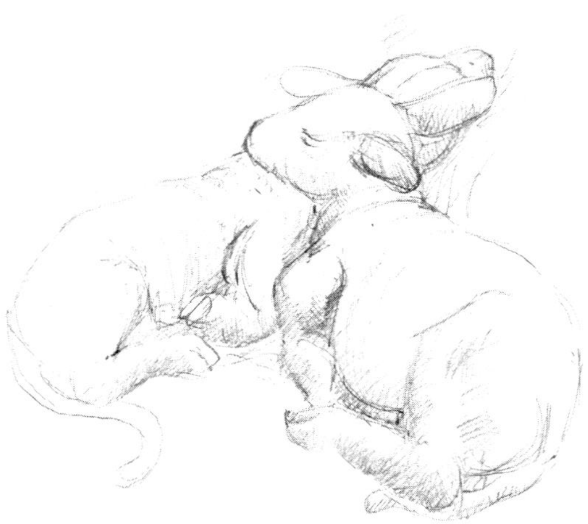

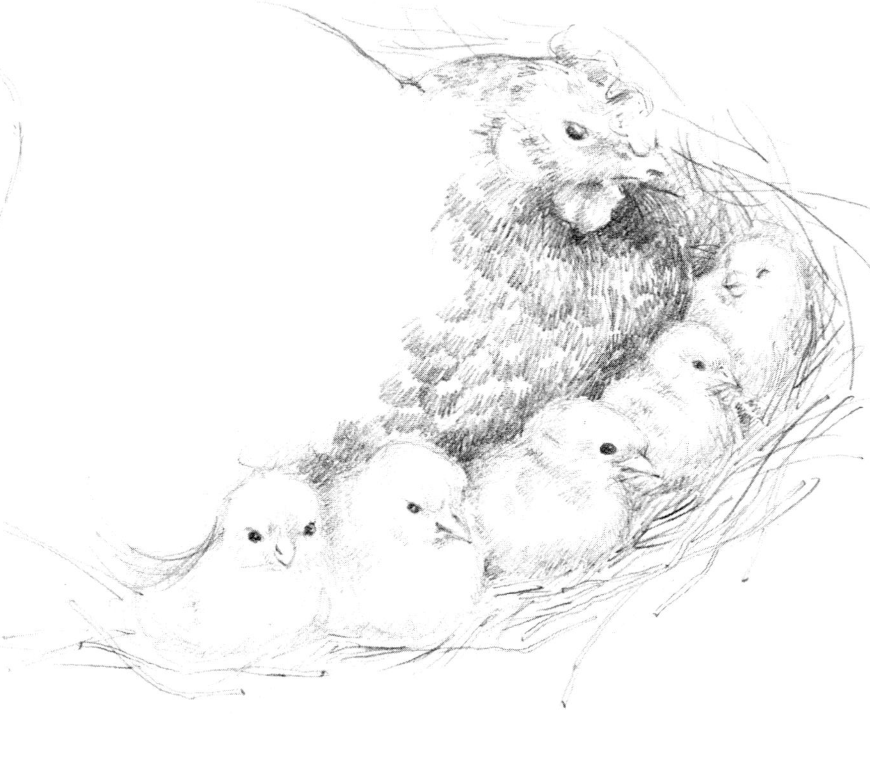

Young animals present an artist with the same problems as old ones, and your approach should be the same. Proportions, of course, are very different. The head is often big in relation to the body, in most cases the legs are longer than you would expect, and the coats or skins of the young look soft and new. Newly born animals of one kind or another can be seen on farms or at markets throughout the year, but spring is by far the best time. I drew the calf opposite at a local market in March. The sketches of lambs here include a more finished drawing of one sitting warmly on its mother's back.

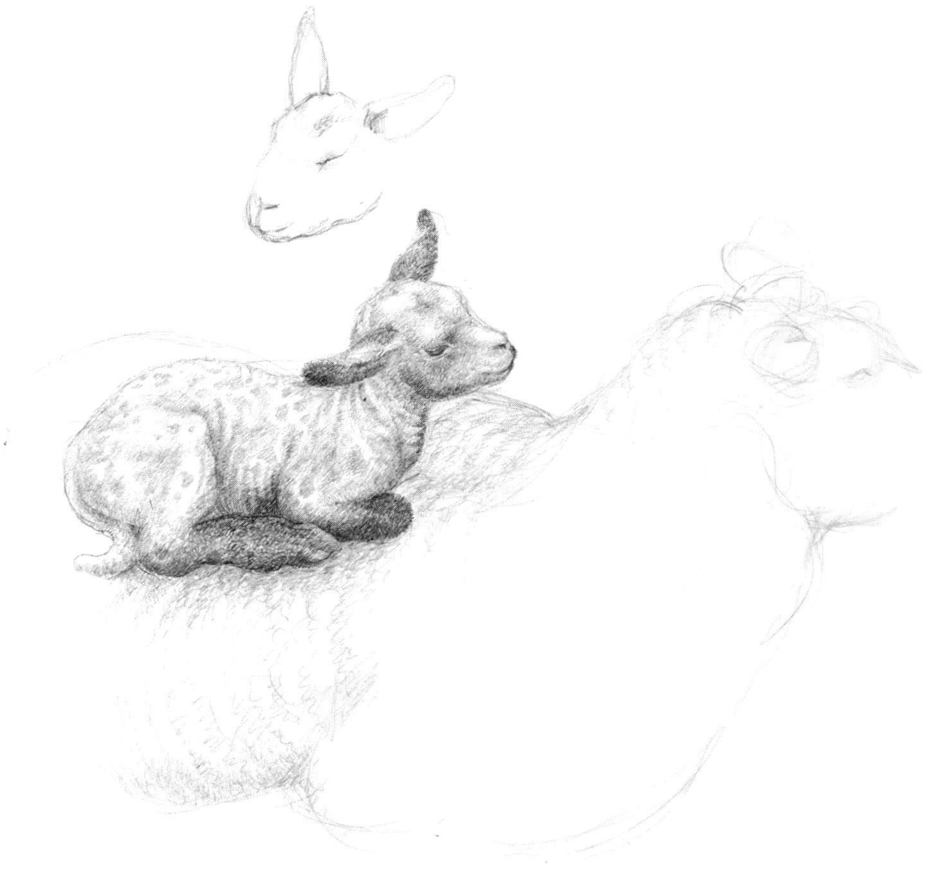

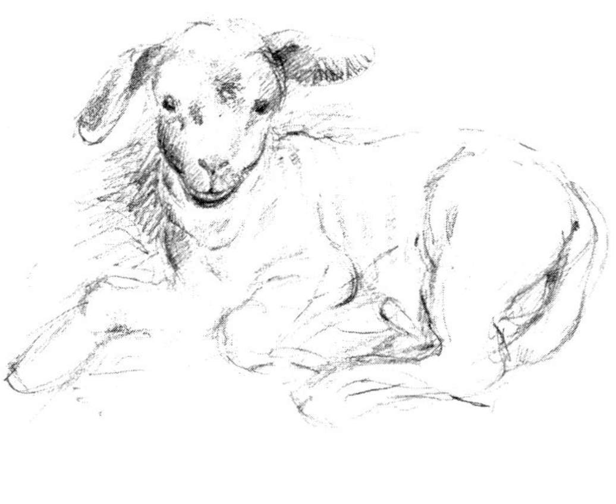

In this drawing I paid as much attention to the surroundings as to the calf itself. She moved round and round me as I drew, but she paused from time to time to study me, and I used these moments to study her.

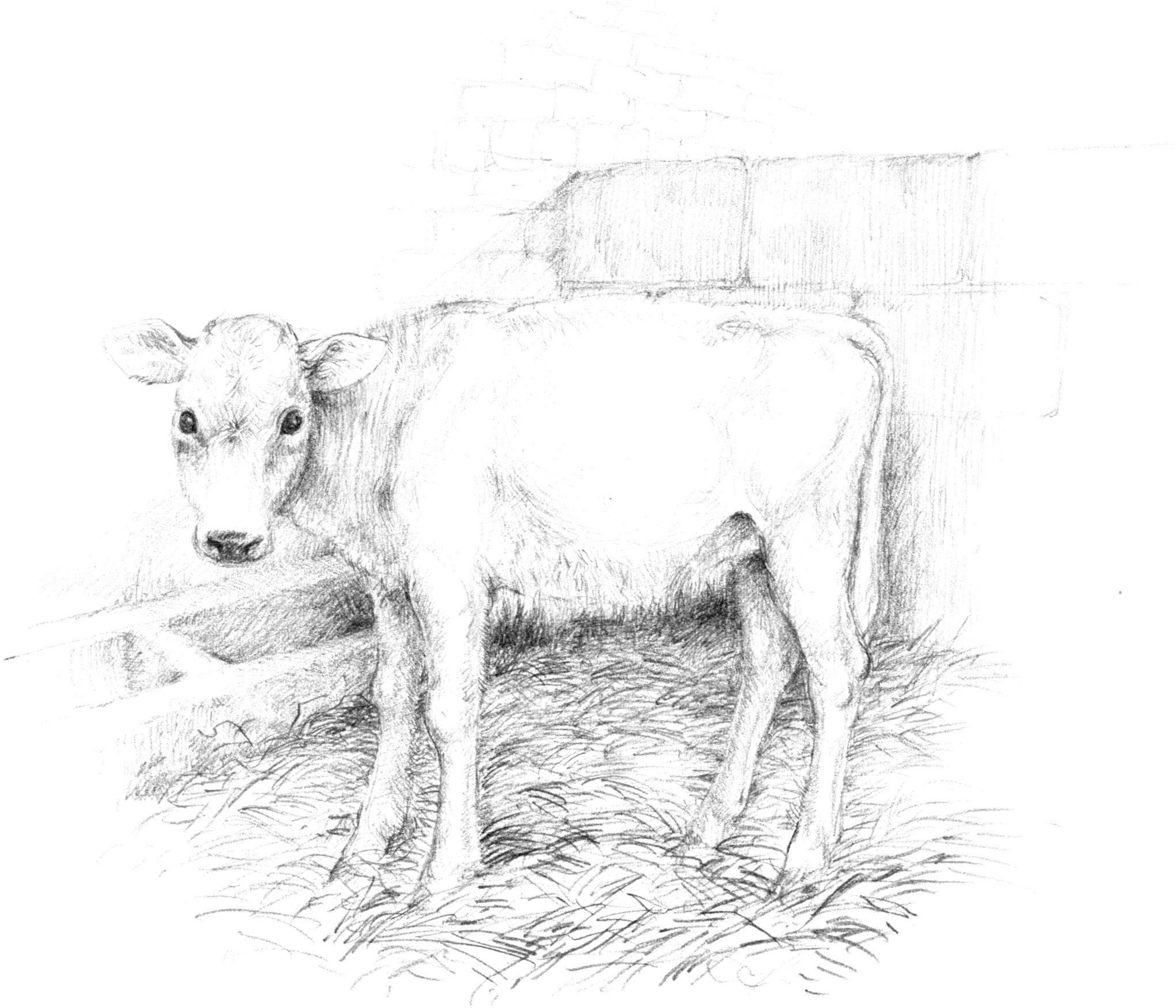

The piglets opposite were very new and might have been made of pink satin. Notice how they fit together—like a jigsaw puzzle.

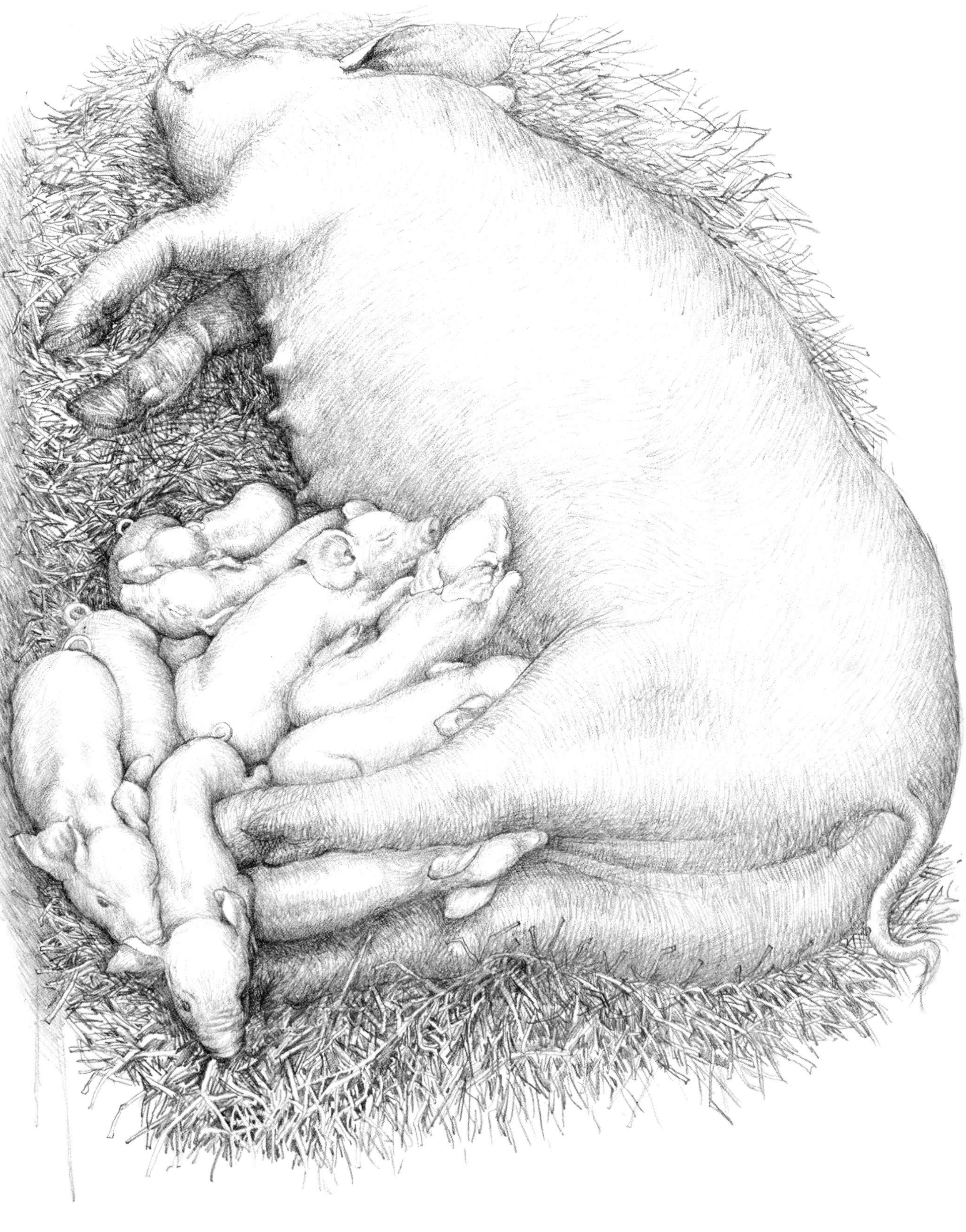

In general

When you go out drawing, you will almost certainly meet interesting people as well as see interesting places. If you want to draw on a farm, ask the farmer for permission first—you will find many farmers helpful, and some will give a guided tour, showing you animals you wouldn't otherwise have seen.

When you are with animals be careful not to frighten them with any sudden movements. Once you have settled down to draw, they will generally take little or no notice of you and will make excellent subjects as a result.

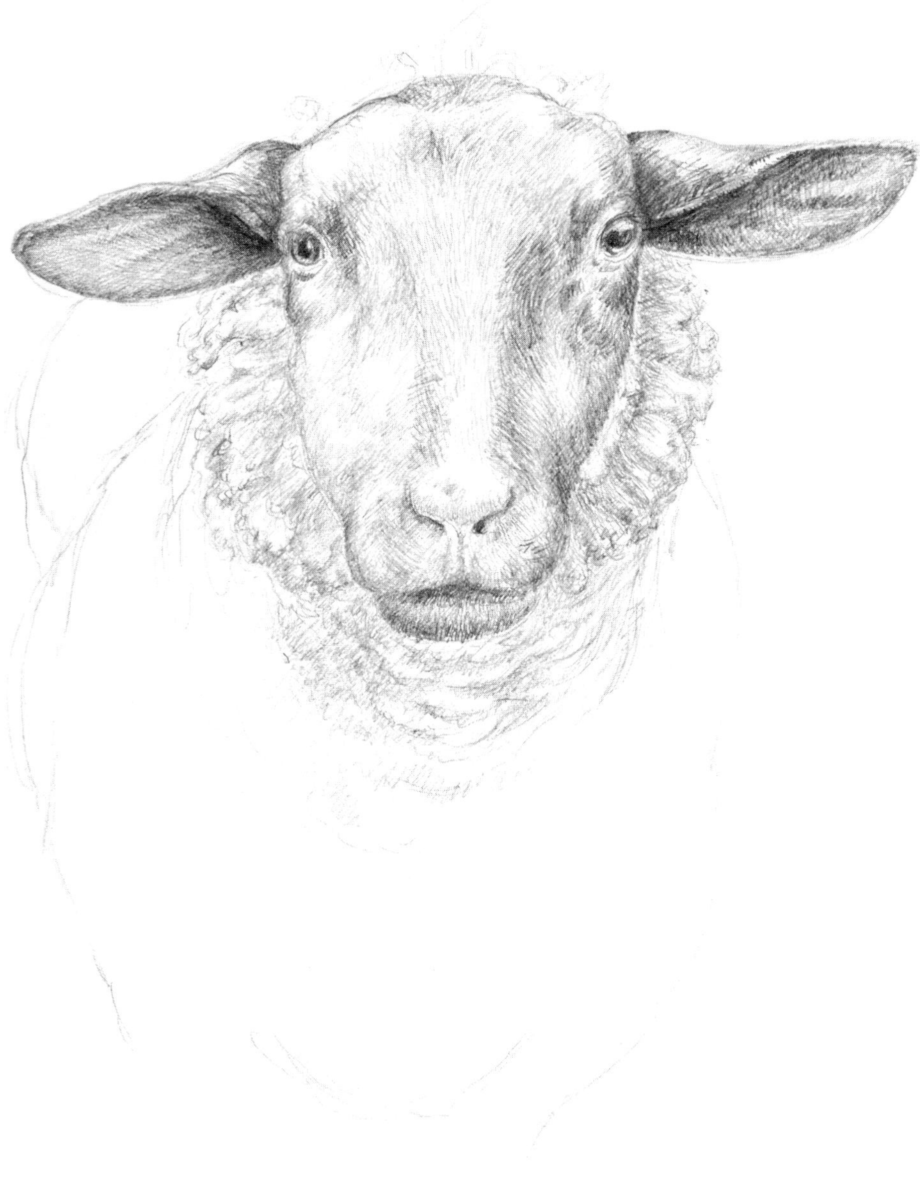

Imagination and fantasy

Imagination is of course an integral part of all drawing but it is fun sometimes to let it take over completely. For this design of a cockerel, I drew a circle with a pair of compasses and sketched a bird that would fit comfortably into it. I put in grasses on the left to balance the tail on the right and then covered the bird with patterns based on the plumage of different breeds of chickens. Finally I added a plain border, because the finished drawing seemed too complicated for the patterned border which I had originally intended.

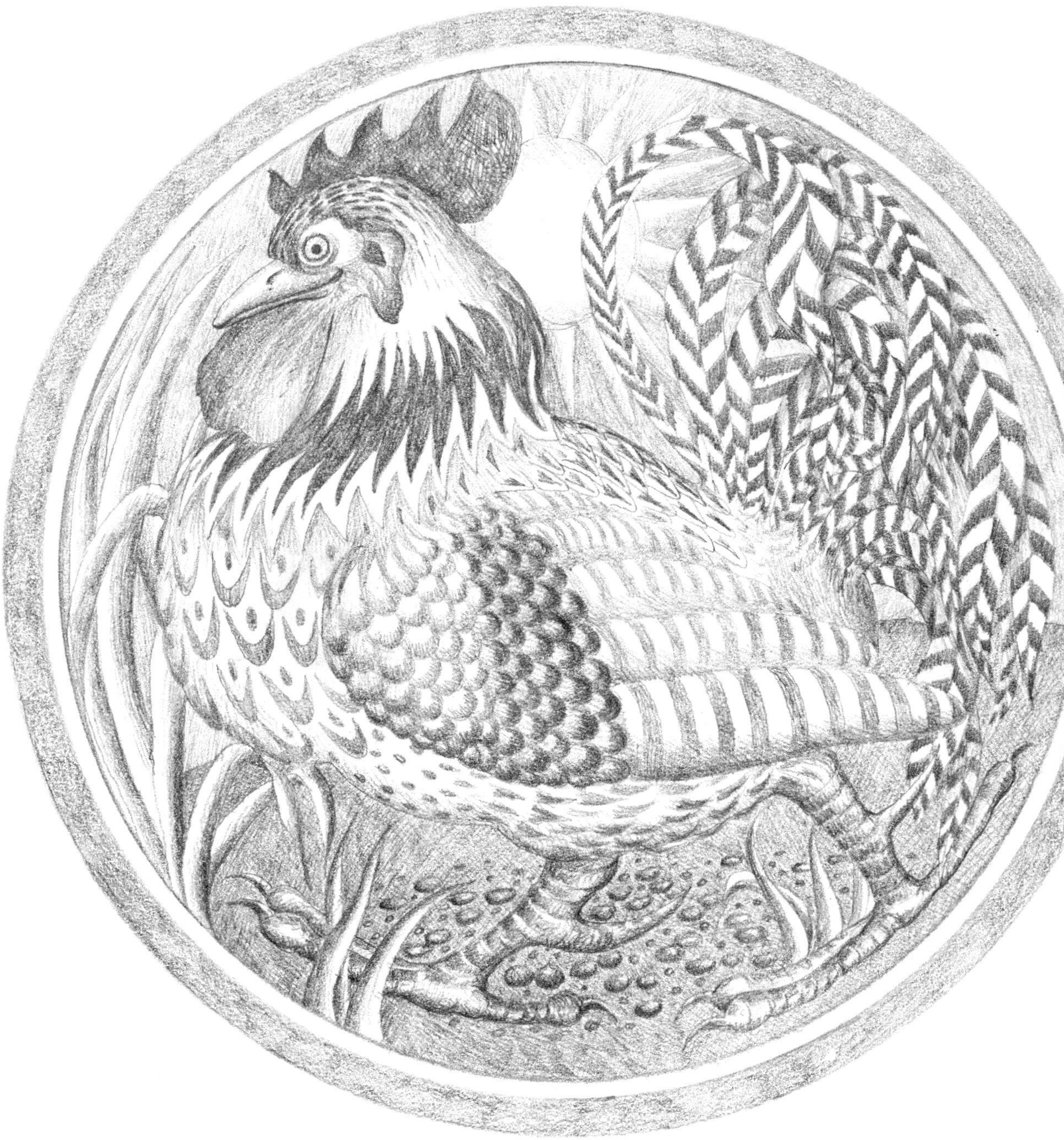

The drawing opposite is pure fantasy. If you embark on something like this, you can invent your own rules within your drawing. You can stray as far as you like from reality; all that matters is that the whole of the finished drawing is convincing. I drew this one entirely out of my head, although I had to use some observation drawings (such as those below) to help sort out a few problems of anatomy. I couldn't, of course, find drawings or photographs which showed the exact poses I wanted, but there was enough information in those I selected to fill the gaps left by my imagination.

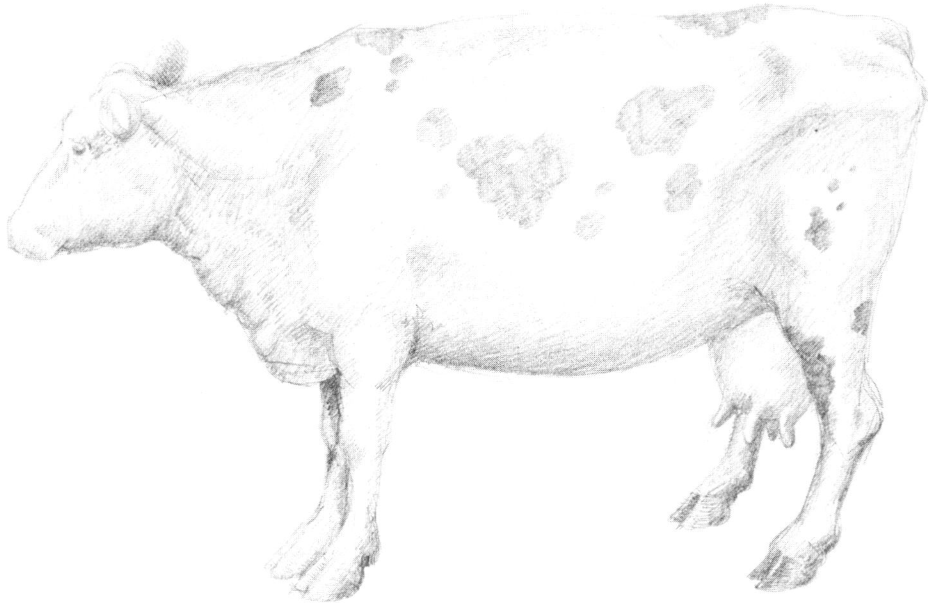

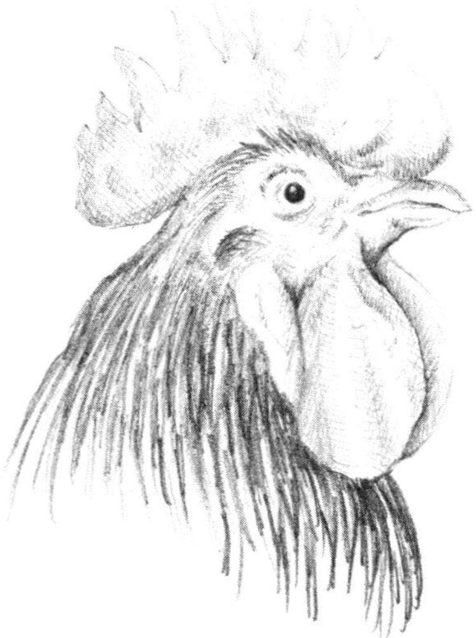

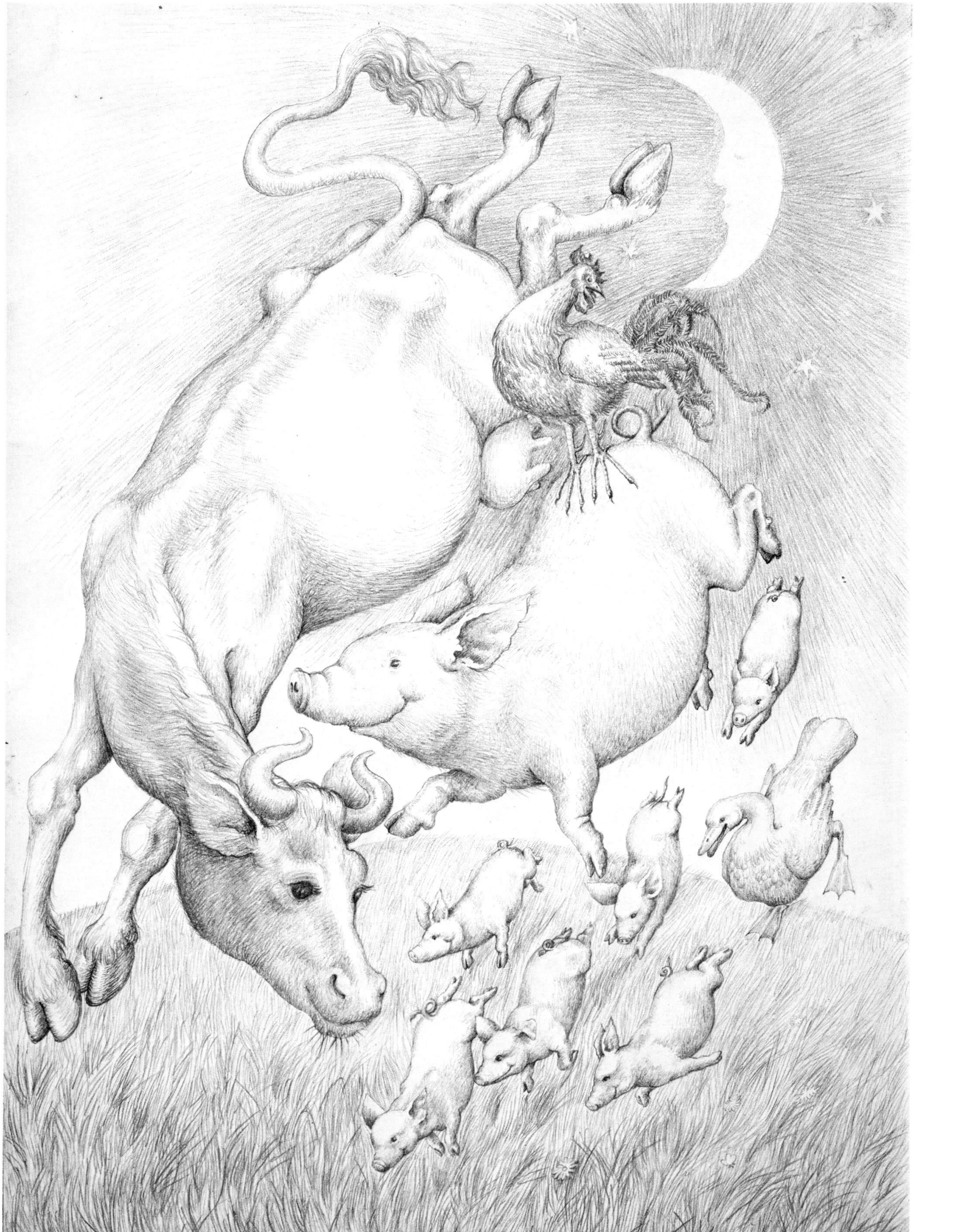

Anatomy

To understand the shape of a horse, it is helpful to know something about its anatomy. Museums with natural history departments often have skeletons that you can study and sketch, and many books contain skeletal sketches. A drawing such as the one here or that on page 14 shows which bones come near to the surface and therefore affect the horse's outline. It also shows the angles made as one bone joins another. This kind of information will help you to be accurate and realistic when you draw a living horse.

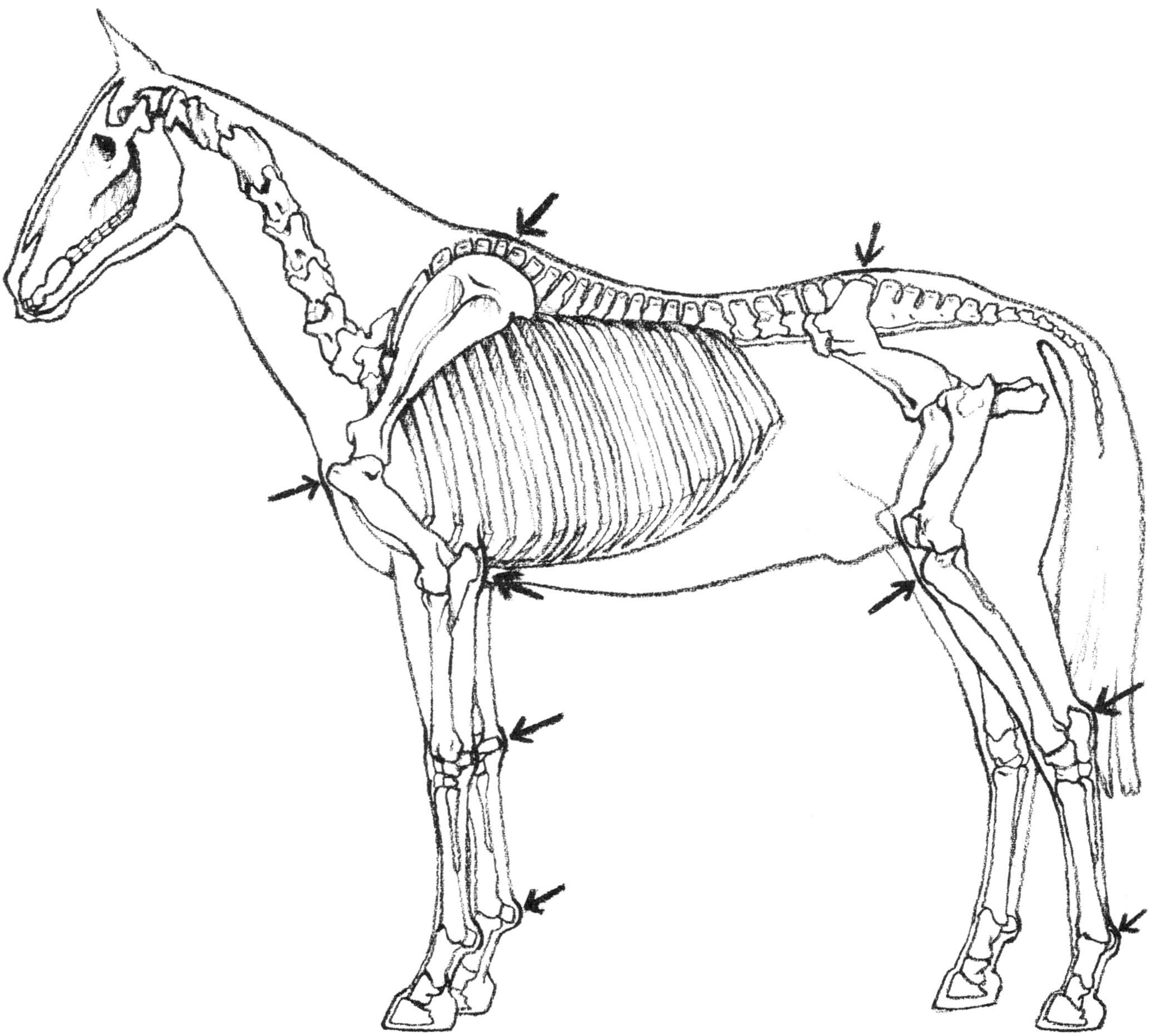

Shown here are the muscles which directly affect the surface area.

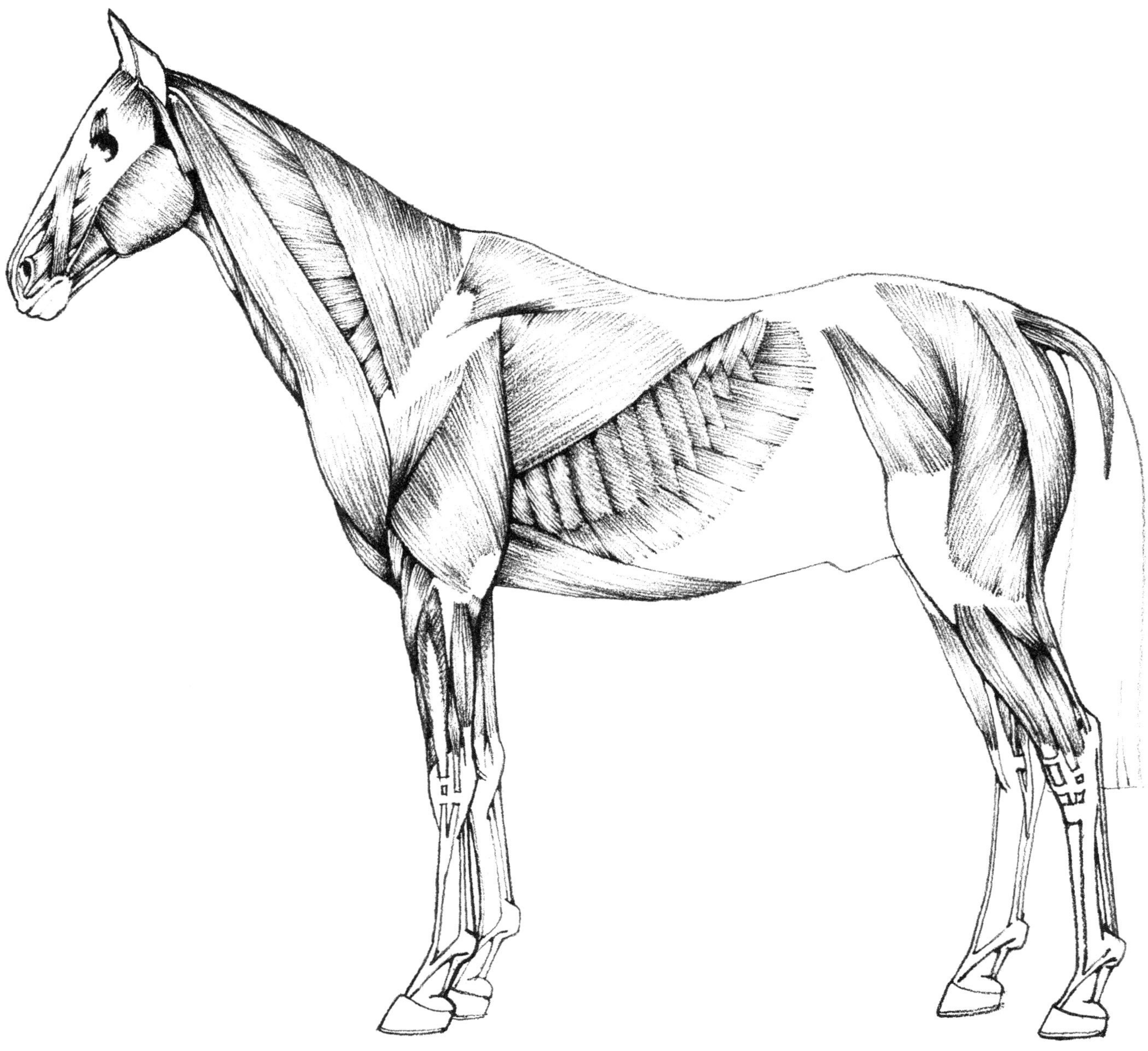

Proportion and structure

In order to get the proportions of your drawing right, and also to capture the feeling of movement contained in the animal's pose, refer to the advice about dogs and cats on pages 101 and 126–7 and compare it with the drawings here.

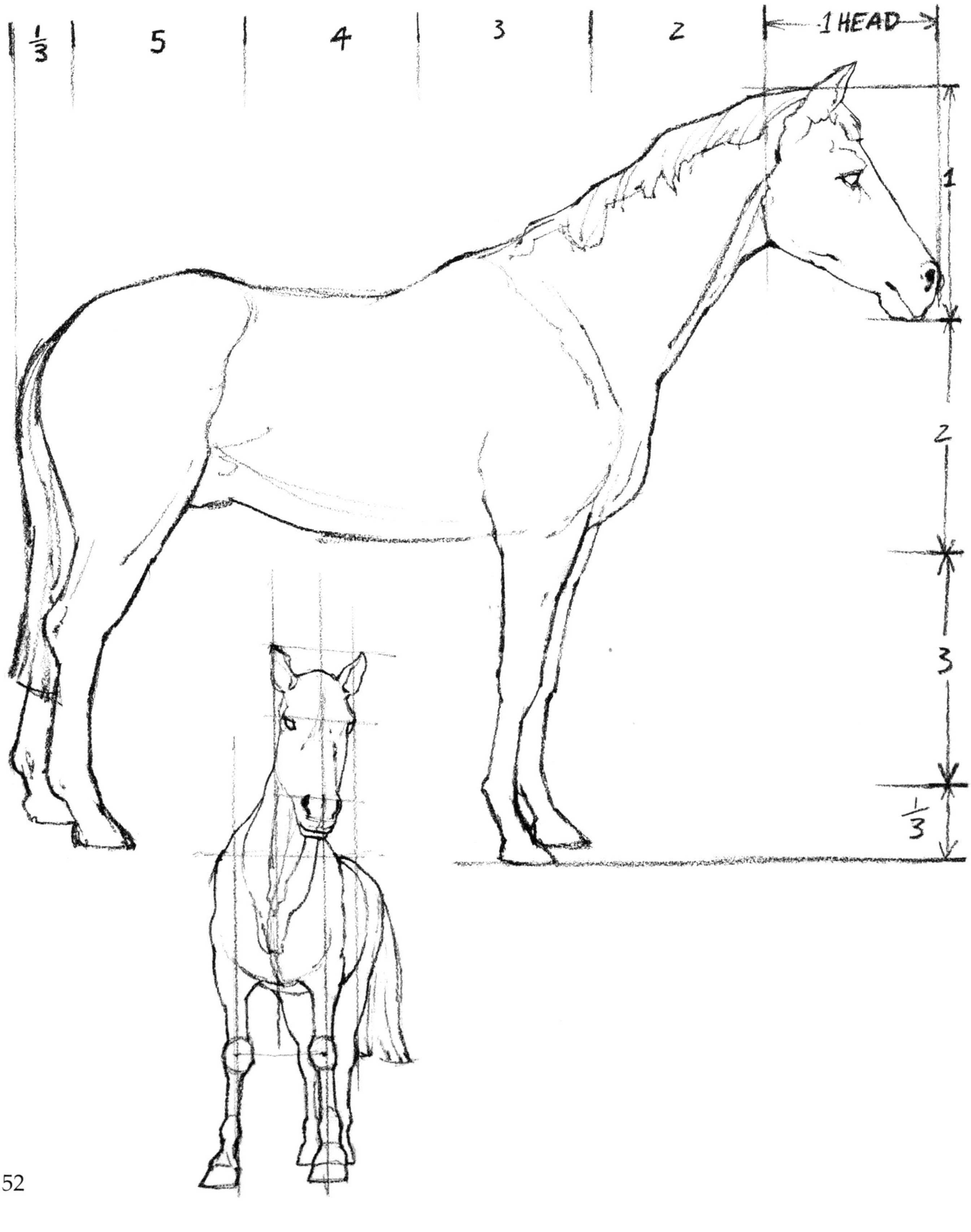

Drawing parts

Study the various parts of the horse's body separately and in detail. A body is symmetrical, which makes the job of analyzing its shape a lot easier. The drawings of heads below show how the structure can be broken down into patterns.

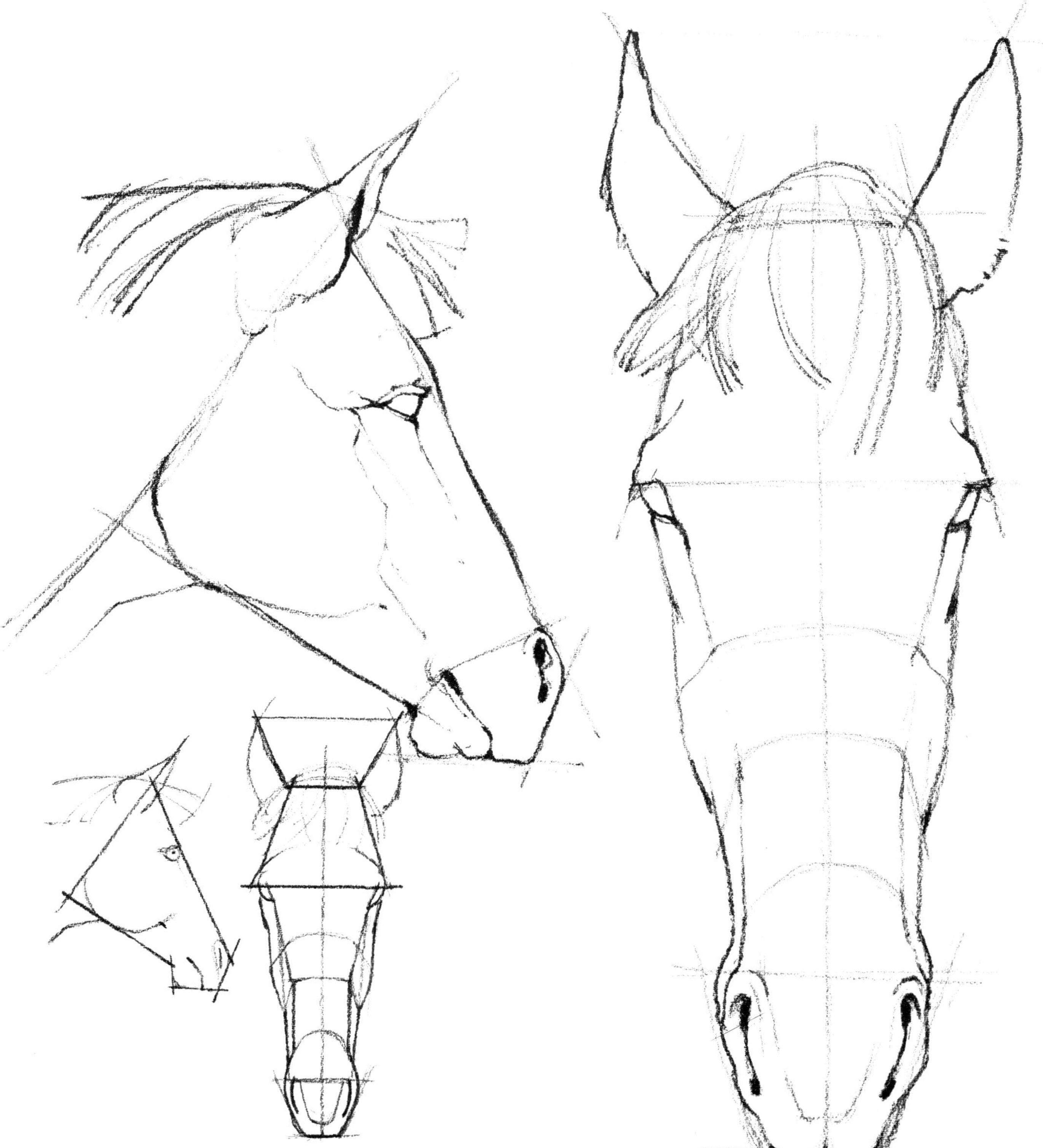

These drawings show the difference in shape between the heads of a workhorse (above) and a racehorse (below).

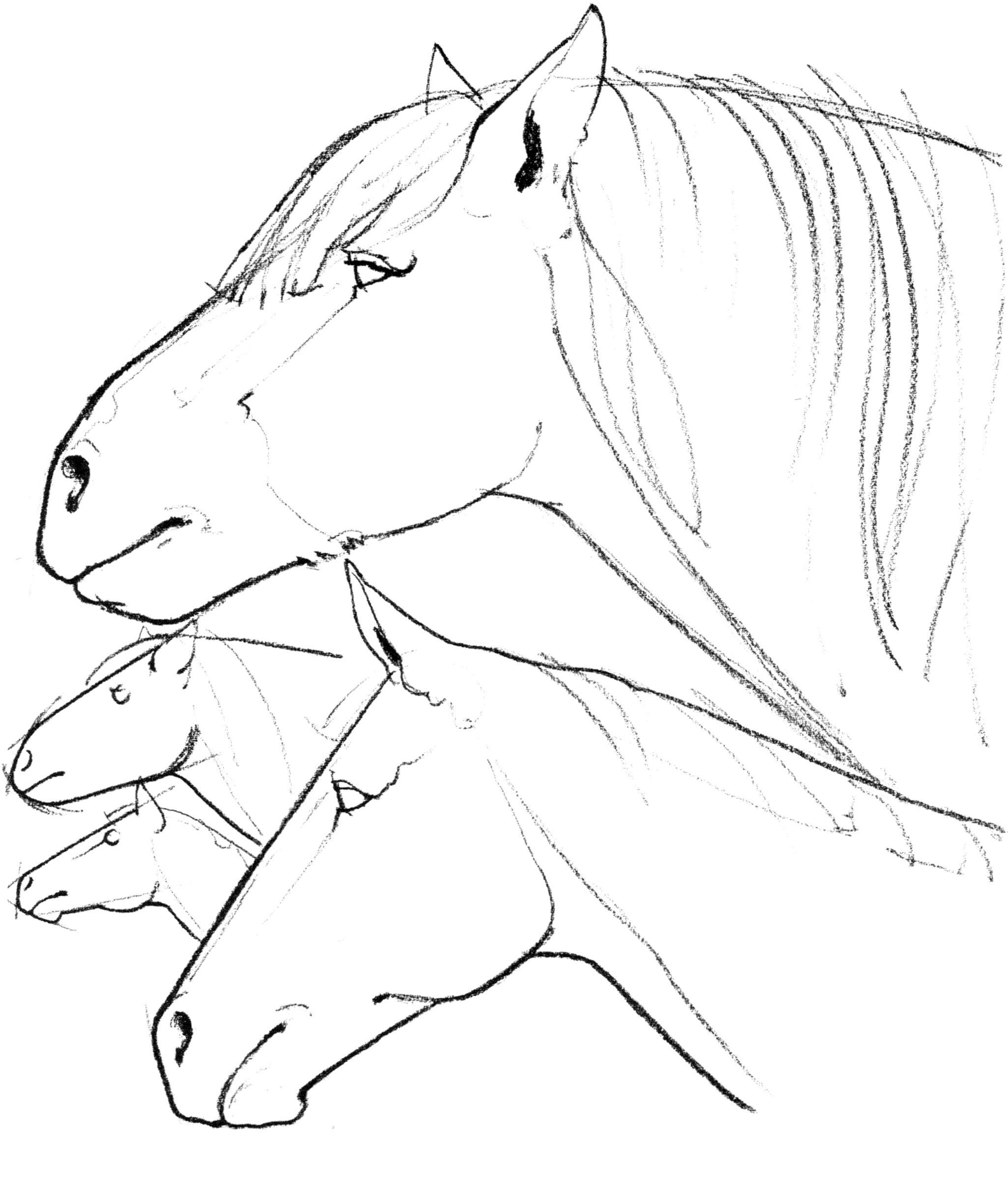

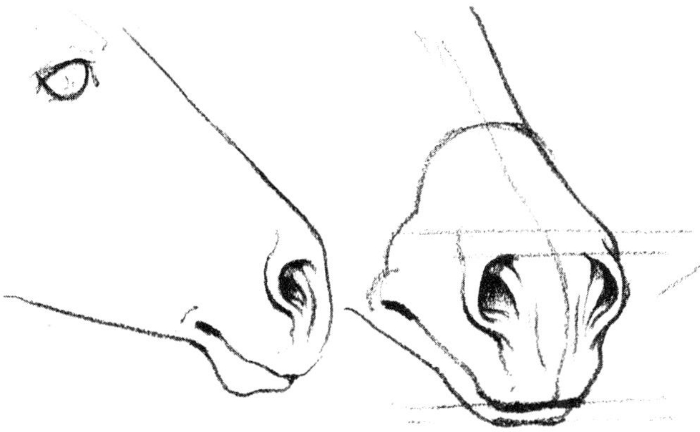

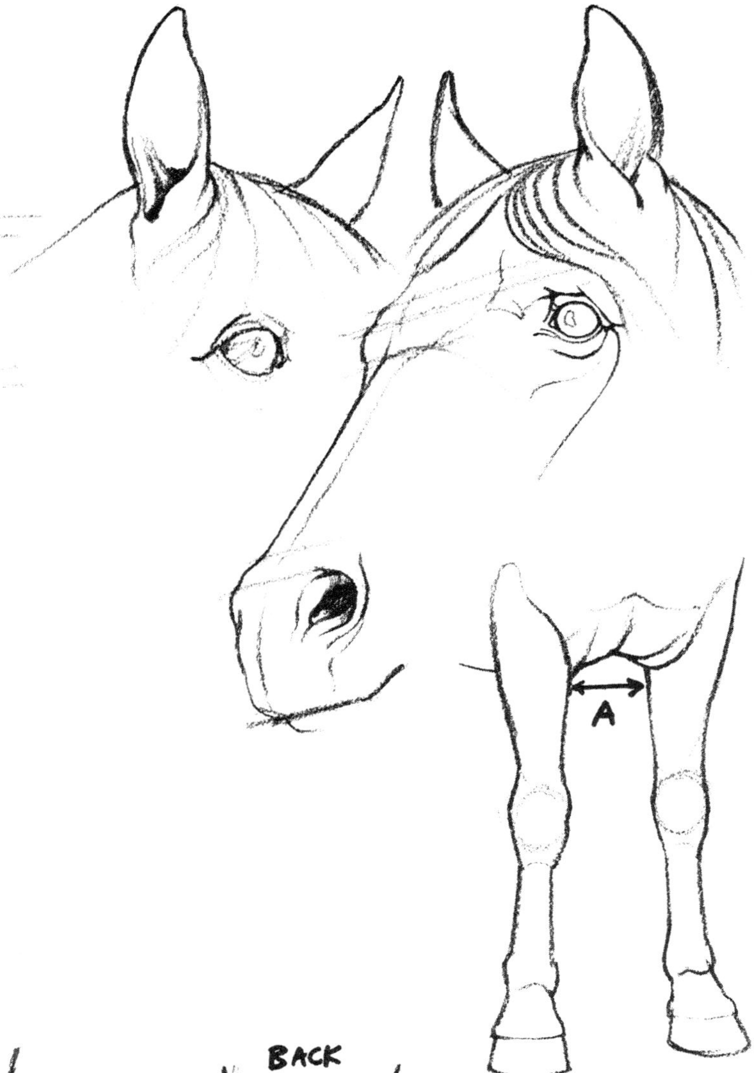

Make detailed drawings of nostrils, eyes, ears, and notice how they fit onto and into the head.

A horse's legs do not come together at the top as a human being's do. There is a gap, marked A here. Study also the different angles made by the front and back legs.

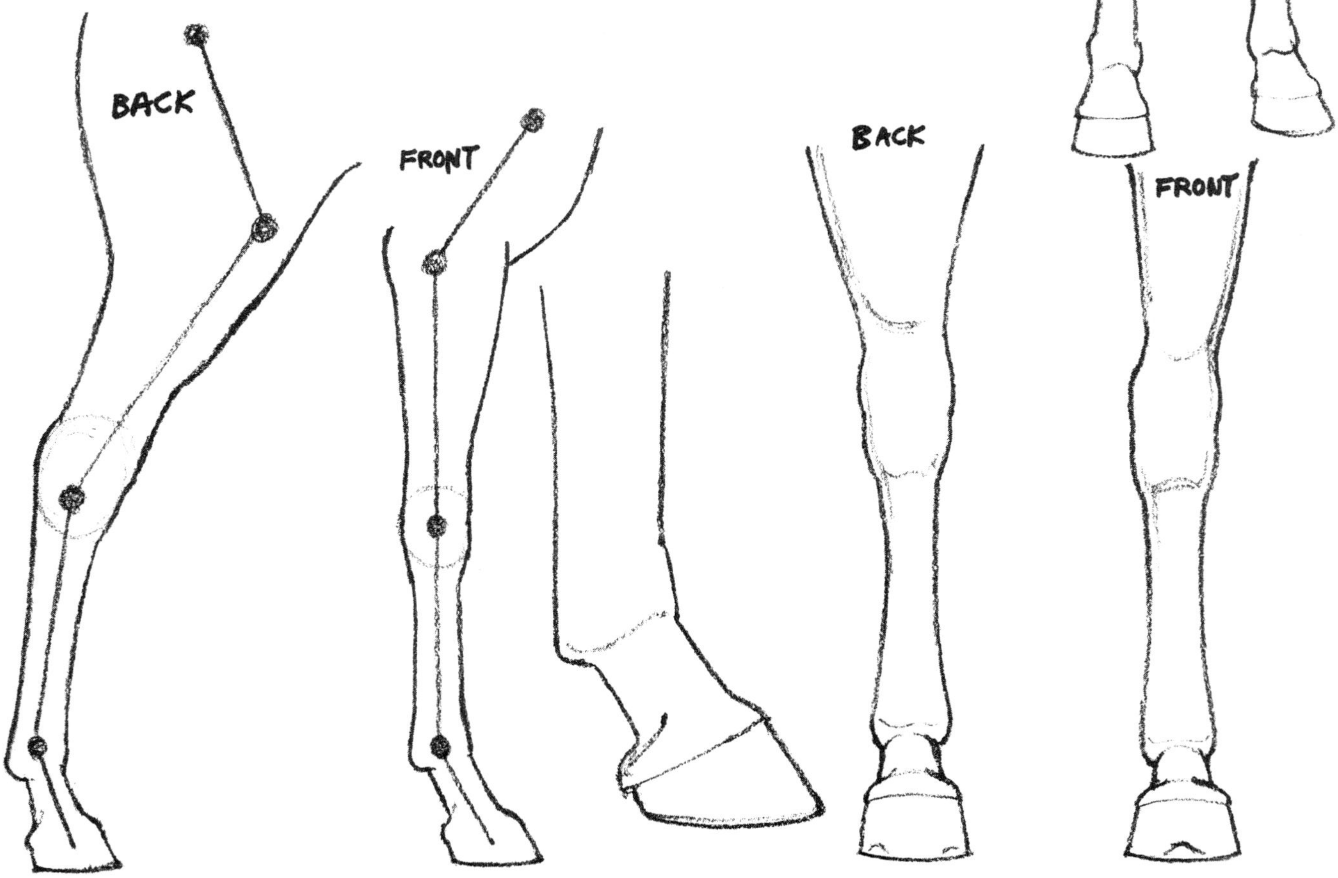

Draw various features from different viewpoints to get an overall knowledge of their structure. This is a slightly unusual view of a horse's head. The sketches below and on page 58 show the difference between the legs of a powerful workhorse and a hunter.

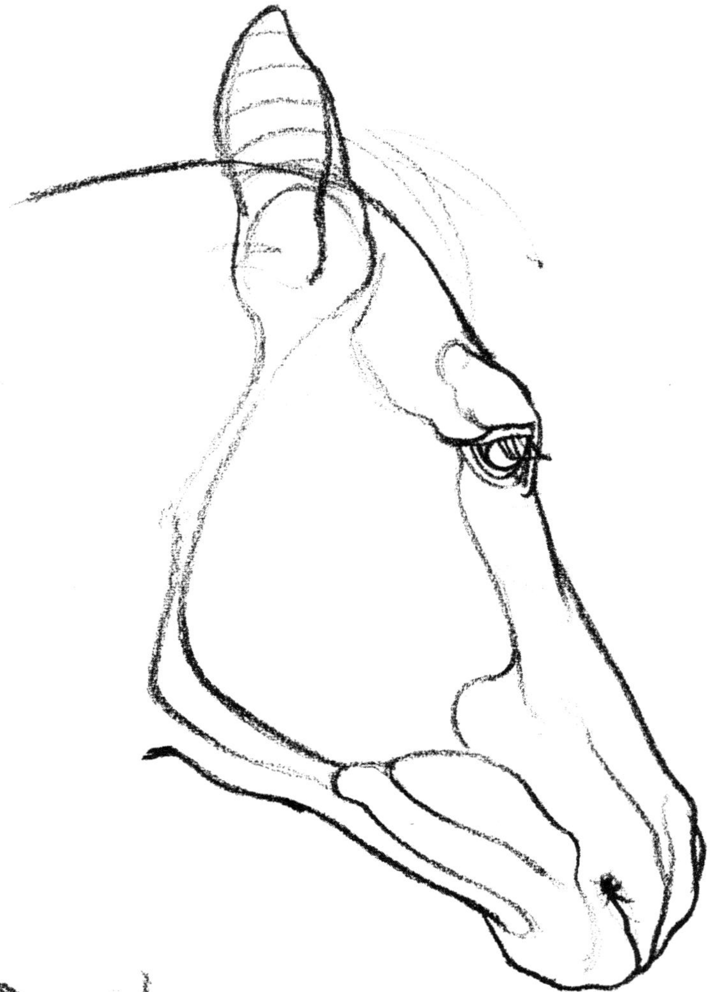

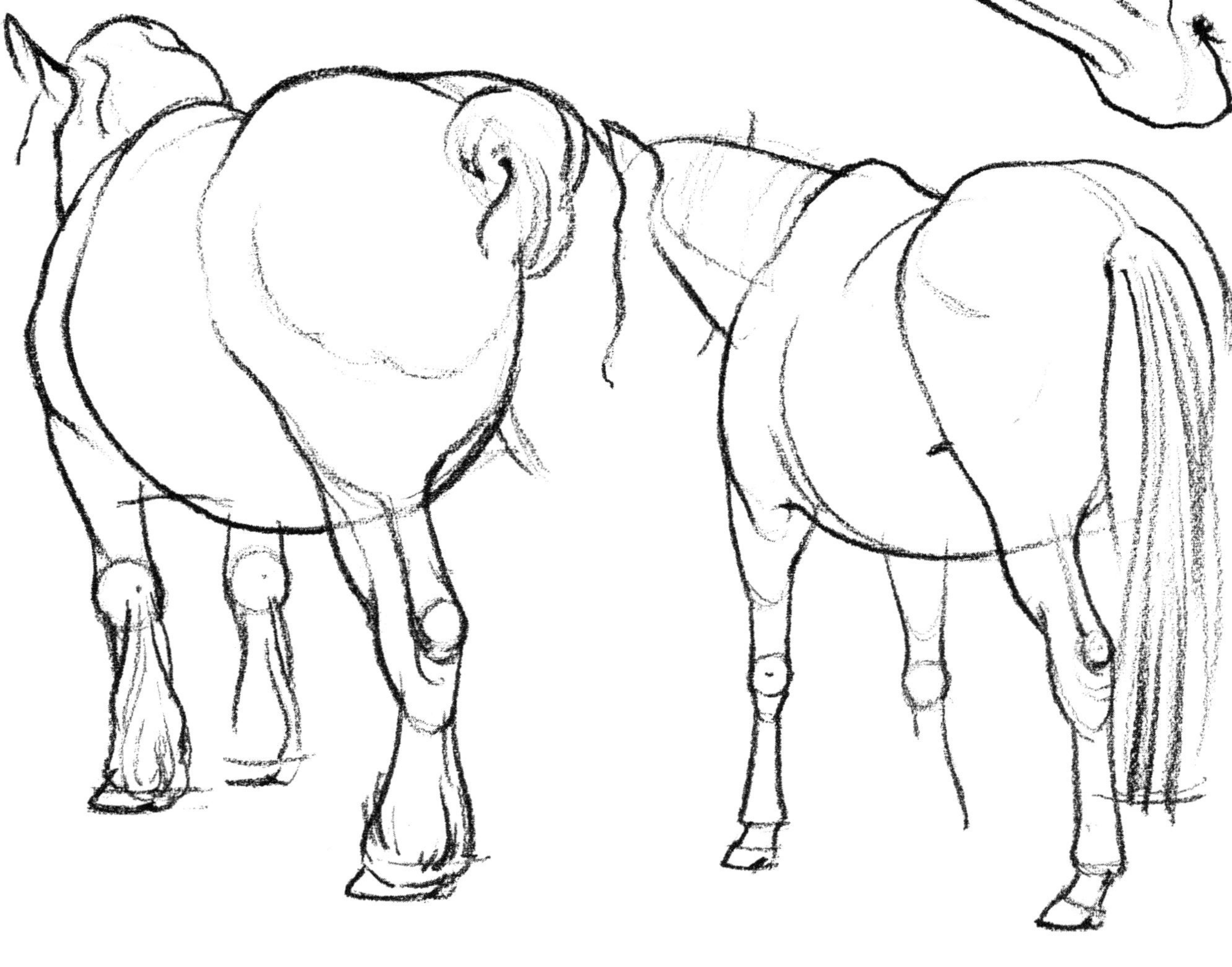

Body shapes

To understand the body shapes better, try breaking them down into a series of simplifed sections. (If you work from photographs, you will have plenty of time to make your own analysis—but make sure to use good quality photographs only.) Then try fuller drawings of different kinds of horse as in the following pages.

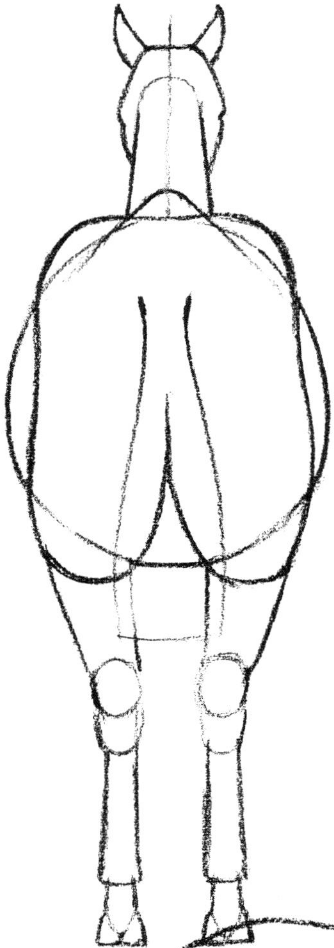

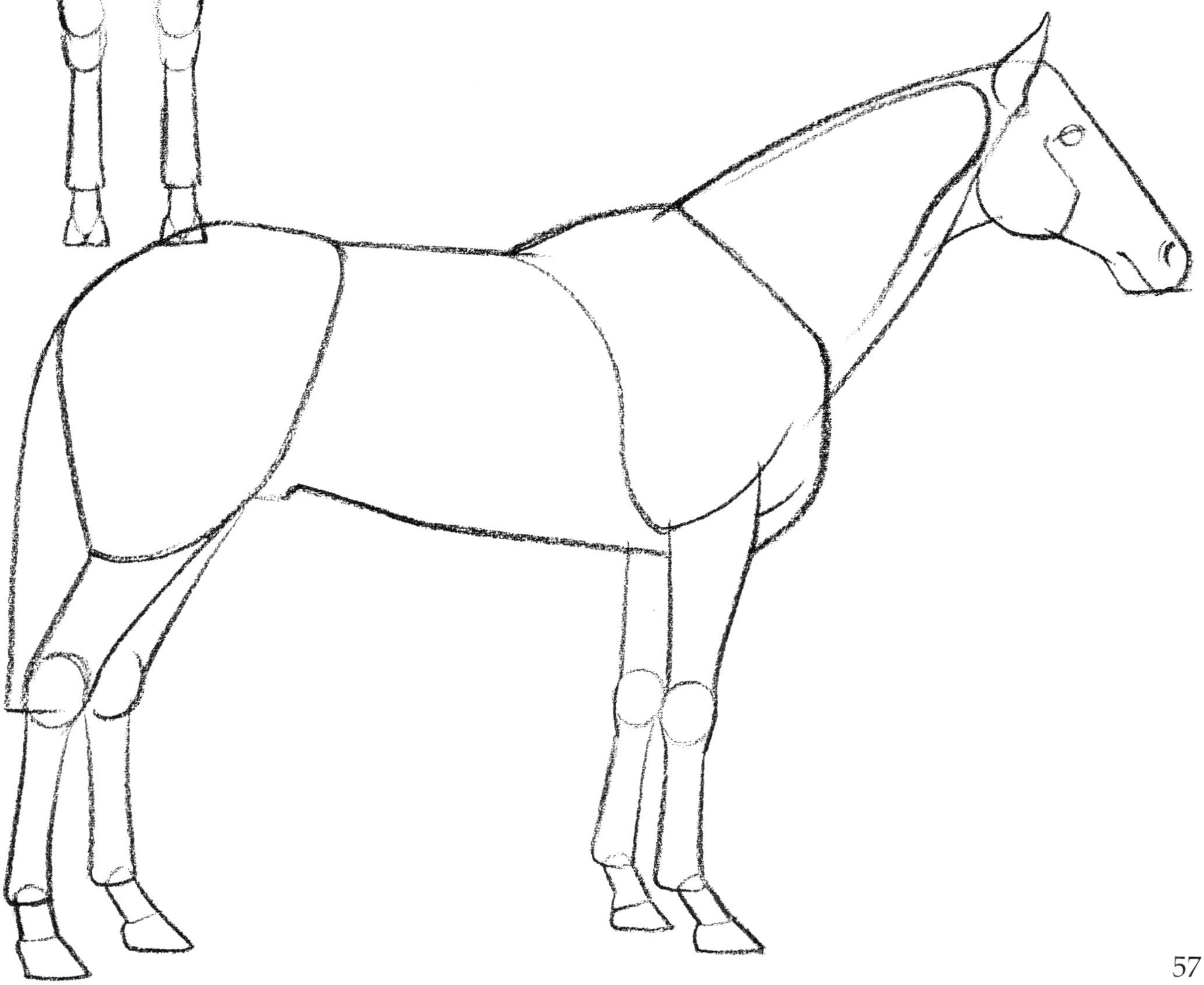

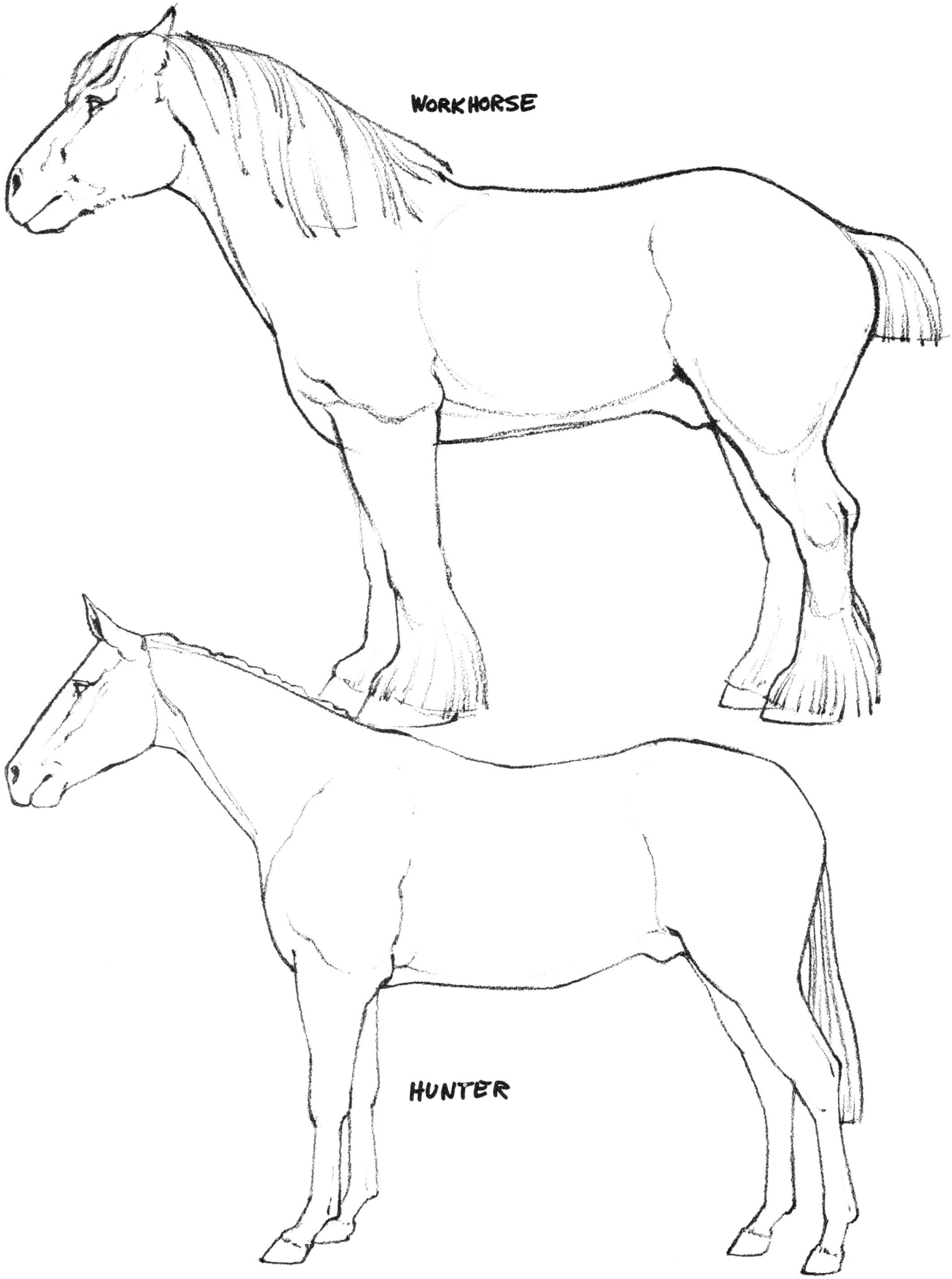
WORKHORSE
HUNTER

The bottom drawing is of a Welsh Mountain pony, the top one of a Shetland. Notice the difference in structure.

PONIES

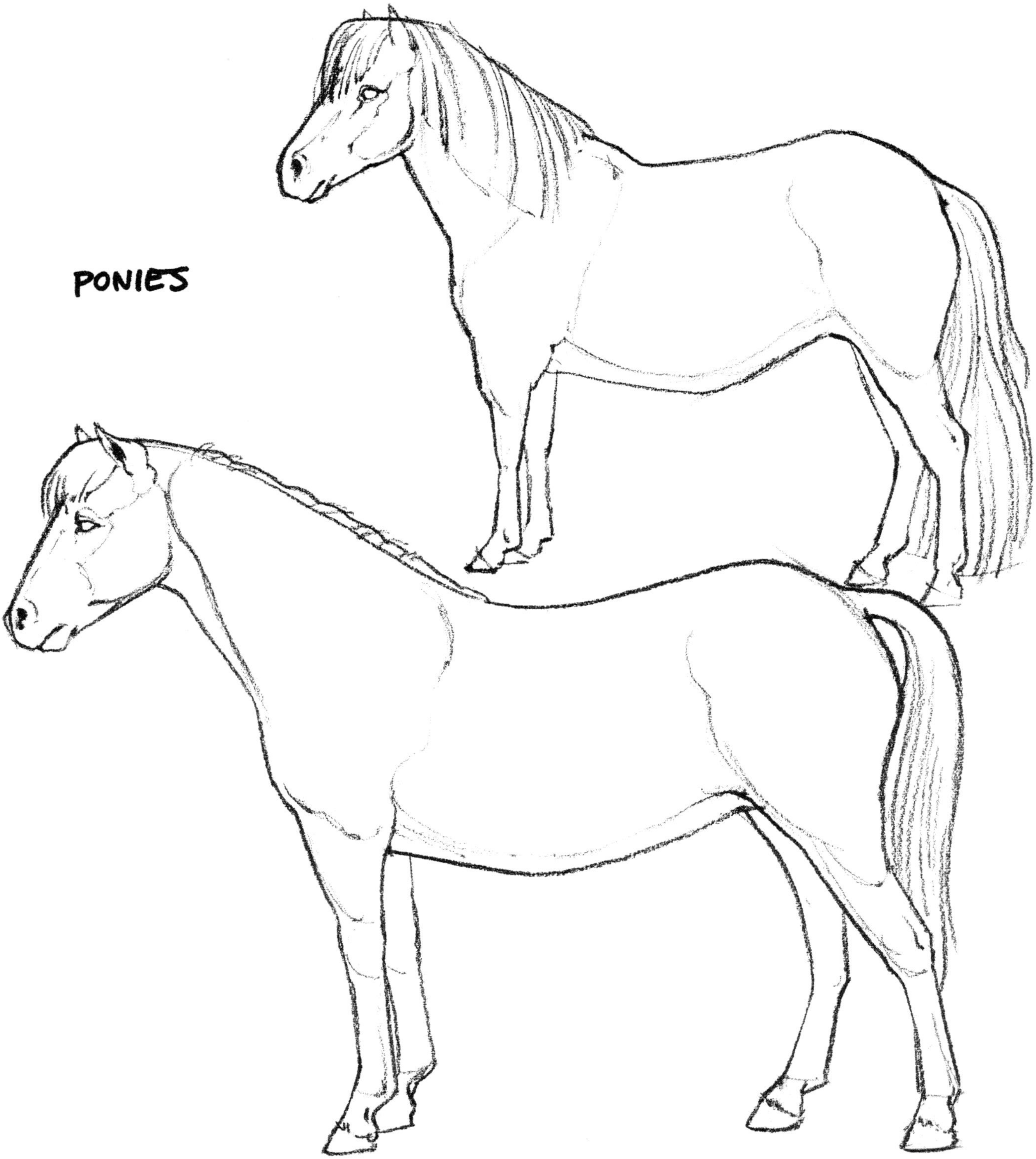

Compare the proportions here. A foal's legs, for example, are very long in relation to its body.

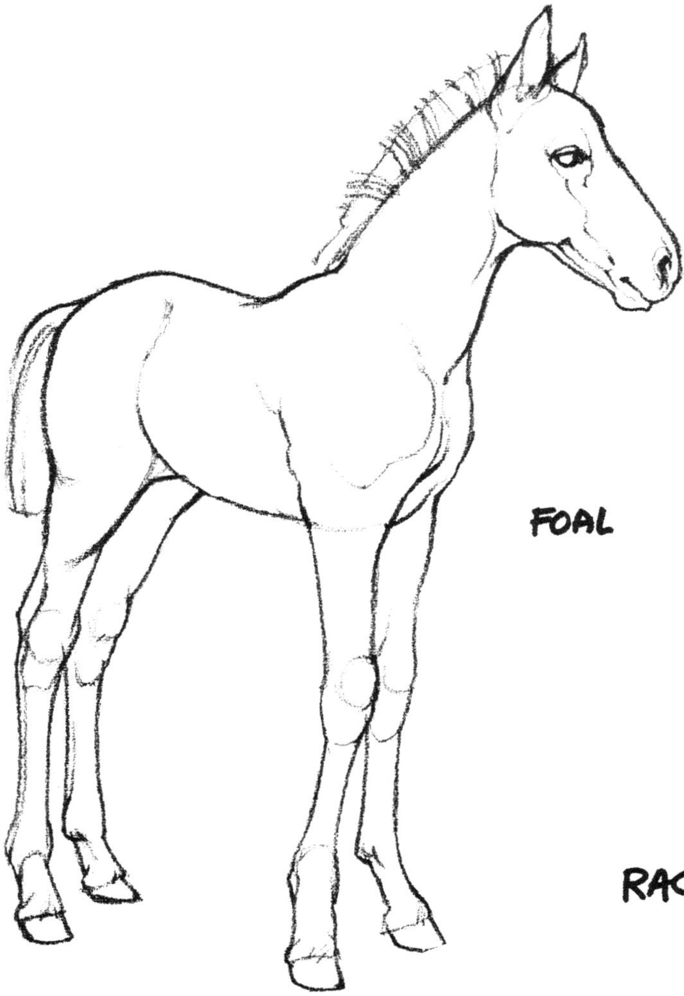

FOAL

RACE HORSE

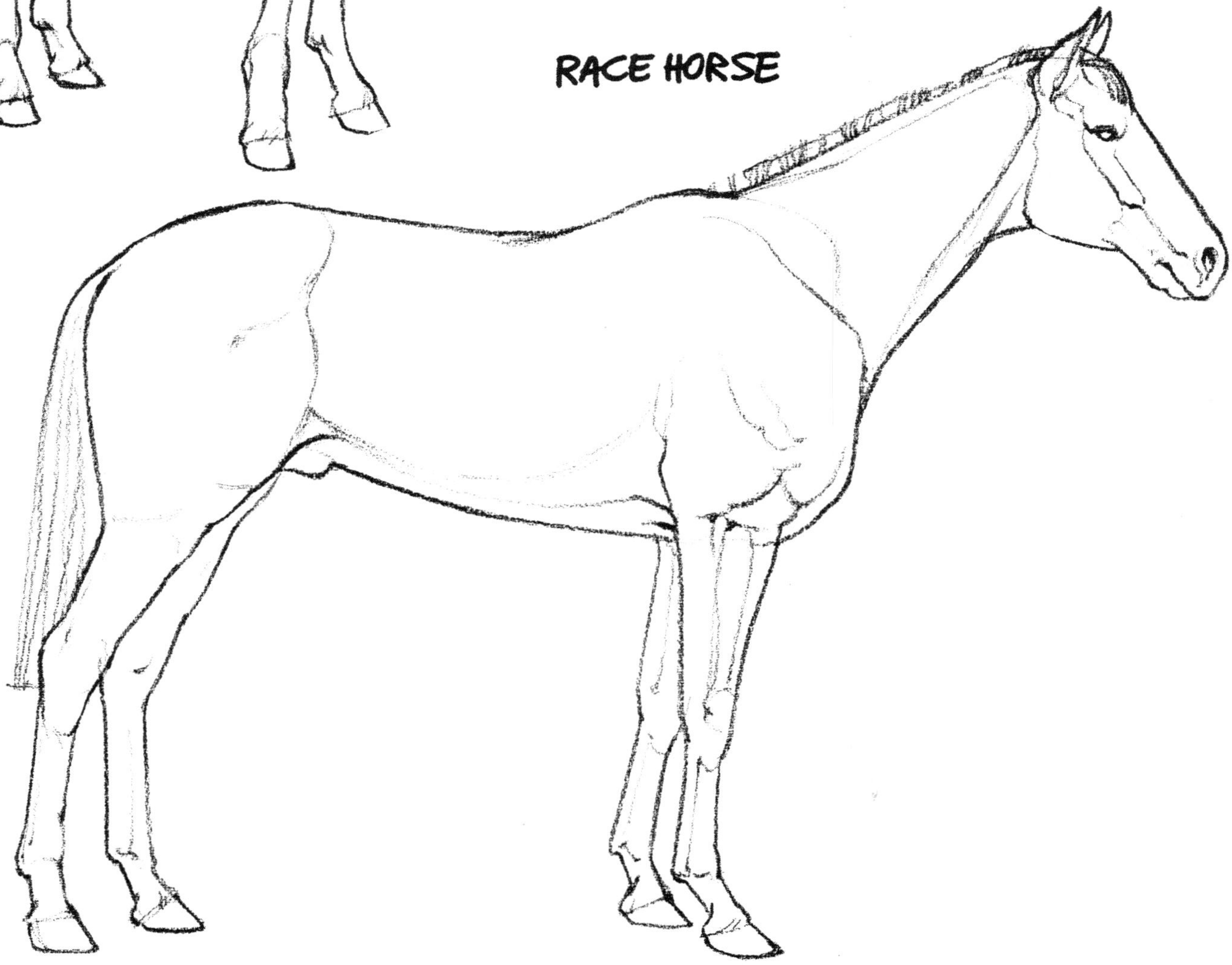

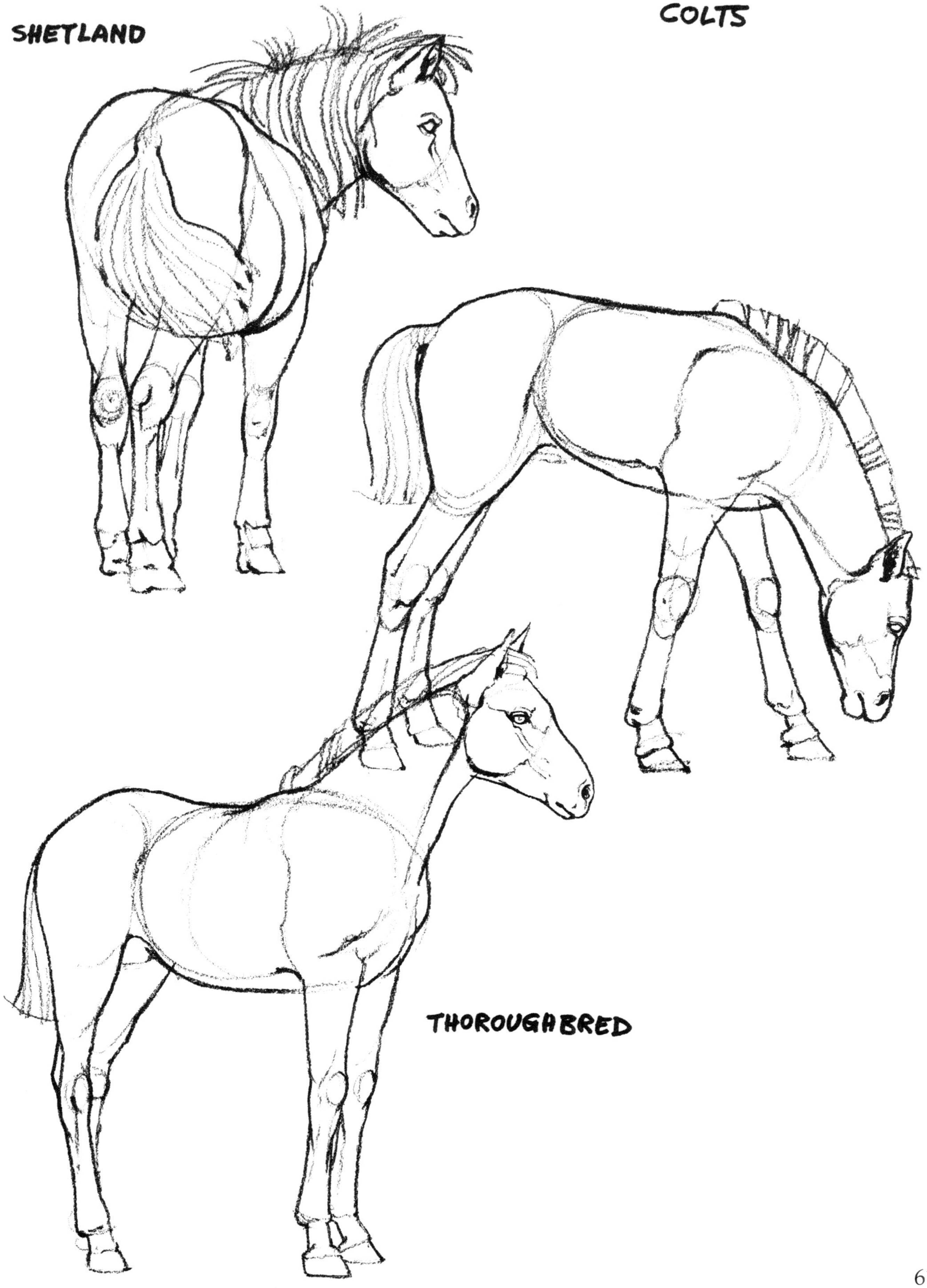
COLTS
SHETLAND
THOROUGABRED

Step-by-step: the head

Here and on the following pages, drawings are developed from first basic lines to completion. In the first stage of any drawing, it helps enormously to add imaginary construction lines like those marked below. These are lines that you won't in fact put in once you become practised—but even then your pencil will go through the motions of adding them, while it only contacts the paper when drawing the actual features.

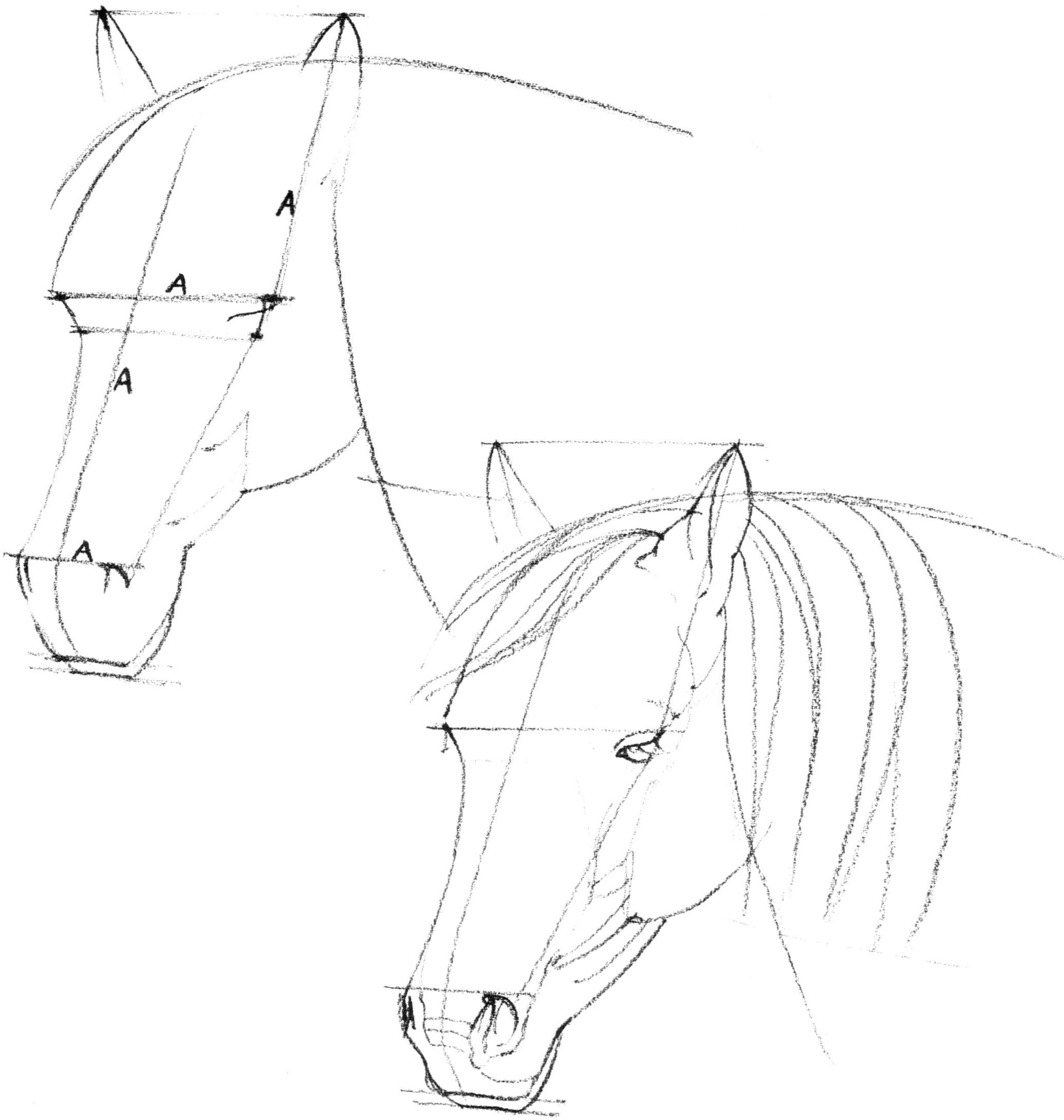

At every stage in a drawing, compare the length, width and shape of the various areas. Check, for example, whether the distance between the eyes is the same as the distance between eyes and nostrils. Don't put in the final shading without noting first where the light is coming from.

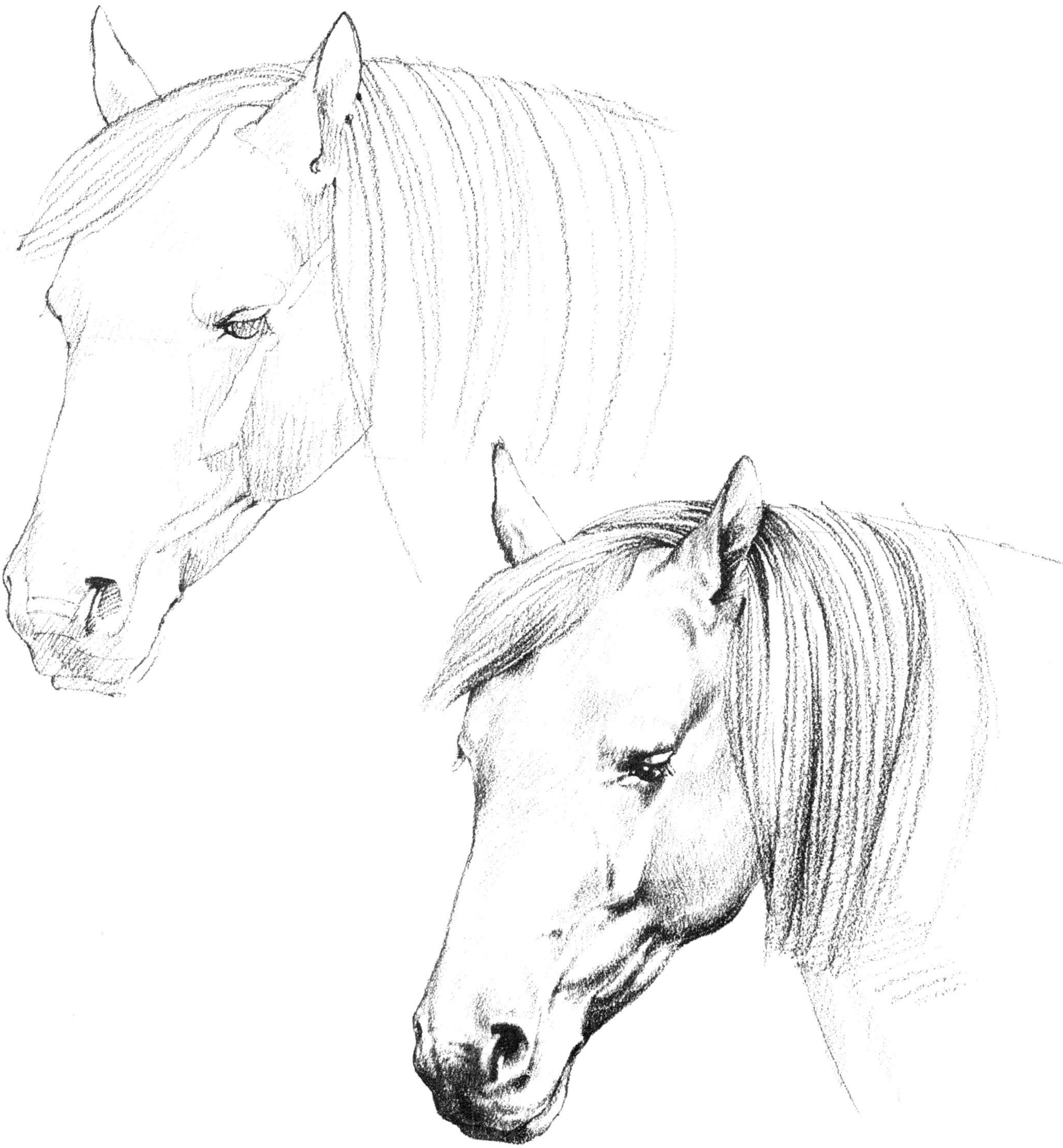

Step-by-step: the body

When starting a drawing, it sometimes helps you to see your subject in its simplest form if you half-close your eyes. By doing so, you shut out most of the detail, which makes it easier to concentrate on basic shapes. The drawing here was made with a B pencil on cartridge paper.

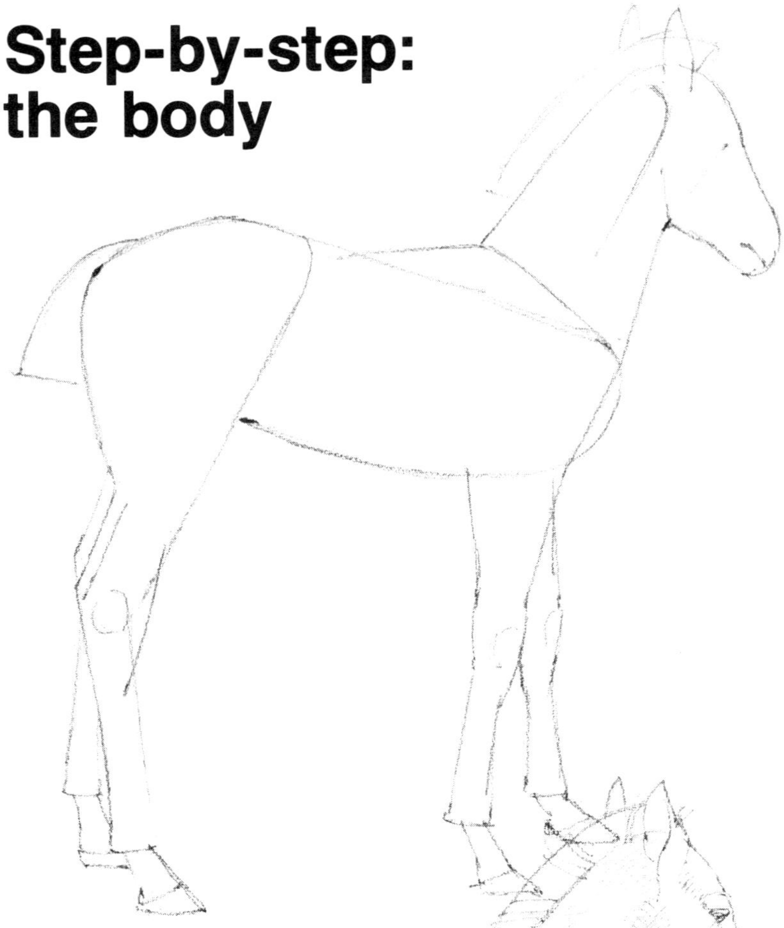

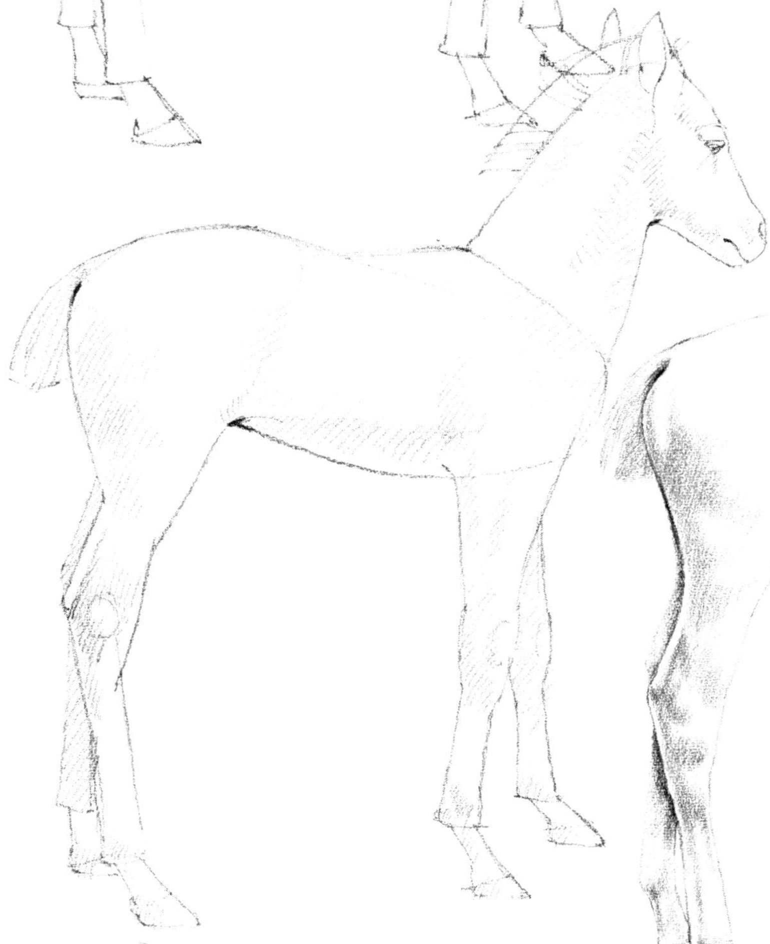

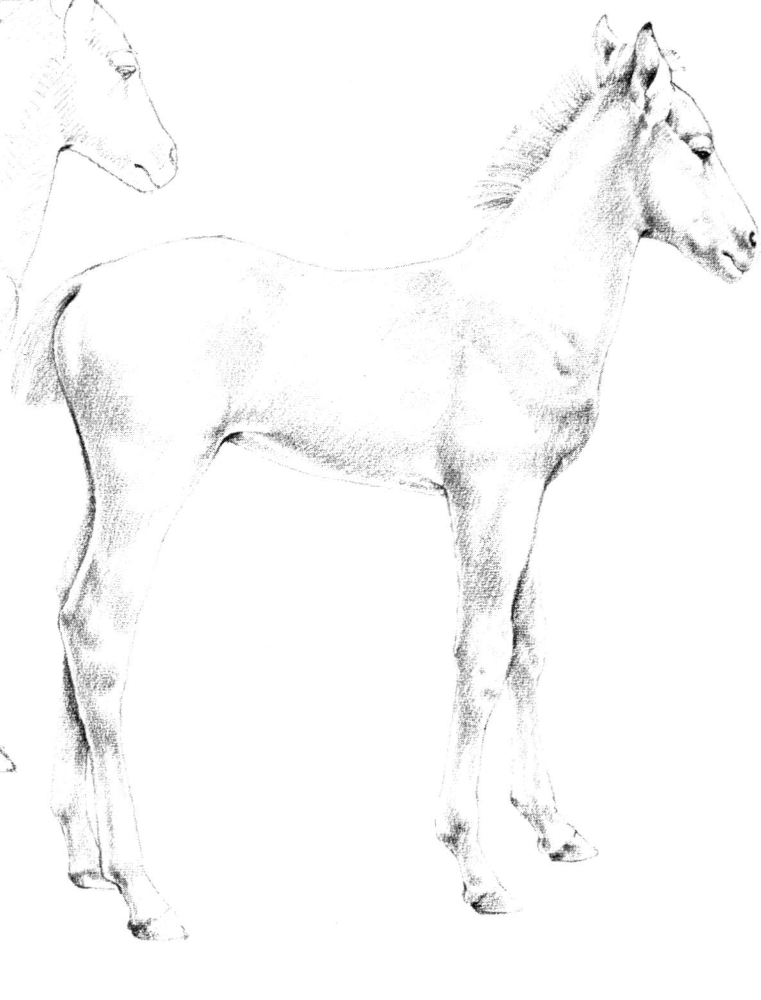

The basic shape of this Andalusian was sketched in with a carbon pencil; the drawing was finished with a stick of charcoal.

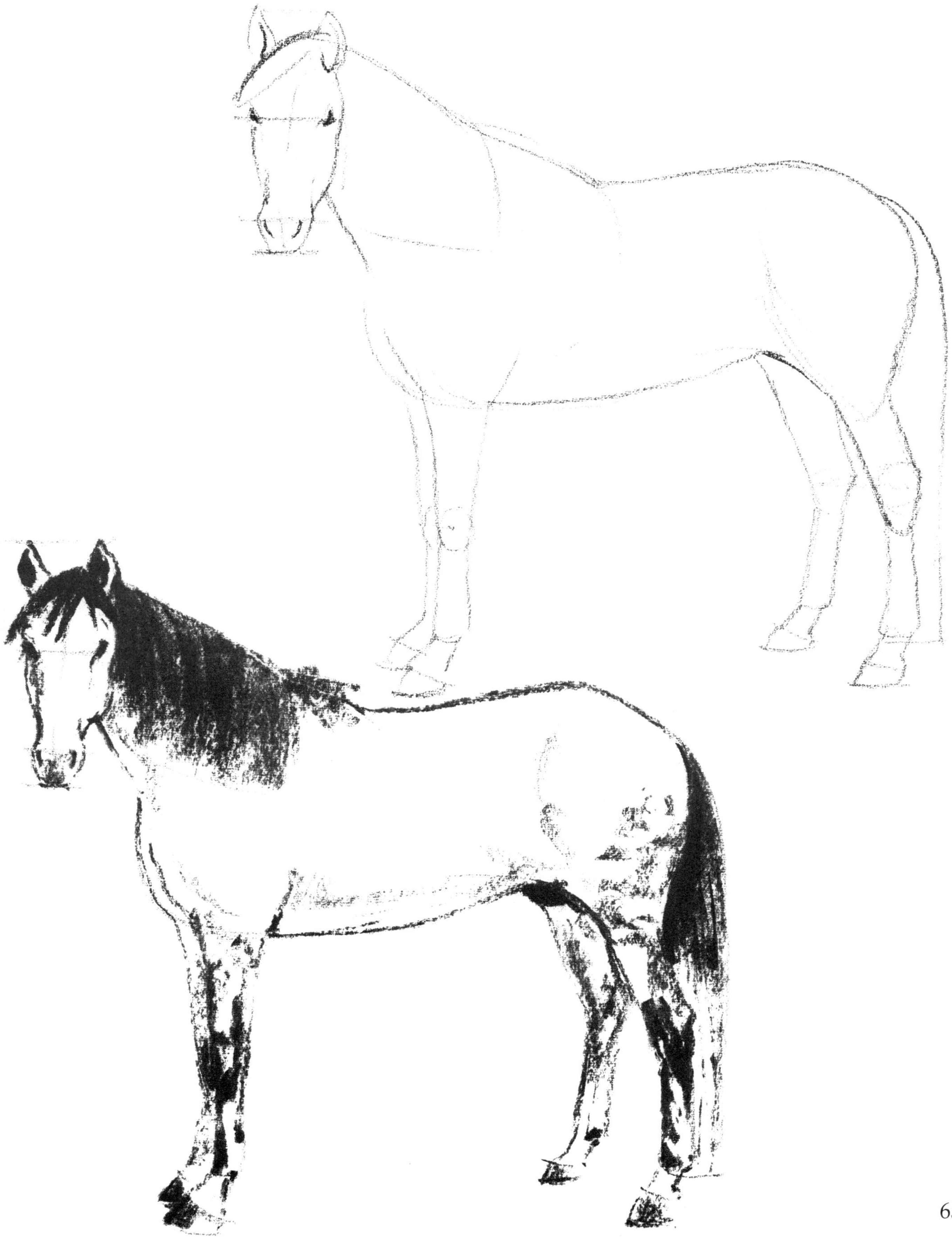

This drawing of a Percheron is more ambitious. The basic lines were drawn with a 6B pencil and then shaded. The result was rubbed with a French Stick (tightly-rolled card) and highlights and spots picked out with a putty eraser.

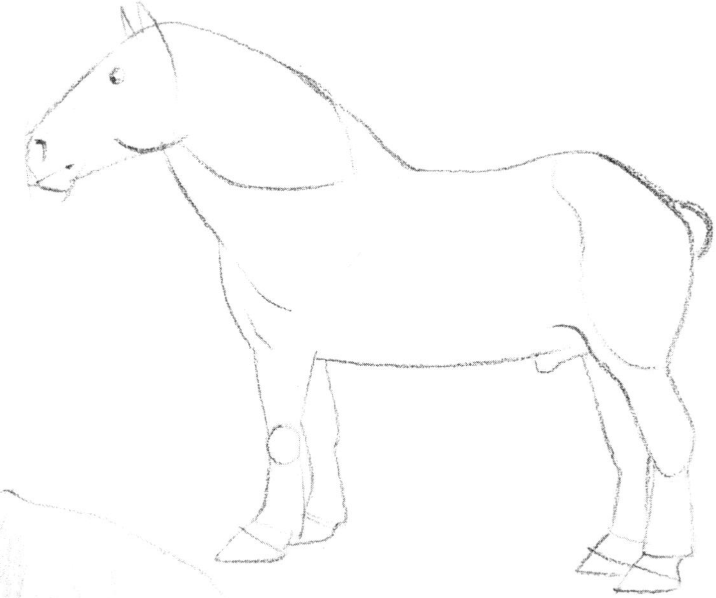

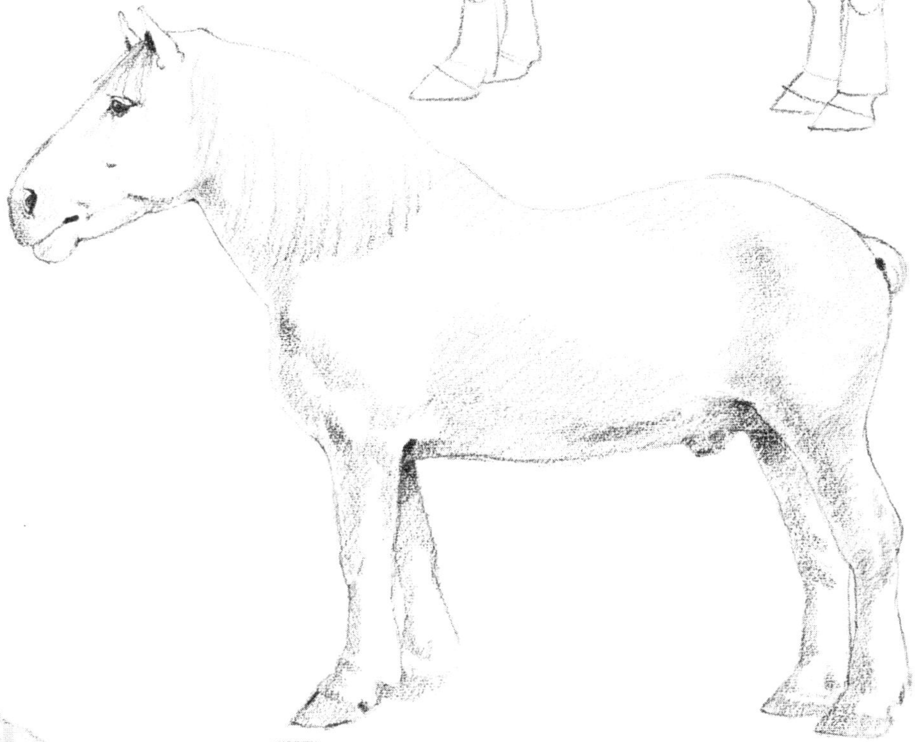

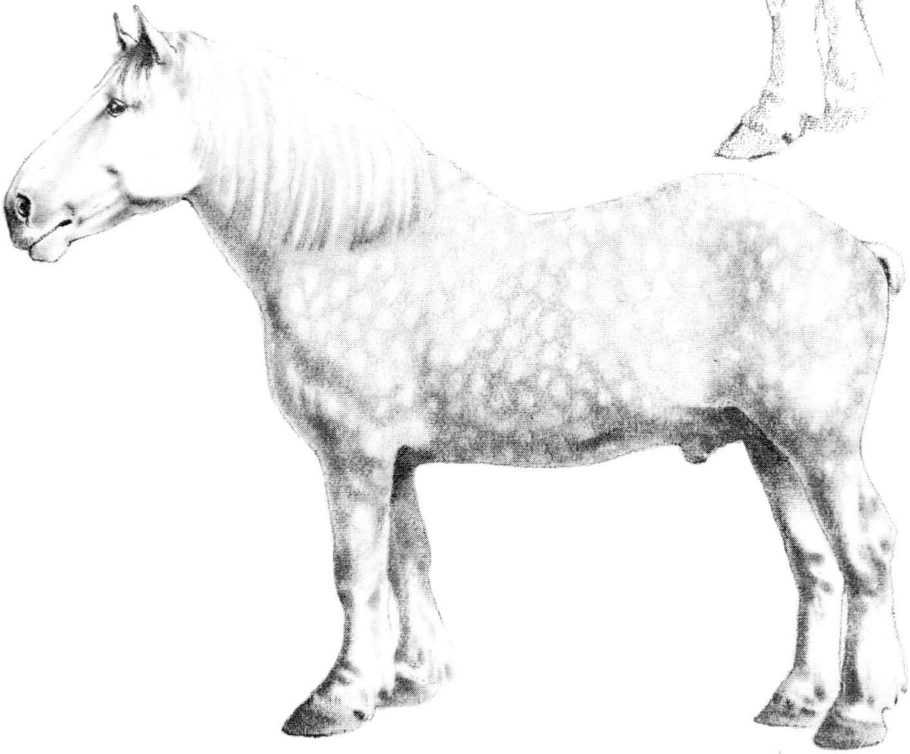

Here, I drew the pony's basic lines with a 2B pencil and, using the pencil's guidelines, added the details with a fibre-tipped pen. Finally, I lightly brushed one edge of the line with clean water. This is not an easy technique to control.

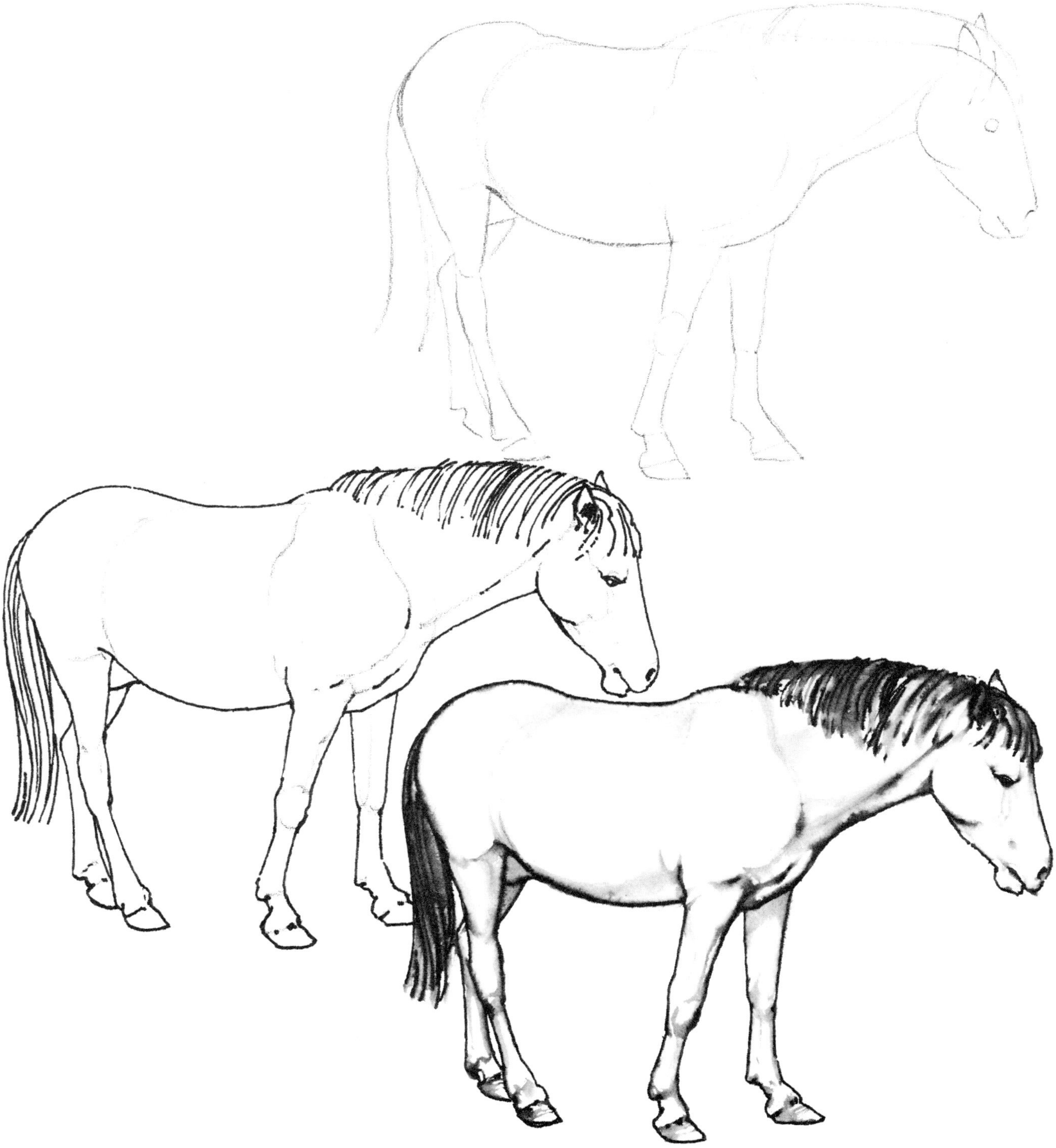

This Pinto's basic lines were drawn with a carbon pencil. The drawing was then developed in pen-and-ink and dabbed with a finger. Finally, a light wash was applied with a brush.

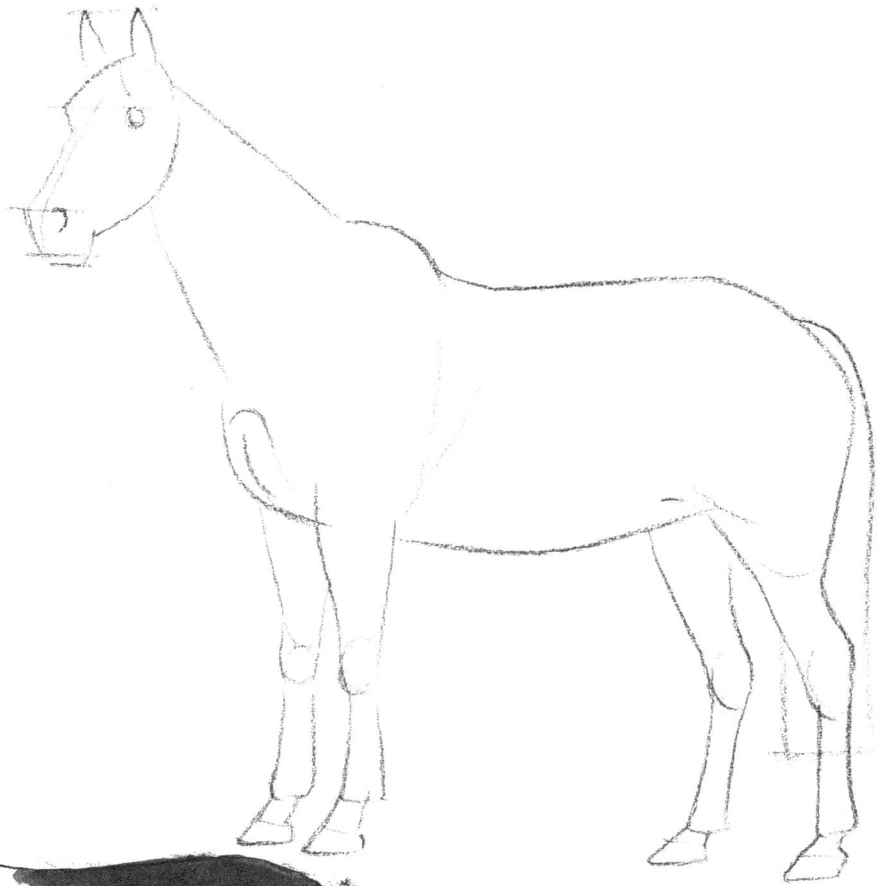

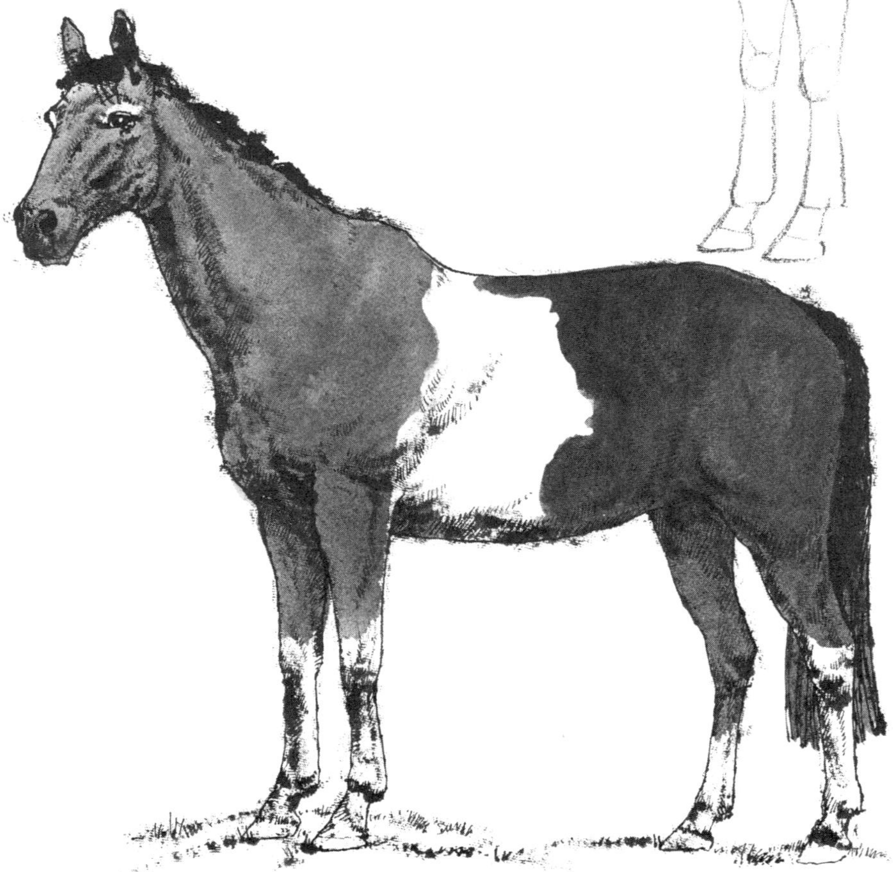

Unusual positions

Go for unusual positions; be adventurous. The drawings on this page and overleaf are examples of somewhat unusual front and rear views.

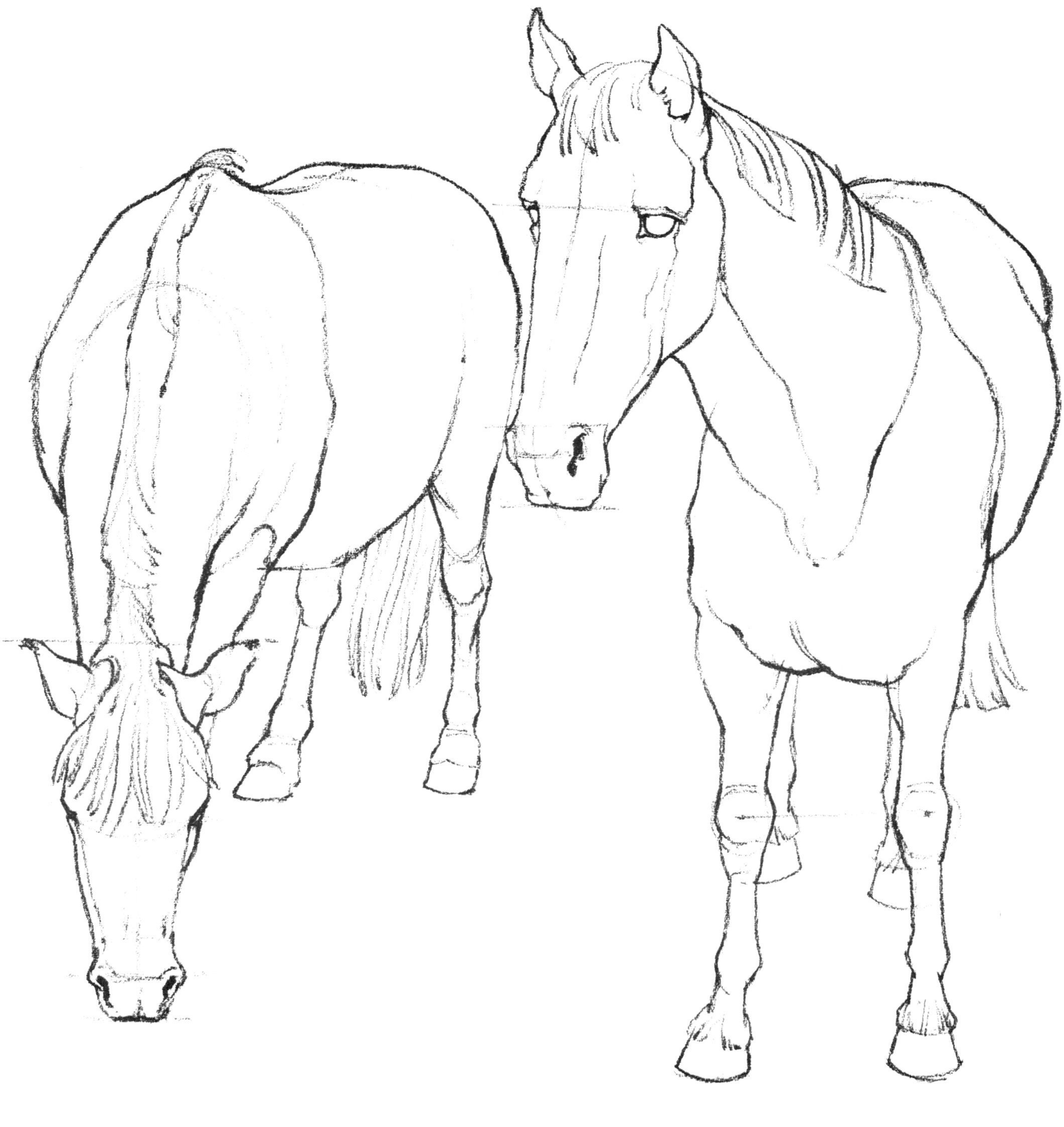

Like the drawings on the previous page, this one was made with a soft charcoal pencil. Notice that the unusual viewpoint brings out the rounded shape and shows how one part of the body fits into another.

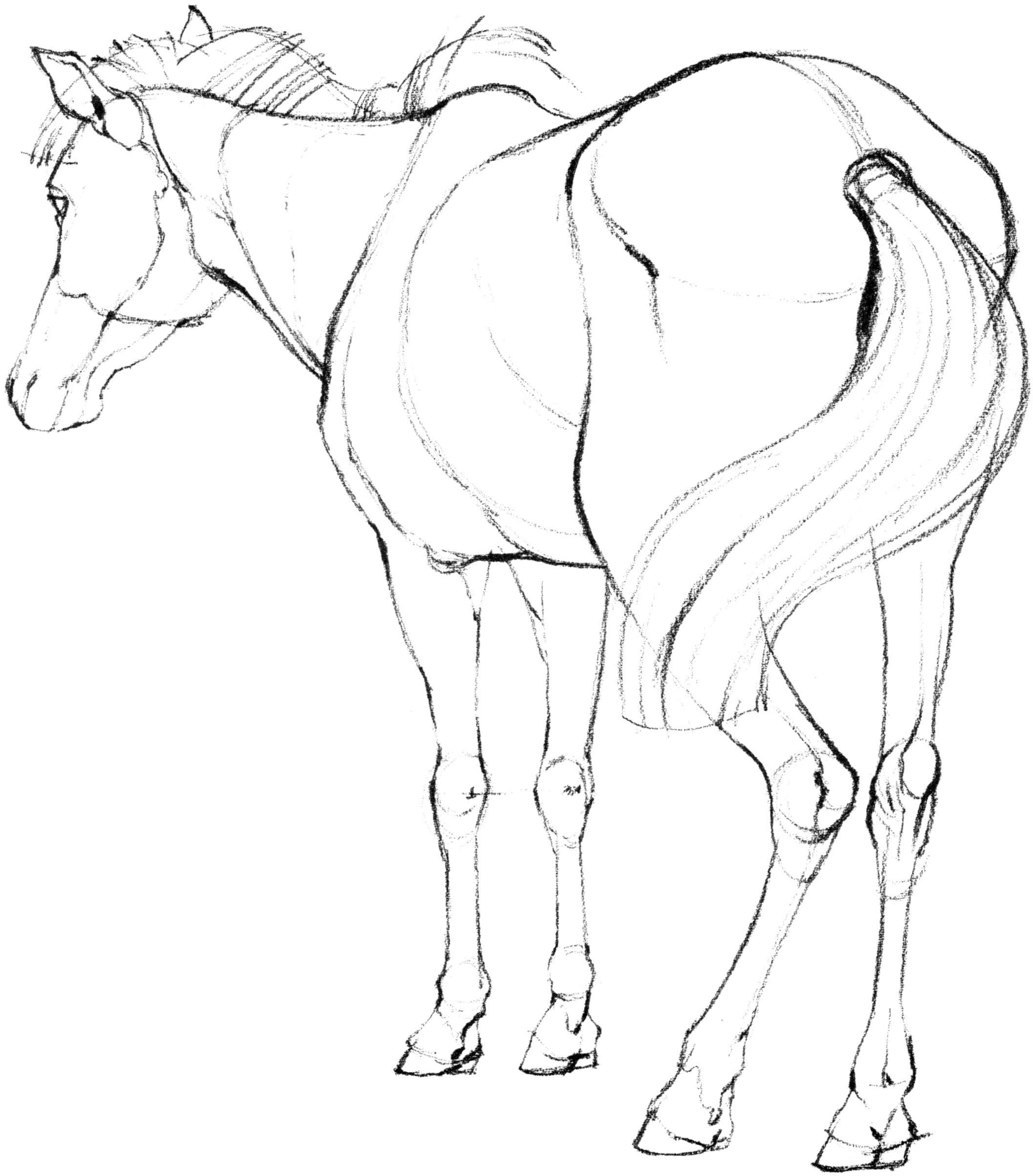

Drawing movement

Drawing a moving animal is not easy. If you are a beginner, you would be wise to start with a horse whose movements are minimal—one who is grazing or walking leisurely from one grazing spot to another, for example. Again, don't limit yourself to a single, obvious, viewpoint.

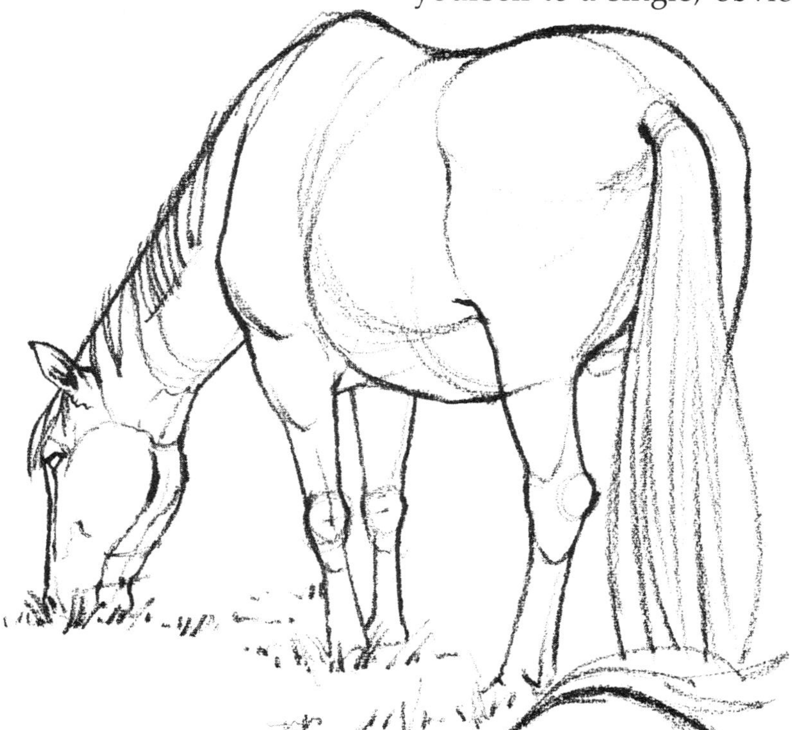

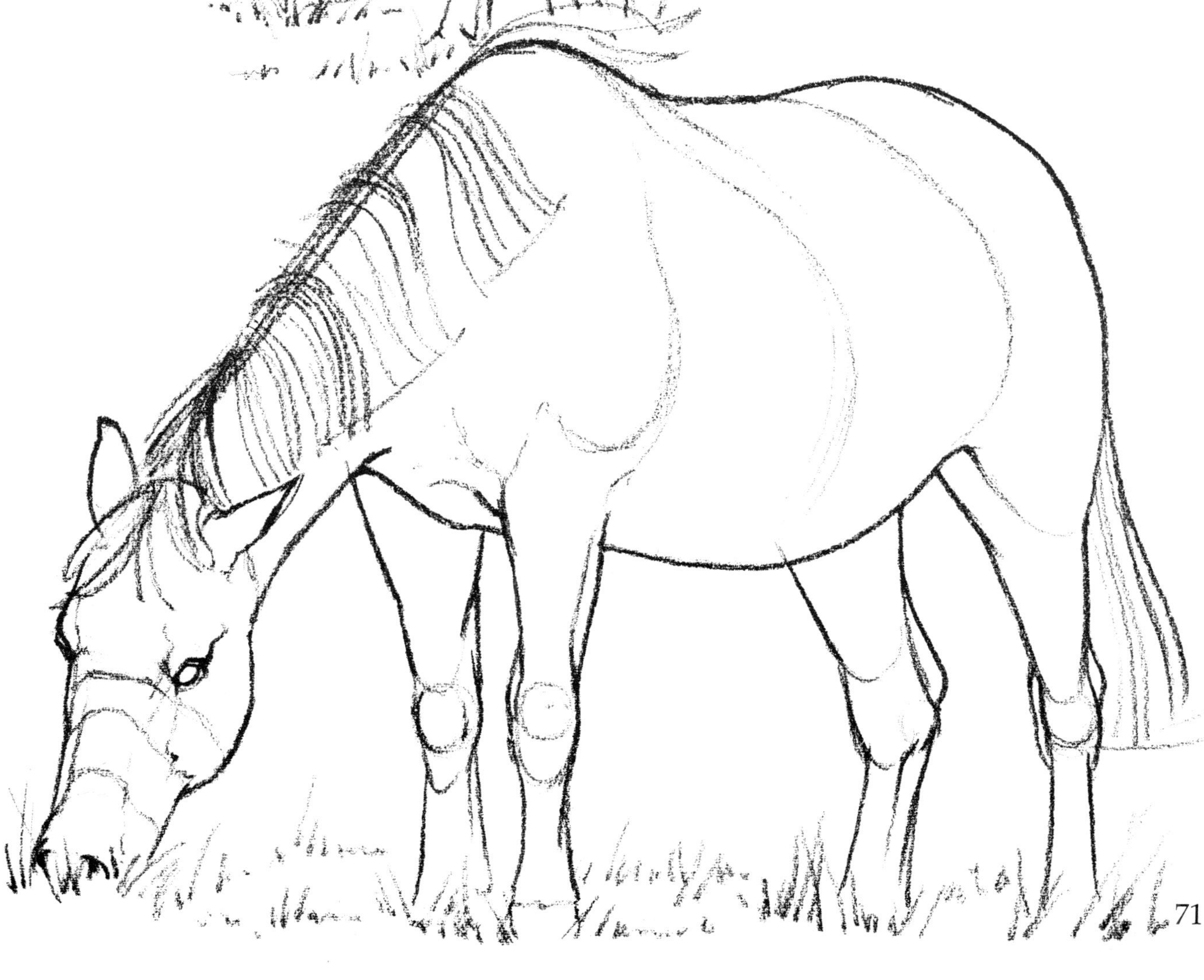

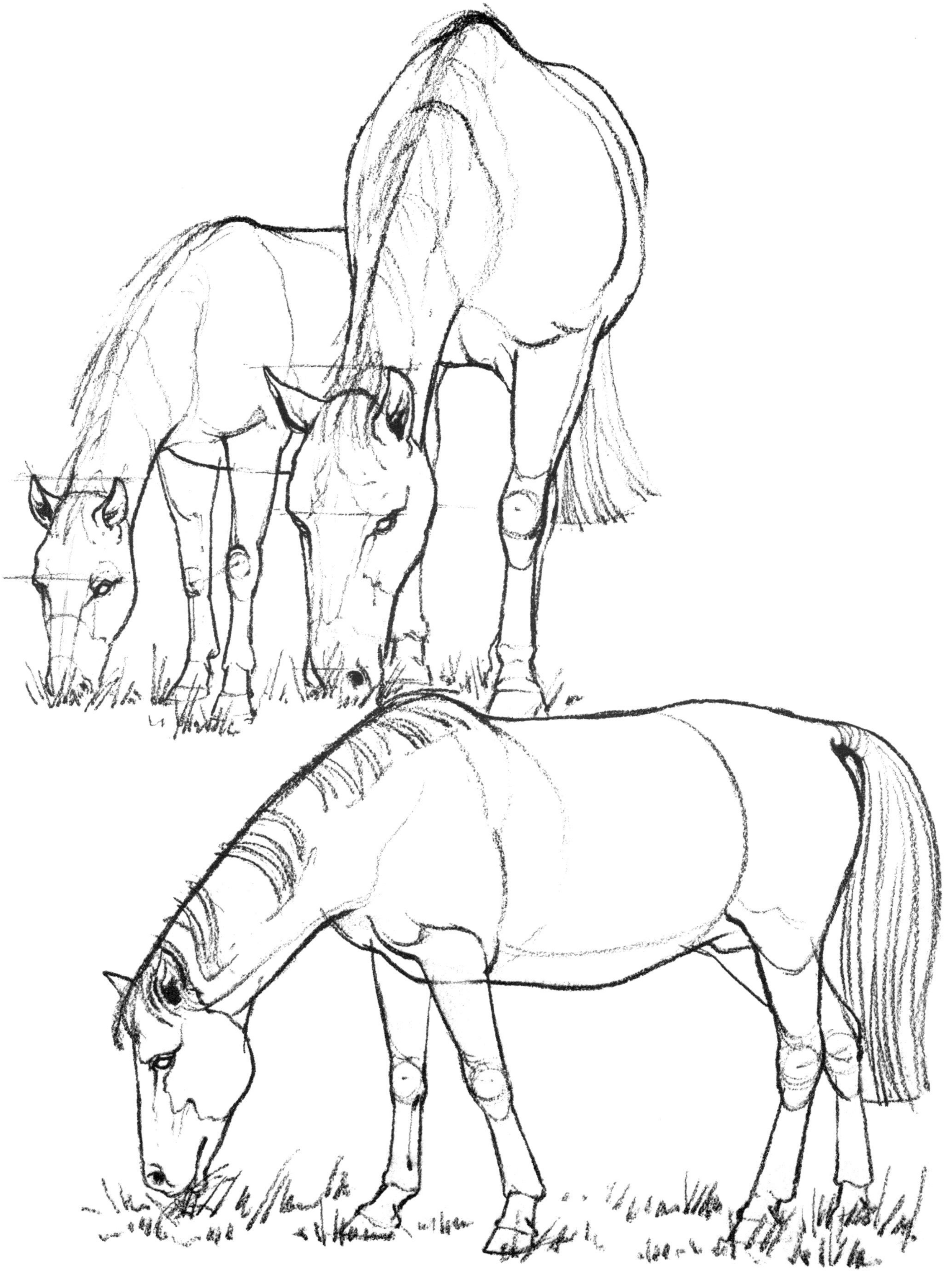

When the horse is moving, watch it closely for a while, before drawing, to study its shape and body movements. Then quickly draw as much as you can from memory, concentrating on the basic form rather than detail. Don't worry if your first results are not successful. Go on to make other quick sketches.

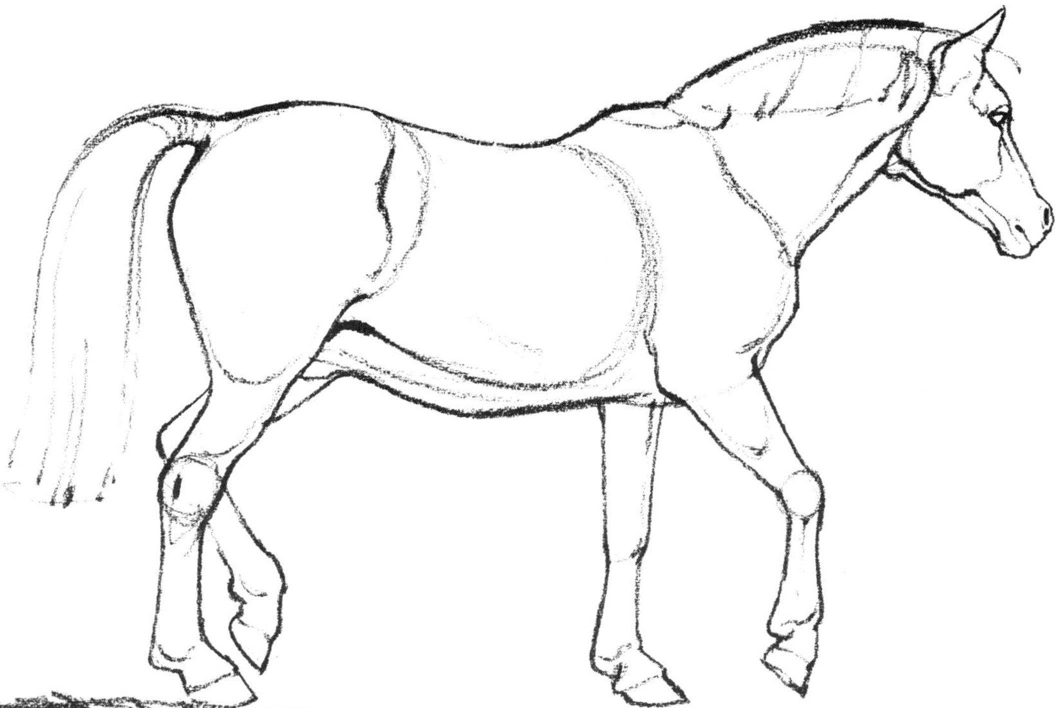

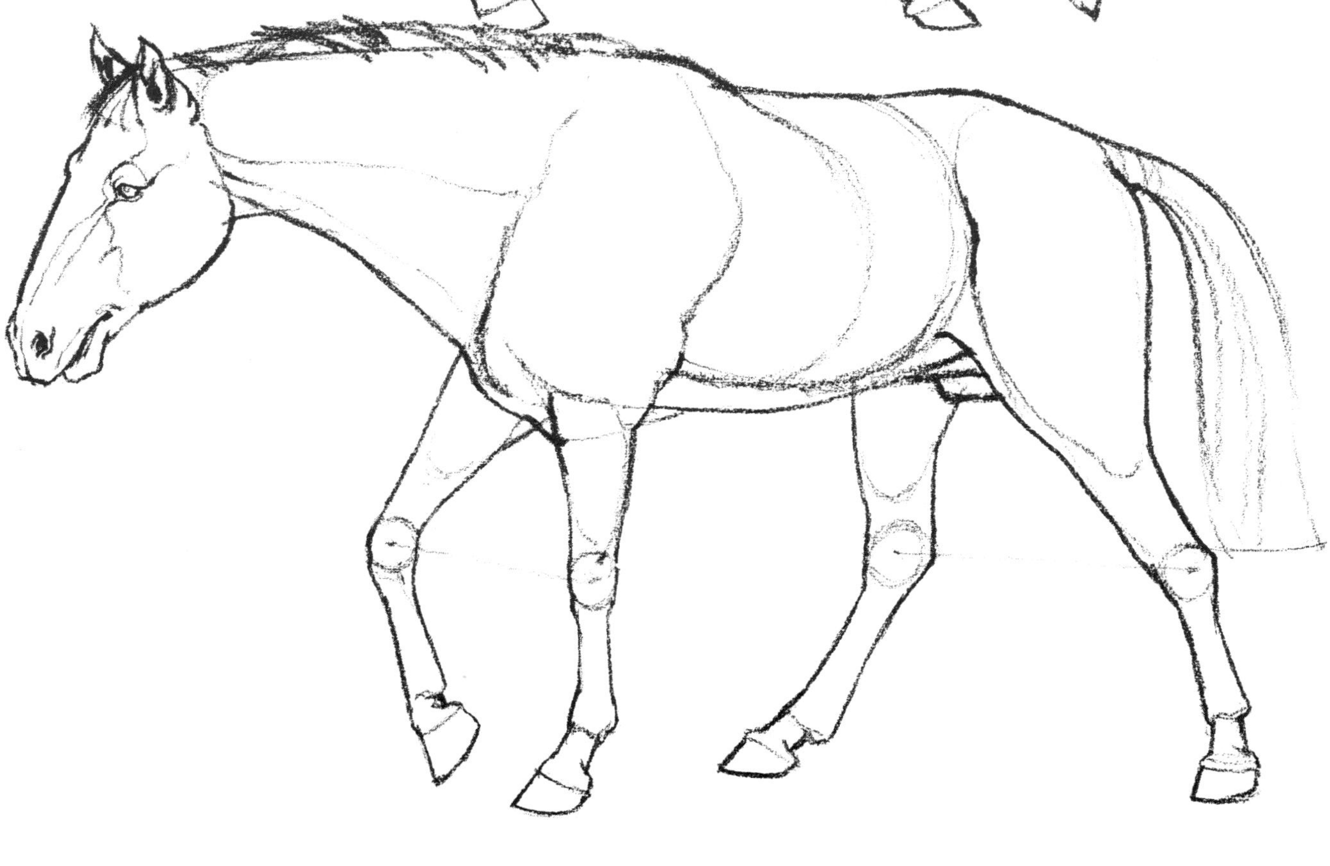

With practice your observation and memory will both improve until you are able to reproduce most of the lines of the body. You can add facial details when the horse is standing still.

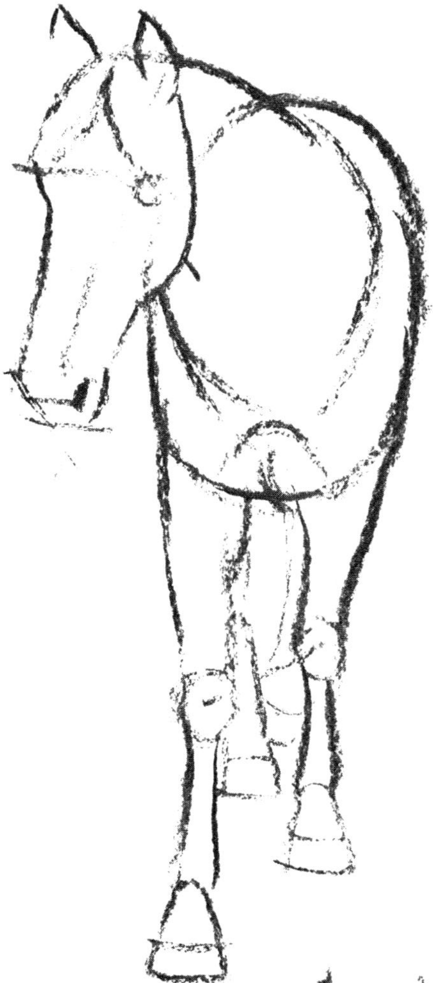

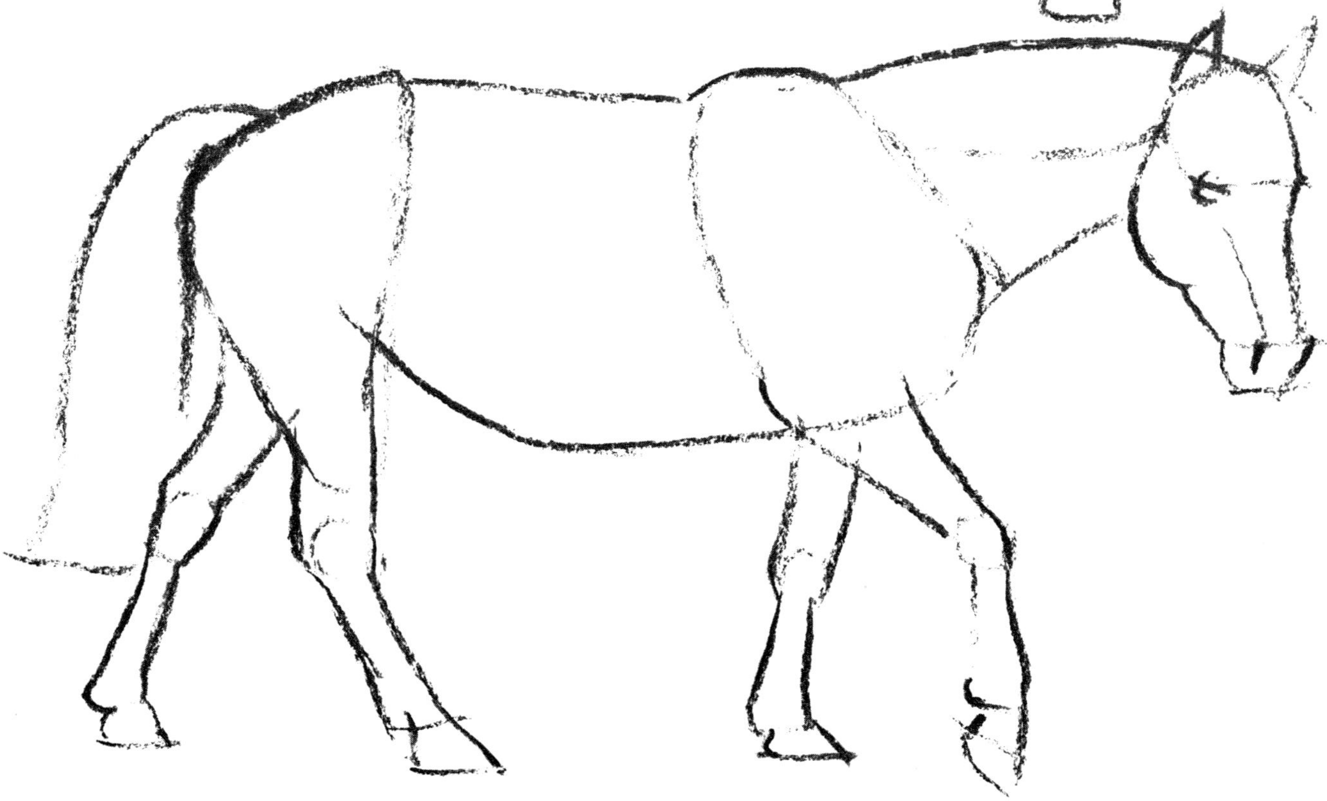

Horses running or jumping are difficult for a beginner to draw from life. It may be better to use photographs. But remember once again to use only good-quality ones; and draw quickly to encourage your observation and get movement into your lines.

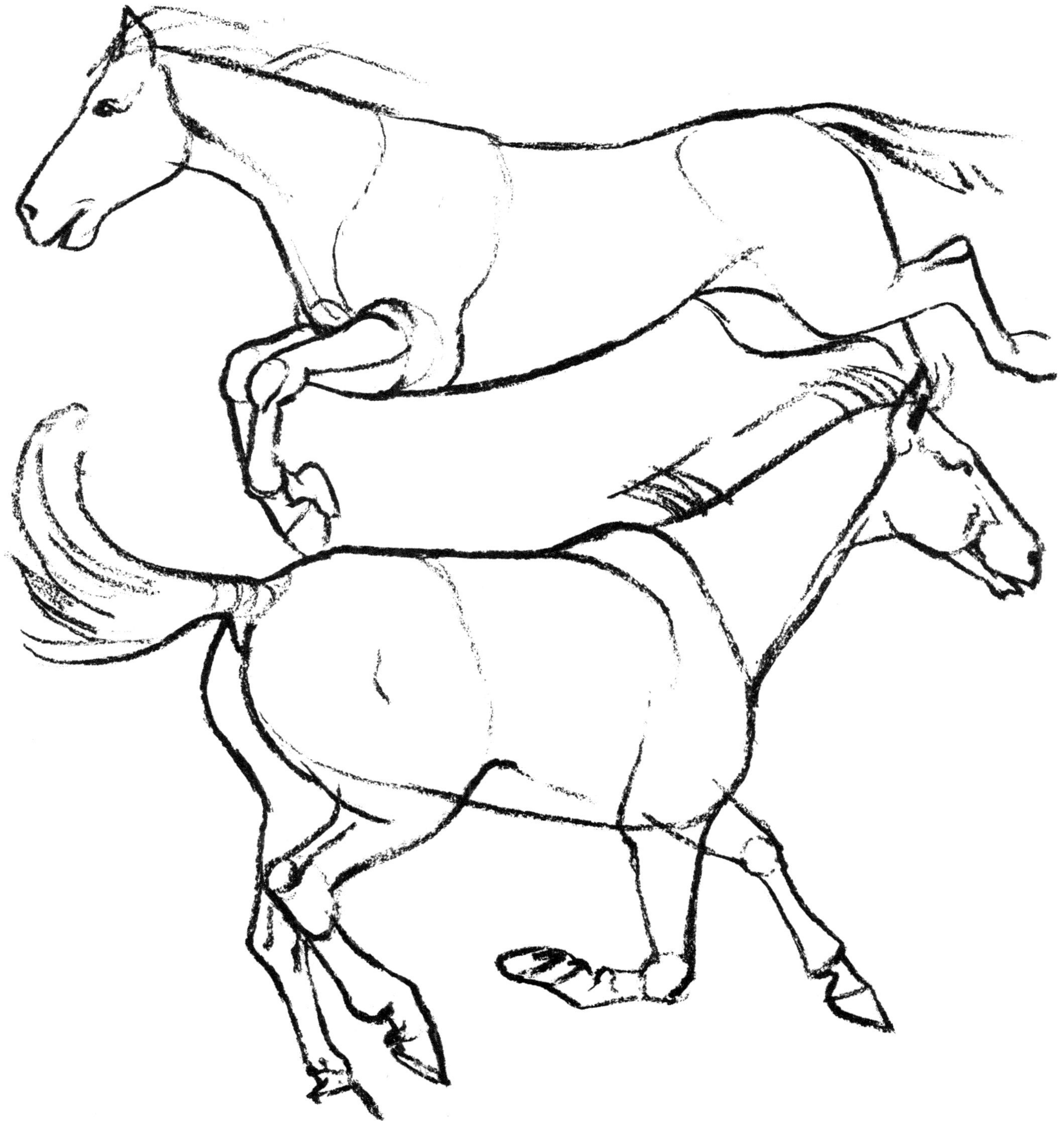

Here are two 'jumping' drawings made from the same photograph. A shows the anatomical form, B the basic lines.

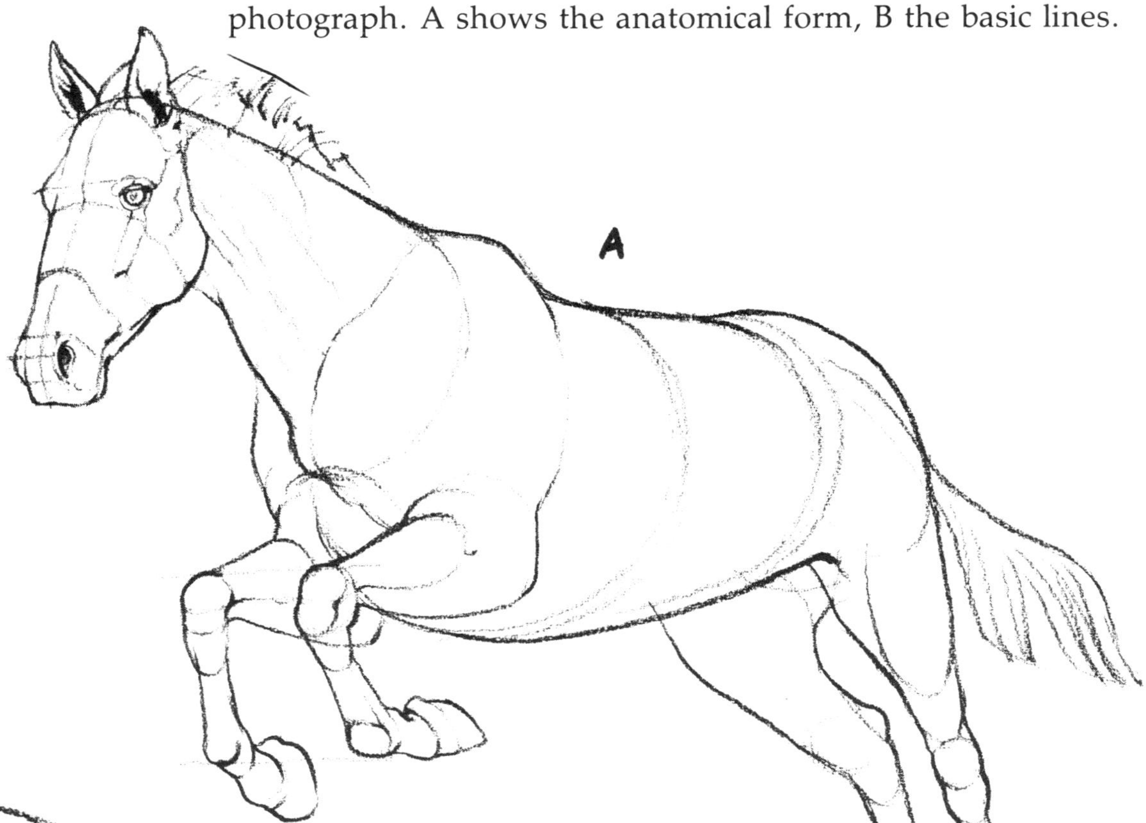

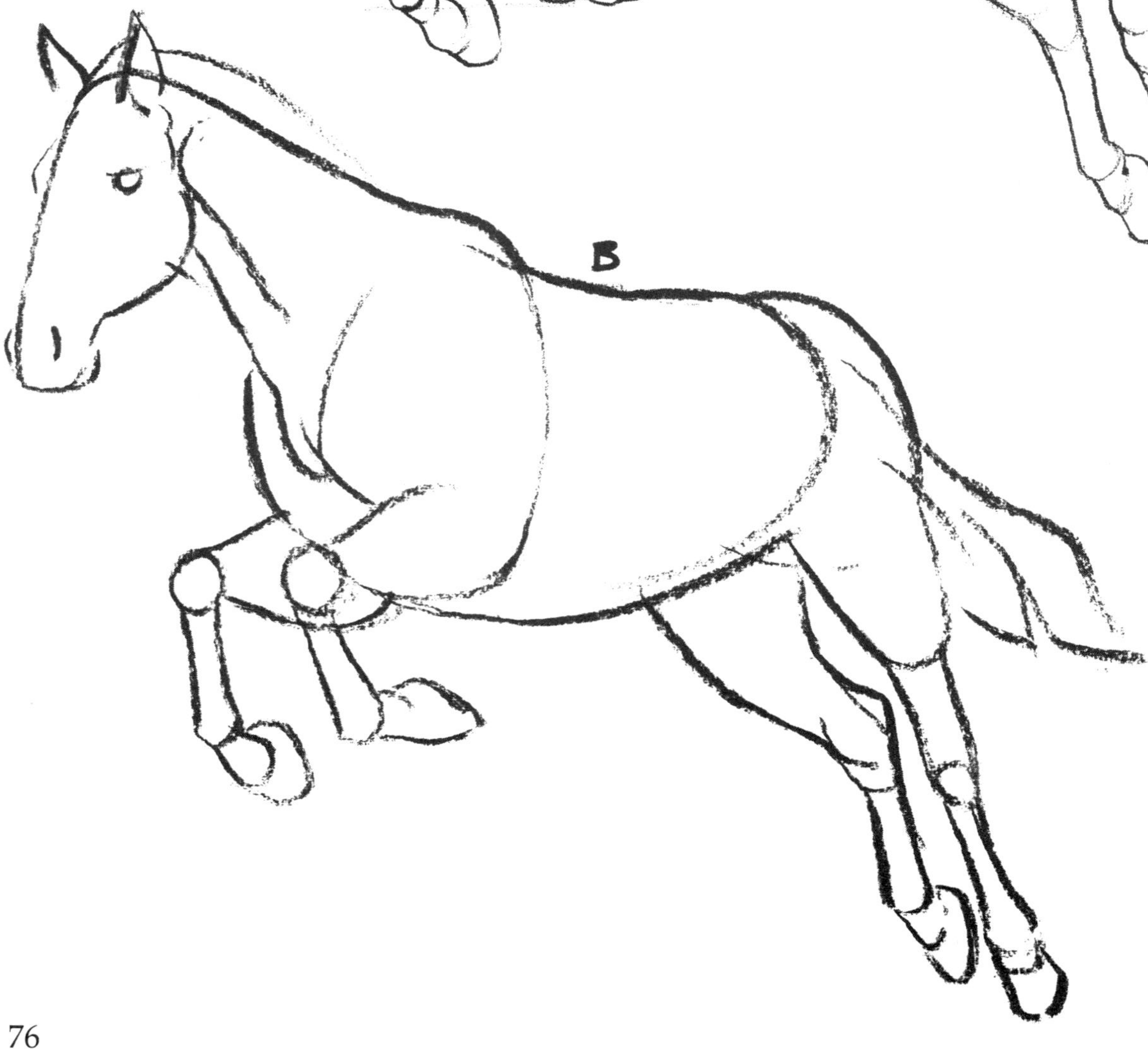

Different techniques

The Przewalski below was first lightly outlined in pencil. I then used masking fluid to paint all the areas I wanted to remain white—on each side of the pencil lines. When this was dry, I painted the whole area with Indian ink (the right-hand side of the drawing has been left at that stage). When the ink was dry, I used an eraser to remove the masking fluid. (See also pages 143 and 145.)

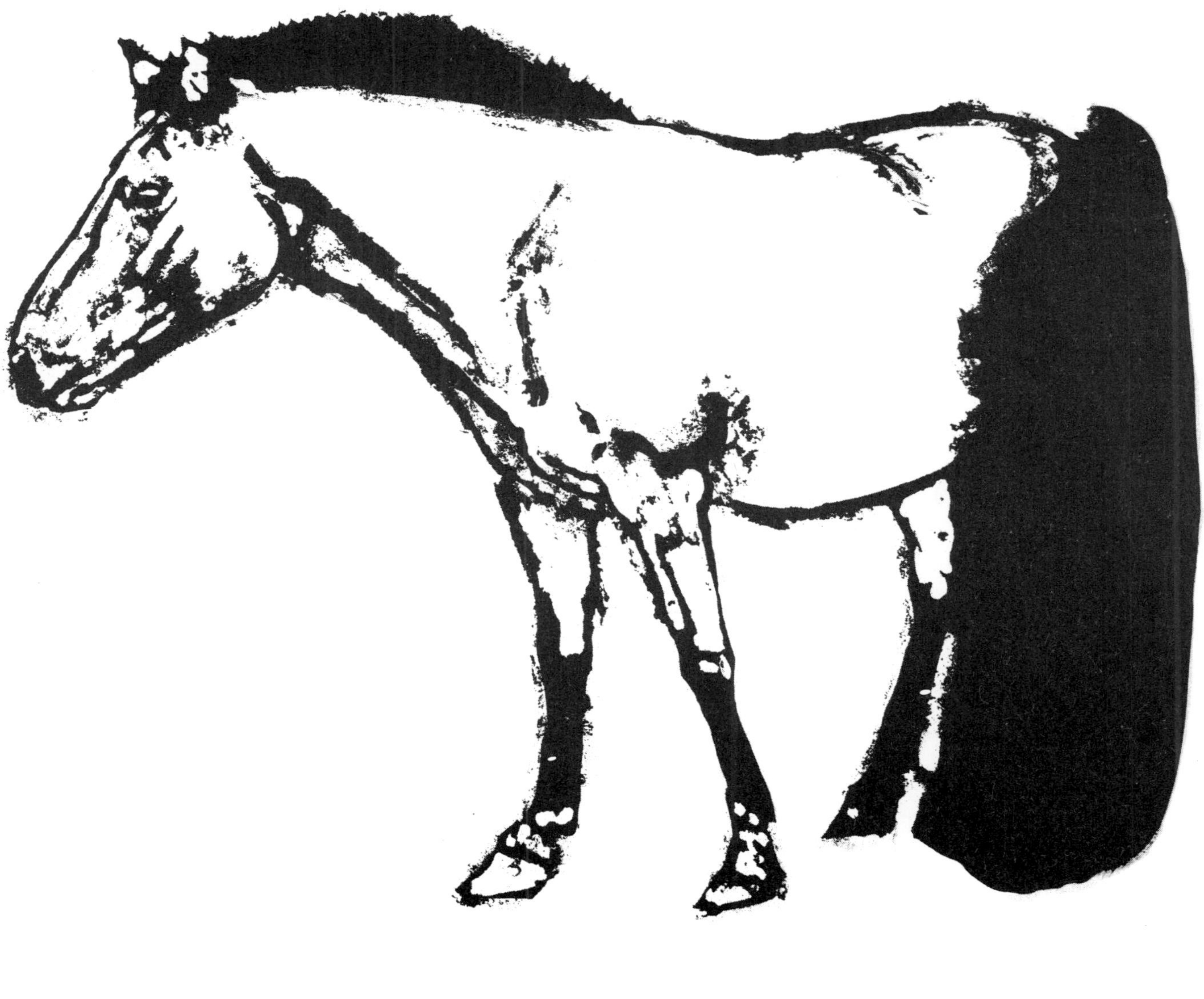

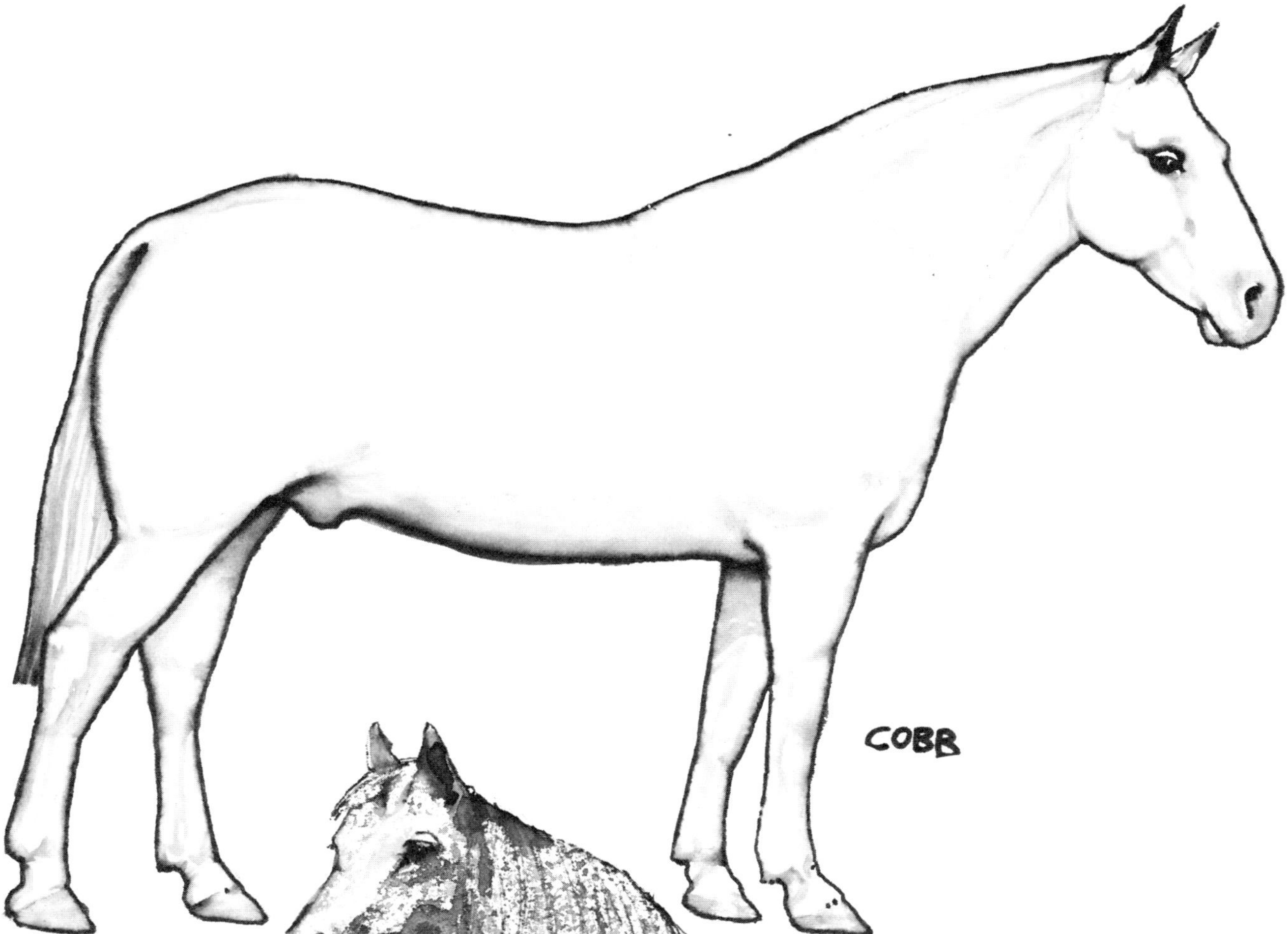

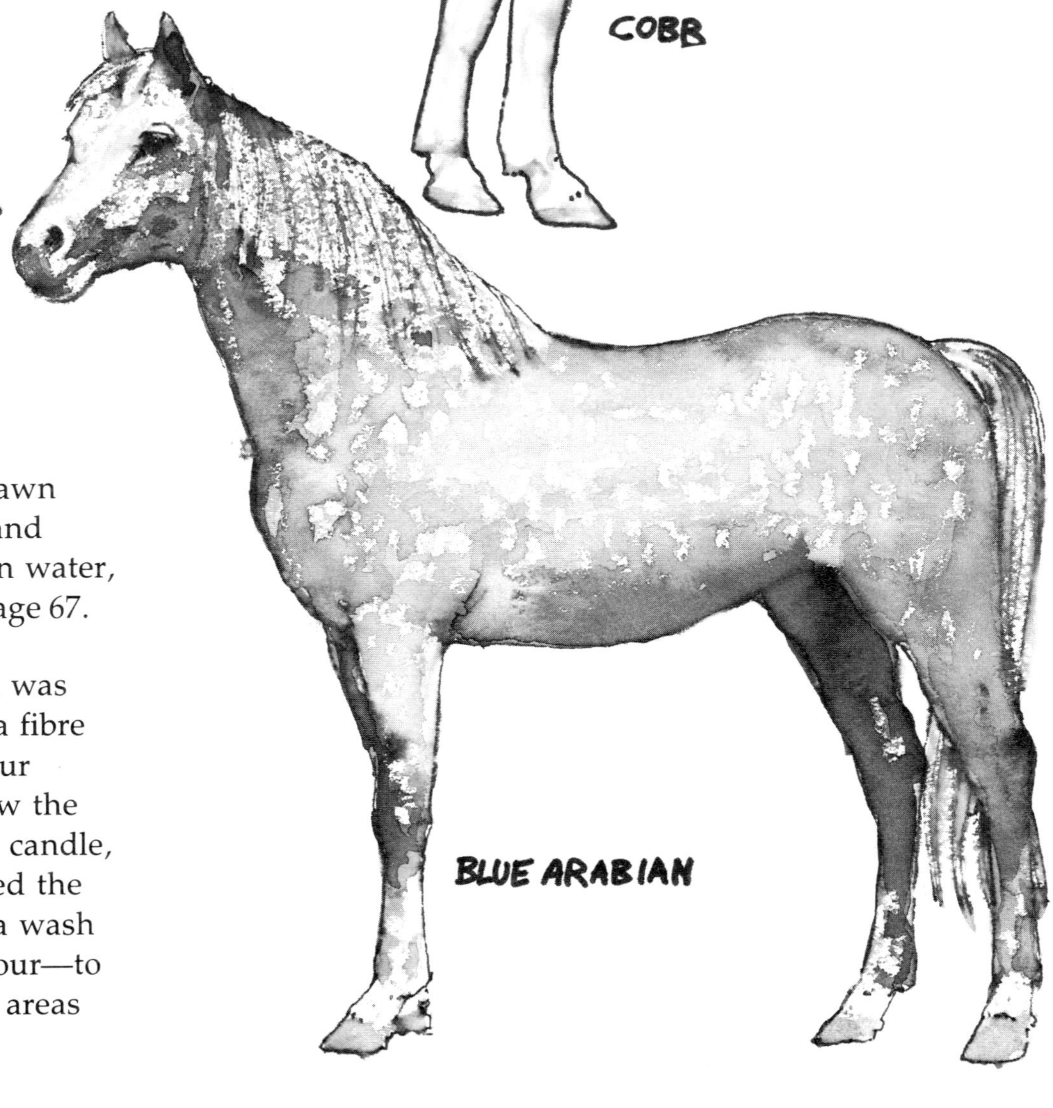

The Cobb was drawn with a fibre pen and painted with clean water, as described on page 67.

The Blue Arabian was first drawn with a fibre pen on watercolour board. I then drew the light areas with a candle, and finally covered the whole area with a wash of black watercolour—to which the candle areas were resistant.

The Clydesdale here was drawn with a felt marker—which is ideal for portraying the strength of the horse, although not a good medium for detail.

The Morocco Pinto was drawn with a brush and black watercolour paint on watercolour board.

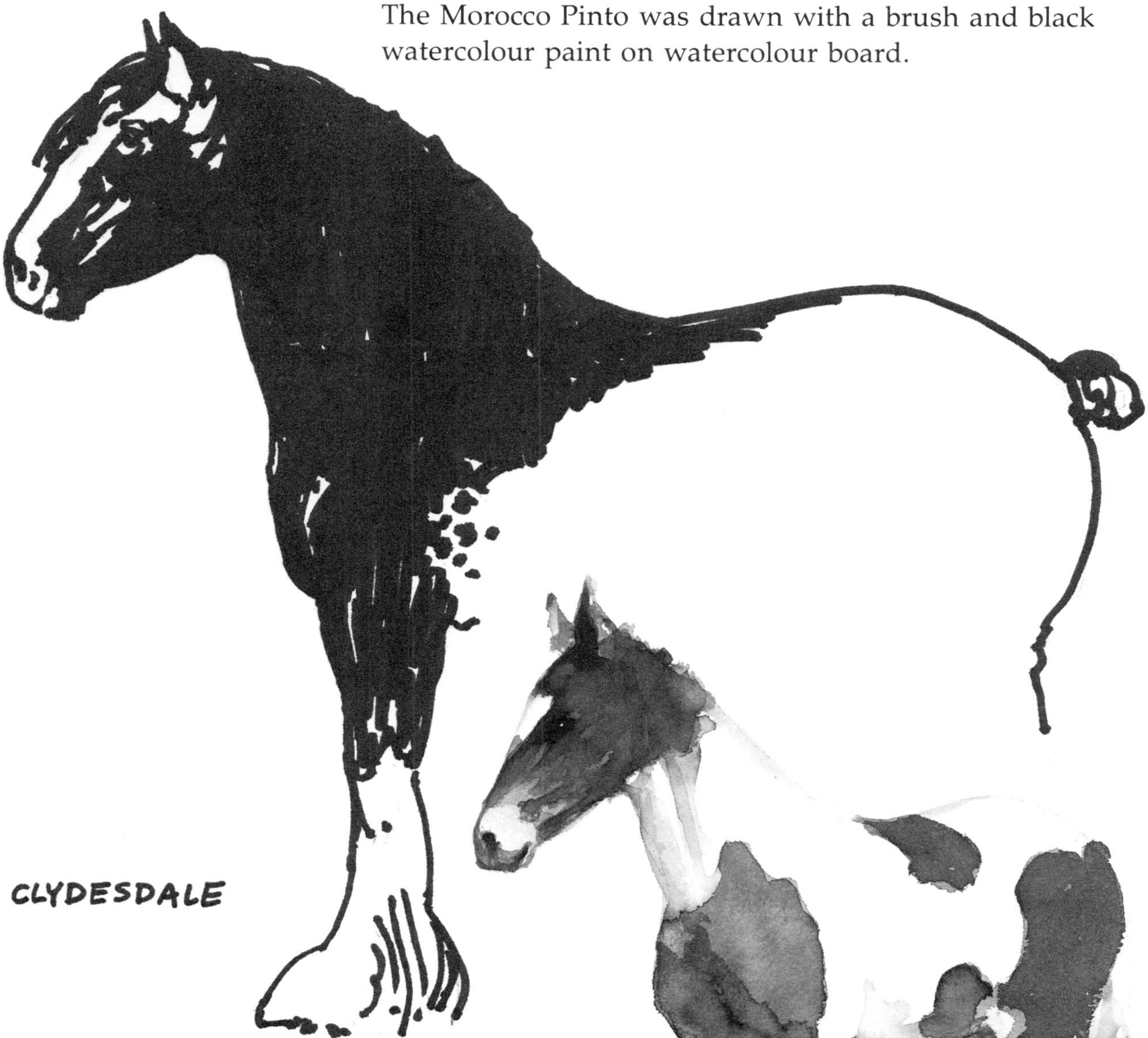

CLYDESDALE

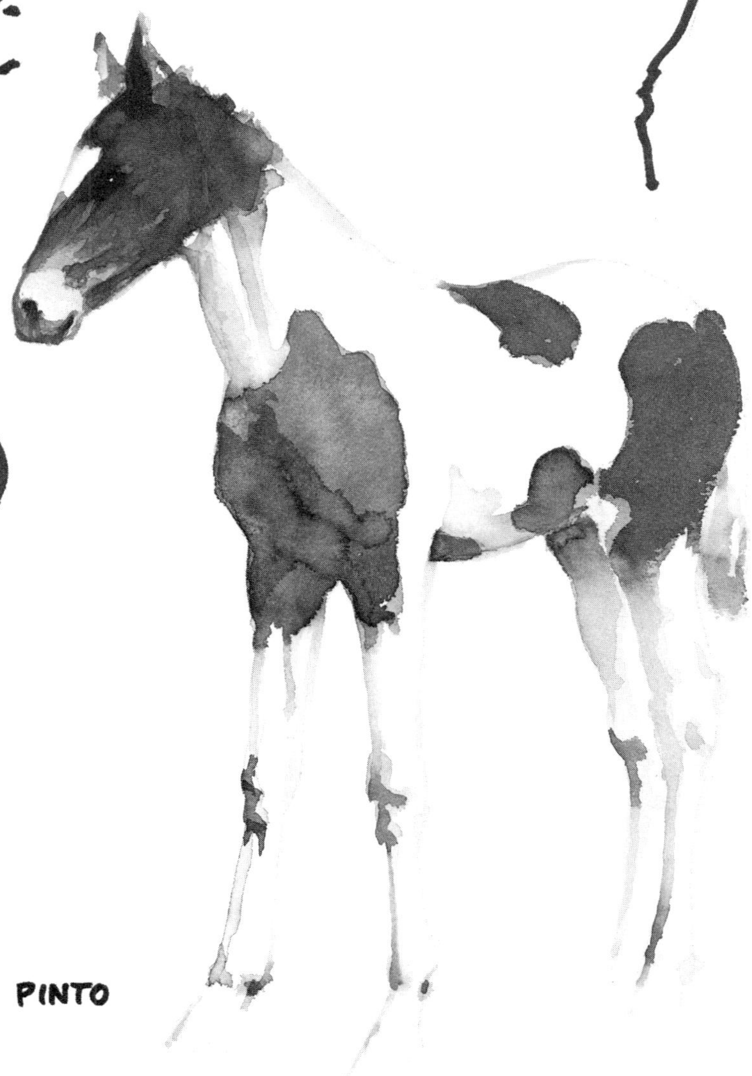

MOROCCO PINTO

This is a Tennessee Walking Horse, drawn with a stick of medium-thick willow charcoal. I used the side of the stick for the broad strokes on the body.

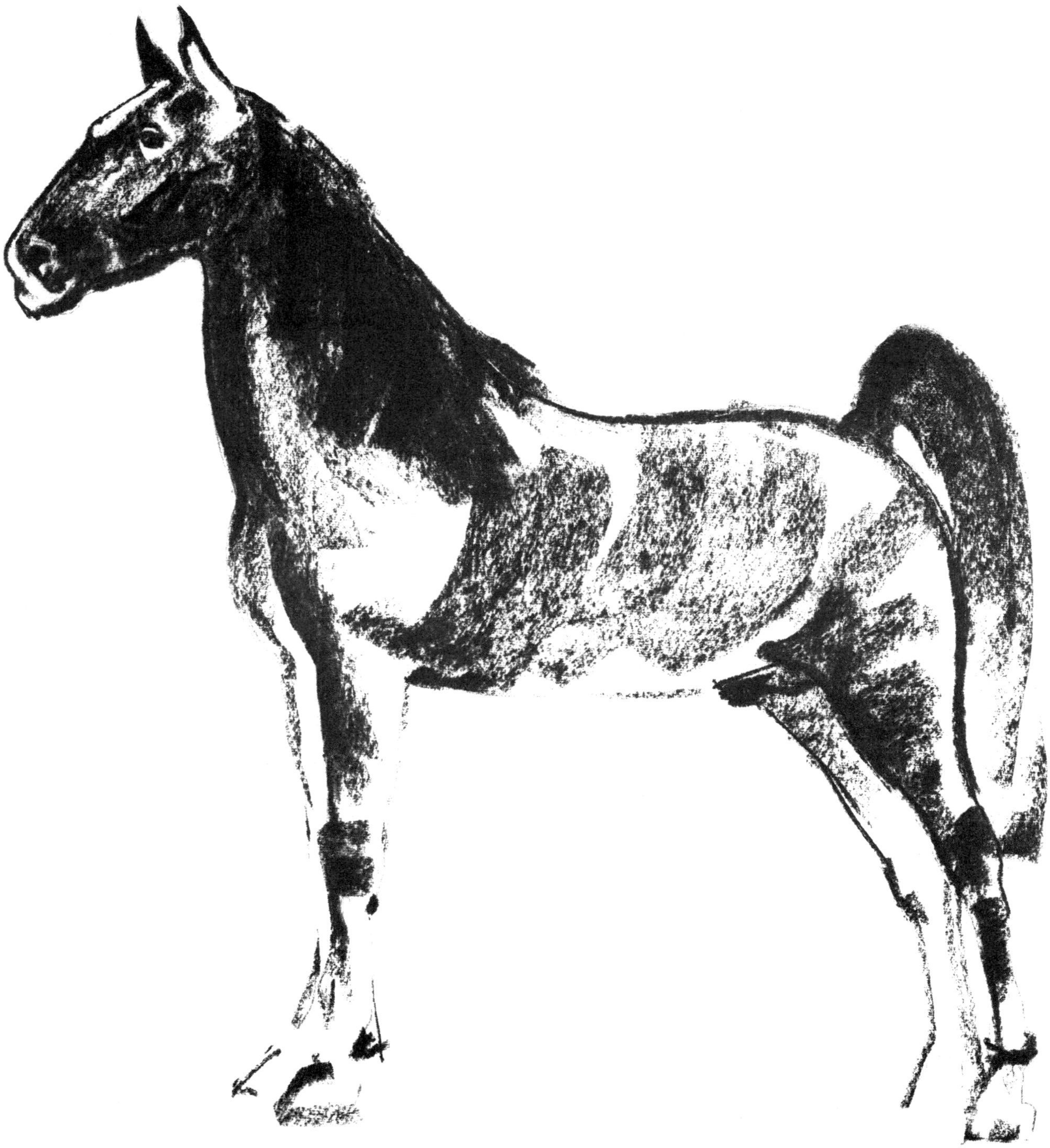

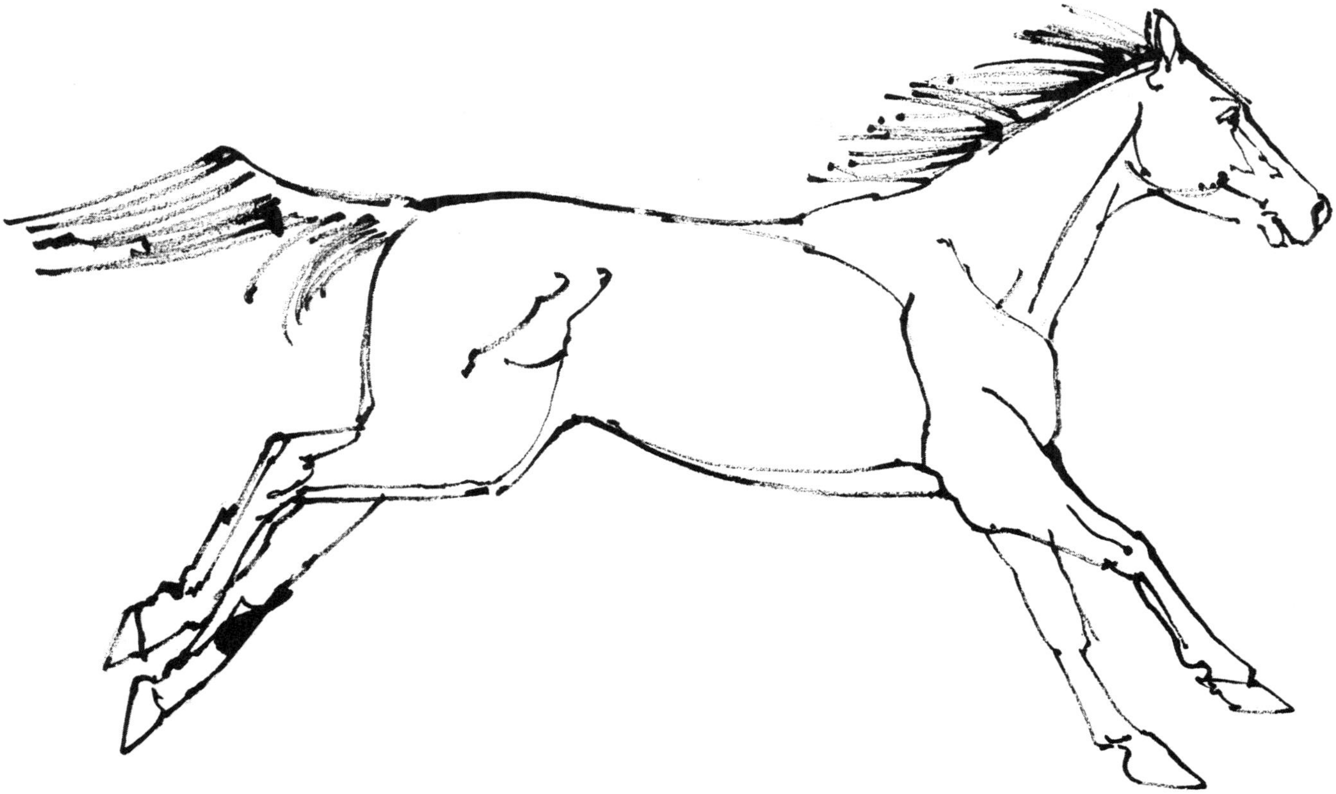

To capture the movement in these horses, I drew with the handle of a brush dipped in ink.

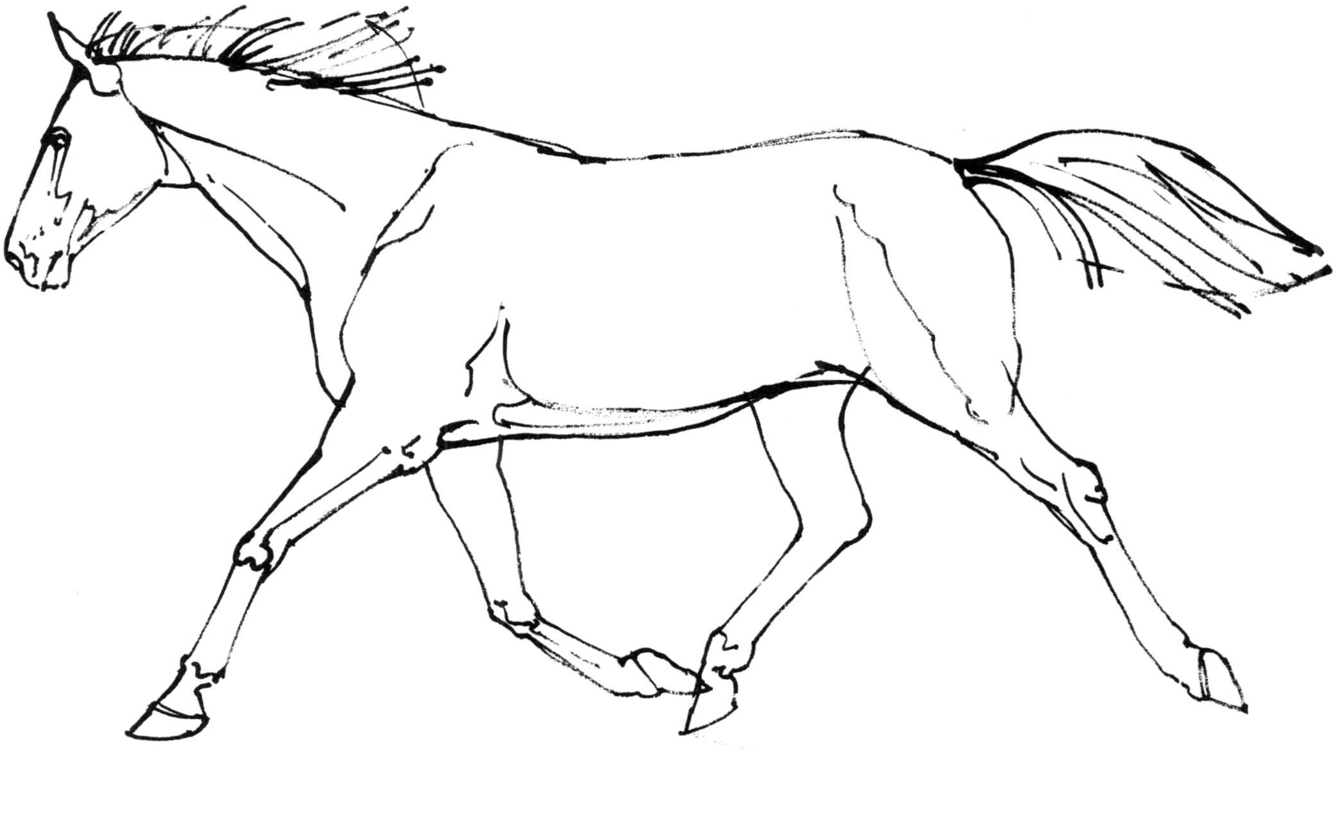

The Mongolian pony (top) and the Ardennais (bottom) were drawn with a wax crayon on a rough-surfaced cartridge paper.

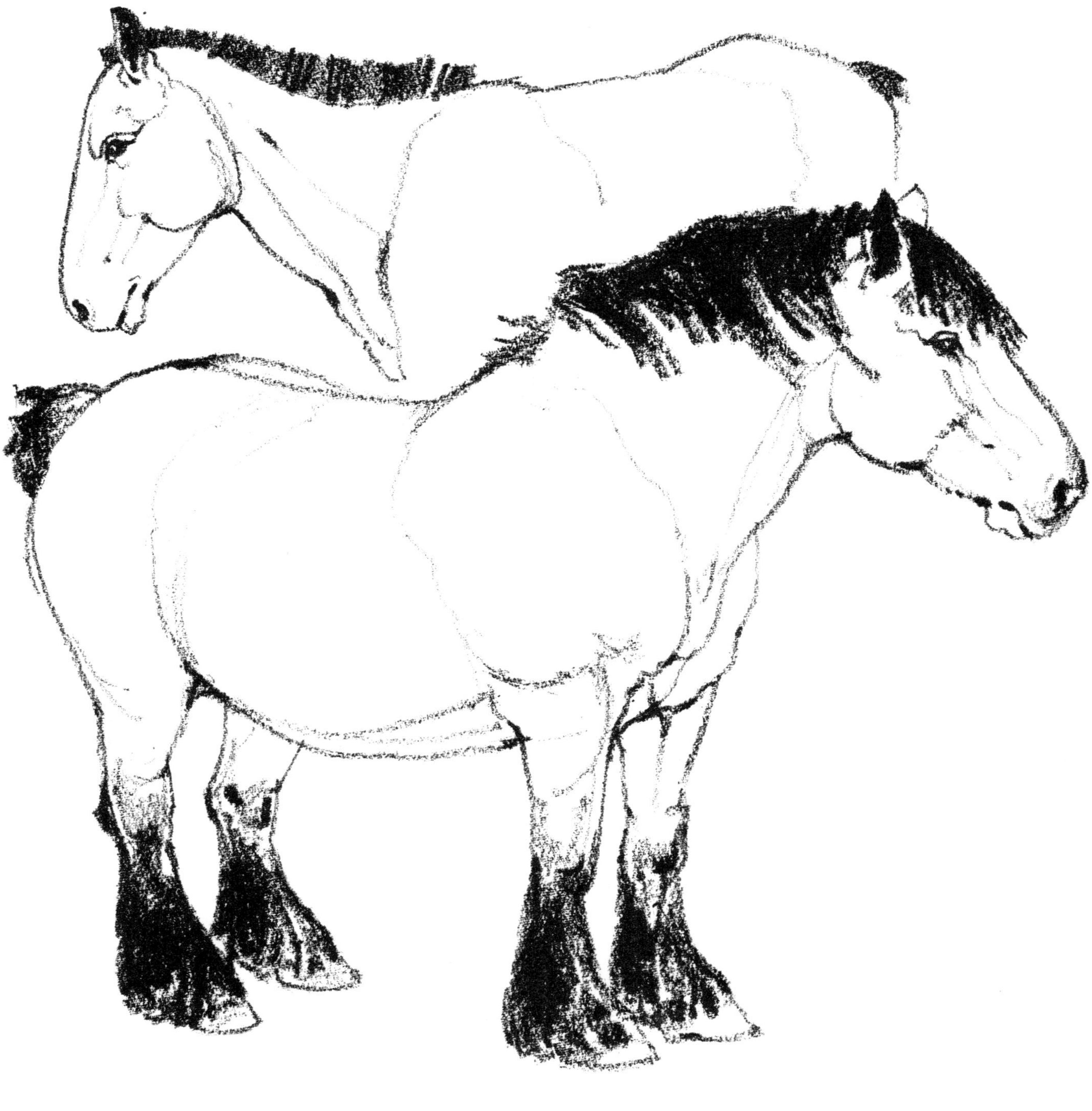

A fibre-tipped pen—used for this drawing—is a very useful medium for sketching.

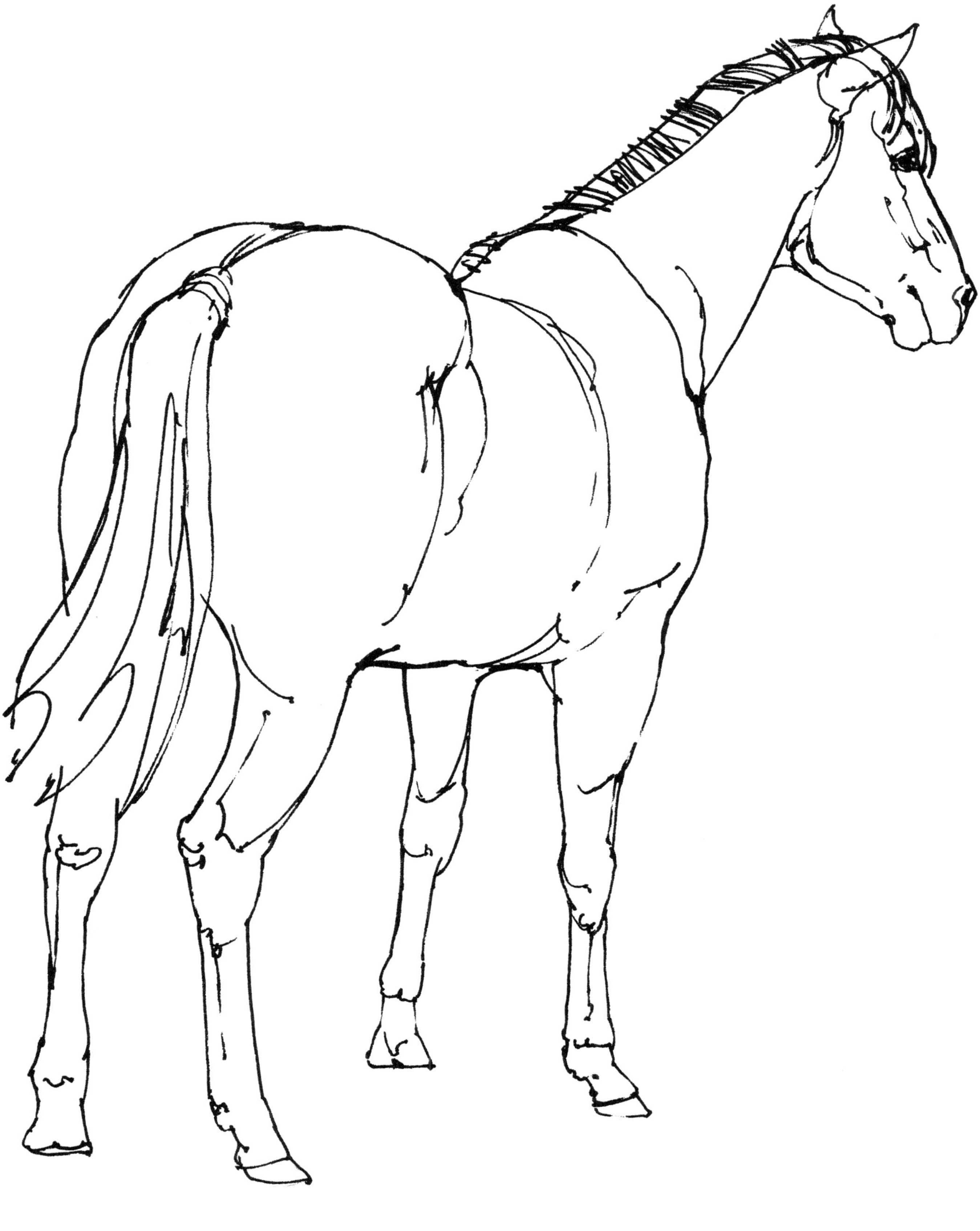

Pastel crayon on rough cartridge paper produced the bold treatment here of a pony. The edge of the stick made the fine lines and the side made the broad ones.

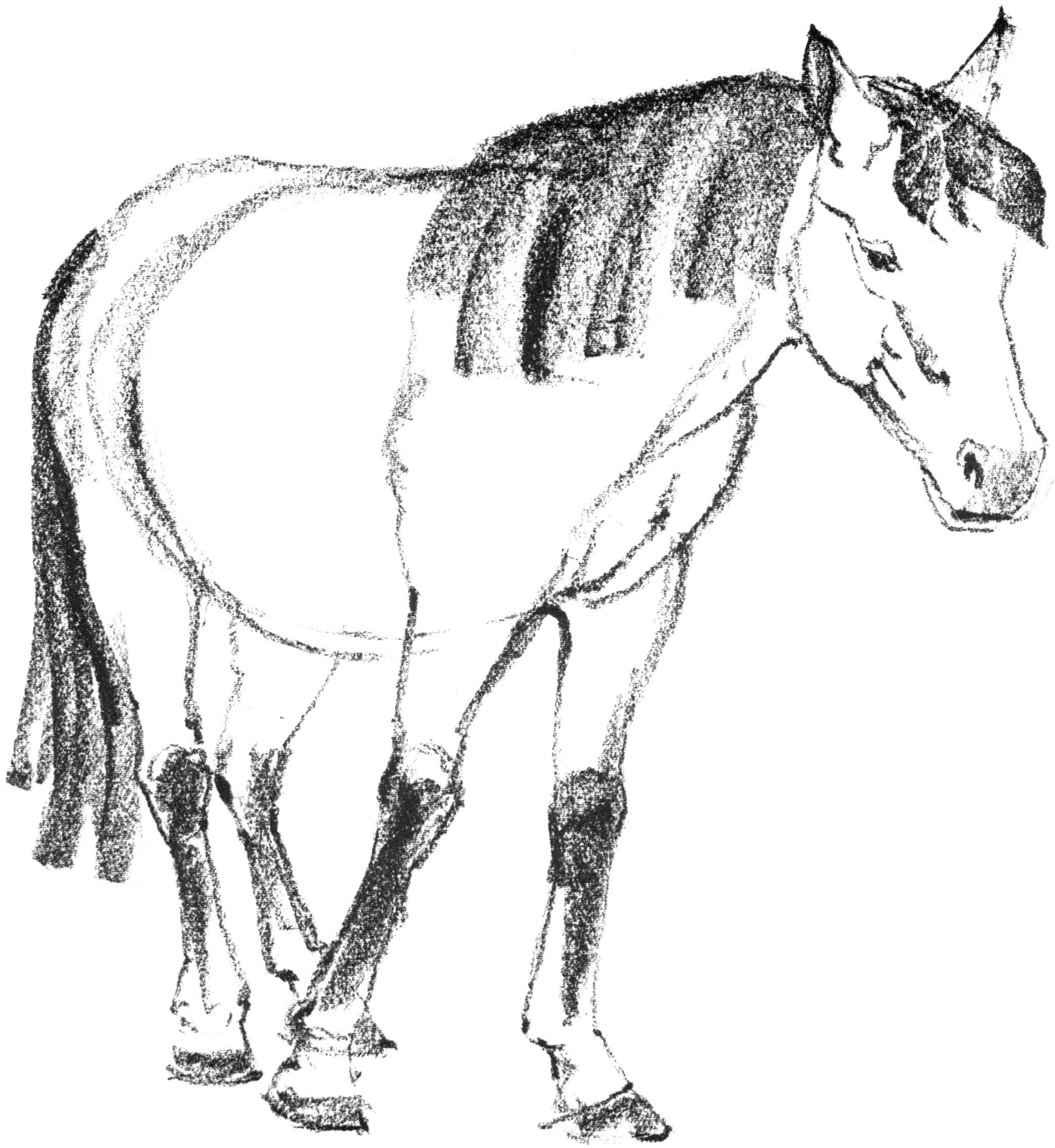

This is a pastel drawing on Ingres paper—of a Dutch Draught Horse. I used only black and white pastels: the middle tone is provided by the paper.

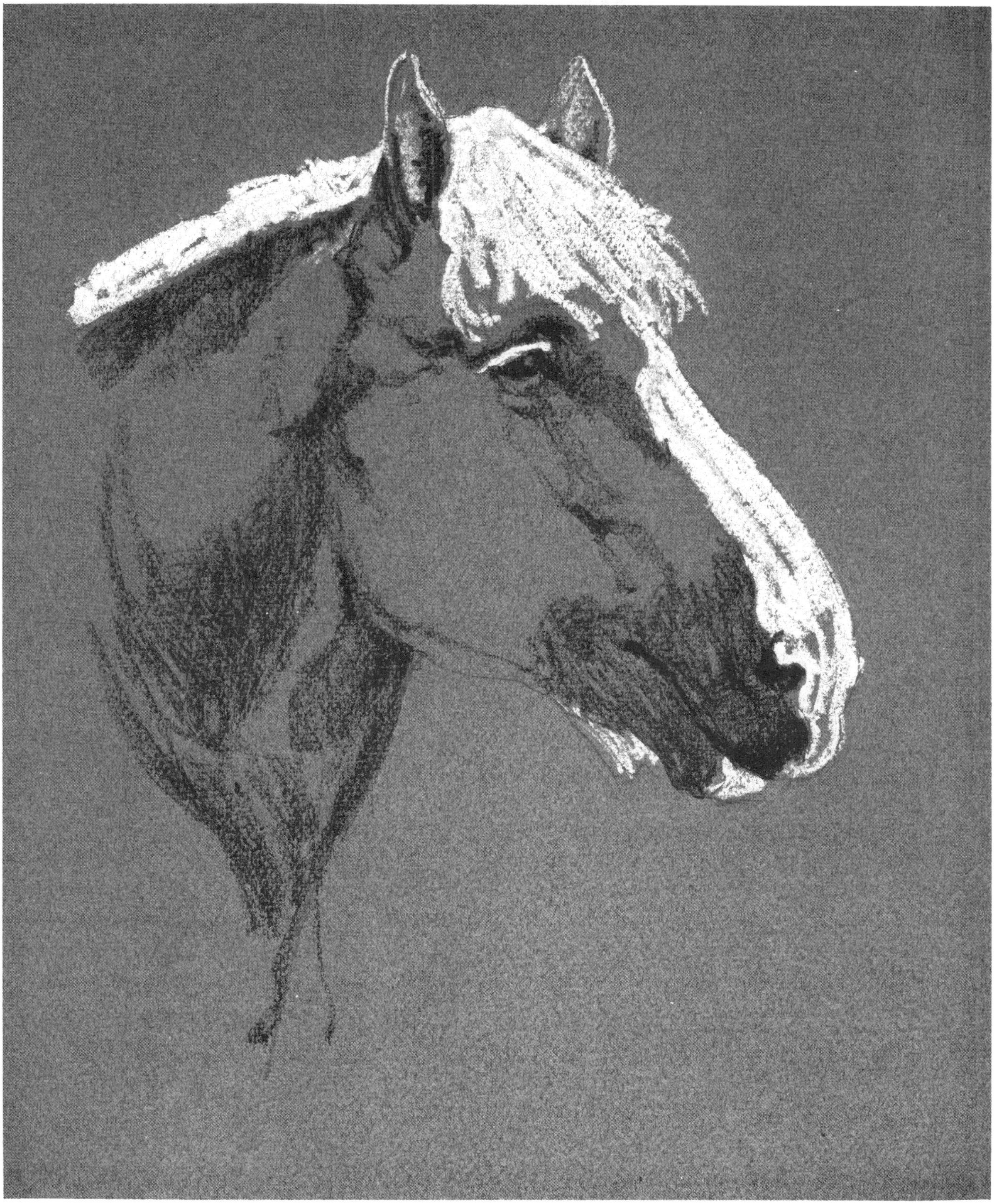

Dogs

Jeremy Morgan

Anatomy

Although different breeds of dog vary considerably in shape and proportion, their basic anatomy is the same. (See also page 101.) A look at the bone structure will help you to understand the exterior shape. For instance, the joint half way up the back leg is really the heel, and the joint above it corresponds to the human knee. Notice the relative positions of the other joints, the shape of the rib-cage and the angle of the shoulder-blade.

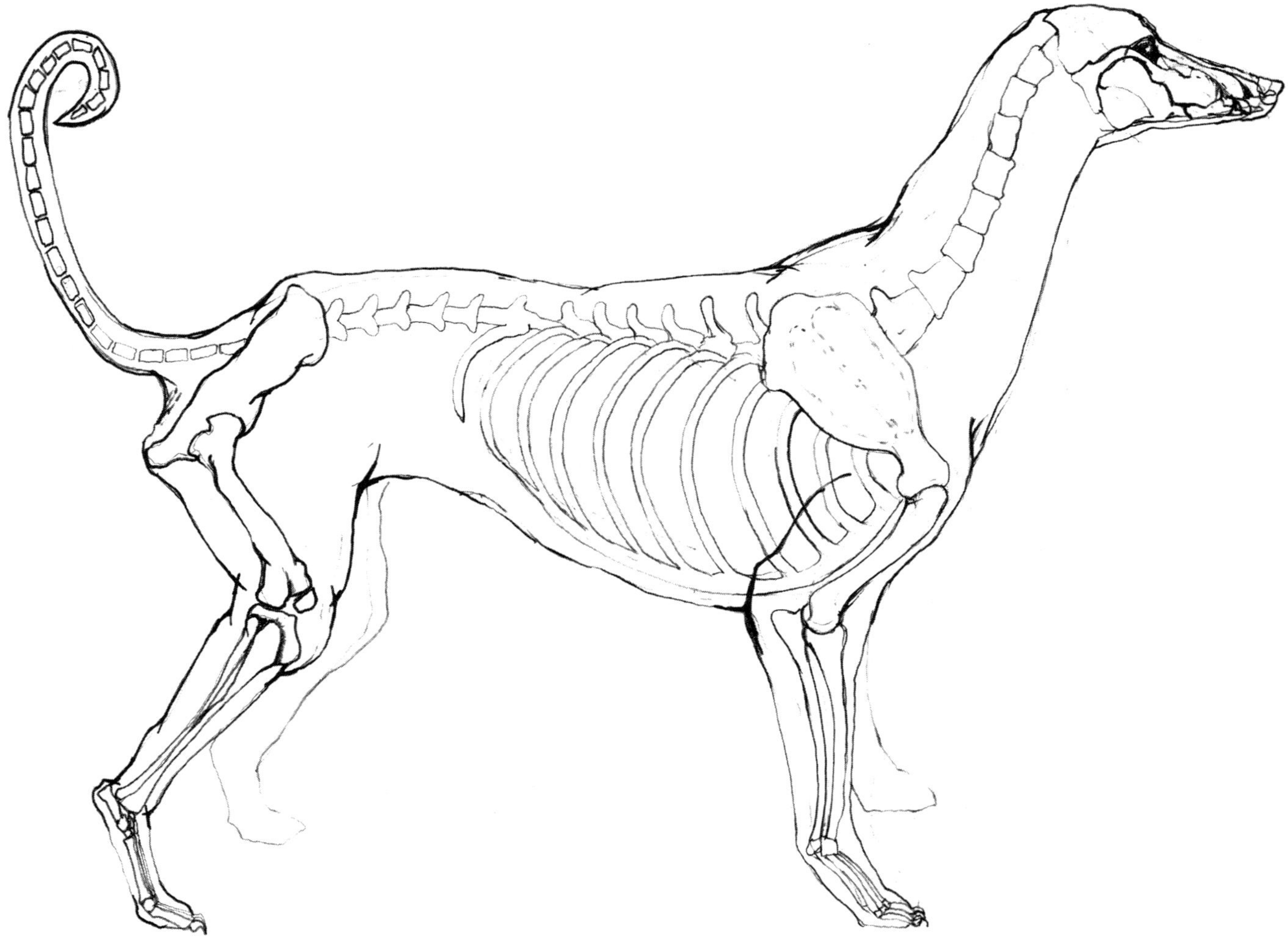

In the lower drawing opposite, notice how the muscles are folded round the skeleton. Watch a smooth-haired dog in action to see how its joints and muscles move.

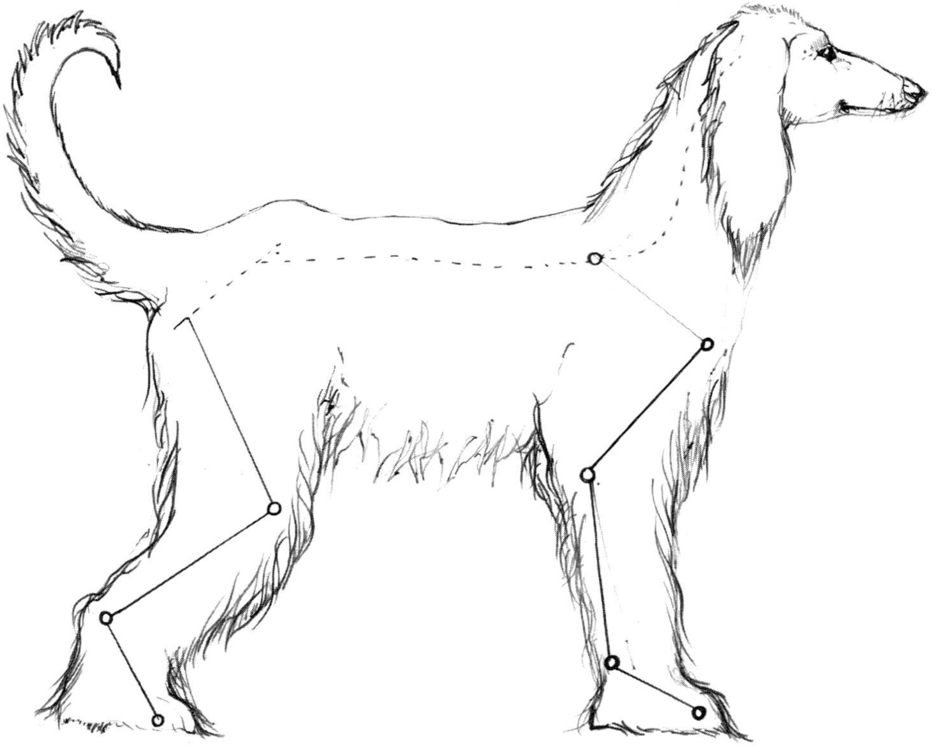

By studying the animal's structure in this way you will be able to make your drawing more accurate and therefore more realistic.

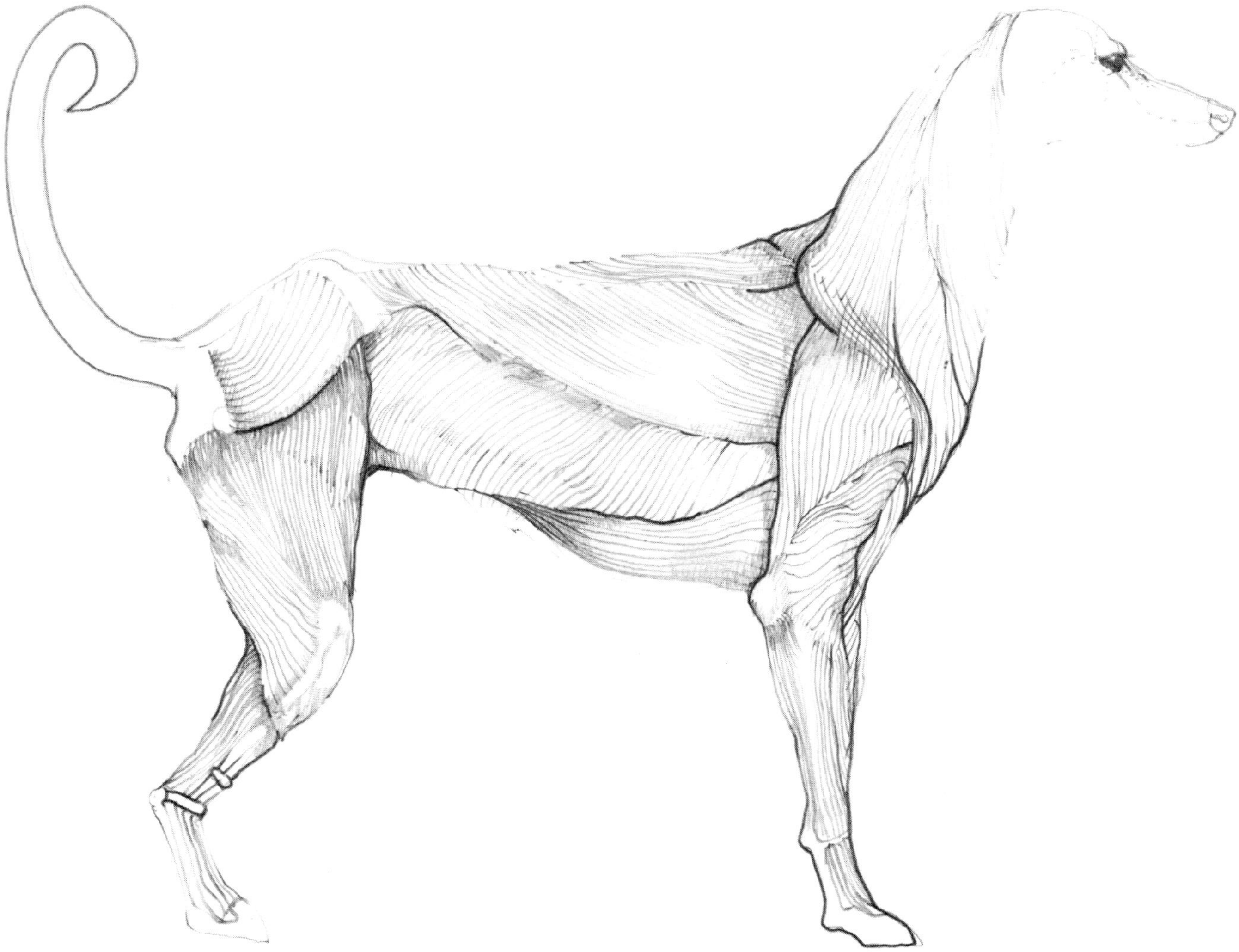

Basic shapes

Look at the overall shape of your subject and the character it conveys. Watch how the muscles tense up when a dog is alert or in movement, and how the shape alters completely when a dog sits down.

When drawing a dog, notice that it is made up of different parts held together by joints and muscles covered by skin and hair. Try to see the shapes created by these bones and muscles.

Remember that all the parts of the body are three-dimensional, and try to suggest this in your drawing. It may help to draw in the contour lines in order to illustrate the volume of the different parts. You can either erase them as you complete the drawing or work over them when you add tone.

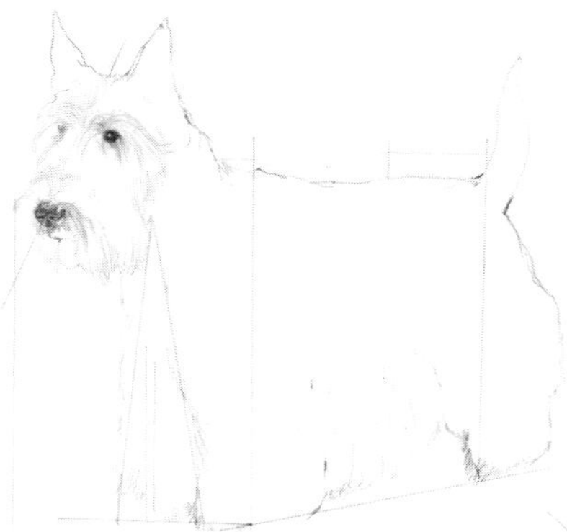

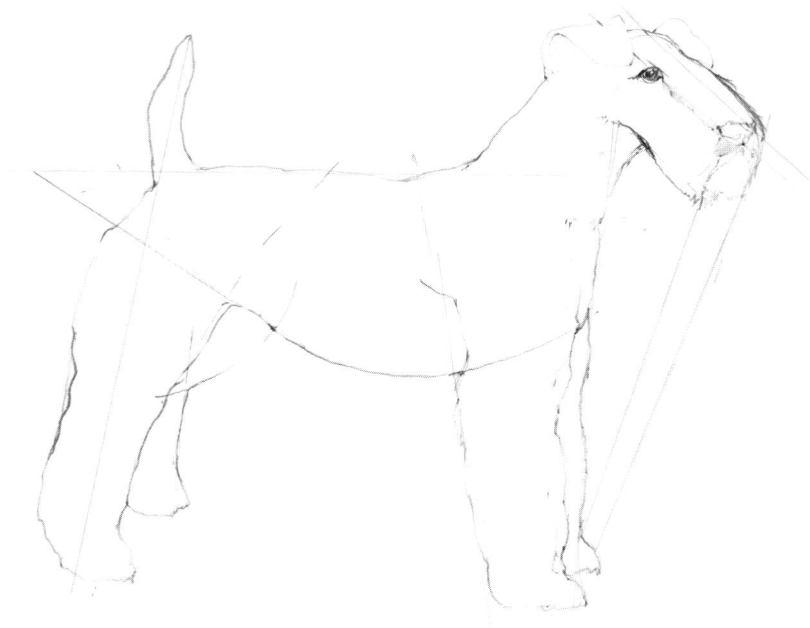

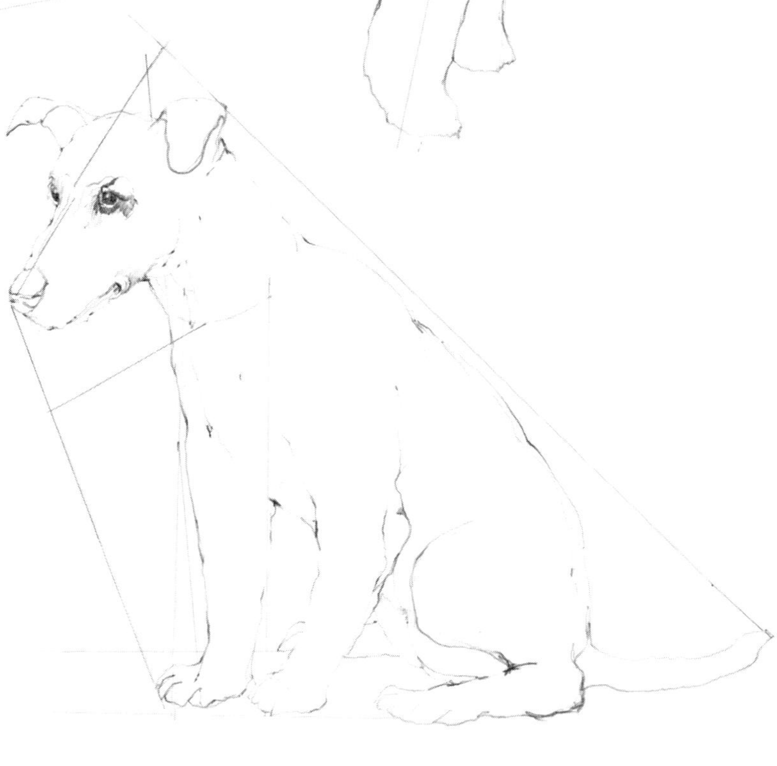

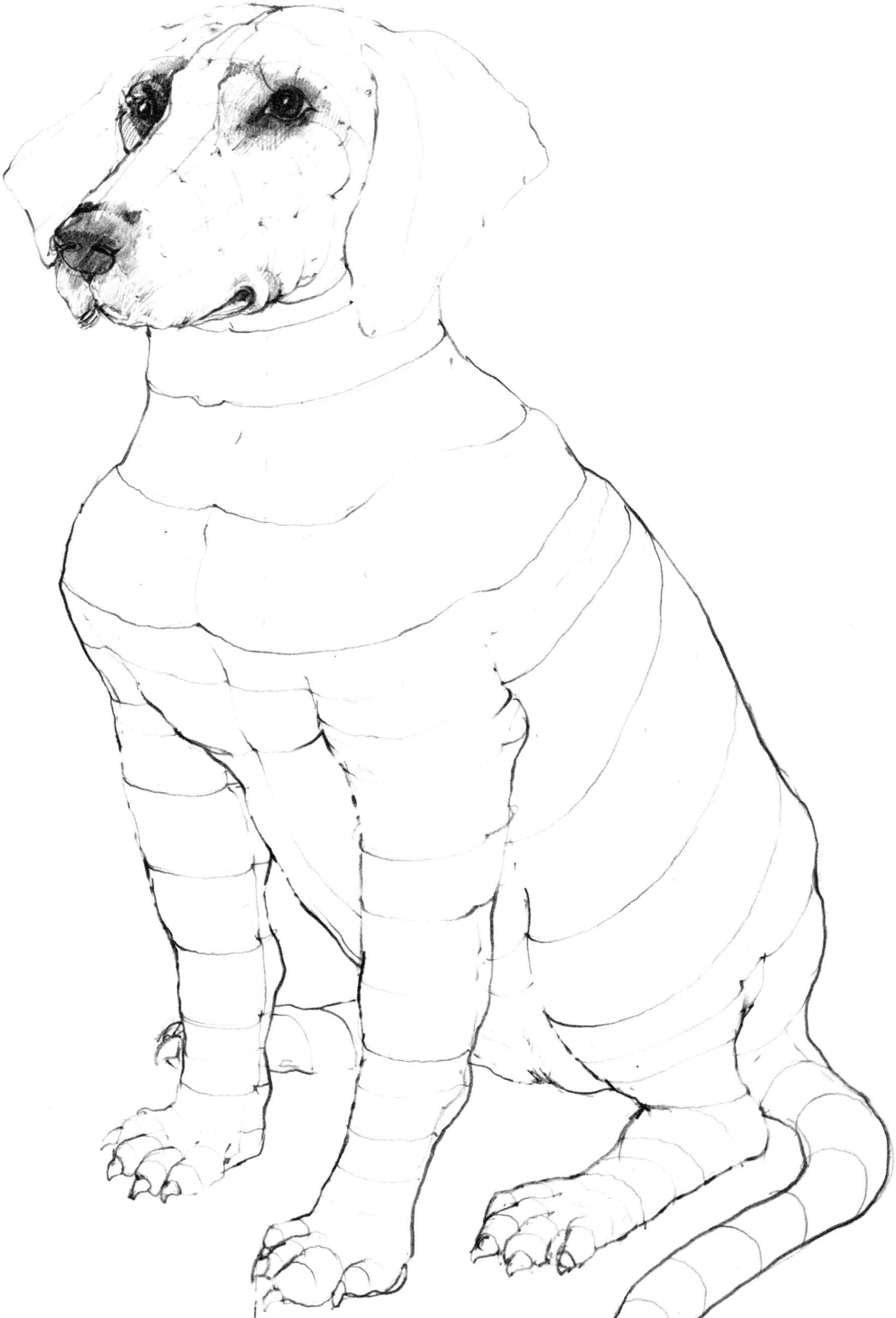

Heads

Dogs' heads vary widely in shape, but there are two basic types: the short, snub-nosed head and the longer, narrower head.

When you begin to draw, look for the basic shapes. Look at your subject from different viewpoints and angles to help you understand the shapes you are going to draw.

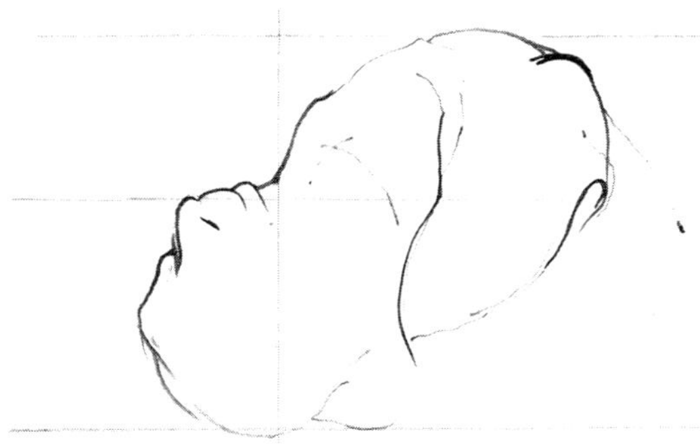

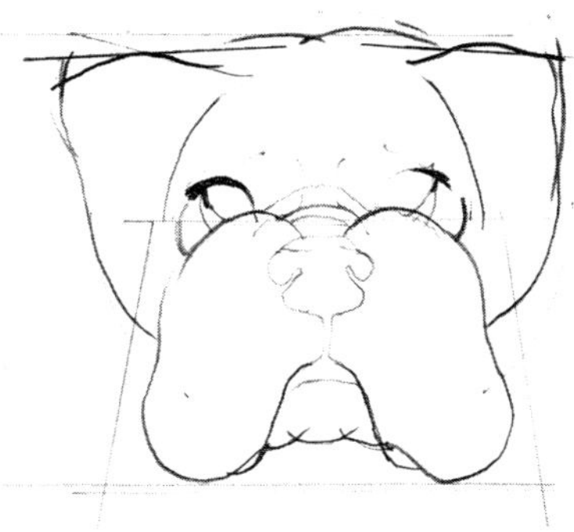

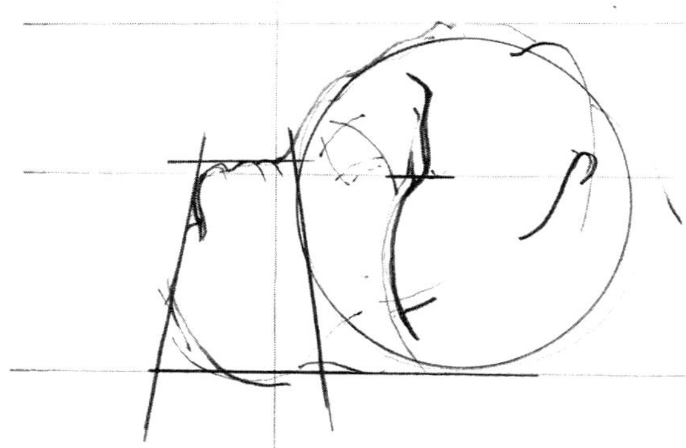

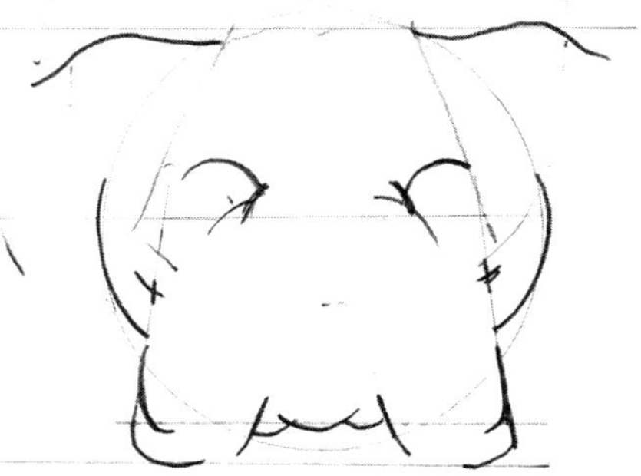

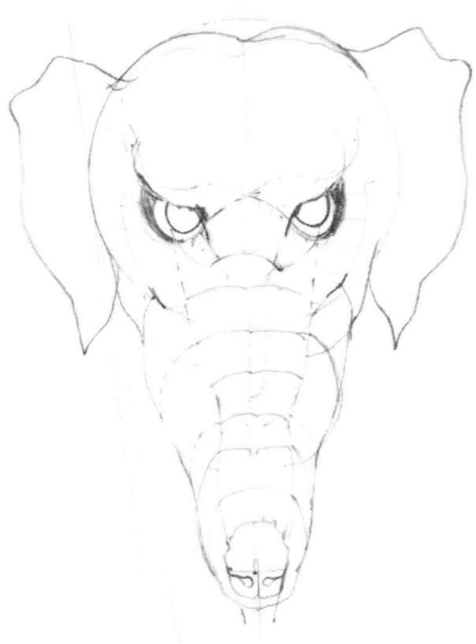

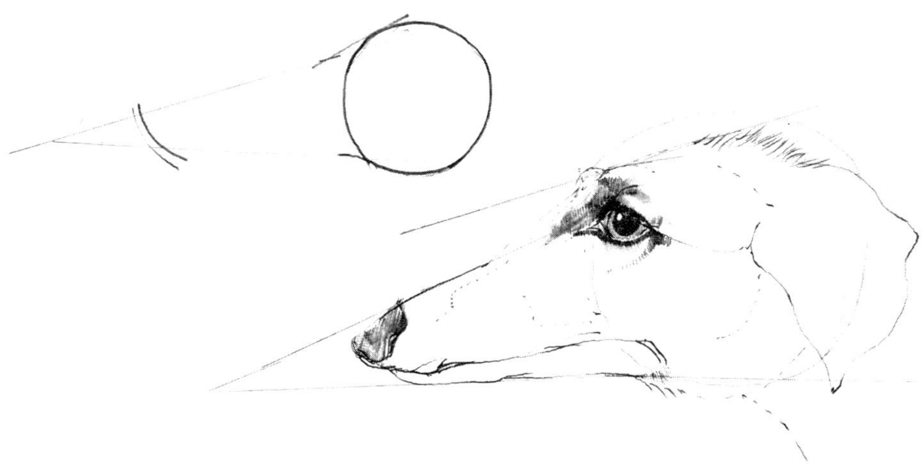

Noses

Notice how the nostrils are folded, how the flesh hangs over the edge at each side. The shape of the nose varies with different breeds.

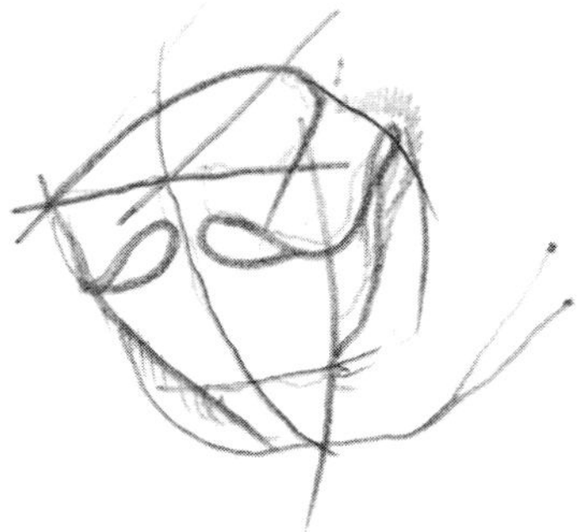

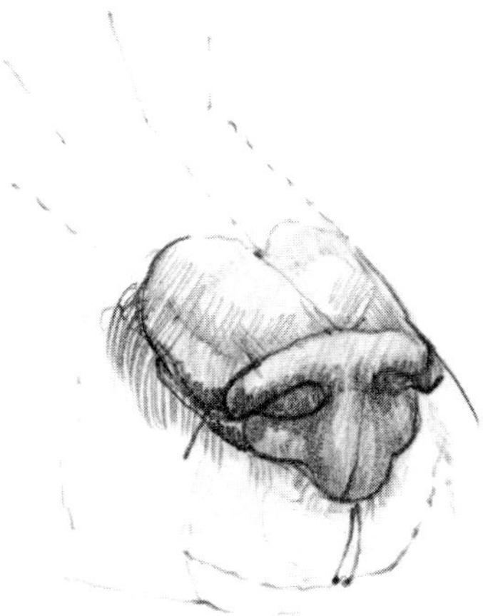

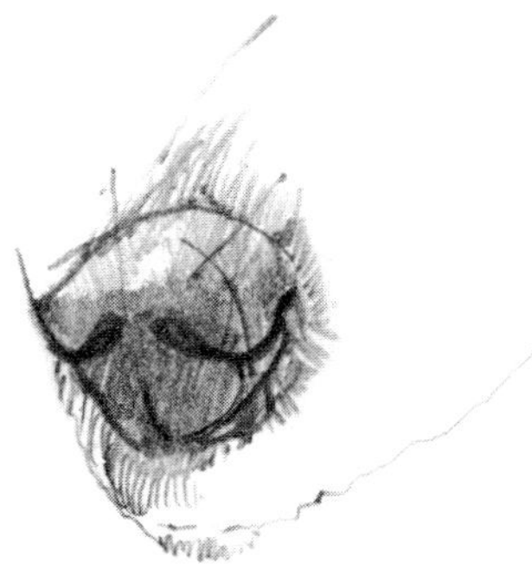

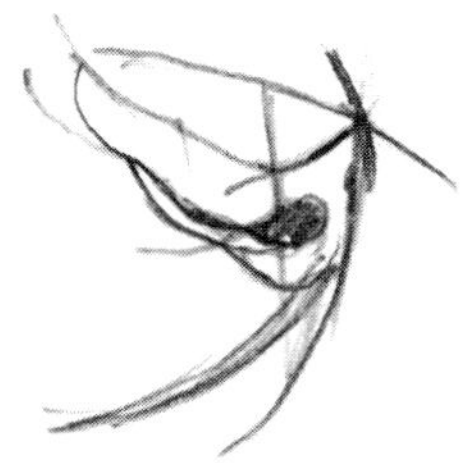

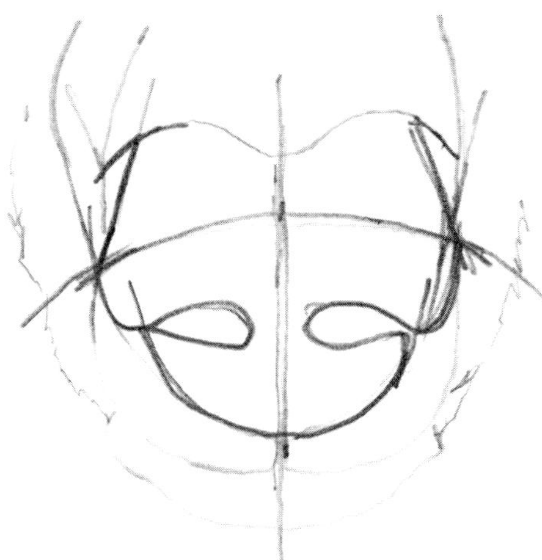

Ears

The shape and proportion of the ears give a dog character and individuality. They may be small and erect, long and floppy, rough or smooth. Notice their structure and how they grow out of the head. Their position also conveys mood and expression.

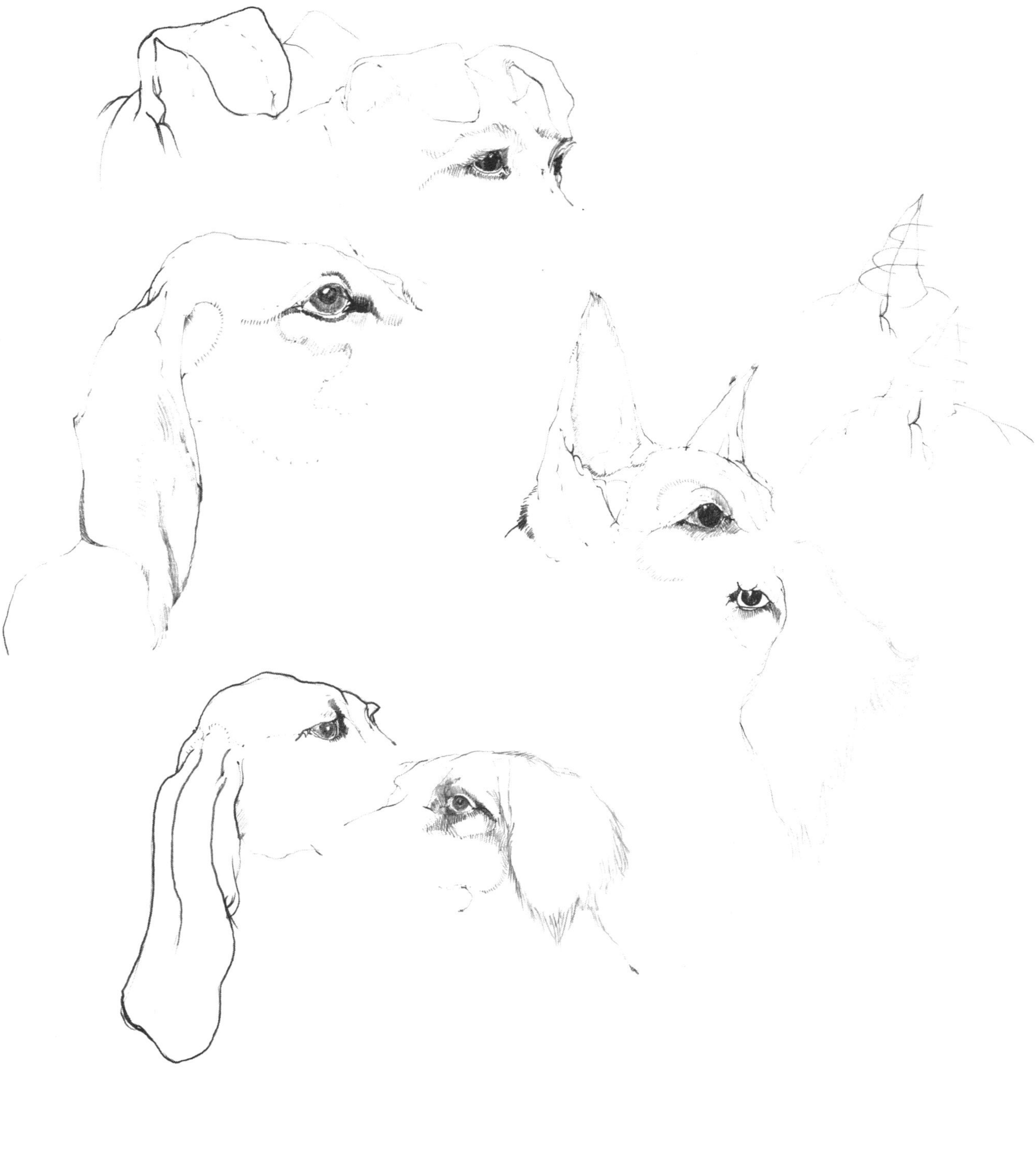

Eyes

The eyes are the most expressive feature, so spend some time studying them and drawing them.

Remember that the eye is a sphere, of which only a small part is exposed. It is mobile and very fragile and is protected by a part of the skull above it and the muscles around it.

Pay careful attention to the folds of skin which also have a protective function and which affect the shape of the eye. Look for the position of the highlight on the eyeball.

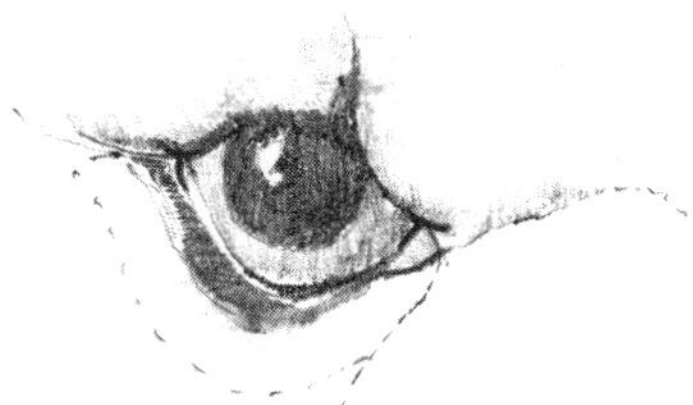

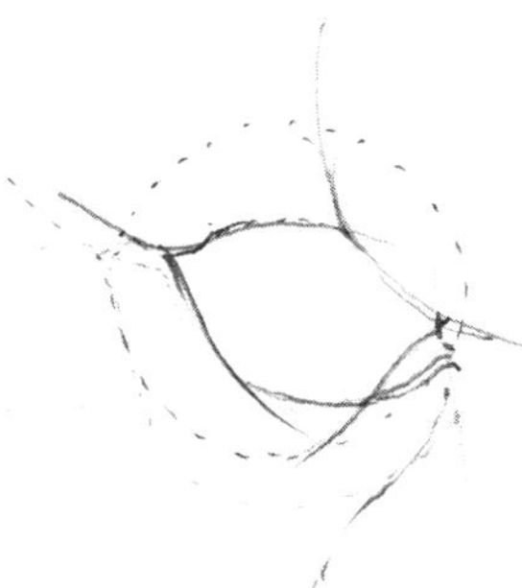

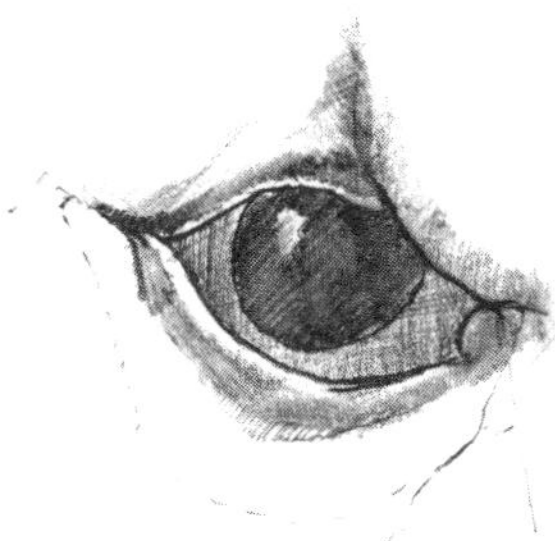

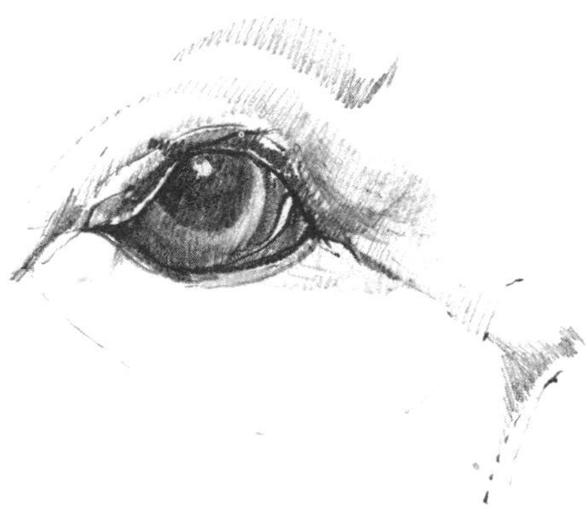

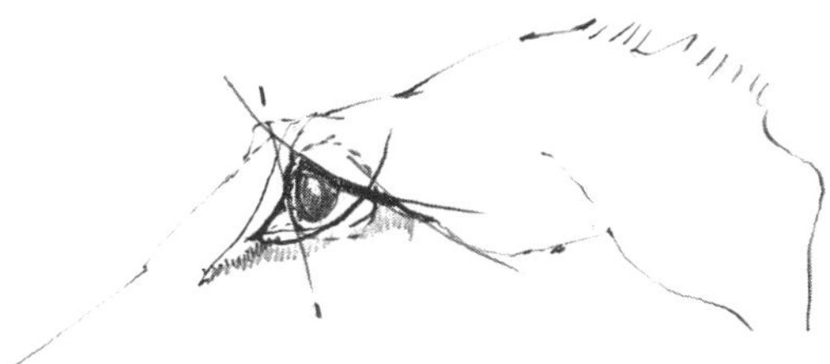

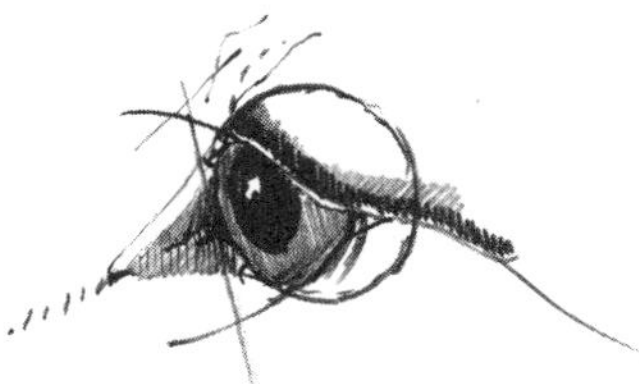

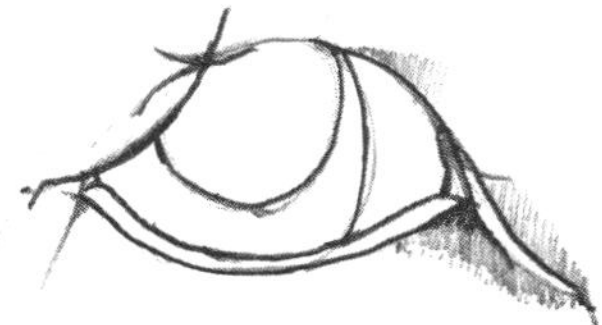

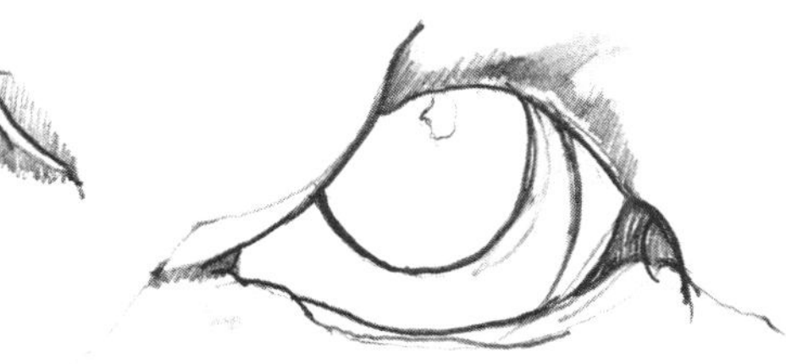

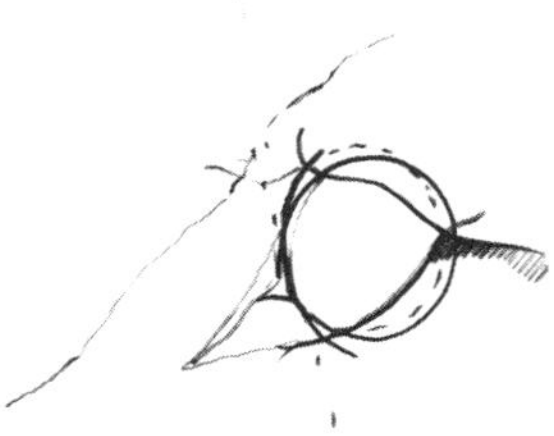

Legs and feet

The legs are also an important part of the character of your subject.

Remember that the legs and feet support all the weight of a standing dog; look carefully at the angles, and observe how the paws spread out as the animal stands firmly on the ground. Compare the characteristically loose and folded skin of a puppy's legs with that of an adult dog.

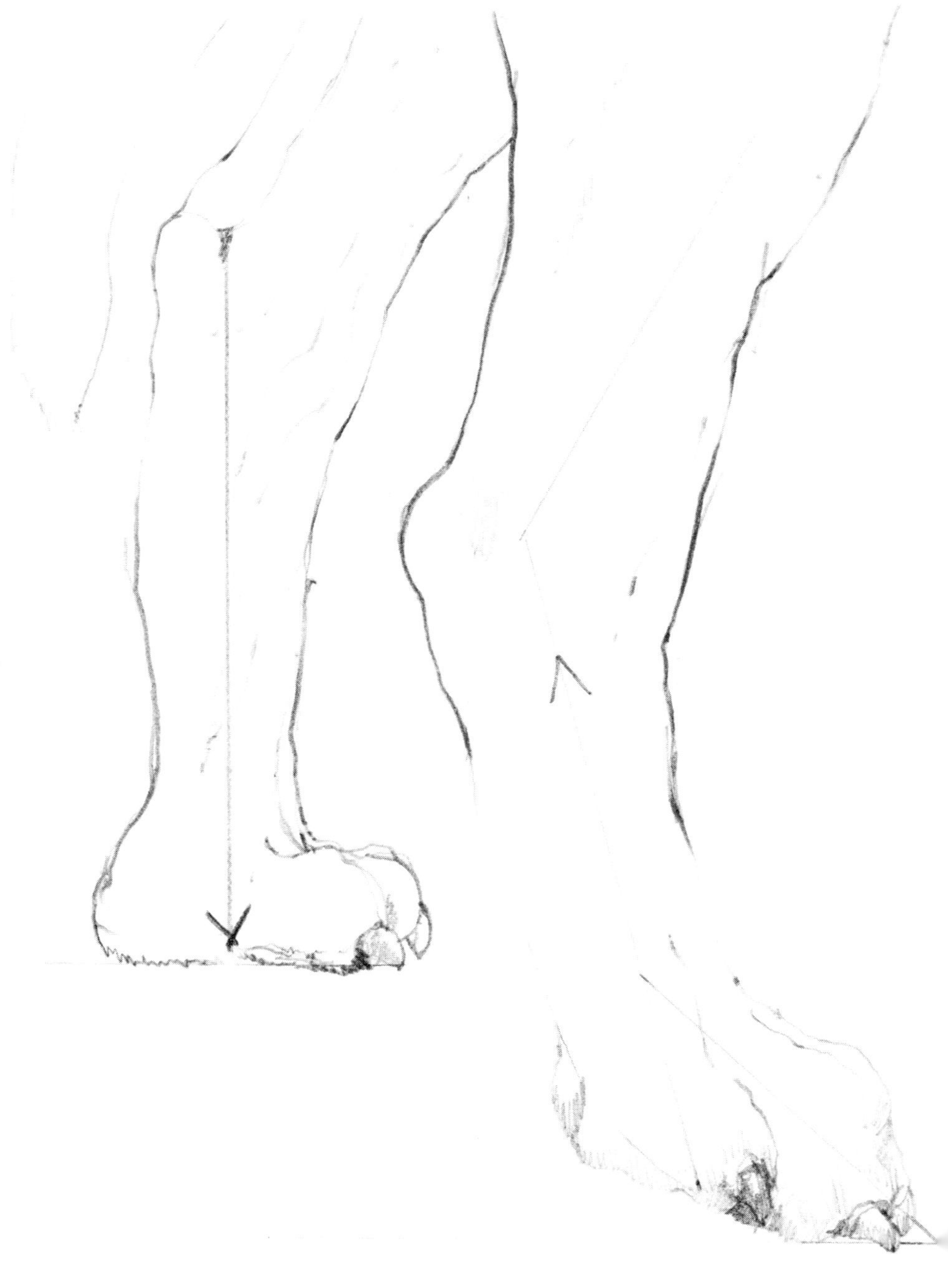

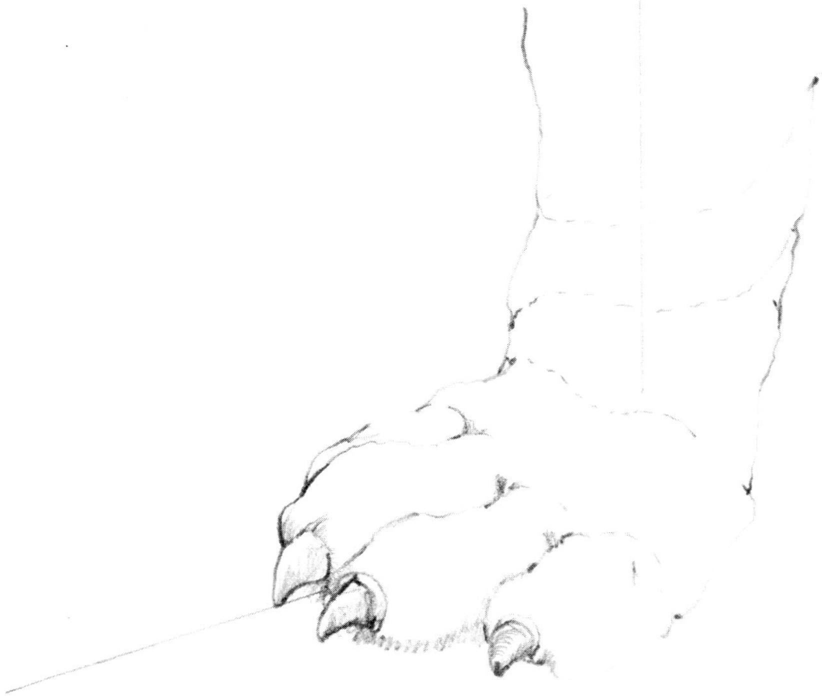

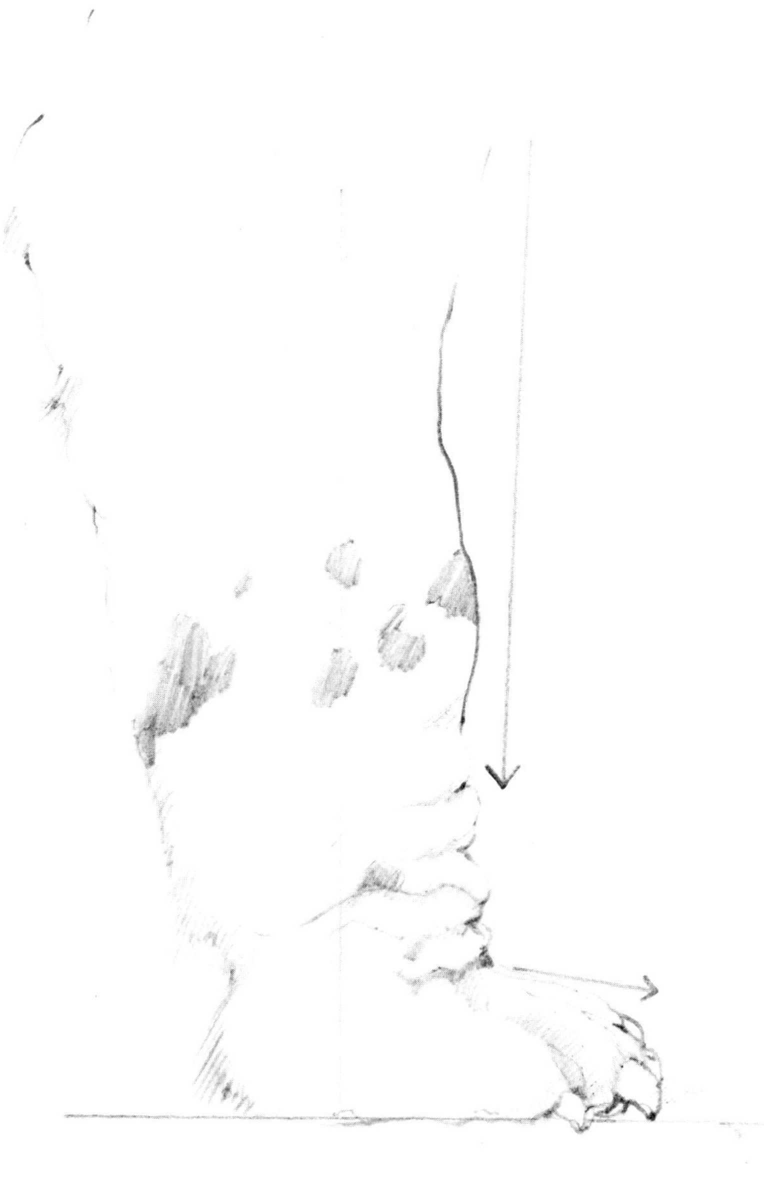

Step-by-step: the head

The basic shape of this long-nosed mongrel is a cone with a half-sphere (the main skull cavity) at its base. The surface of the cone is broken up into different facets or planes (for example, A, B and C on my drawing).

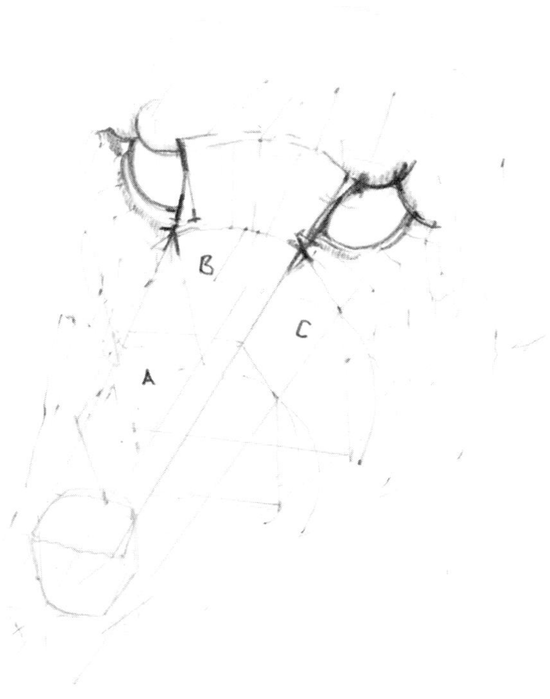

Begin by lightly drawing the basic shapes. Notice how they change if the head moves to one side or the other. Then study specific areas—around the eyes, the top of the skull, the nose. Look for the different planes and the points where the surface changes direction. Keep moving across the drawing, from one part to another, so that you begin to understand the structure.

Next begin to work on specific areas in more detail—the shape of the eyes, nose and ears.

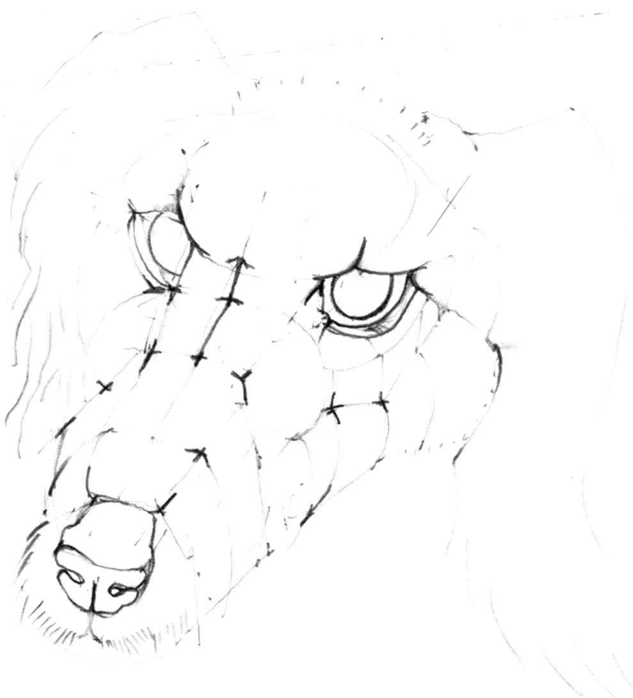

Finally, to give your drawing a feeling of solidity, put in the tonal quality—the areas of light and shade across the surface and around the forms, and the way in which the hair lies.

You can follow this same sequence with any shape of head.

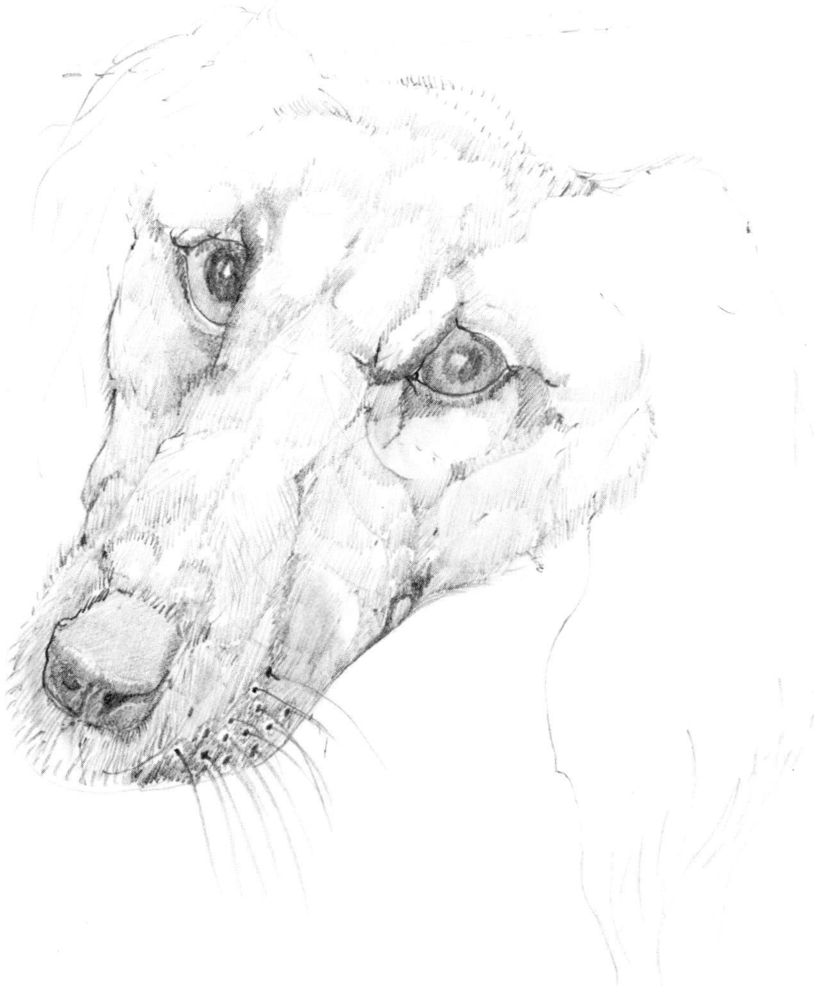

Step-by-step: the whole dog

Observe carefully the posture and the relative proportions of head, body and legs.

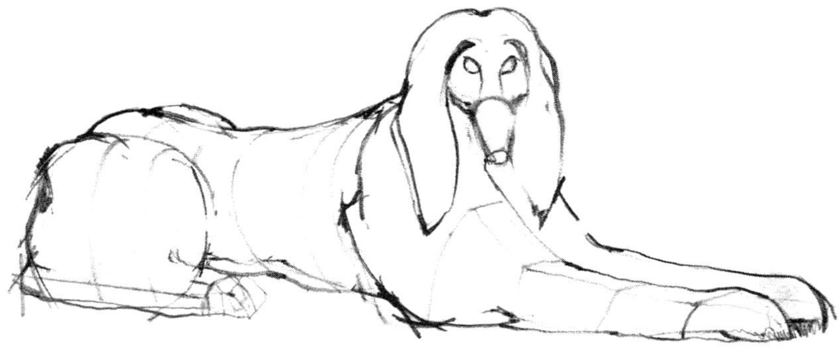

Think about what aspect you want to project. As you draw, look continuously at your subject and notice the particular shapes and characteristics.

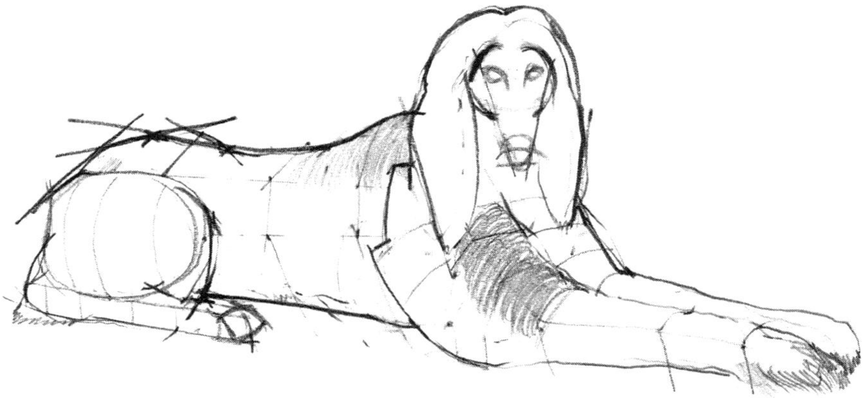

Begin by drawing very freely the overall shape. Look for curves, horizontal and vertical lines. Notice how one part flows into another, and the rhythm of the lines.

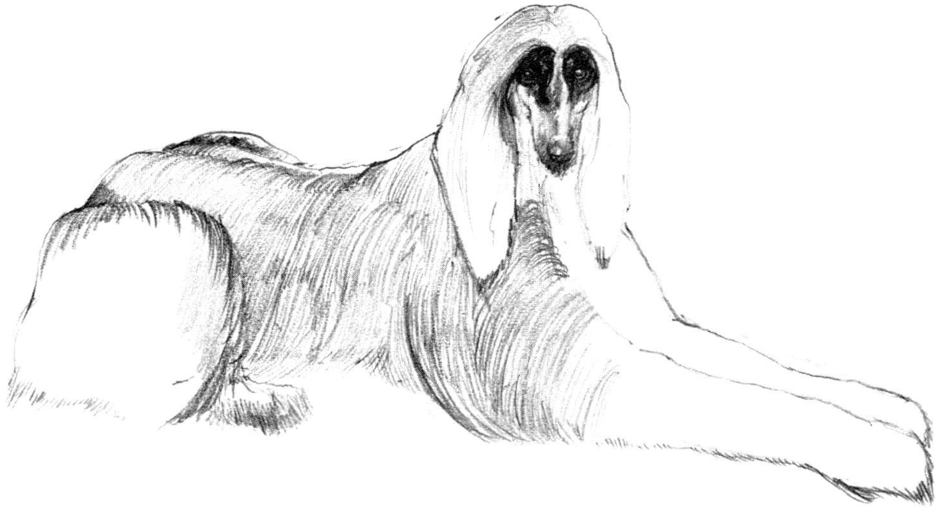

Then look more carefully at how the individual parts relate: notice how and where the legs emerge from the trunk, how the rib cage hangs, the line of the neck, and how the muscles affect the outline. Try to draw exactly what you see—don't invent lines that you think should be there.

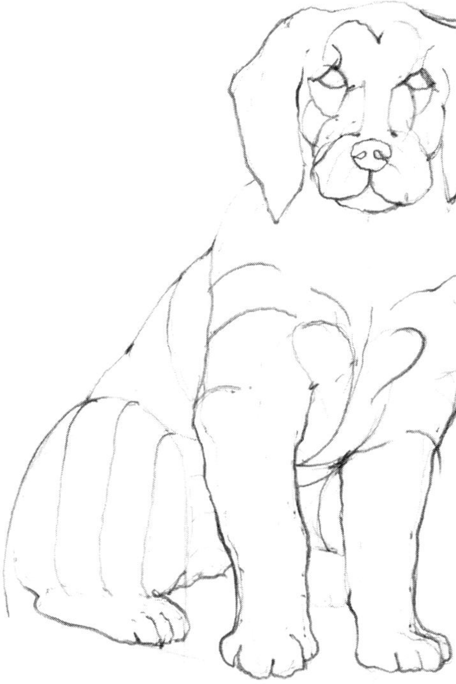

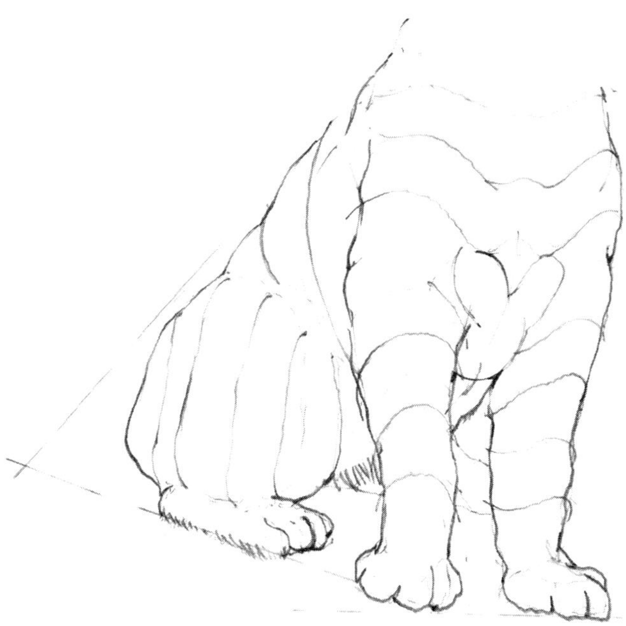

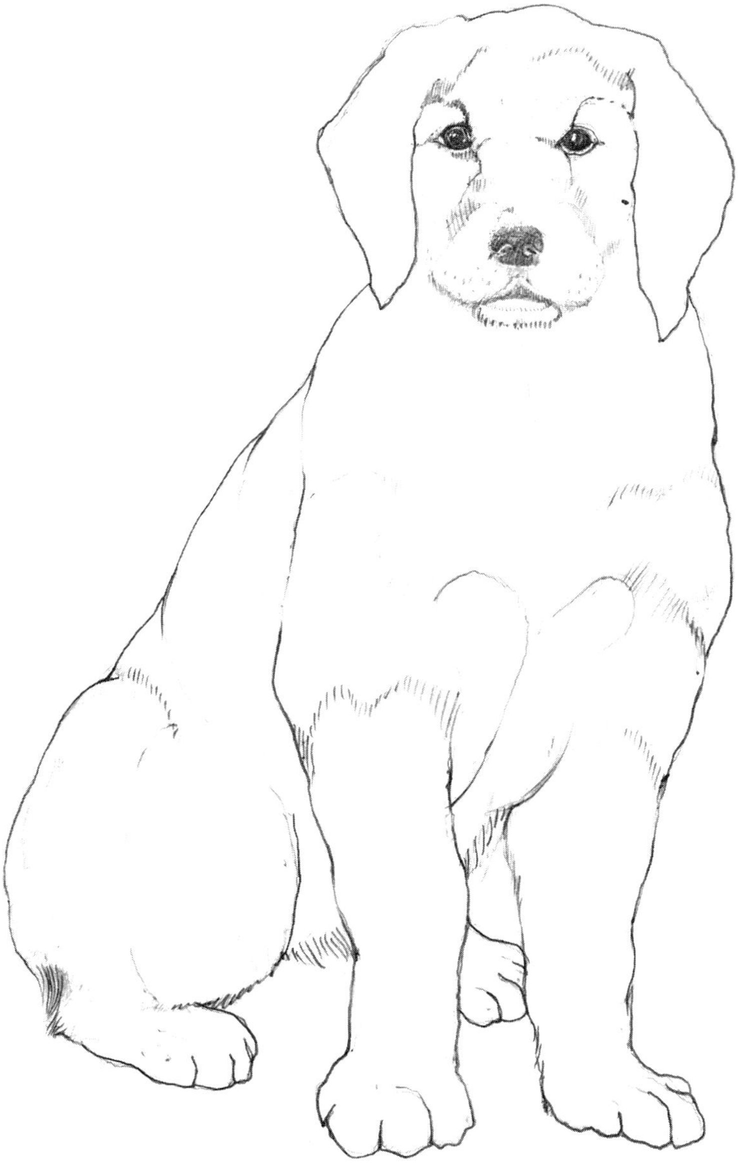

All these observations will help you to understand the underlying structure and make your drawing look three-dimensional. When the basic shapes are right you can add tone and detail.

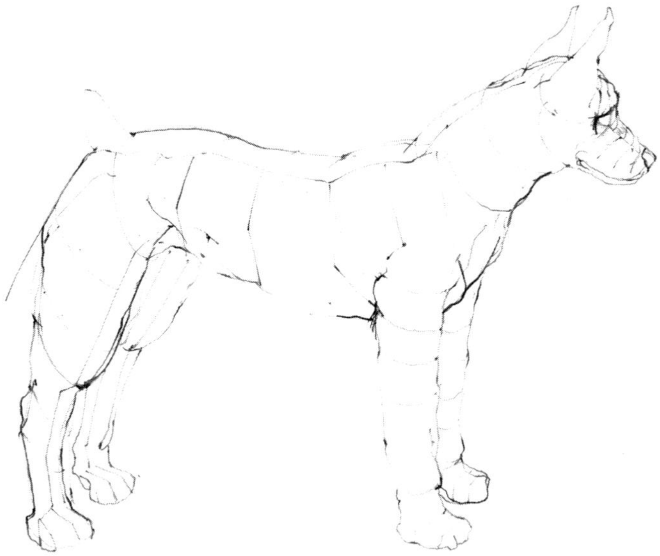

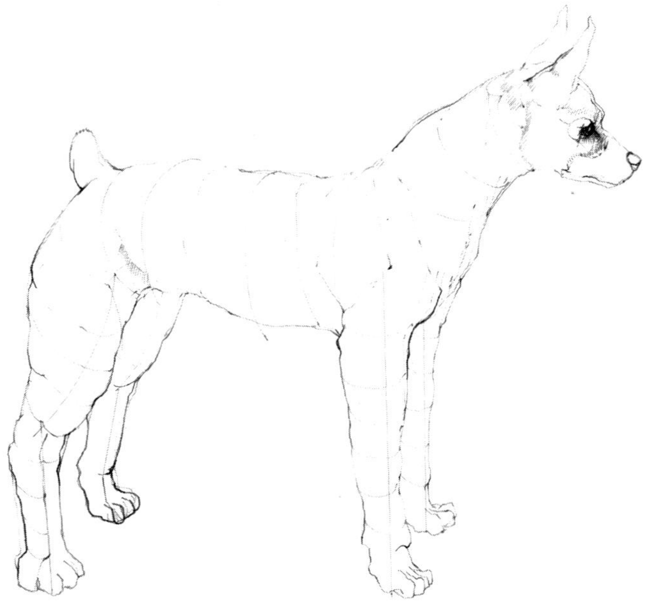

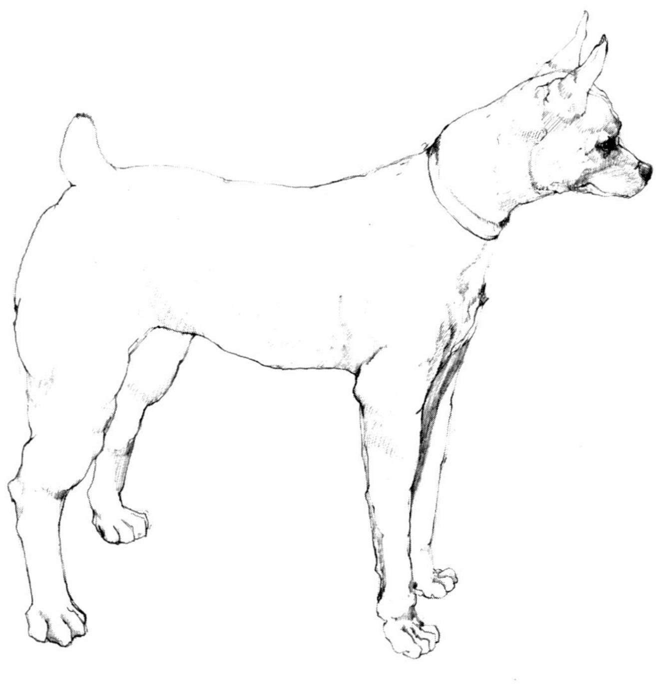

Proportion

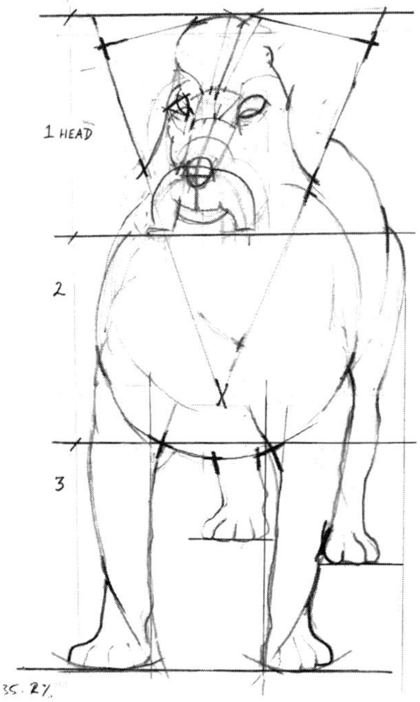

To draw well, you must be constantly aware of the relative proportions of your subject.

One way to check proportion is to use the head as a unit of measurement. Hold your pencil vertically at arm's length, with the top of the pencil in line with the top of the dog's head, then place your thumb on the pencil in line with the chin. Keeping your thumb in position, work out how many times this head measurement fits into the overall height. This animal's head is one-third of the total height.

Remember, though, that the relative size of the head will differ with the breed of dog and the position in which you draw it.

By holding your pencil vertically, at right-angles to the ground, you can also check the angles of the body and legs. This will help to give your drawing accuracy and character.

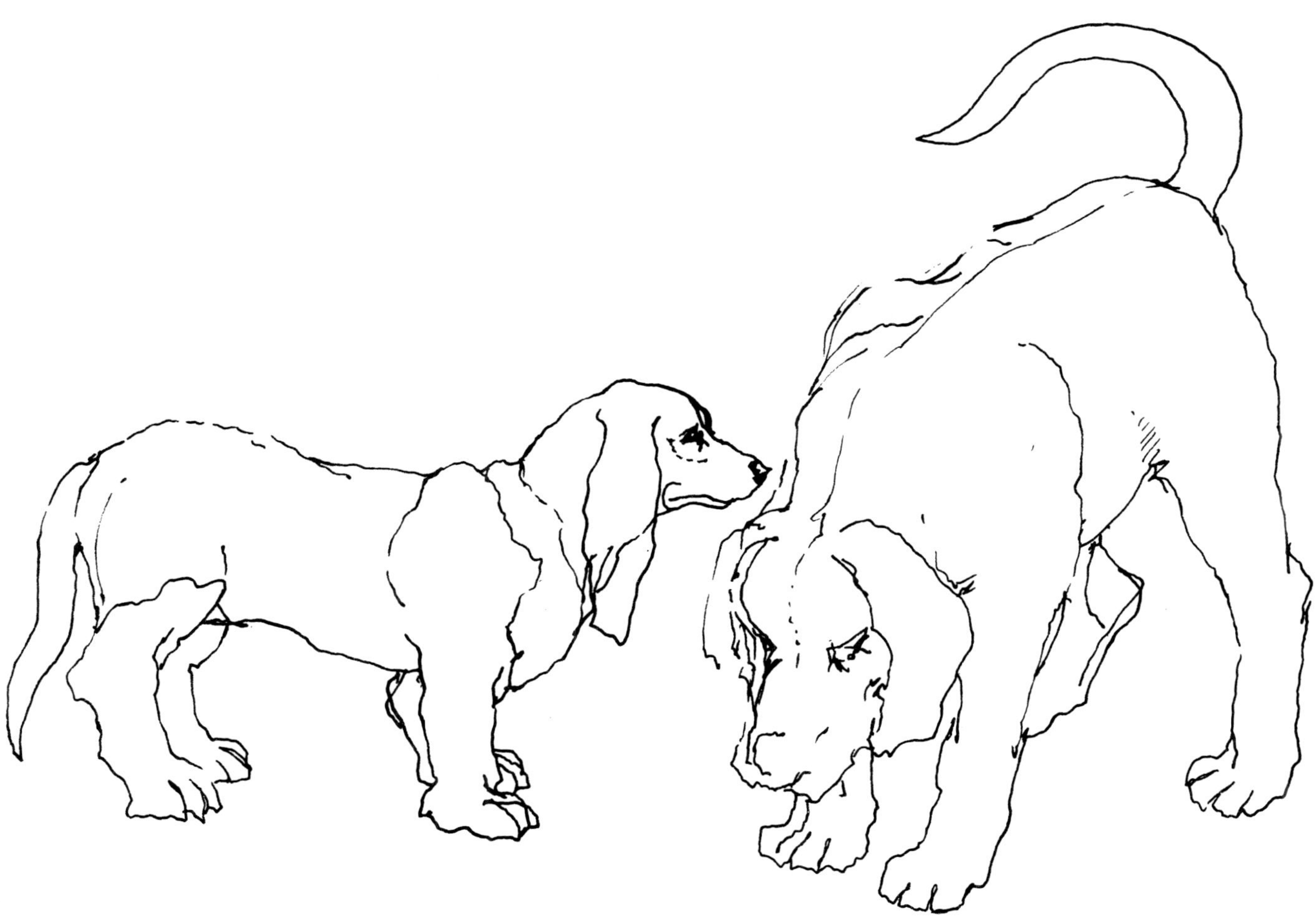

Action

Your interest may wane if you draw dogs only in standing or sitting positions. Try sketching your dog as it eats, stretches or scratches. Then take your sketchbook into the park or garden and watch your dog running around and meeting other dogs.

Don't attempt clean, finished drawings to start with. Draw freely in soft pencil, charcoal or ink. If you don't succeed at first, start again, and keep on trying.

Look at the basic lines of the neck, shoulder and spine, and notice how they alter as the dog moves. Draw in these lines to record what you have observed.

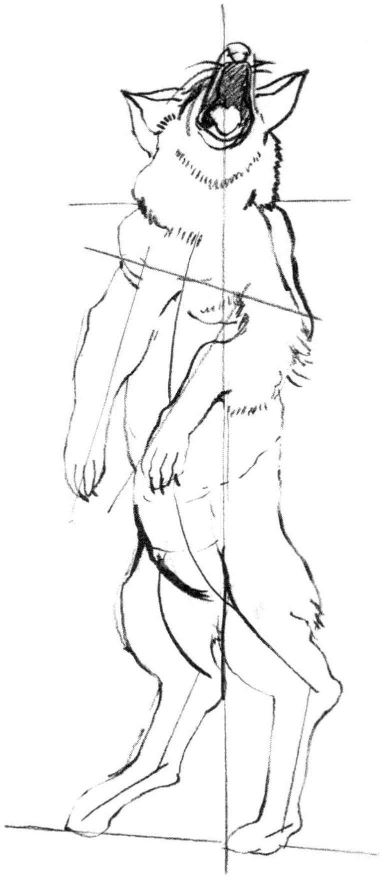

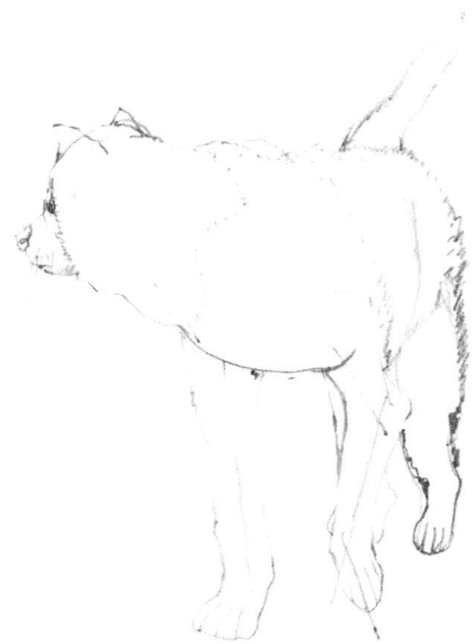

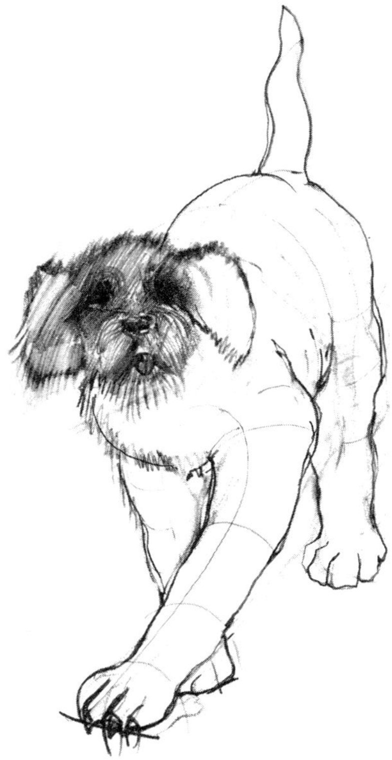

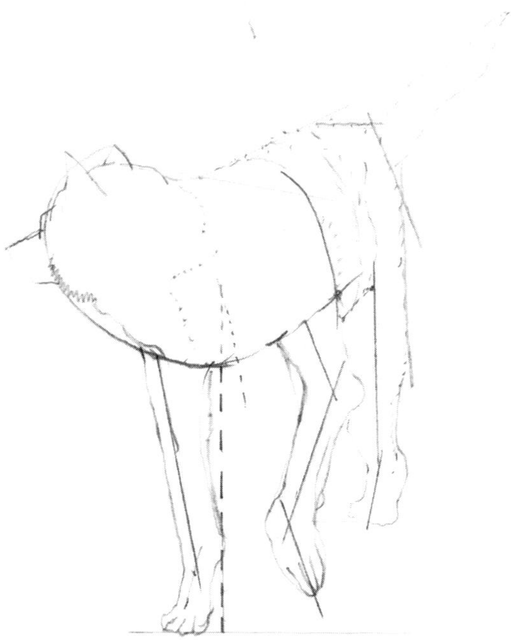

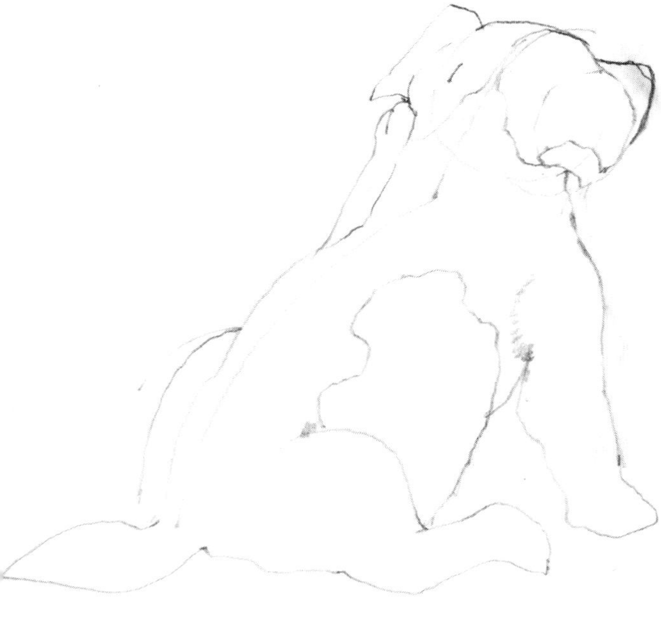

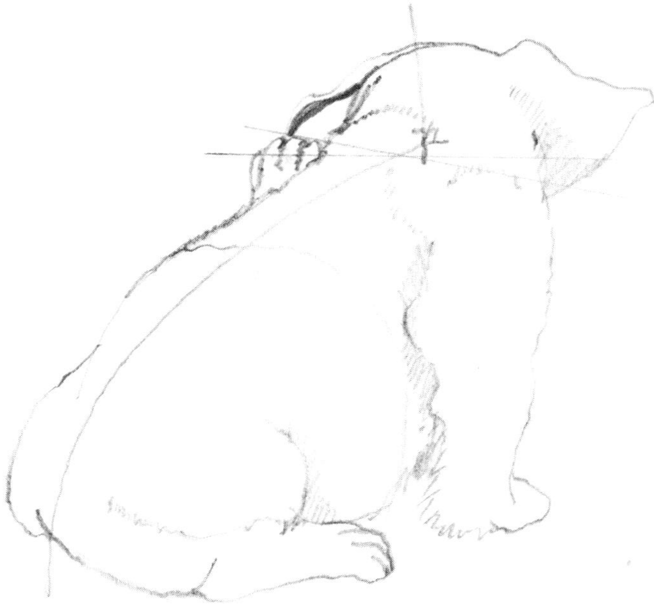

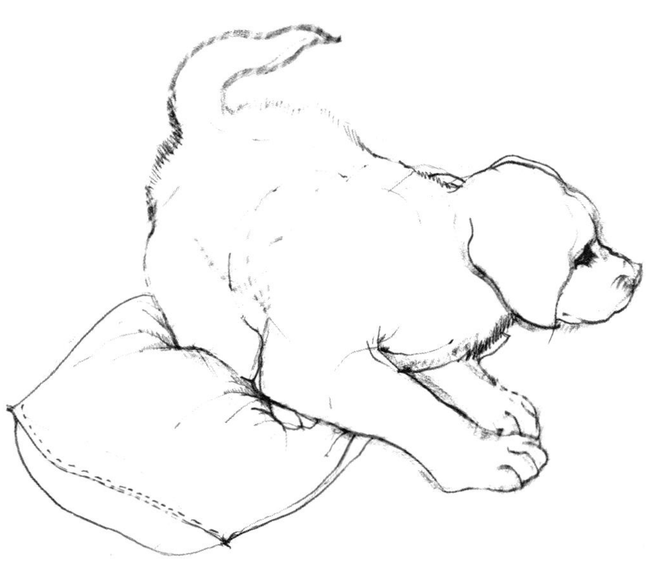

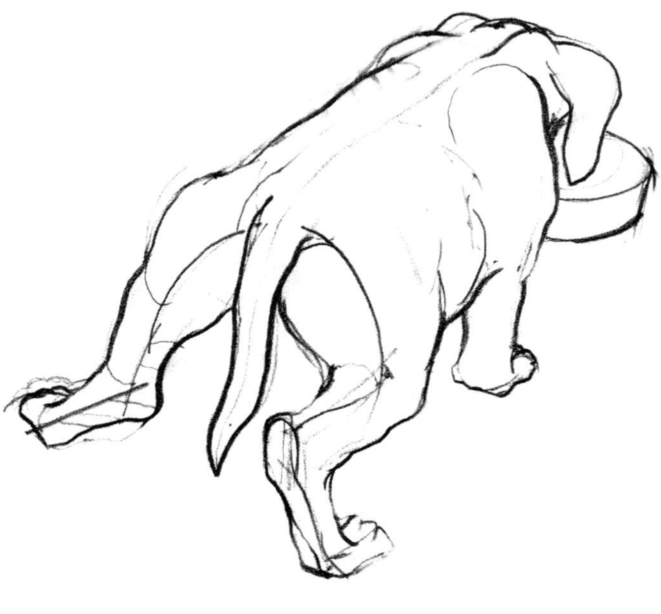

Remember that the legs of a standing or moving animal bear its weight, and that the distribution of weight alters as it moves. Observe the shift of body weight and how the animal maintains its balance. Notice how it carries its tail.

Continual watching and drawing will increase your understanding and help you to record more accurately what you see.

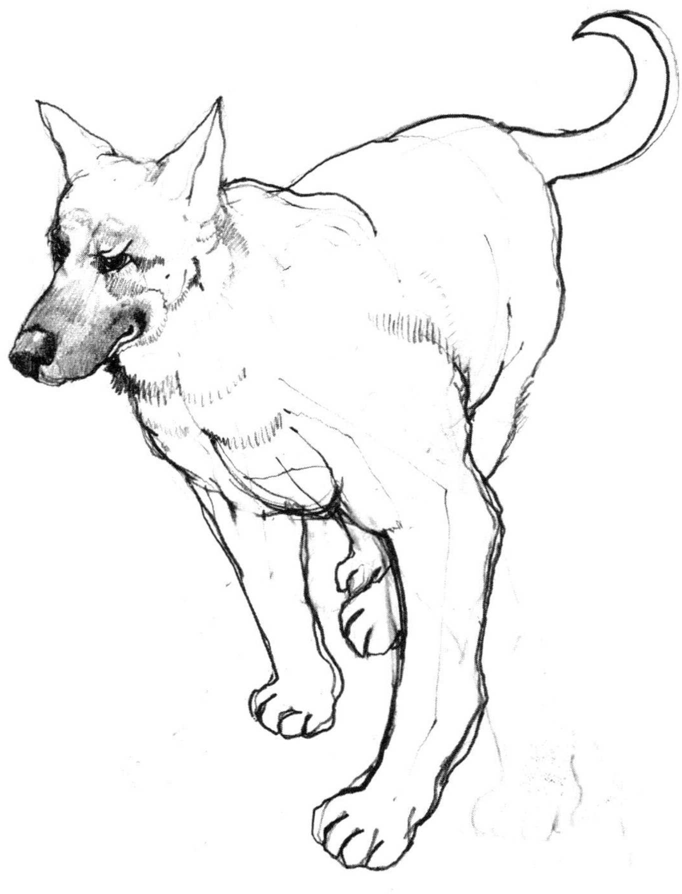

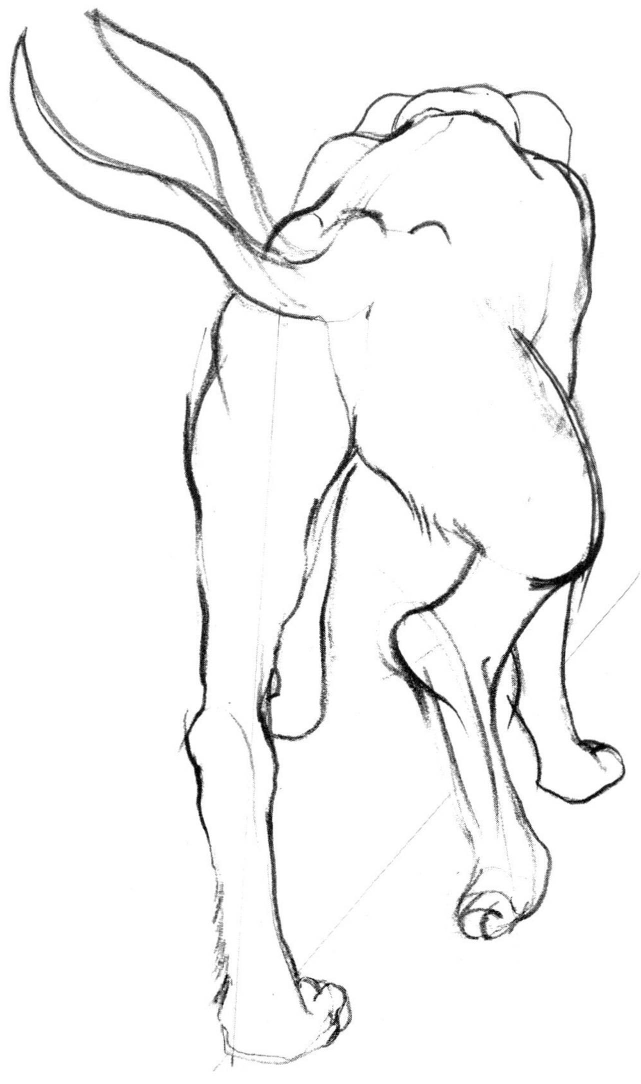

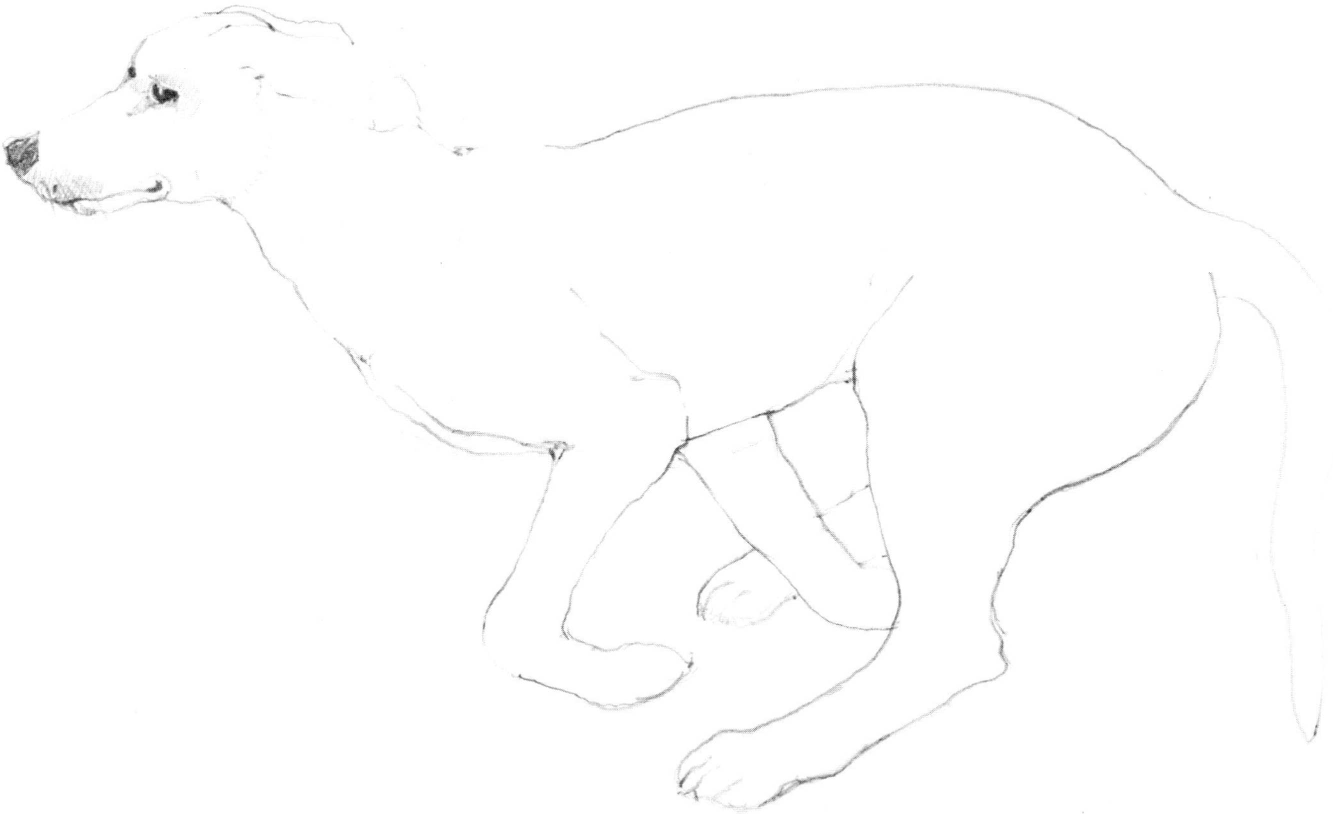

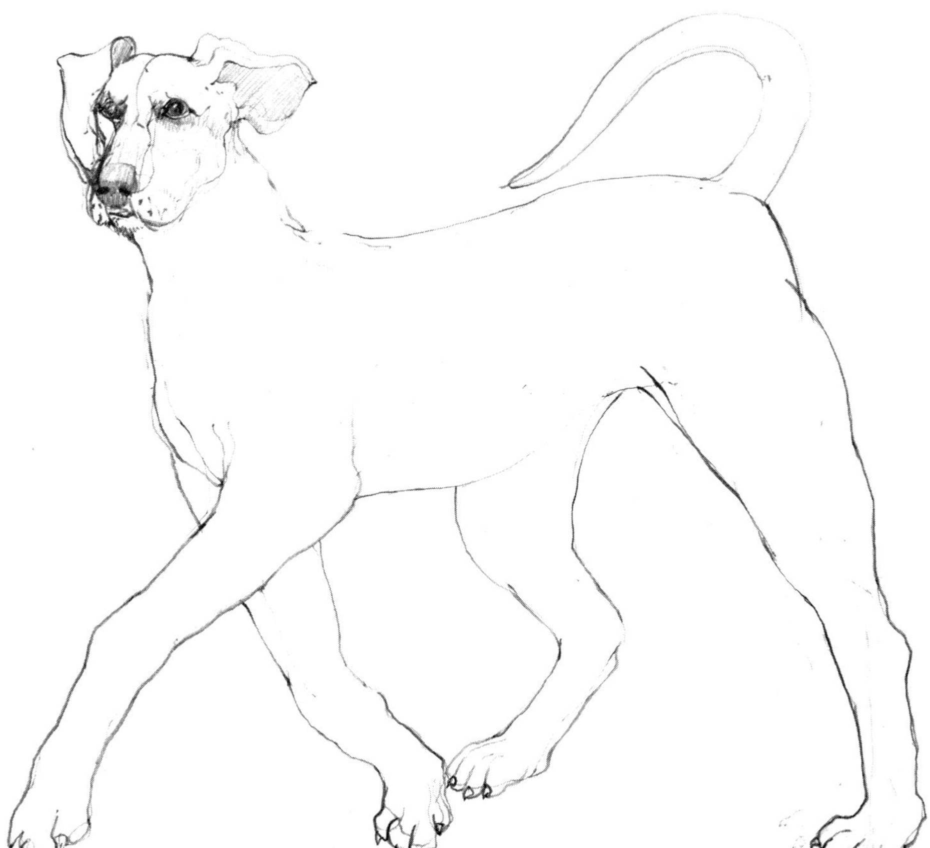

Materials and techniques

As you draw, you will become aware of the variety of shape, size, colouring and texture in different types of dog. You may find that the materials you use for drawing one dog will be less suitable for drawing another.

Experiment with different media to find new ways of achieving various effects in your drawing. This will make your work more interesting.

Be careful, though, not to become too interested in technique alone. It can be used as an aid to help you achieve the result you want, but remember that observation is the surest way to improve your drawing skill.

Try to use whatever media you choose in as many ways as possible; for example, a pencil that draws a sharp line can also be held at an angle and used for shading.

Experiment on a sheet of paper to discover the variety of marks you can make with one drawing tool. This will be useful when you want to combine different media in one drawing. For example, a pencil used for shading may not produce a dark enough tone for certain features such as the eyes, so try using Conté or Chinagraph to give the depth of tone you want.

Discover different ways of conveying the texture of different types of hair—a sharp pencil, or pen and ink, for short wiry hair, charcoal for long, soft hair, etc.

The following pages show examples of the use of different media.

These two heads were drawn with a fine pen and black ink, using a 2B pencil for shading.

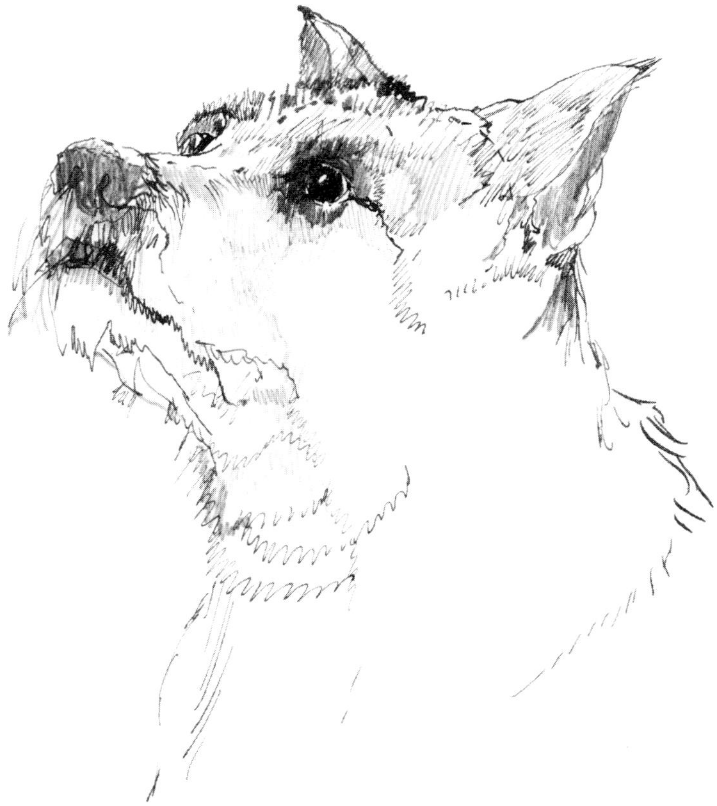

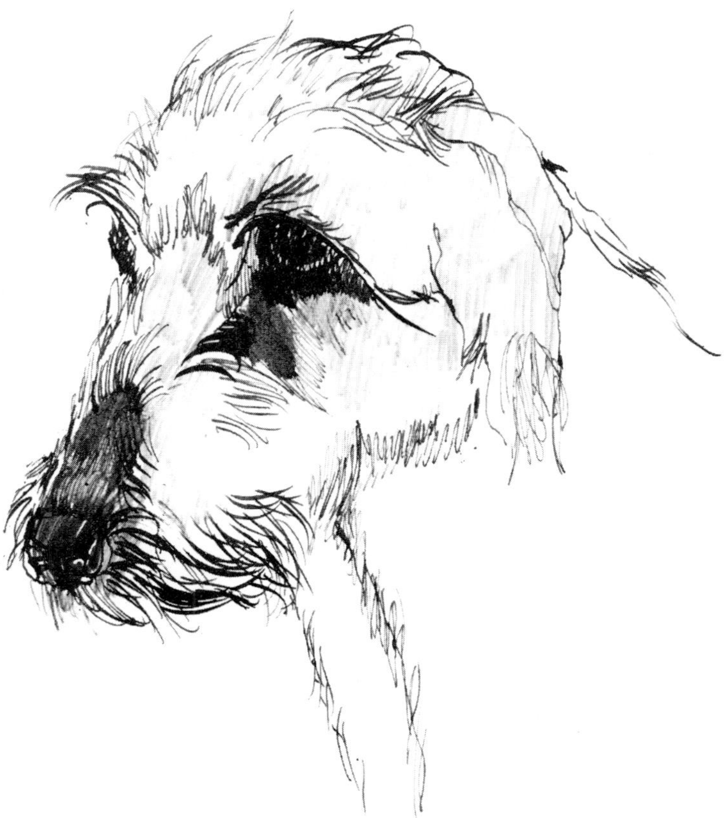

Quick sketches made with a fine felt-tip pen.

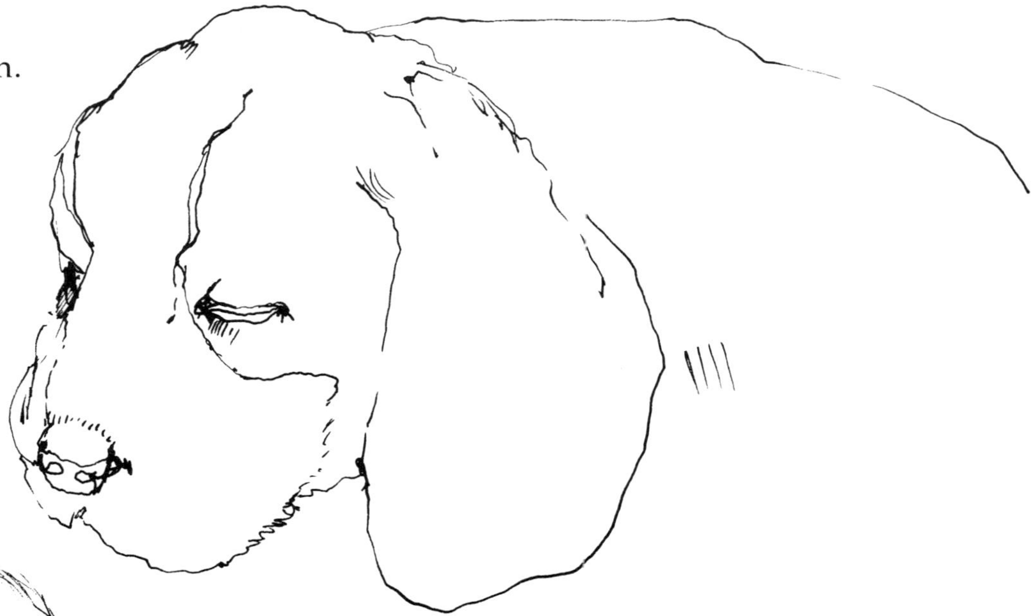

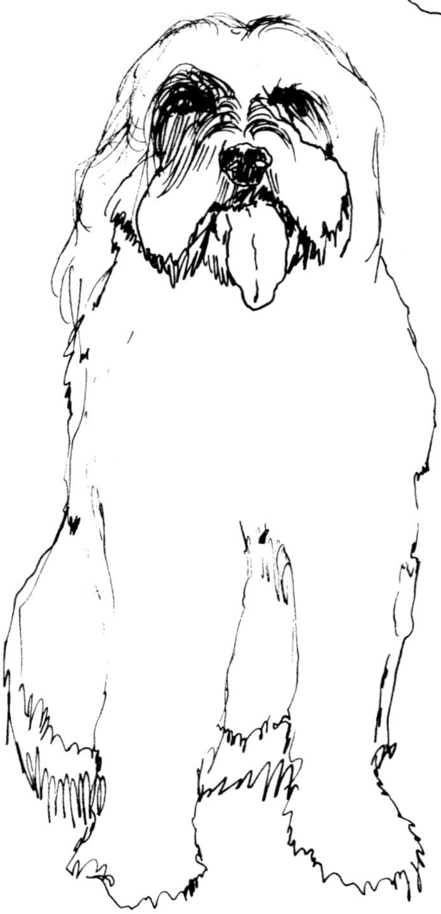

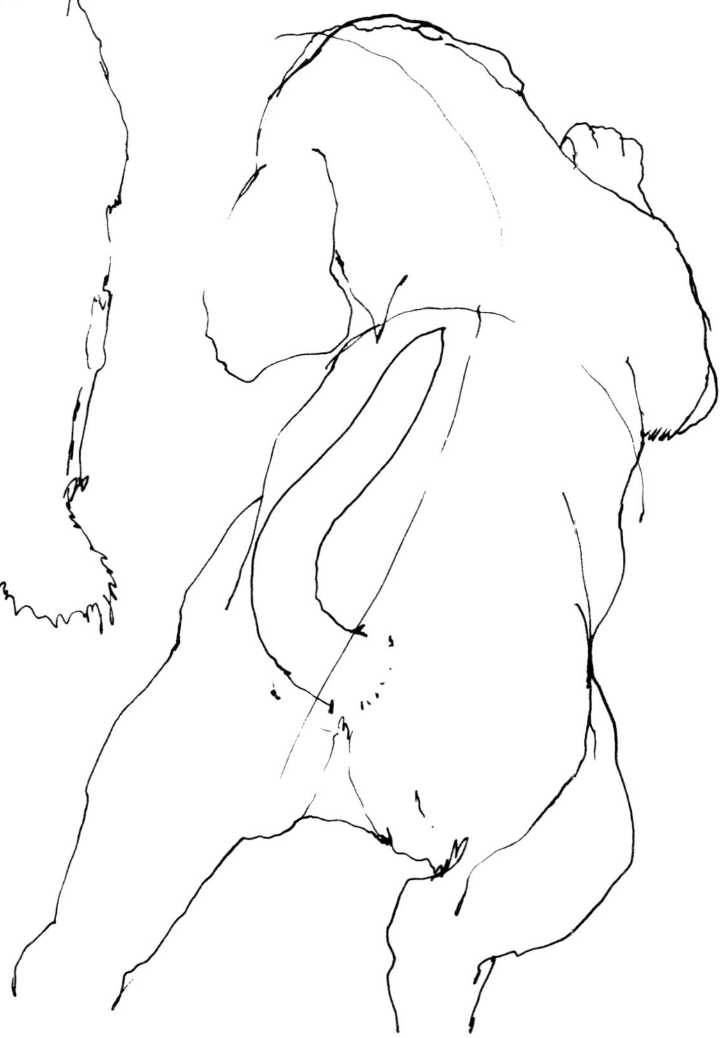

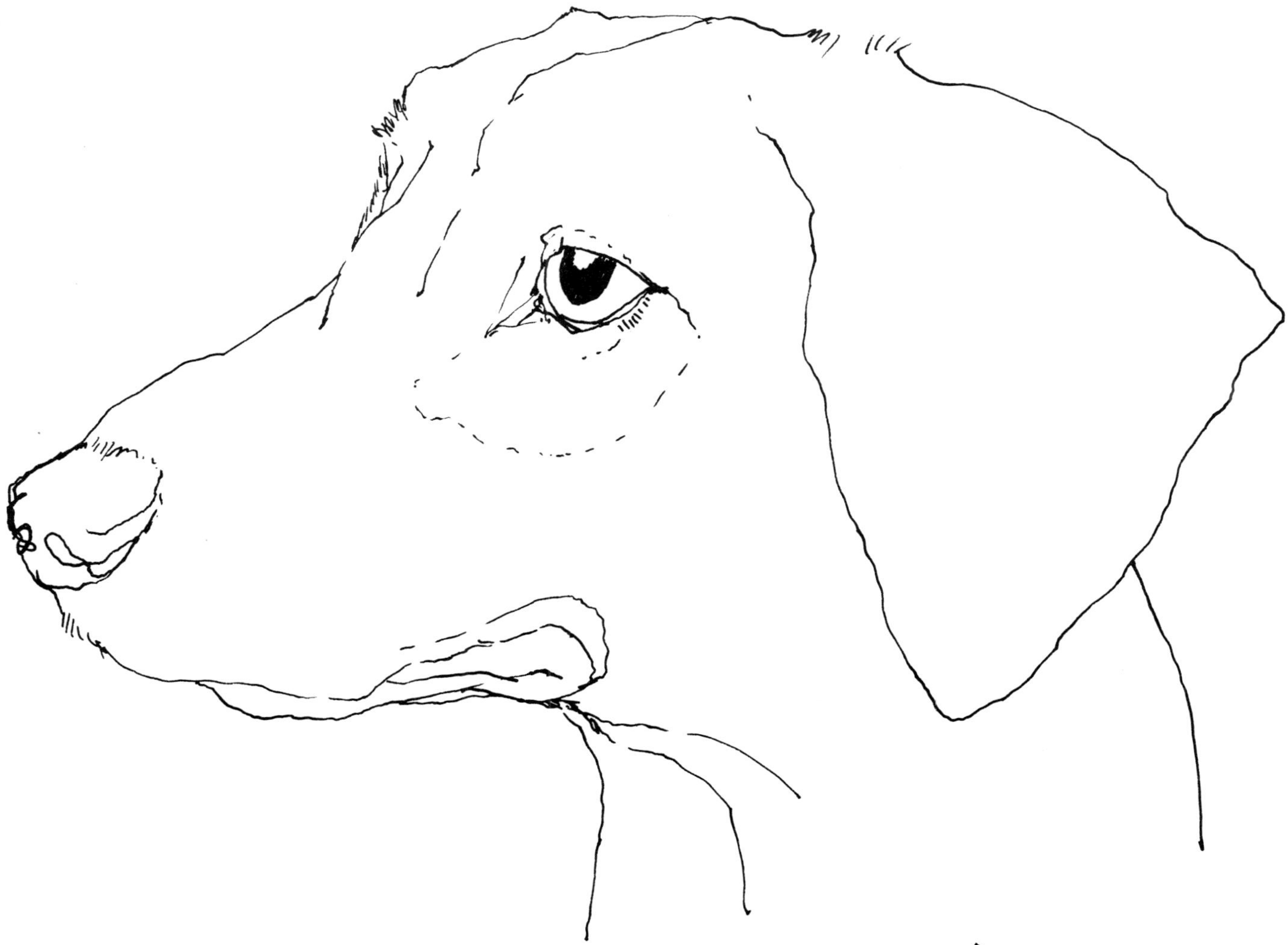

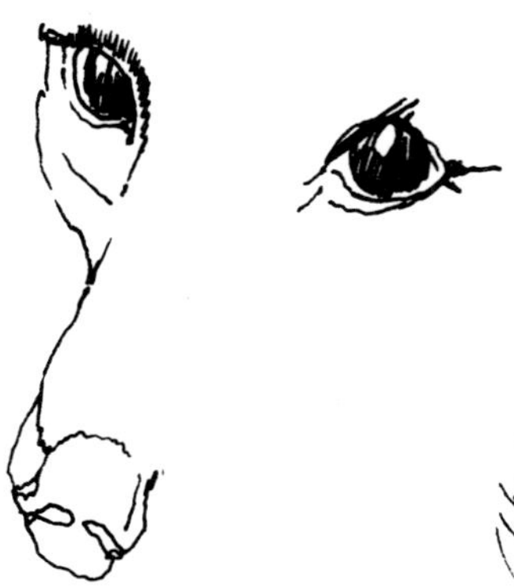

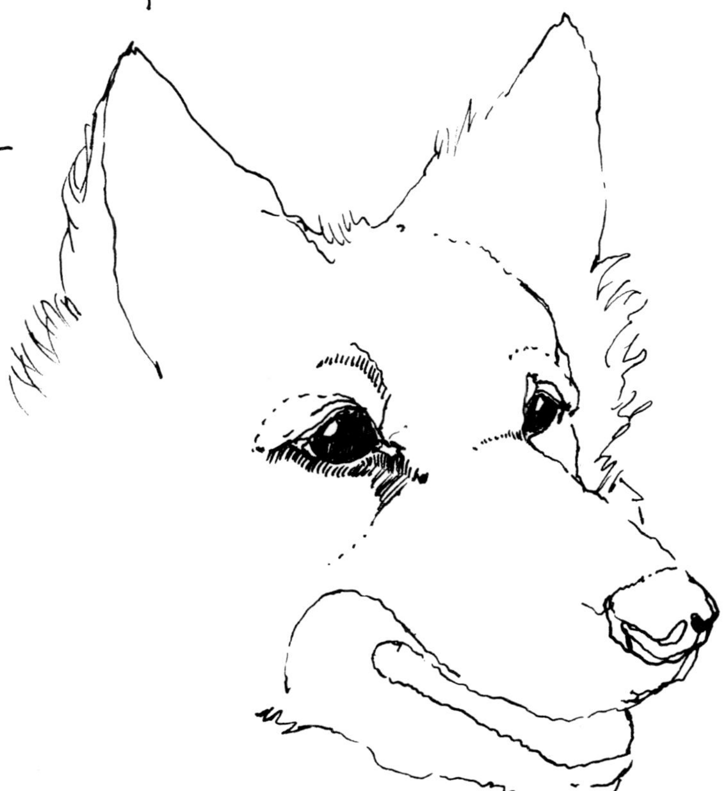

To draw the texture of long hair you can use charcoal and an eraser. Draw lines to show how the hair lies over the body, then gently rub with the edge of the eraser to get tonal and textural effects.

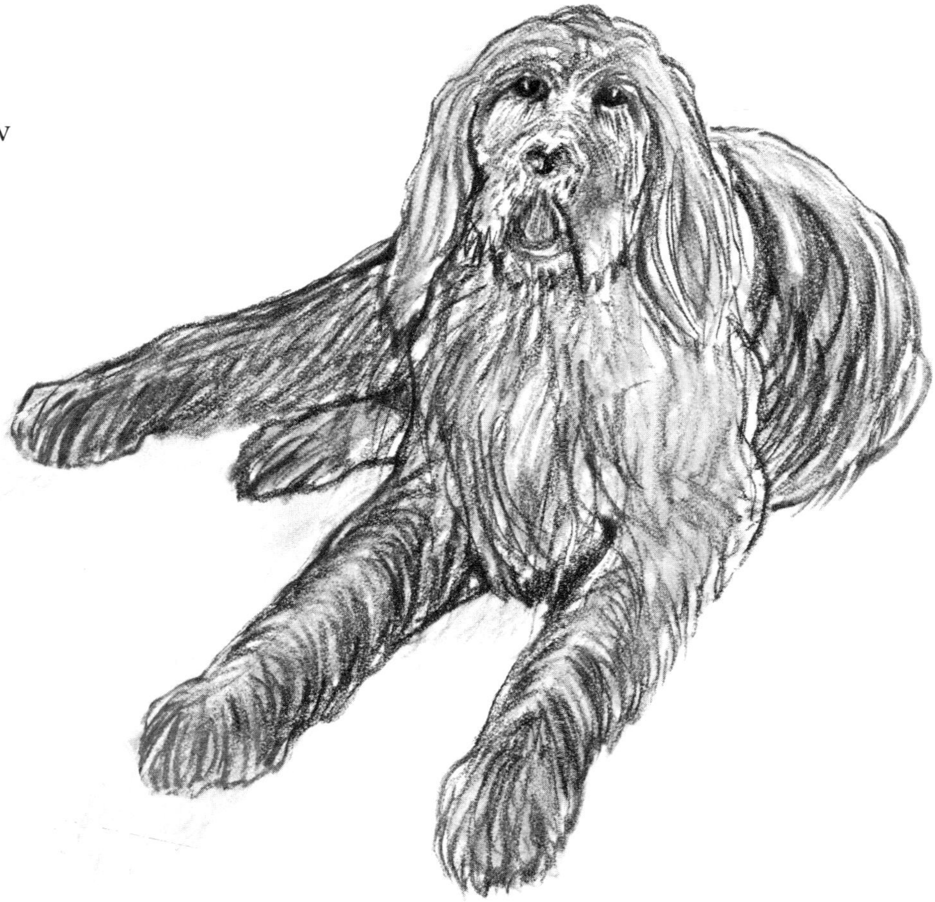

This bulldog was drawn with wax crayon and pencil.

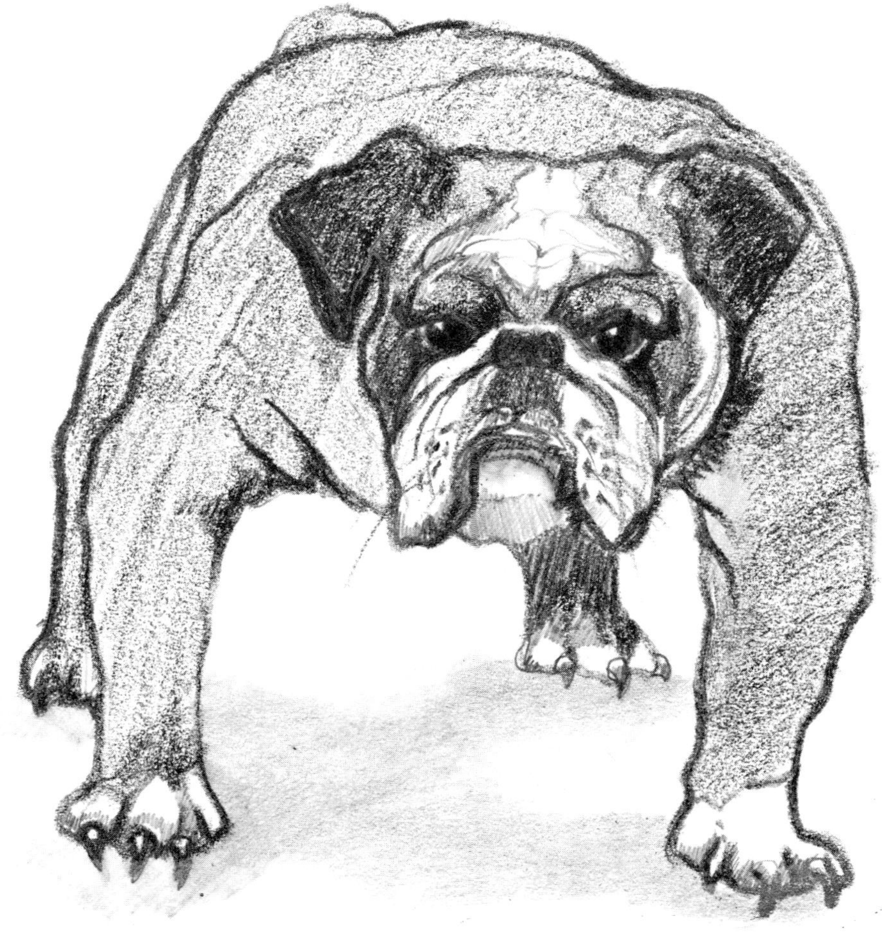

A thick felt marker can be used for quick, bold drawing but is not good for detail.

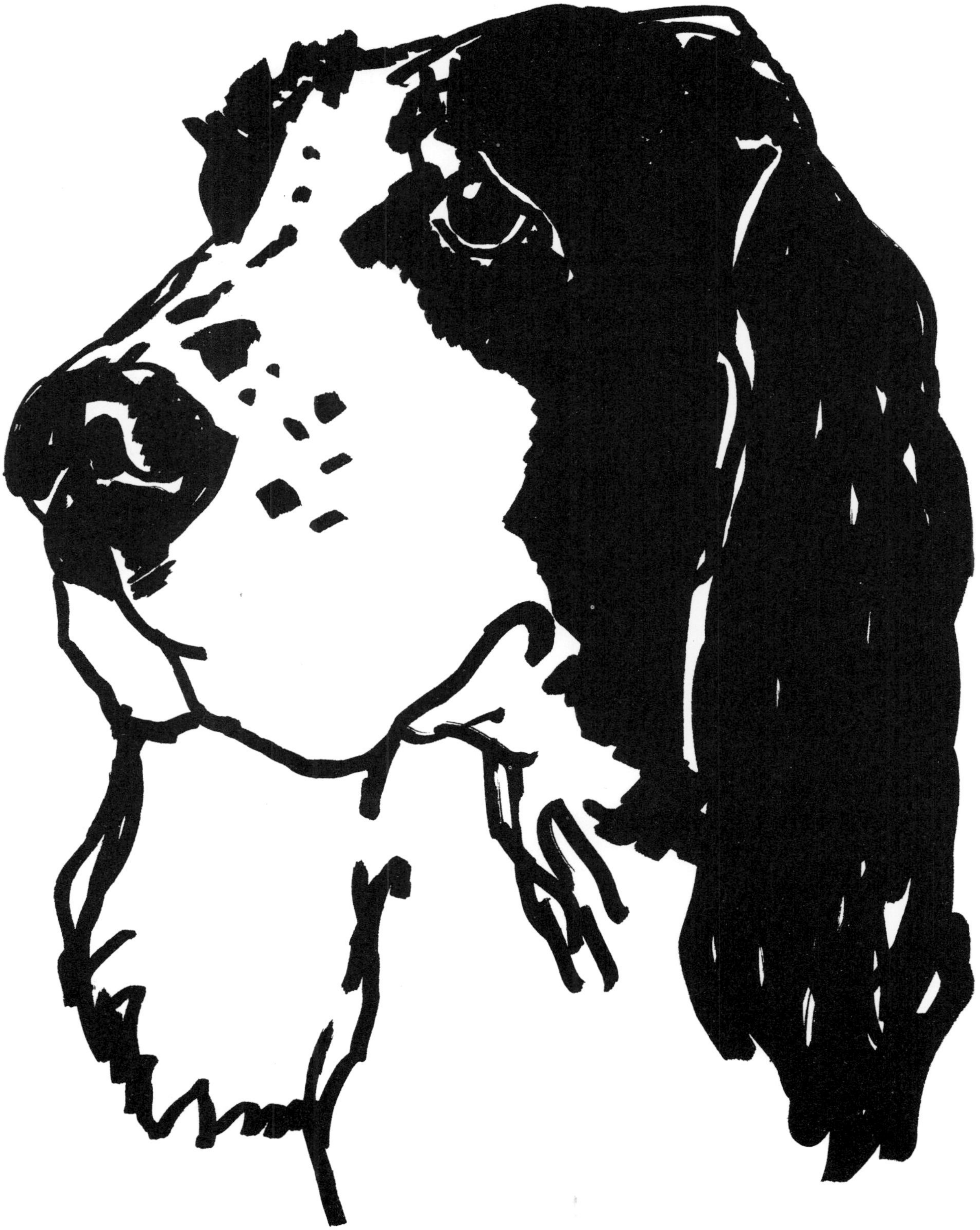

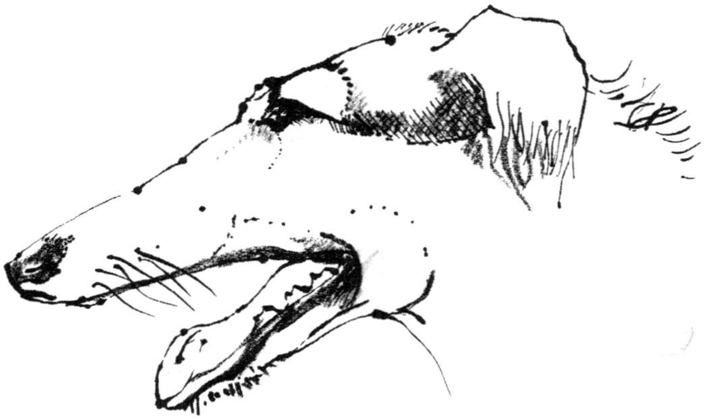

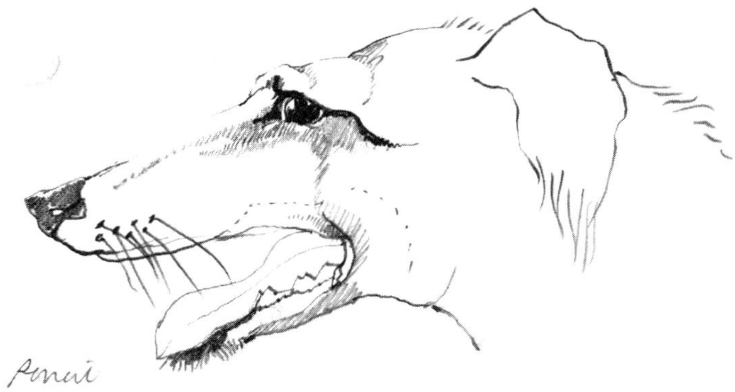

Two drawings of the same head, using a combination of ink and pencil (left) and pencil alone (right).

This boxer was drawn with pencil, Chinagraph and charcoal, using an eraser to vary the tone in some areas.

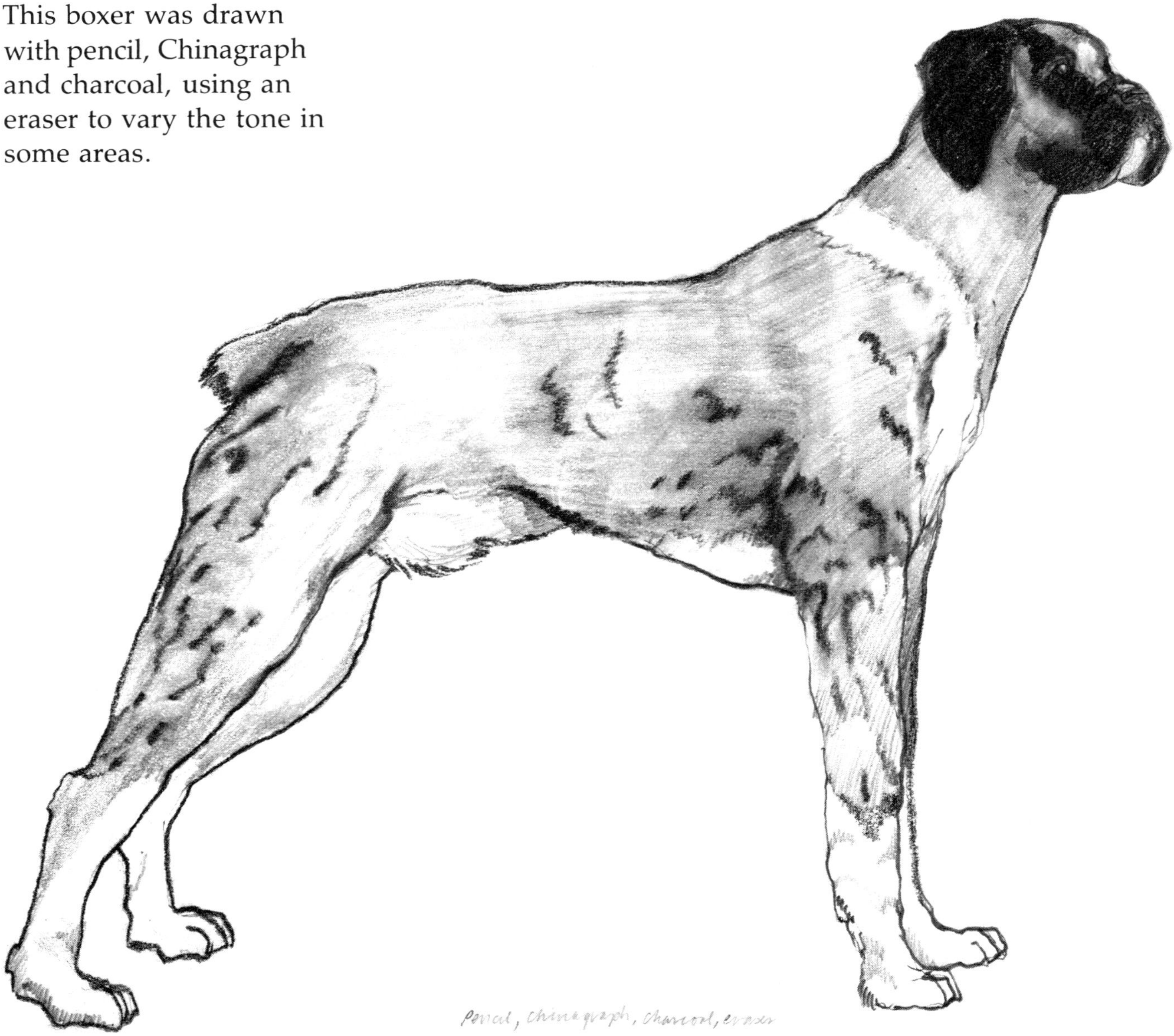

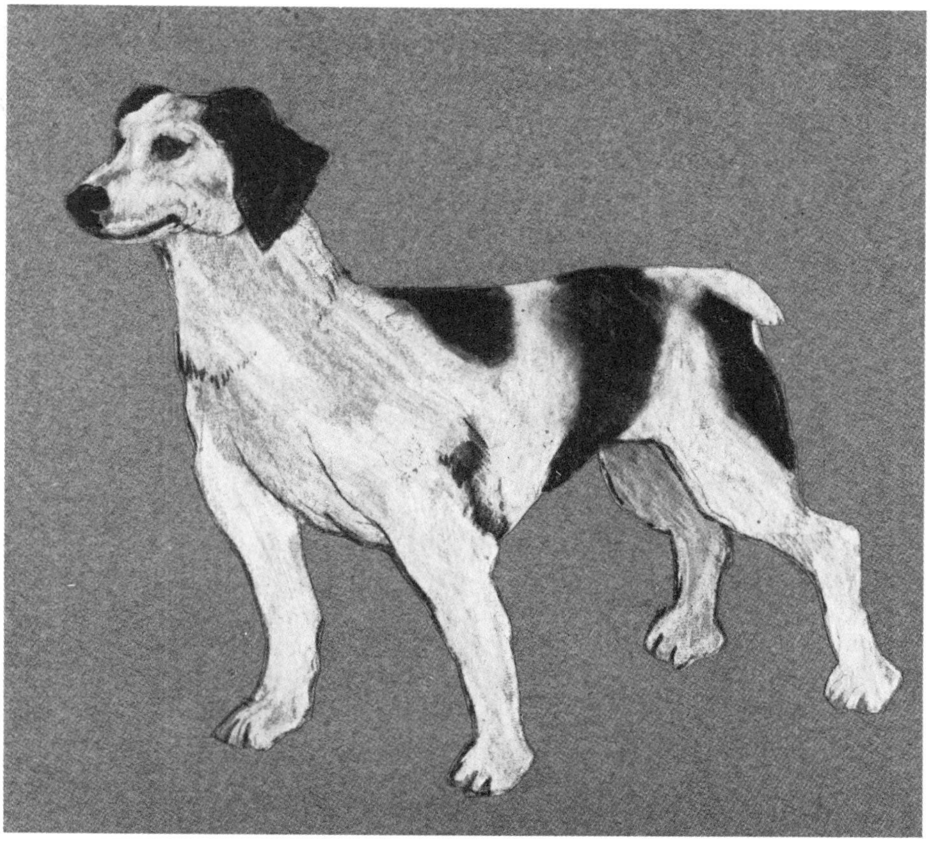

You can draw on coloured paper, using black and white pastels, and the paper will provide a third tone.

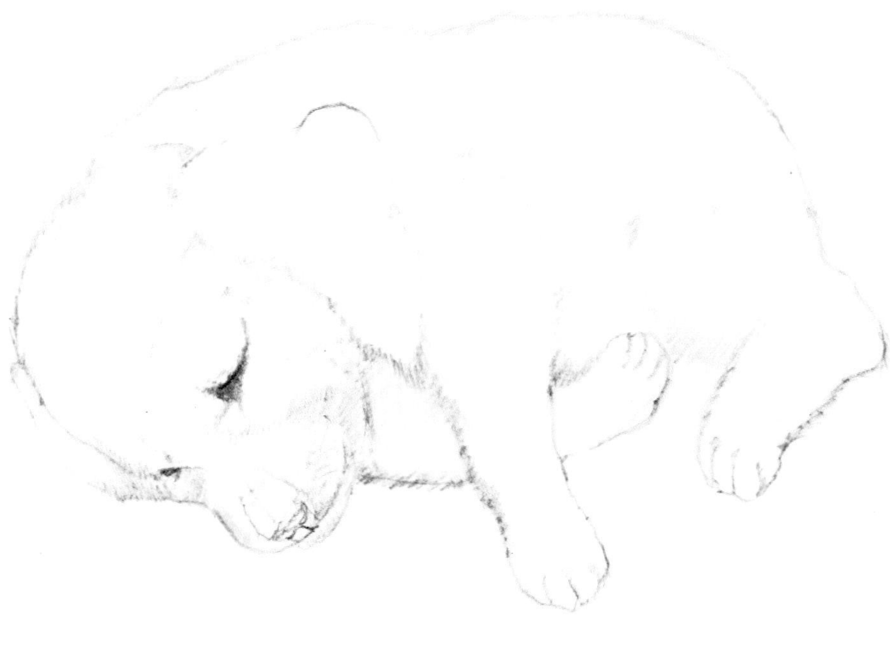

A pencil drawing rubbed with a French Stick.

If you draw with ink on wet paper, the lines will blur to give a soft, furry effect. Additional sharp lines can be added when the paper is dry.

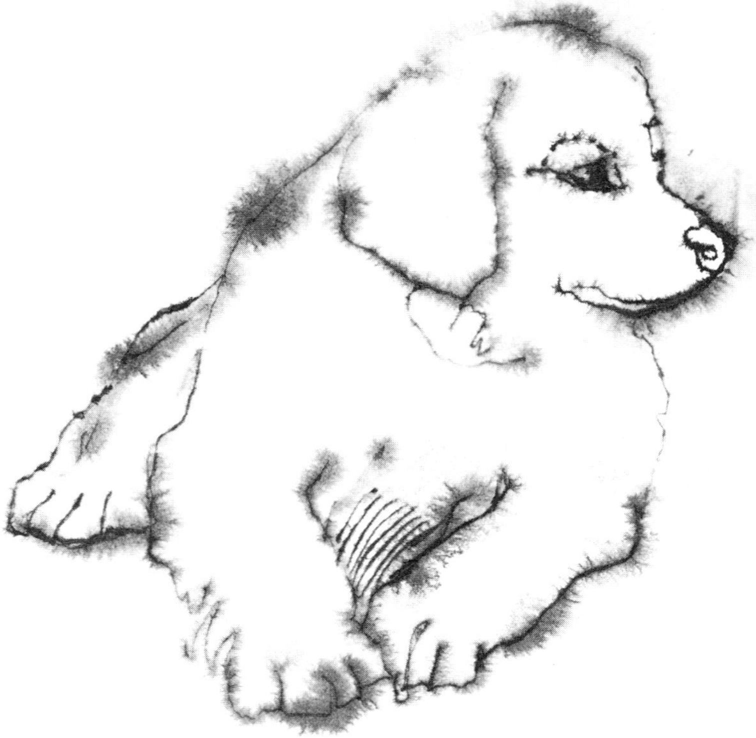

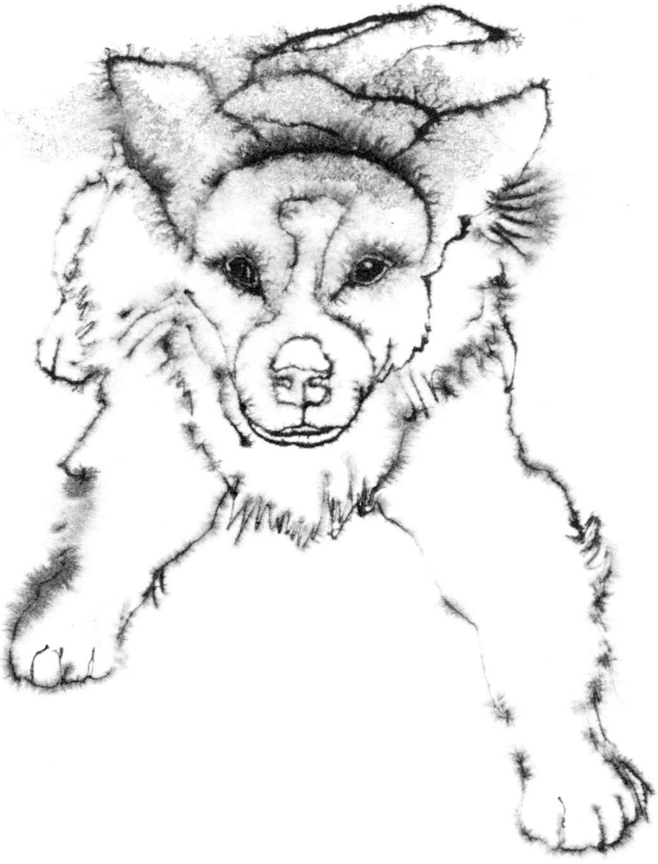

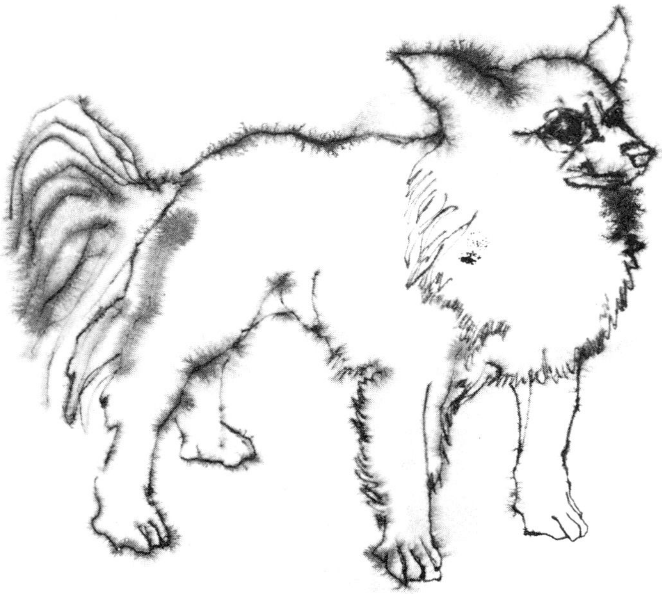

A combination of pen and ink, pencil and wash is a good way to convey the effect of colour variation in your subject.

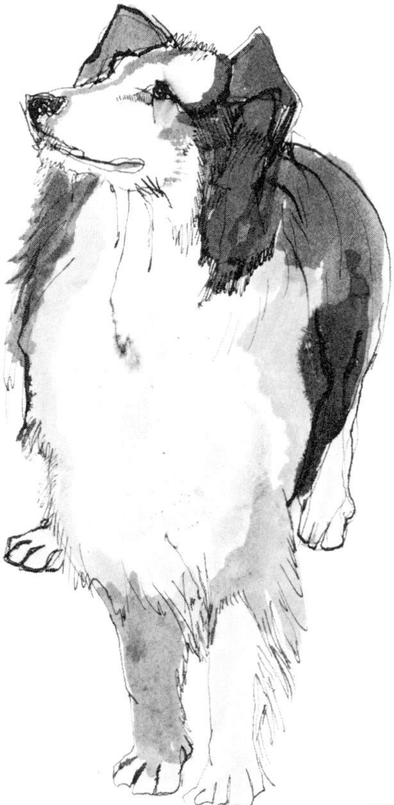

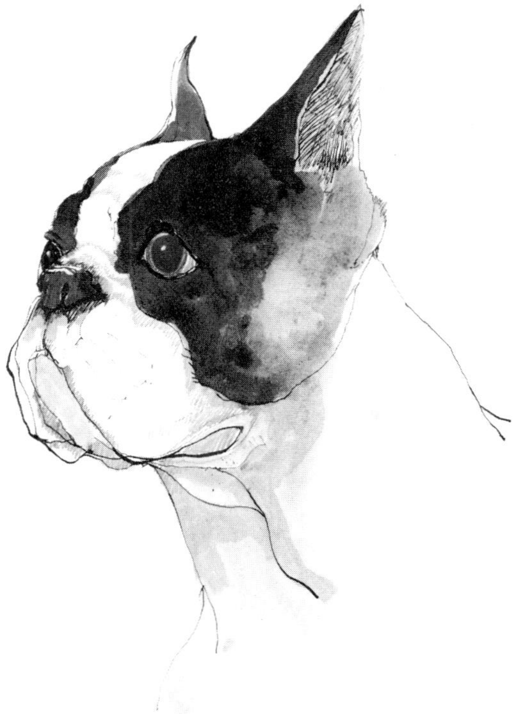

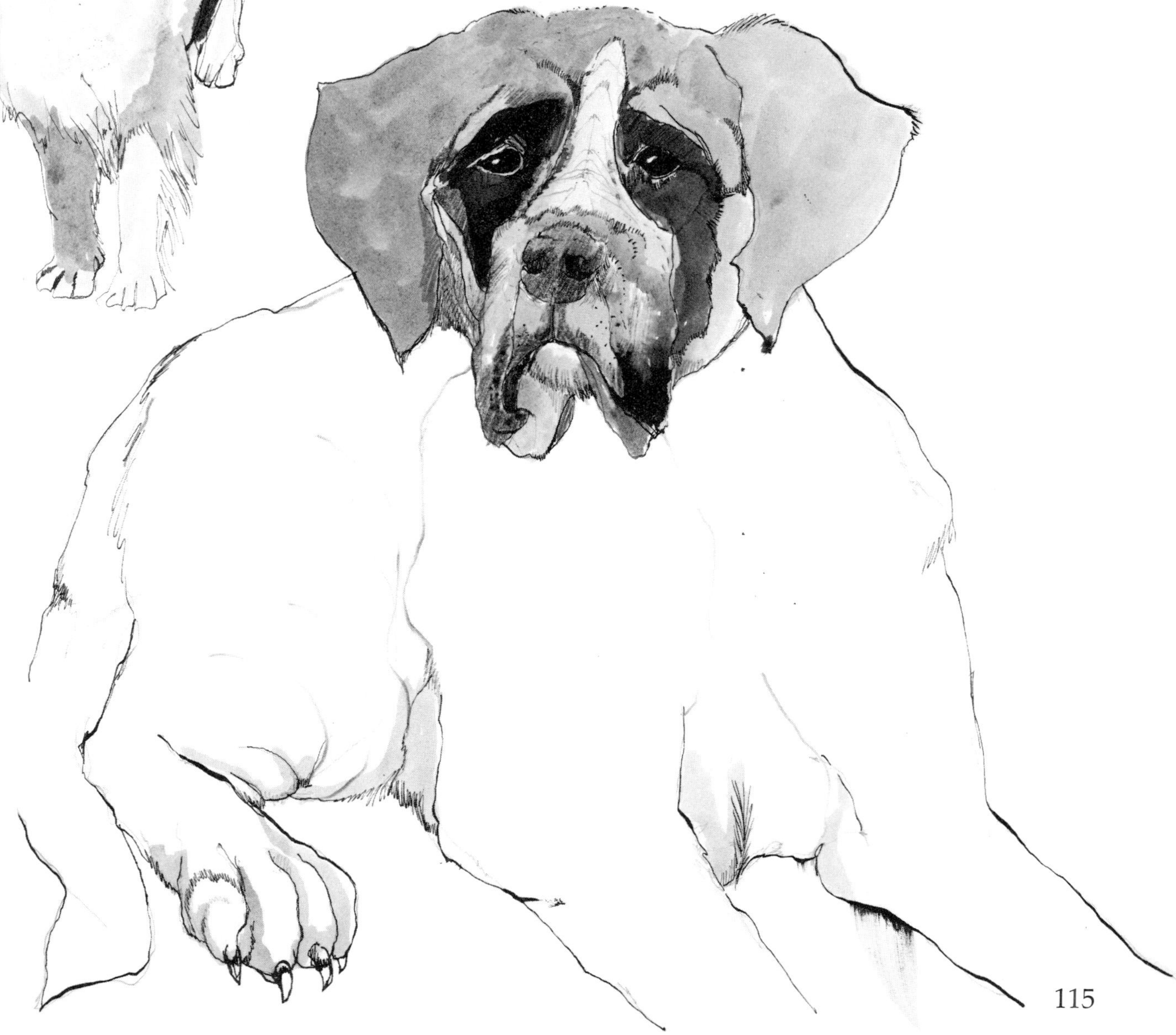

This drawing and the one opposite were done with a soft wax pencil, with the addition of a 4B pencil for shading.

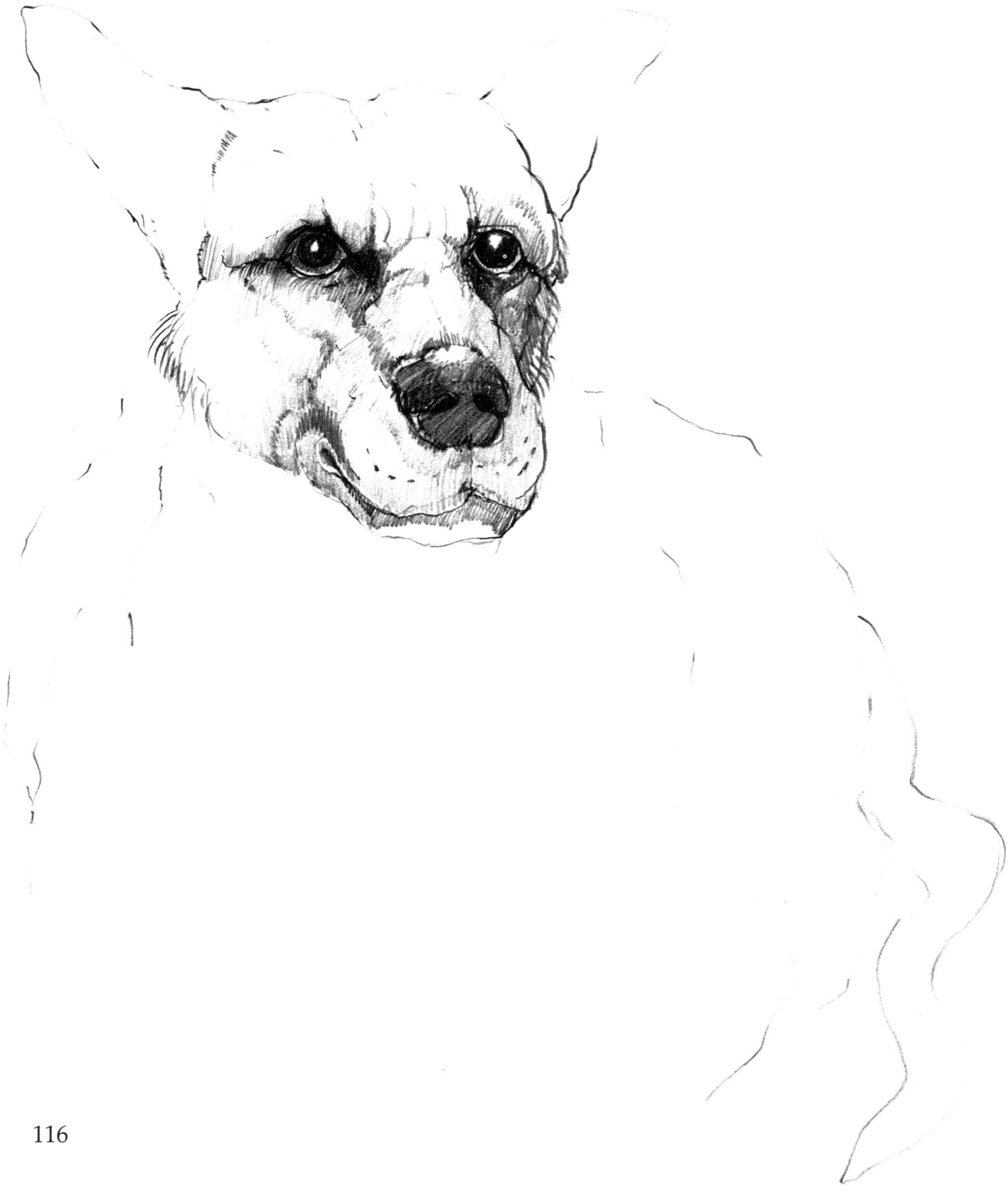

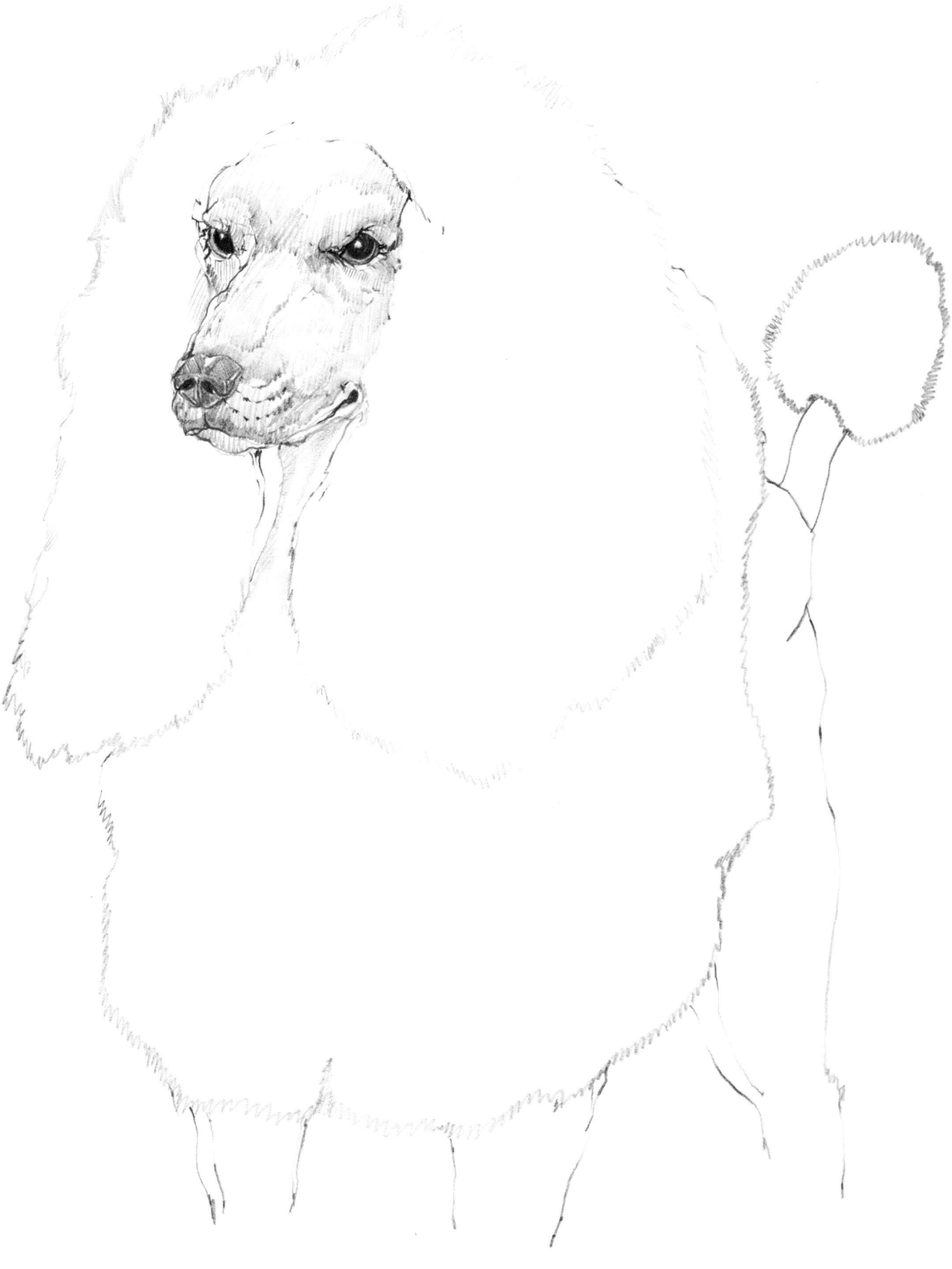

This terrier was drawn with a 4B pencil. Remember to sharpen your pencil frequently to keep the lines crisp and give your drawing sensitivity.

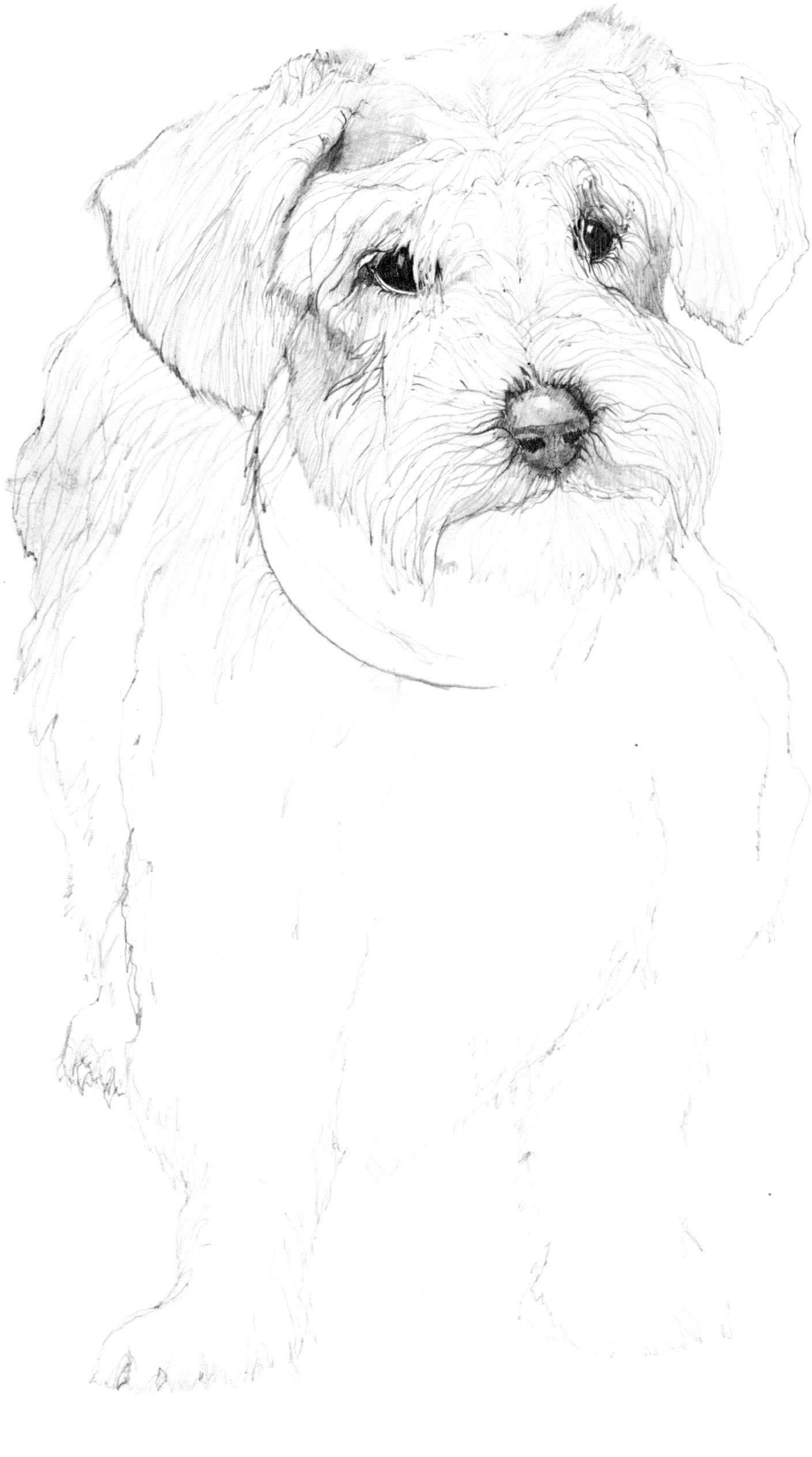

Here I have used 2B and 4B pencils, with charcoal pencil for the darkest areas.

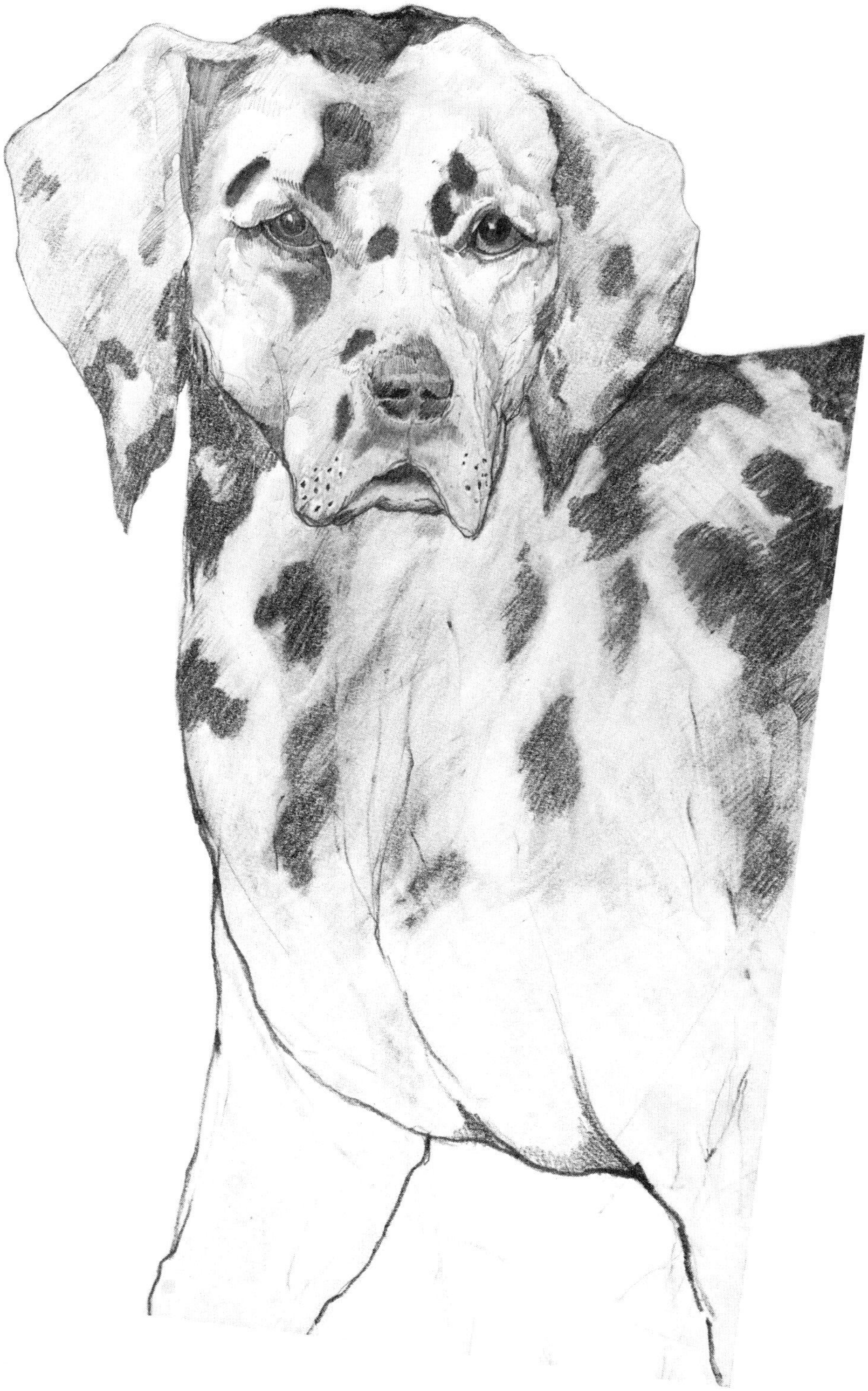

David Brown

The cat's anatomy, shown here, helps to explain the exterior shape. For instance, the joint which you can see half way up the back leg is really the heel. Notice the position of the knee. Look at the other joints marked by arrows. By studying the shape in this manner you will obtain more accuracy and therefore more realism in your drawings.

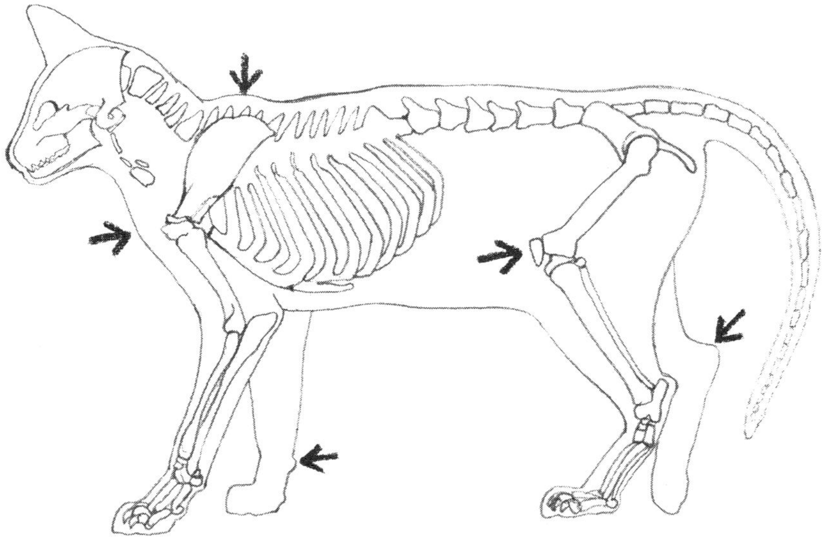

Anatomy and shape

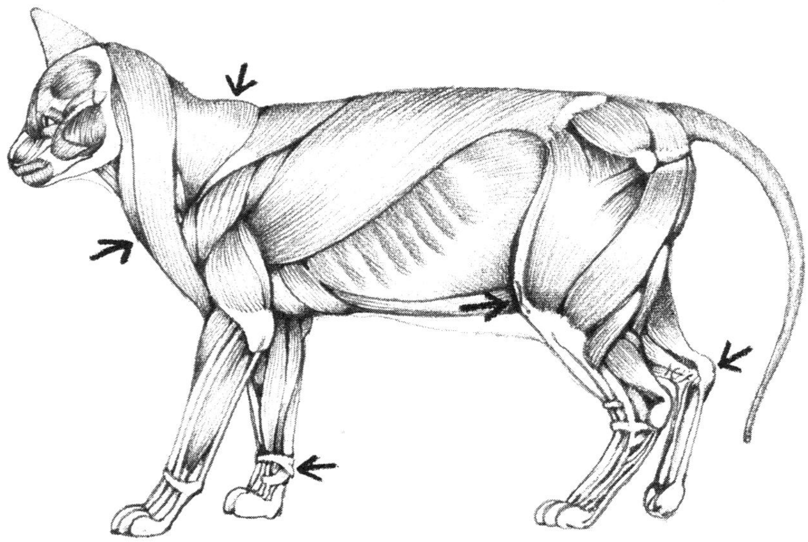

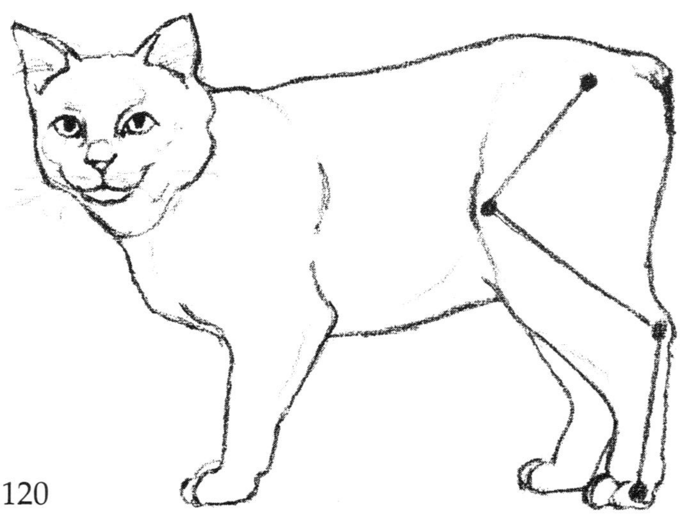

The head comes in two basic shapes: one is wedged, the other round. The first (above) appears in breeds such as the Siamese and Burmese. The second (below) includes such cats as the Tabby and Chinchilla.

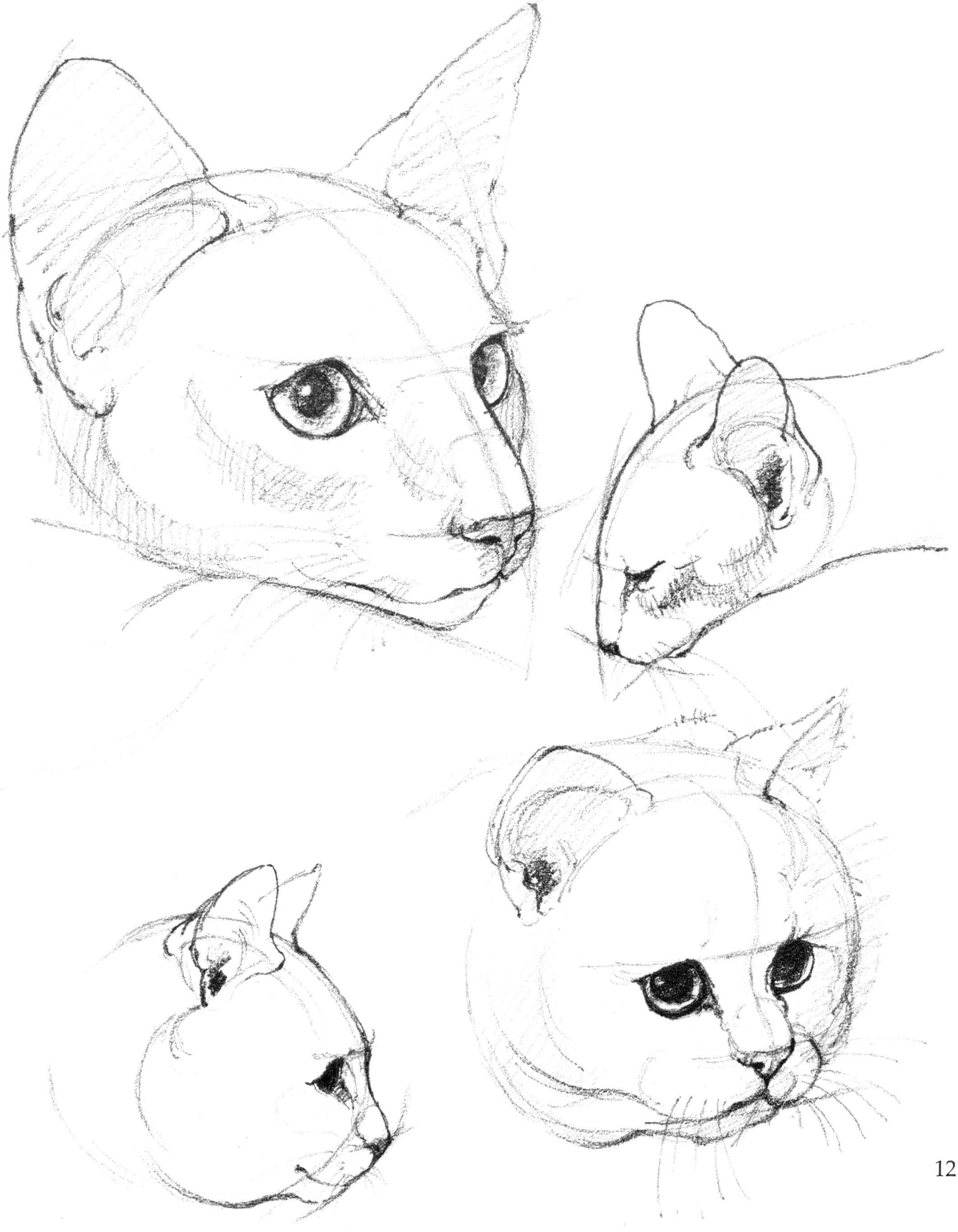

Study your subject closely. Draw each part from every angle until you understand its structure and how it connects to the main part of the body. Note its position in relation to the other parts. A body is symmetrical, which makes its shape a lot easier to analyse. Its structure can be broken down into a series of simple patterns (A) which will help you in your studies.

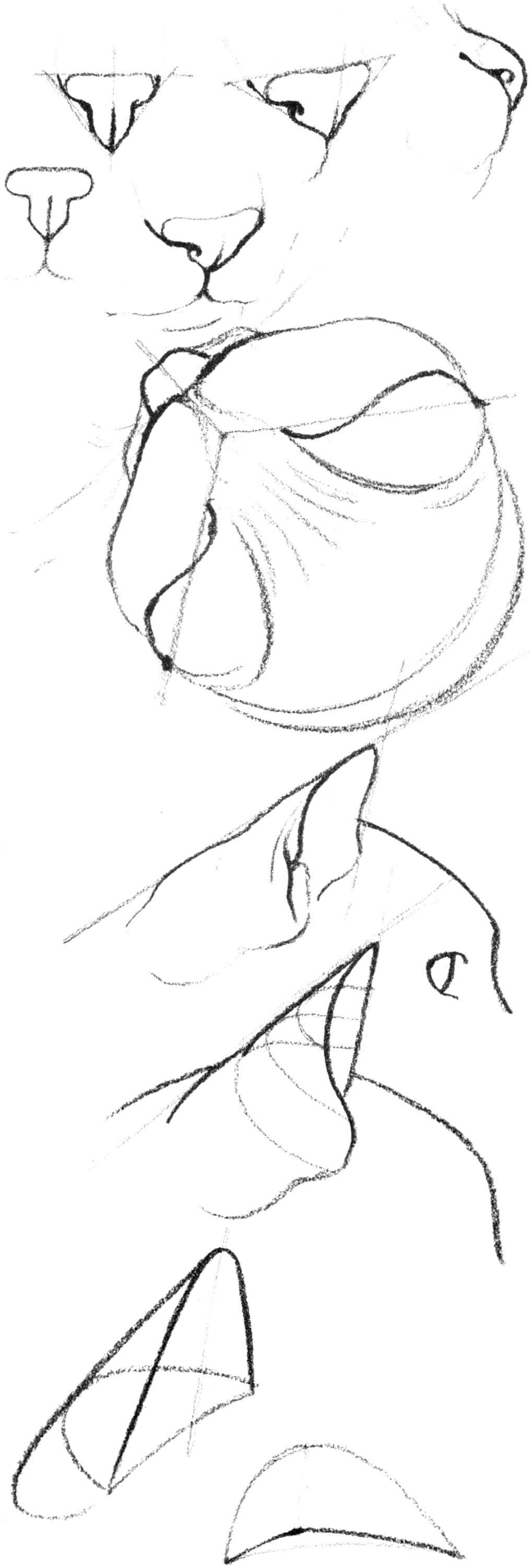

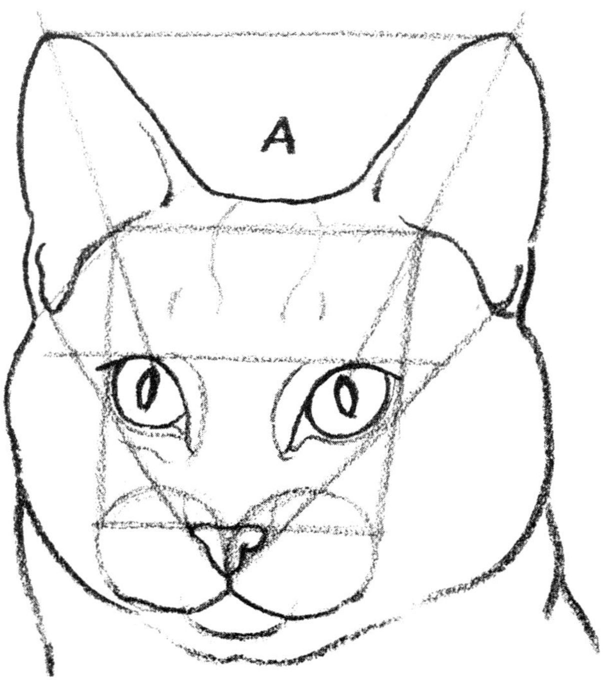

The pupil of a cat's eye opens in the dark and closes to a slit in bright sunlight. When drawing eyes, note the highlights which add to the expression, and remember that the eyeball is rounded, not flat.

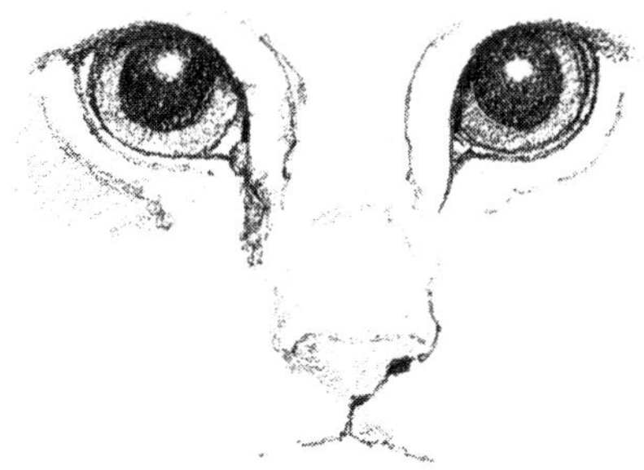

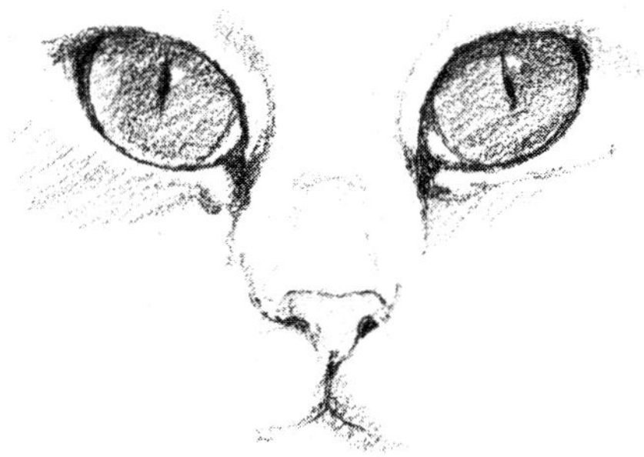

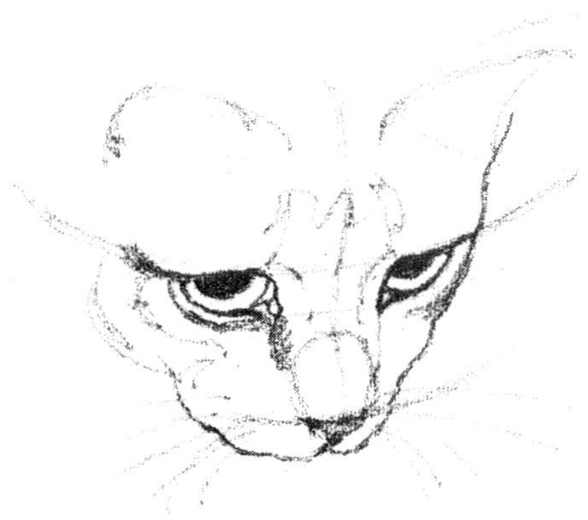

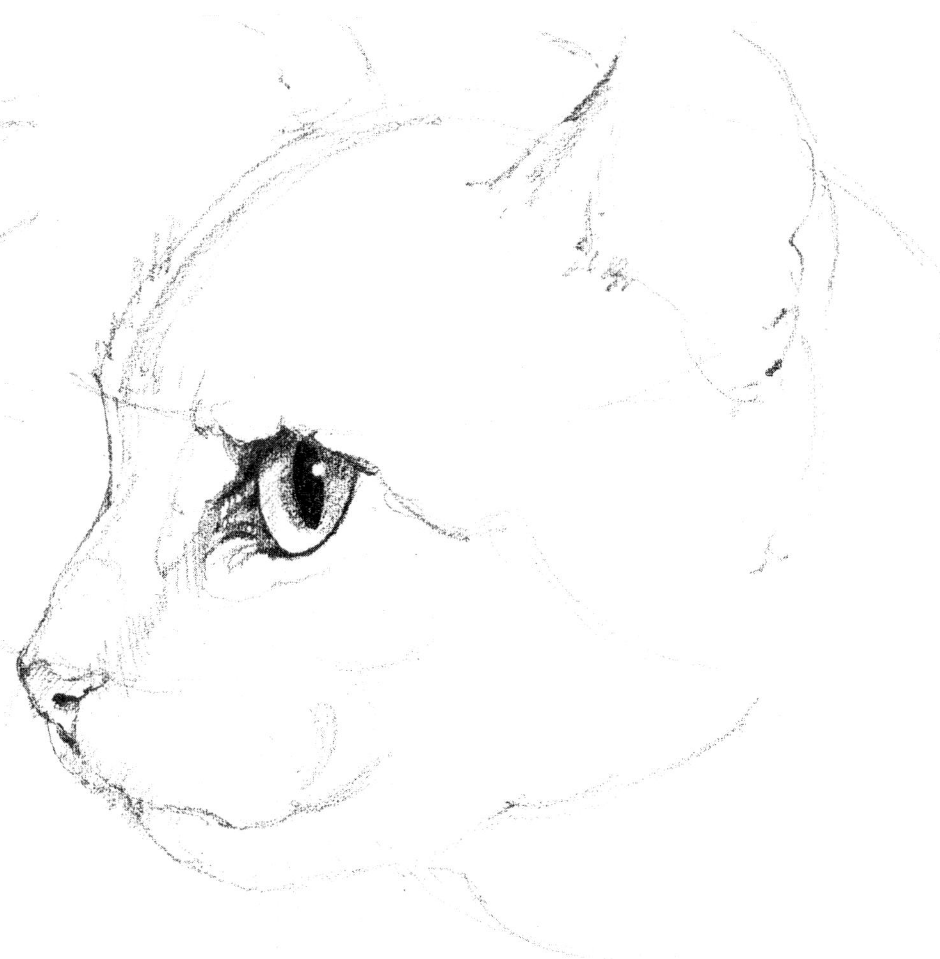

If you have no cat of your own you can learn a great deal about anatomy by studying good quality photographs, especially action ones. These two drawings were done from photographs. Notice, for instance, how the shoulder line is affected by the outstretched front leg. Draw contour lines over the various parts of the body to help you understand its shape.

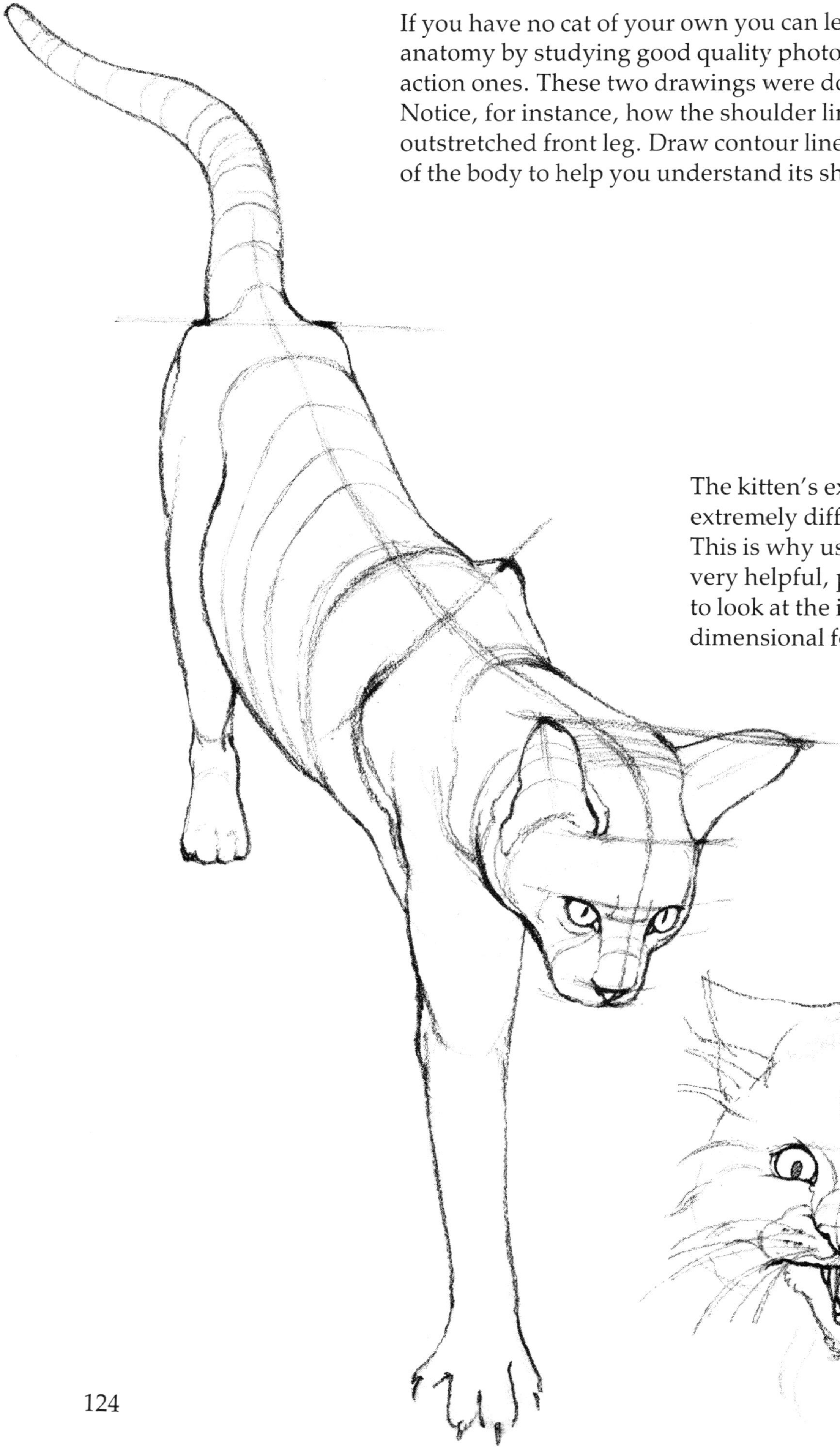

The kitten's expression would be extremely difficult to draw from life. This is why using photography can be very helpful, provided you remember to look at the image as a three-dimensional form.

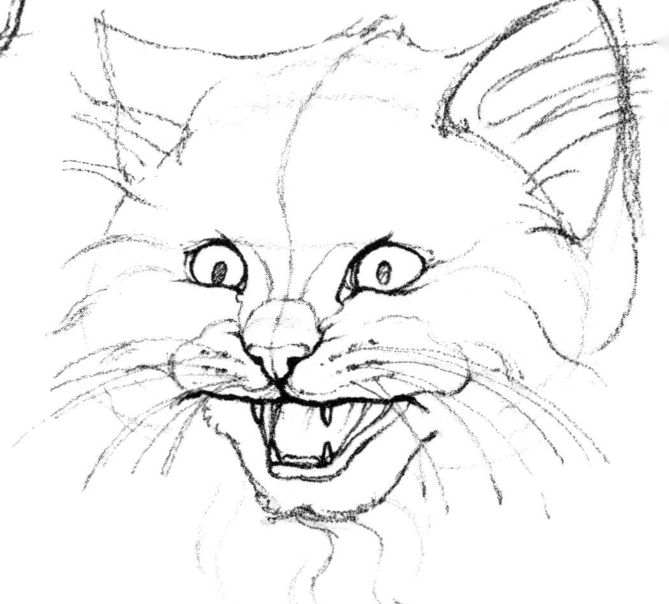

Here are two examples of how *not* to draw from photographs. The head of the cat on the left is flat. No thought has been given to its rounded shape, and it would have been better in this instance to have used a wash of ink or paint rather than using the pencil as a paint brush to produce the dark-coloured area.

The cat on the right is not much better. Again there is a flat cut-out effect, obviously drawn from a bad photograph. Notice the areas of stark white and flat, harsh shading; the dark areas show no detail, even in the eyes.

I can't stress enough that when using a photograph you should treat the image as a three-dimensional living animal, and draw it as such. Always work from a good quality photograph.

Some teachers tell you never to use photographs. I don't go along with this view, provided you adopt the right approach. I have yet to meet a professional illustrator, particularly one with a realistic style, who has not used photographic reference.

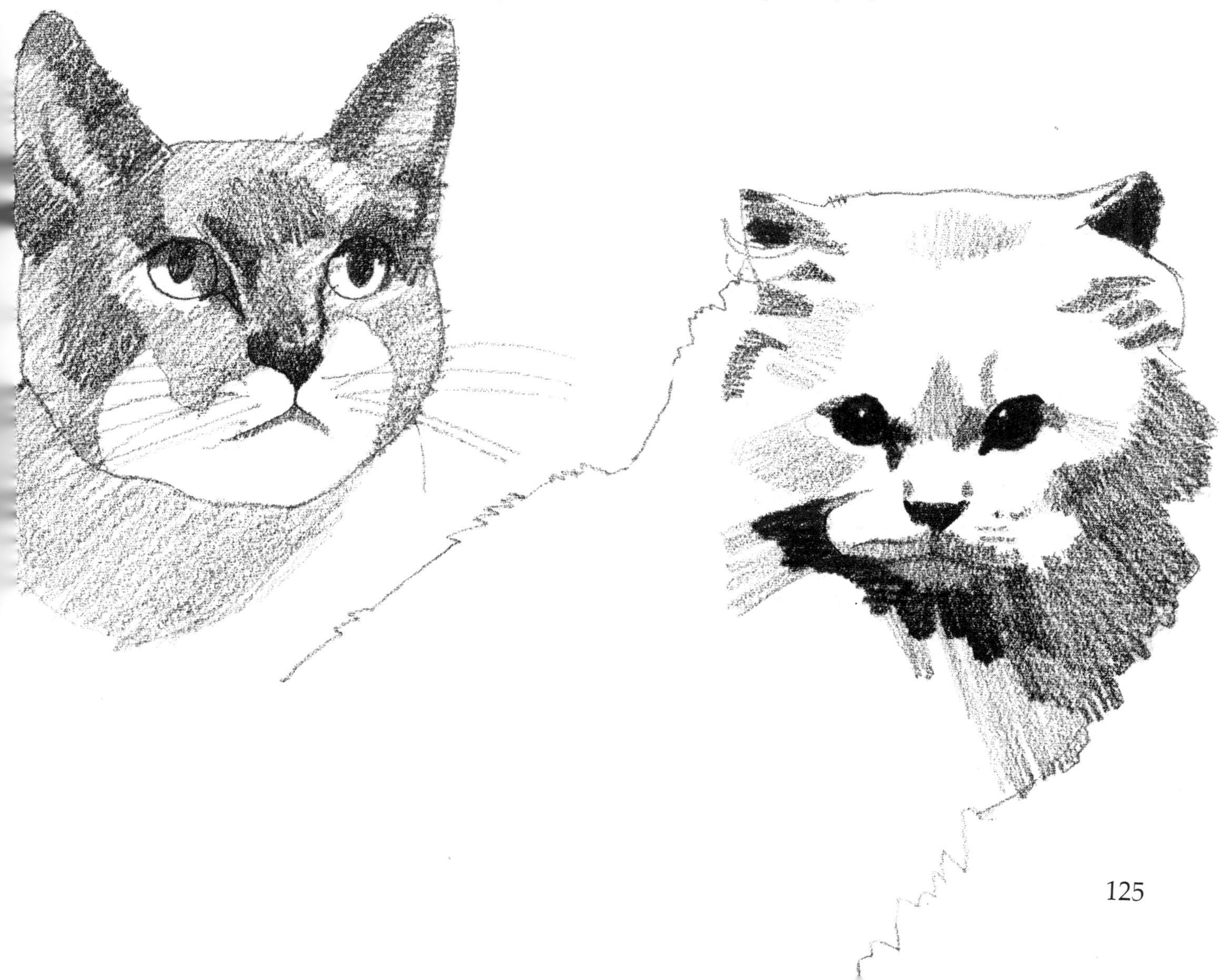

Proportion

The essence of good draughtsmanship is to get your proportions right. This *must* be done at the basic lines stage.

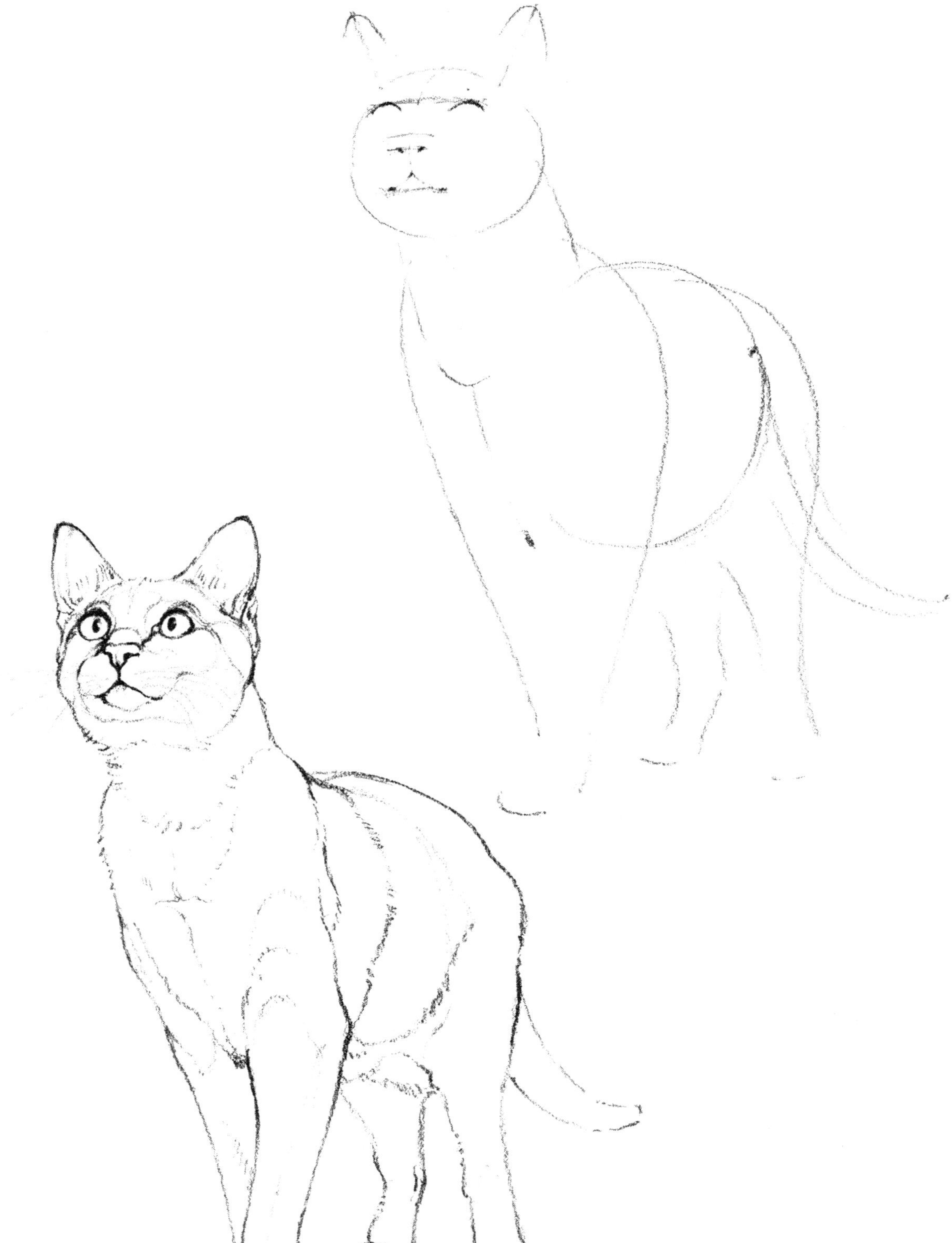

The most common mistake in drawing is getting the proportion wrong. One way to avoid this is to use the head as a unit of measurement. Hold your pencil vertically at arm's length, with the top of the pencil in line with the top of the cat's head; then place your thumb on the pencil and line up with cat's chin.

Use this measurement to work out how many heads make up the cat's height, keeping your thumb on the same spot on the pencil and the pencil at arm's length. For this cat it worked out at 3½.

Now roughly draw the cat's head and using this as your unit of measurement mark out the number of heads you need to get the correct height.

To get the feeling of movement contained in the pose, hold your pencil vertically, making sure it is at right-angles to the floor, and line it up with the cat's nose. Run your eyes down the pencil, noting the position and angle of the various parts of the body in relation to the vertical line made by the pencil. In this instance the head is directly over the cat's right paw, giving the body an interesting swing which you could easily miss by not checking in this way.

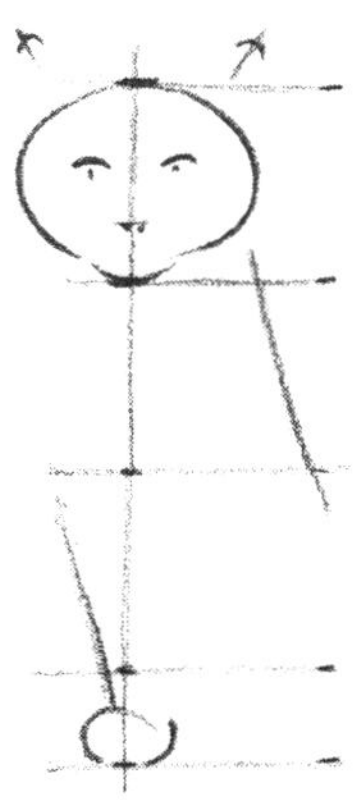

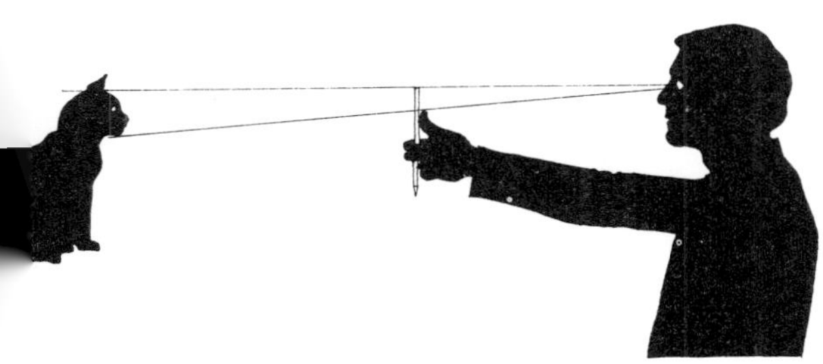

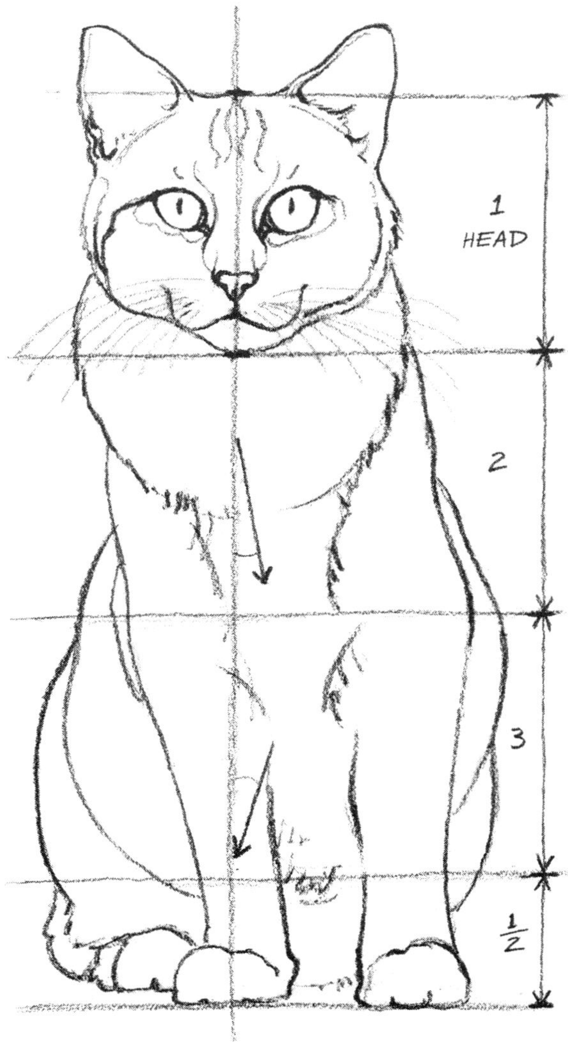

Basic shapes

When starting your drawing, try to see your subject in its simplest form. It may help to half close your eyes. By so doing you shut out most of the detail, which enables you to concentrate on the basic shapes. A charcoal pencil was used here on the final drawing.

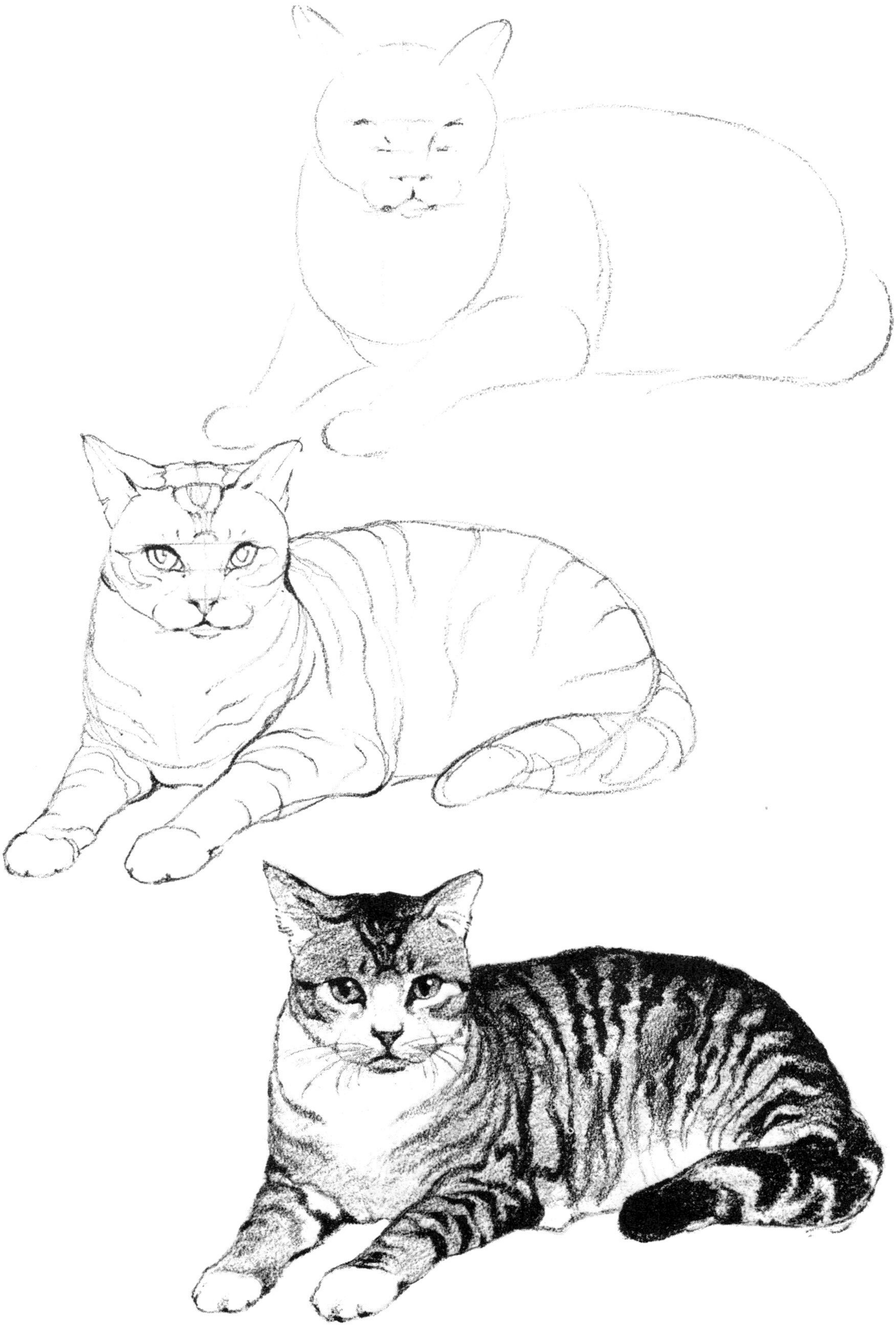

Try mixing your media occasionally. Here is a soft charcoal pencil drawing finished off with a thin wash of black designer's gouache paint. Remember to vary your line, by varying the pressure on your pencil.

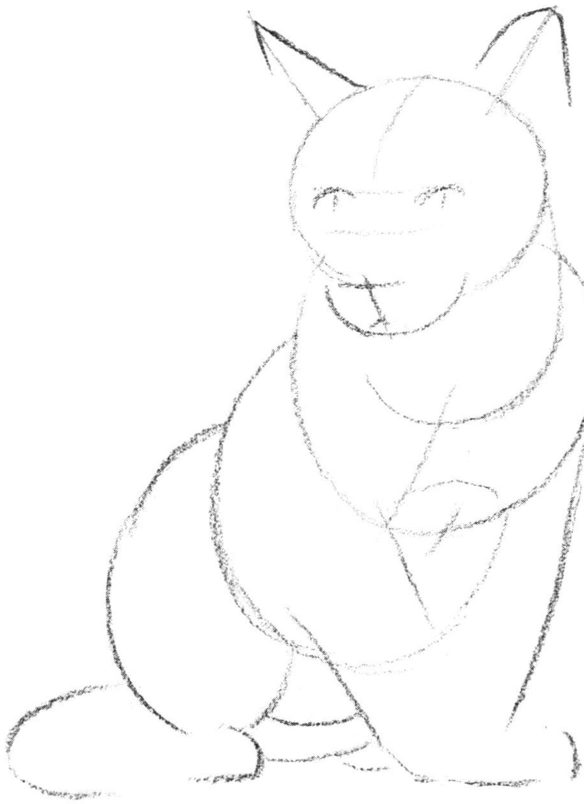

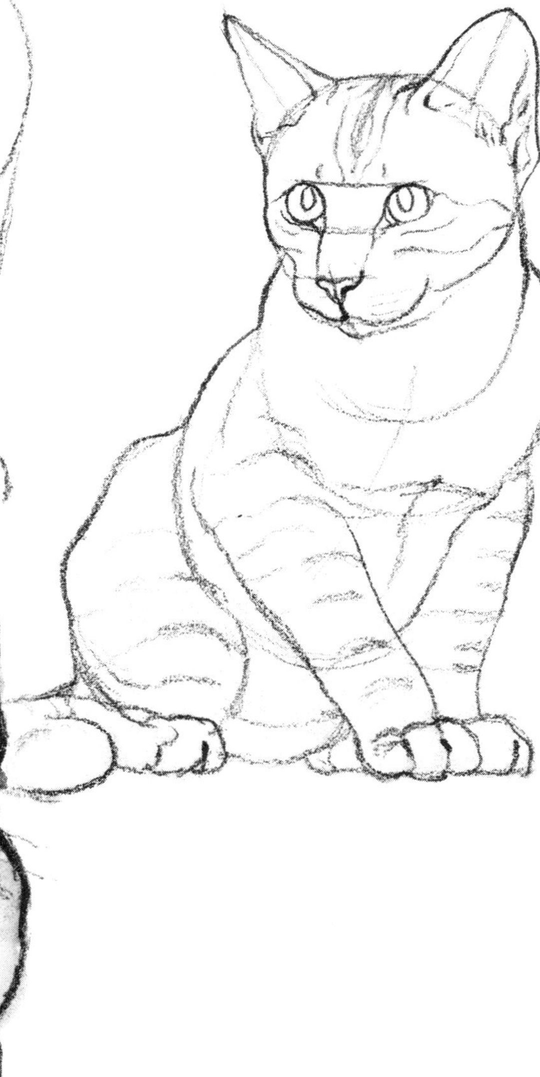

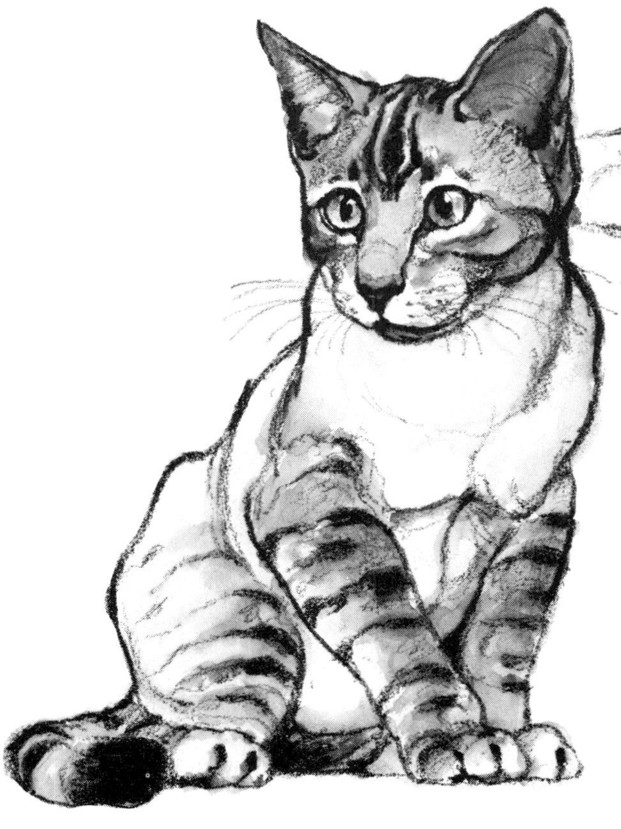

Step-by-step

These pages show the development from basic to the finished drawing. Draw the basic lines and don't be timid about adding imaginary lines such as the ones marked 'A'. These help enormously in constructing your drawing. In time, after a great deal of practice, you will find that your pencil will merely go through the motions of drawing them without touching the paper, and will come into contact with the paper only when drawing the relevant features.

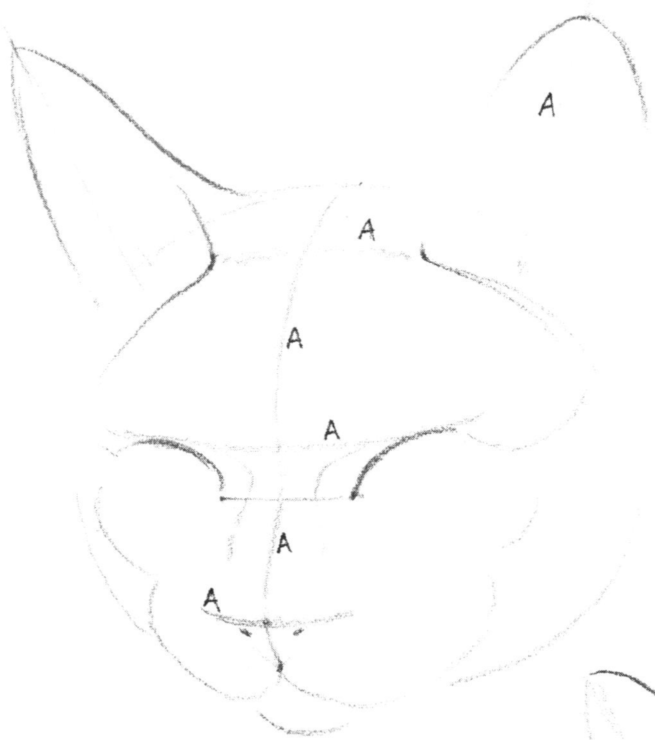

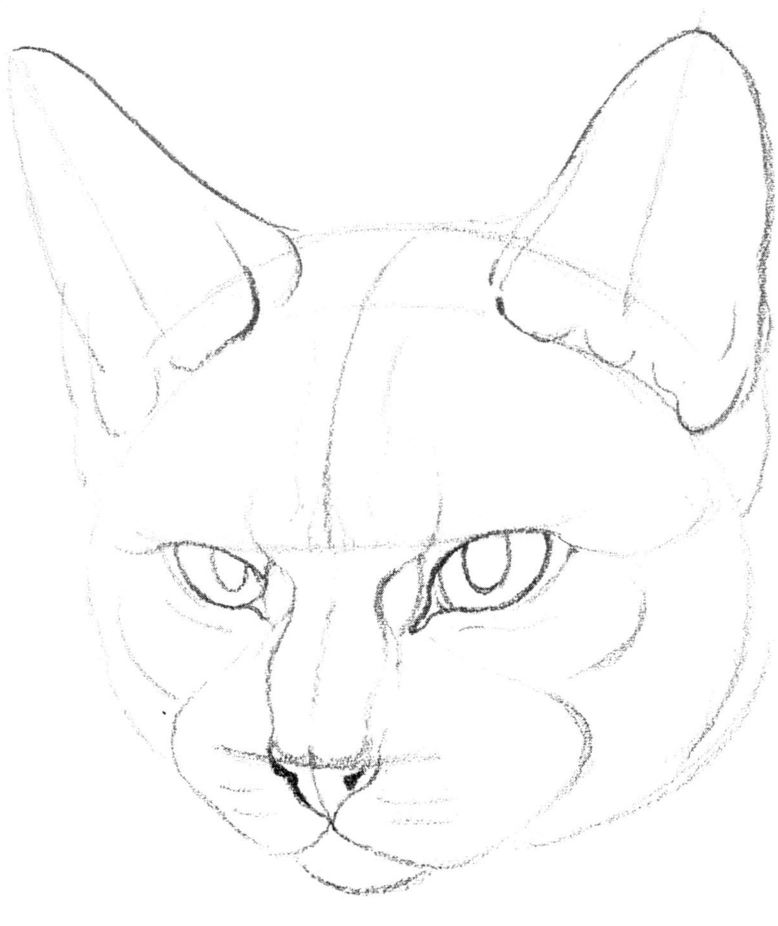

To get the proportions right, you must continually compare the length, width and shape of the various areas. For example, is the gap between the eyes equivalent to the width of one eye? Is the length of the nose equal to the height of the forehead?

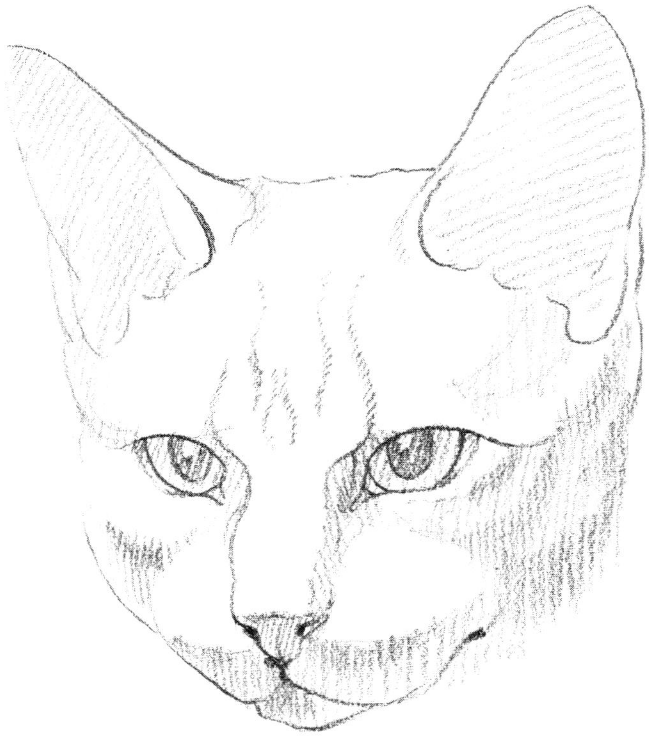

Note the direction from which the light is coming and then put in the shaded areas.

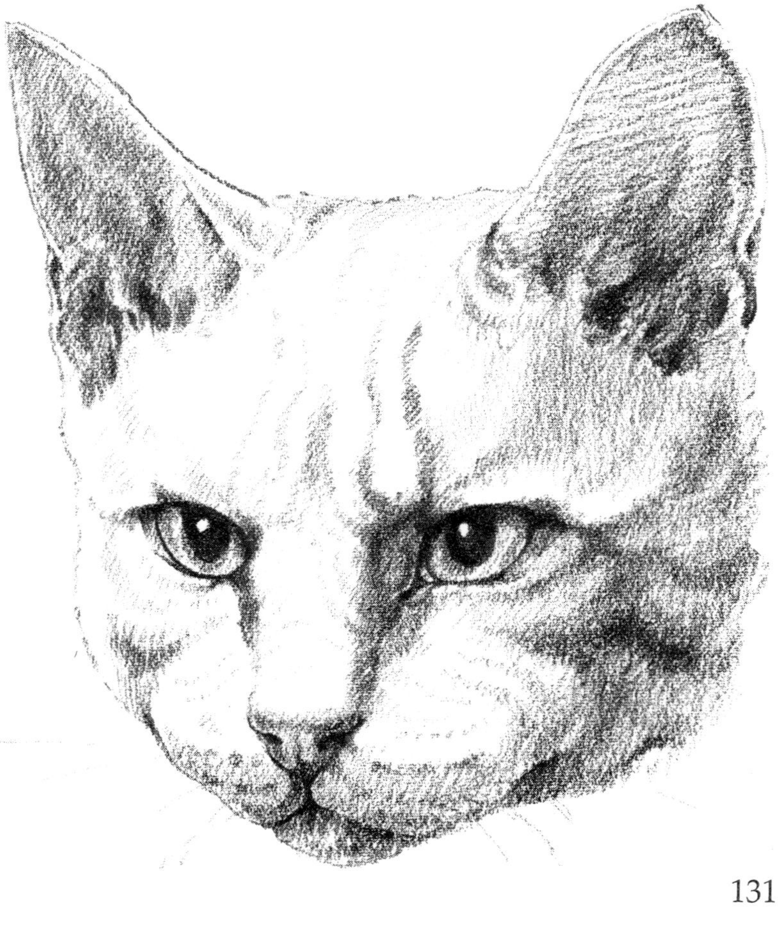

Resist the temptation to draw only straightforward front and side views. Be adventurous, draw from unusual angles.

The basic lines of the Siamese below were drawn with an HB pencil. Notice how imaginary lines were used to help capture the directional swing of the body. Using the pencil guide-lines, details were drawn in with a Pentel fibre pen. The drawing was completed with a brush dipped in clean water.

The lower drawing was done with a carbon pencil on a semi-rough surface.

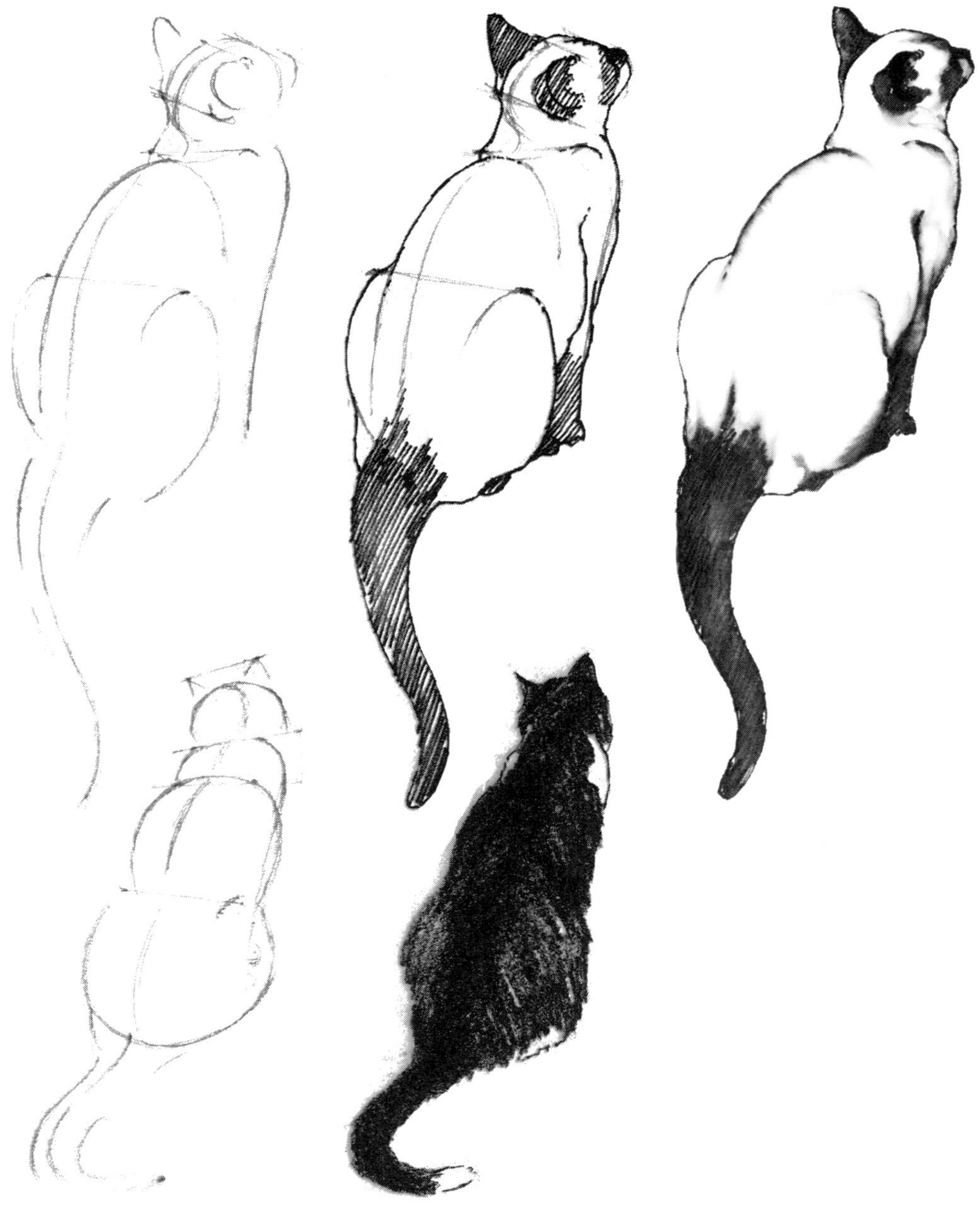

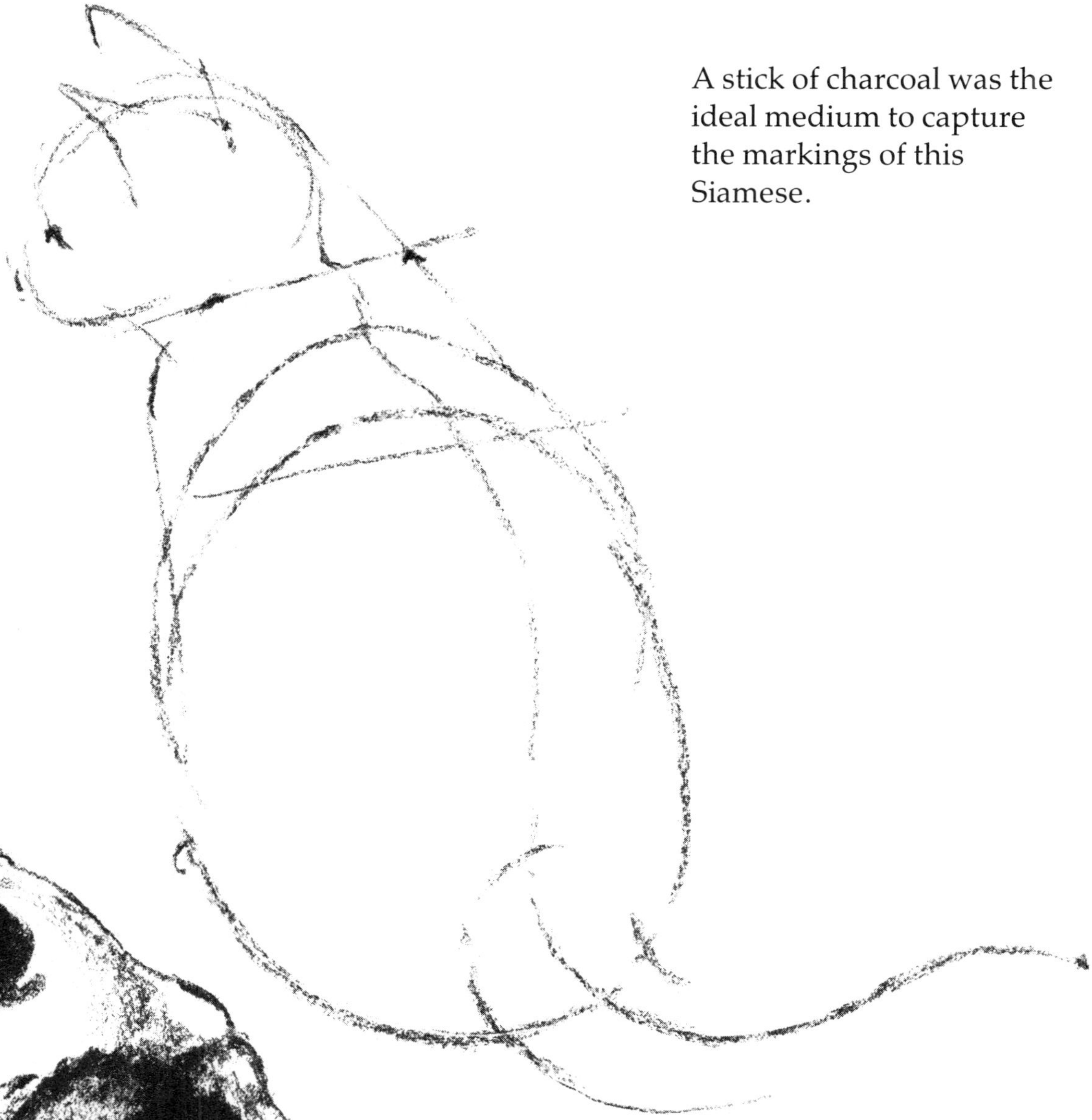

A stick of charcoal was the ideal medium to capture the markings of this Siamese.

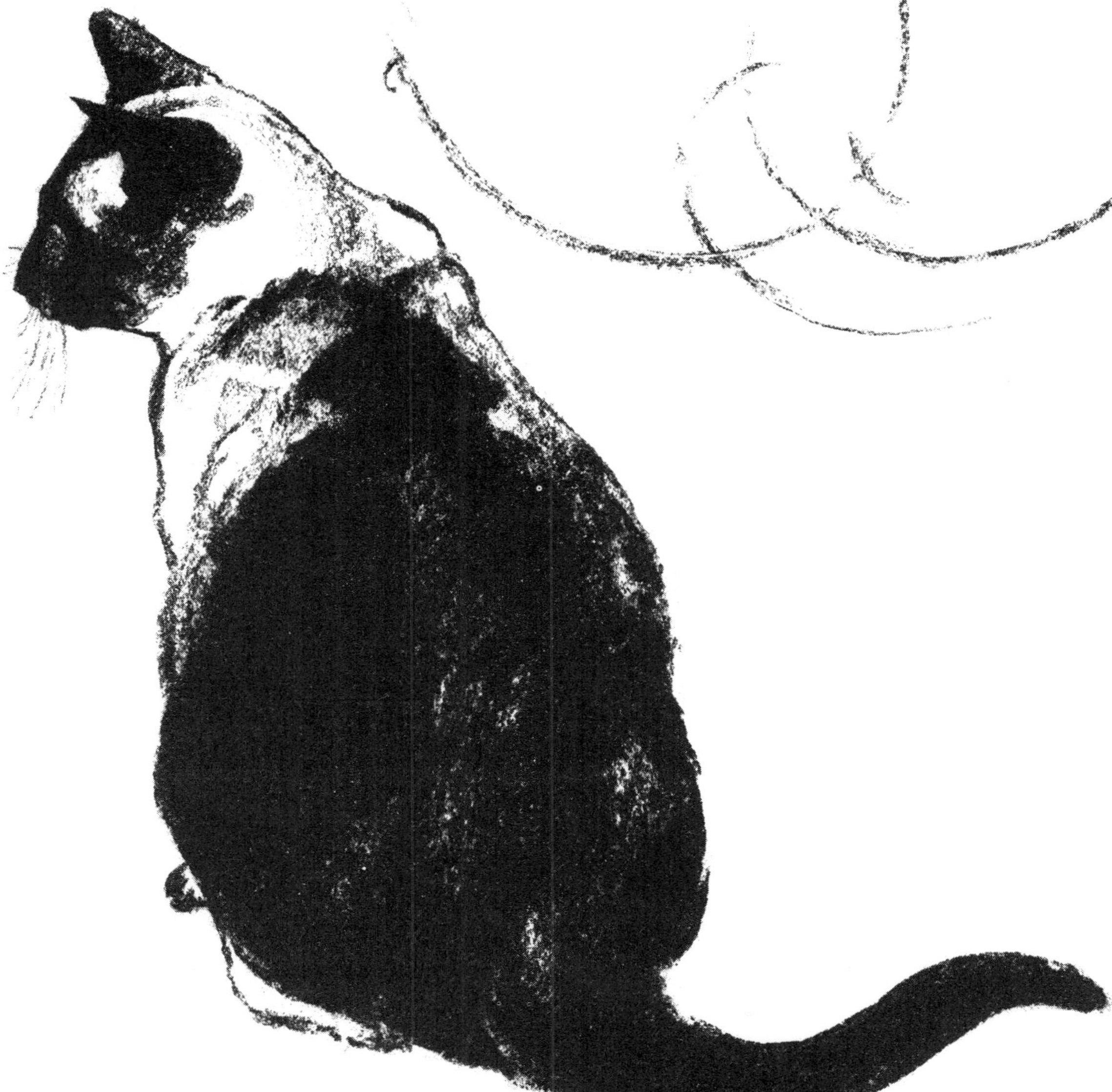

After drawing the basic shape in pencil, this drawing was developed in pen and ink, and then dabbed with a finger dipped in ink; finally a light wash was applied with a brush.

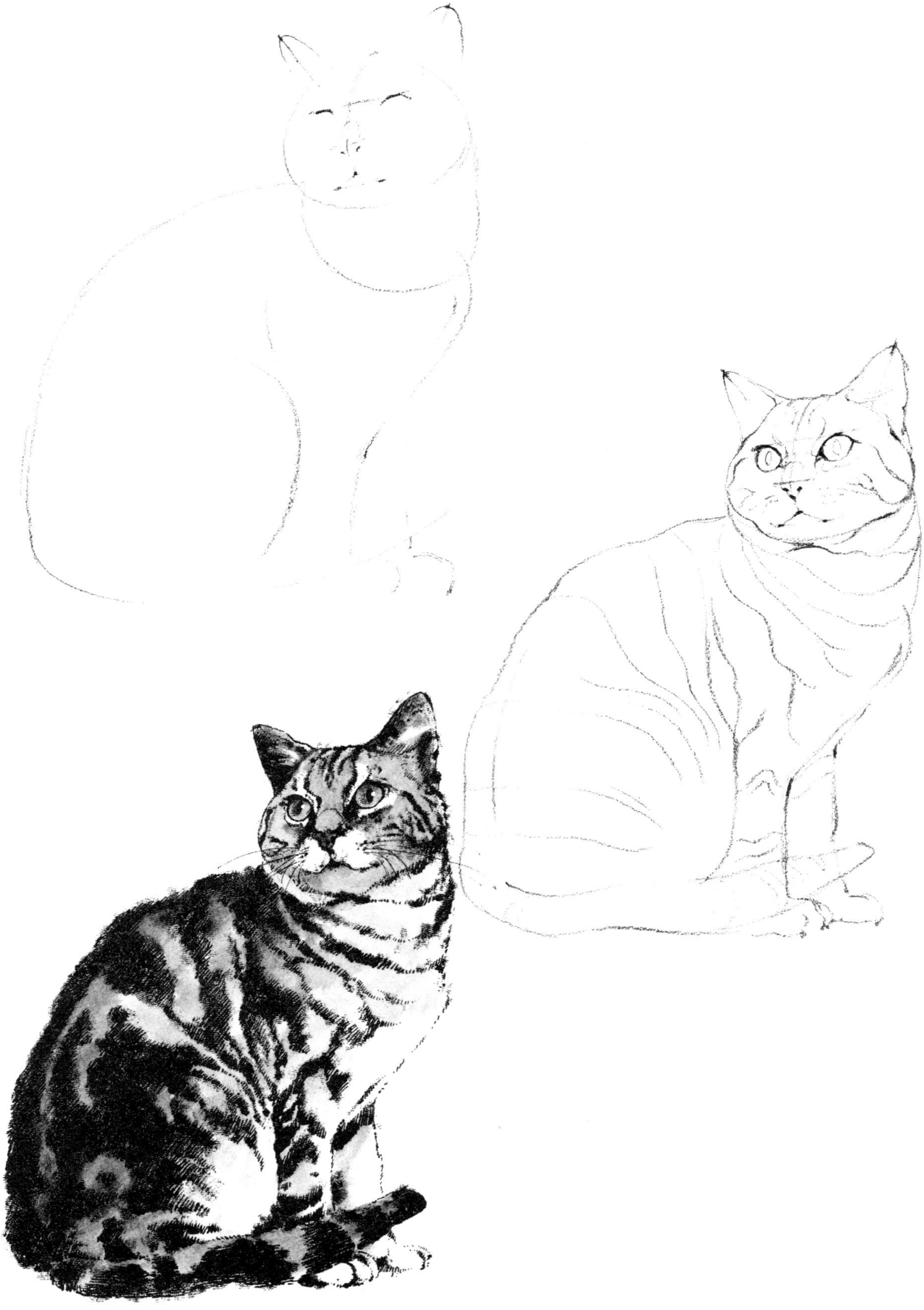

It is more difficult to see the form of a long-haired cat such as this Blue Persian. At first glance all you can see is a mass of hair, but look carefully at the way the hair flows and the shaded areas, and remember what you have learnt about a cat's anatomy.

Vary your line and shading by varying the pressure on the pencil. Look carefully at the finished part of the drawing. See how the line is soft in the light areas and heavy in the dark areas.

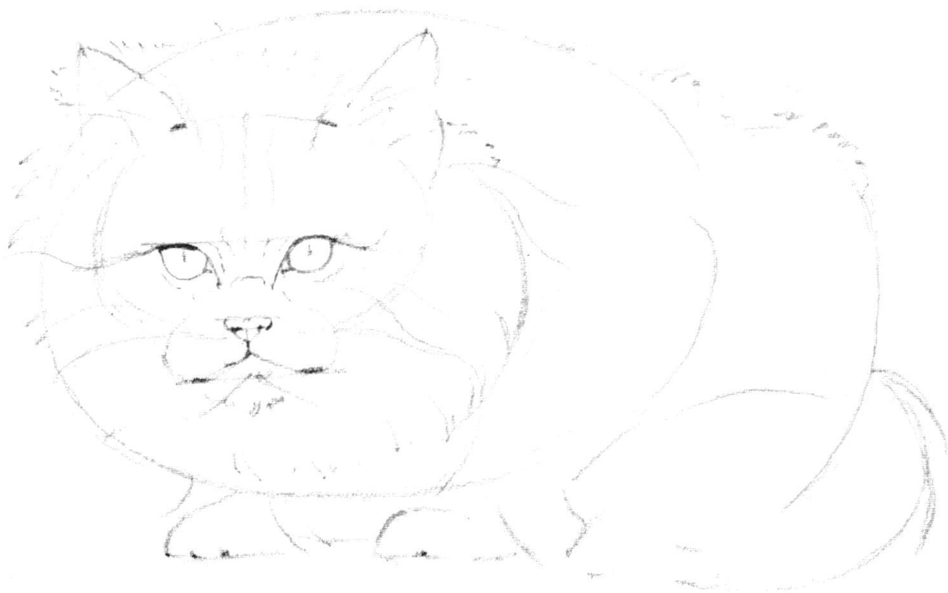

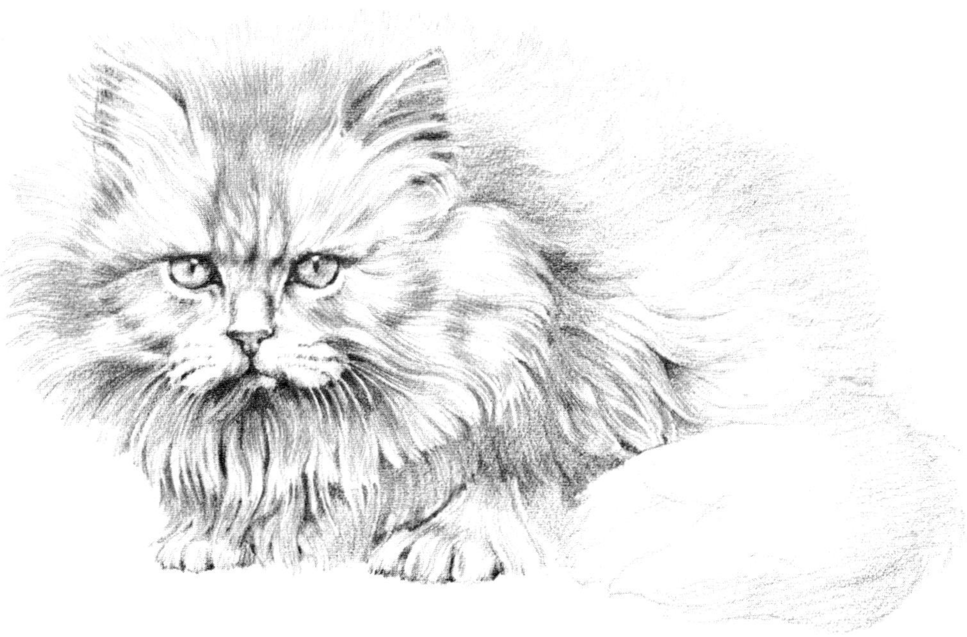

Expression

Inject life into your drawings by capturing the character, movement and expression of your subject.

The ferocity of this Tabby is conveyed by the use of a large fibre pen, giving a bold, gnarled look to the face. The staring eyes complete the picture.

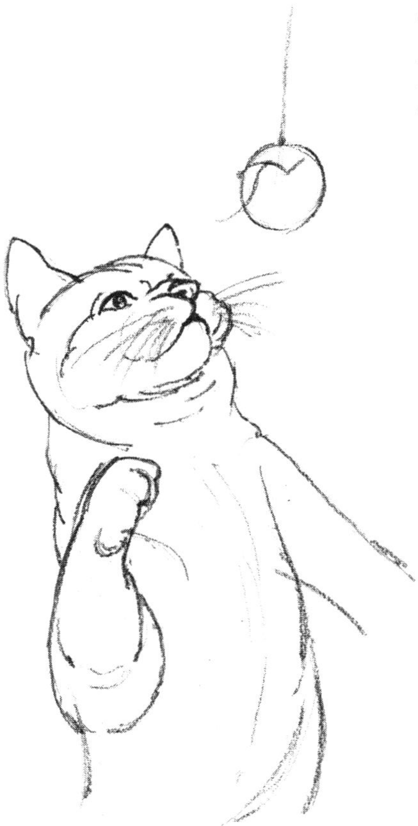

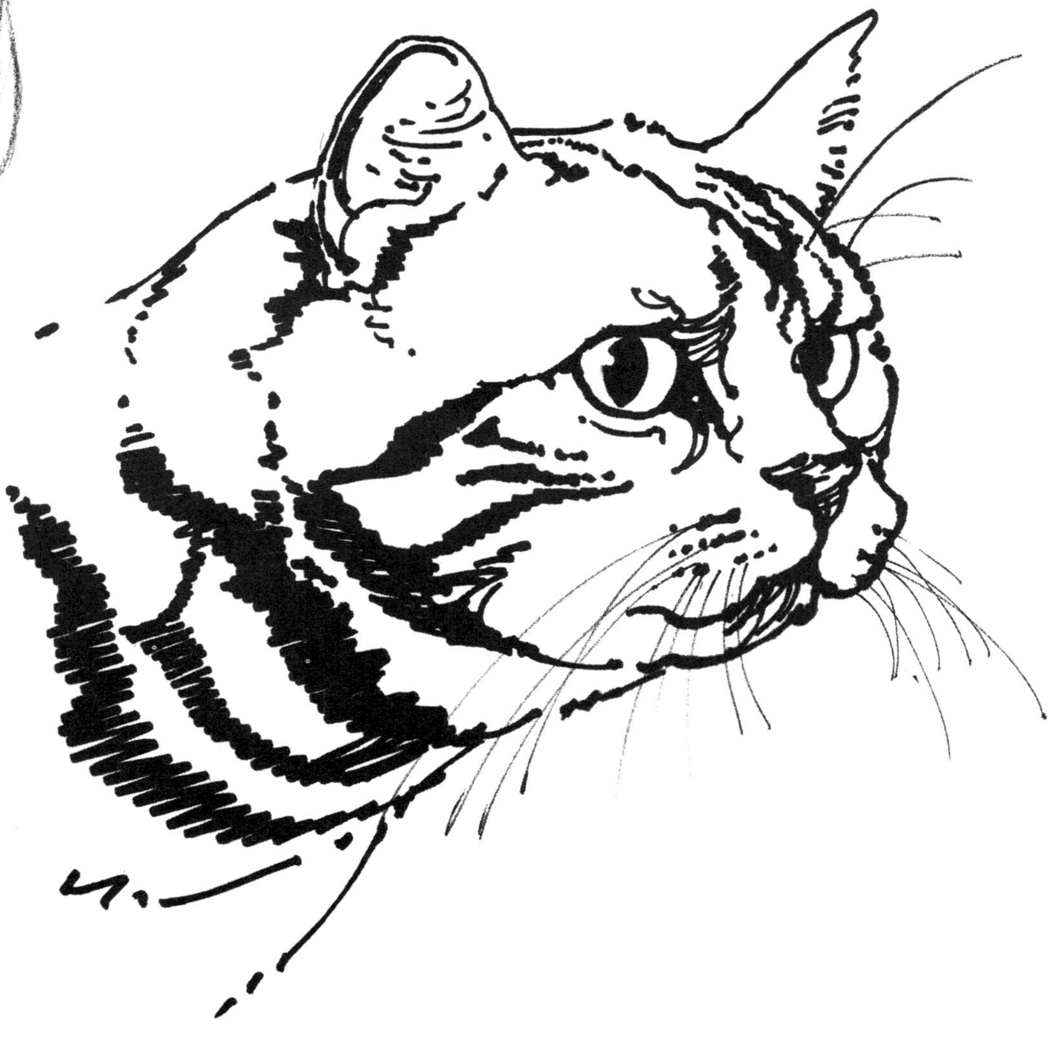

The best way to capture the expression and mood of your subject is by studying the eyes. They are the most expressive part of the body. Cover the drawings on this page with your hands, leaving only the eyes visible, and you will see what I mean.

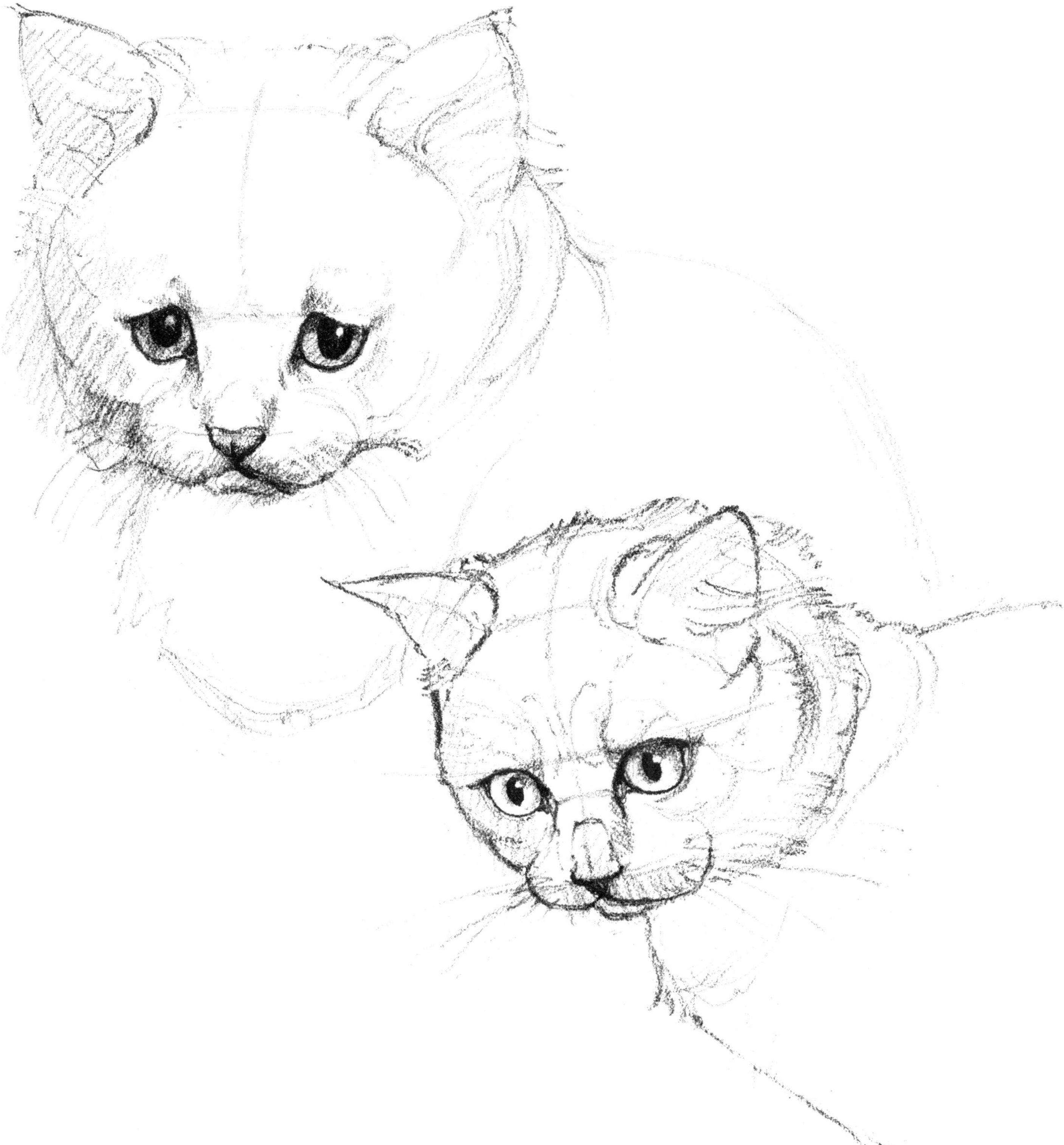

Here are two contrasting moods. The expression of the first cat is alert; it has stopped abruptly to direct a penetrating gaze at something it is not too happy about.

The mood of the sleeping cat below couldn't be more different. Details—such as the way the shoulder pushes the cheek into folds—help to convey its comfortable relaxed posture.

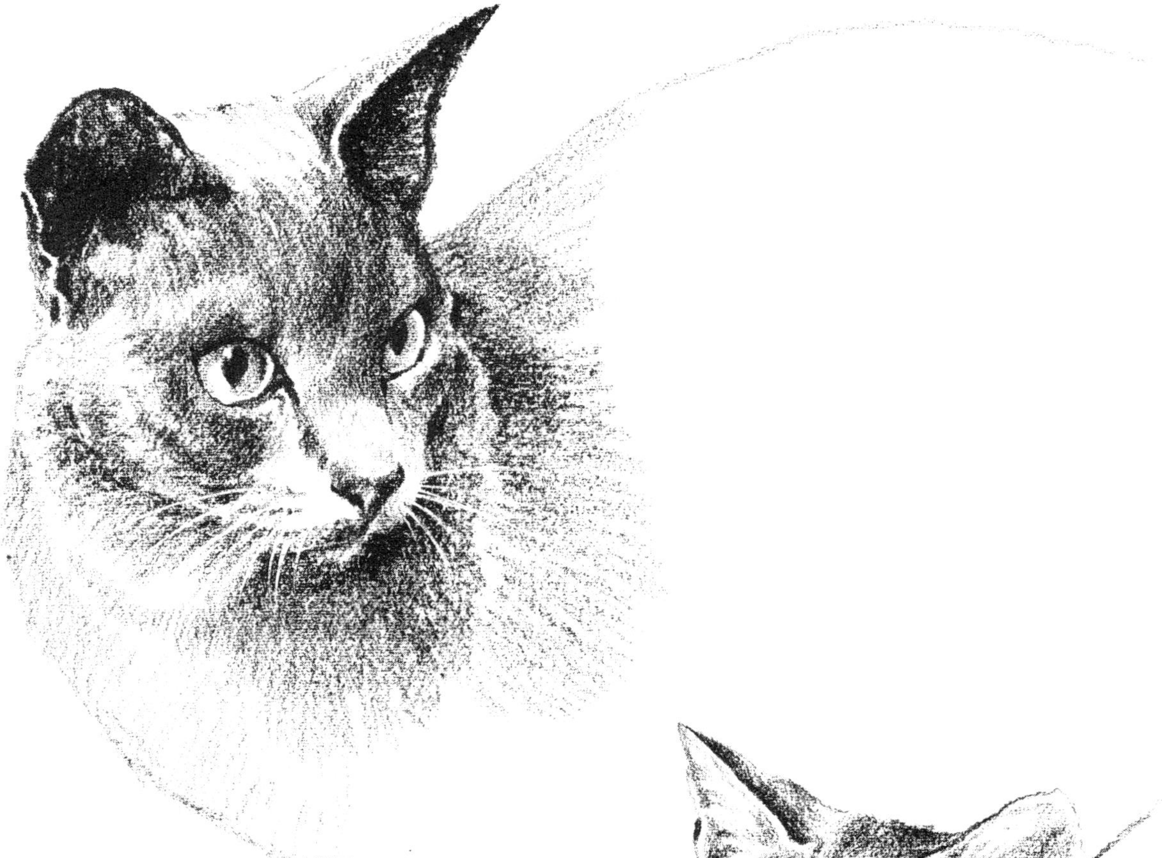

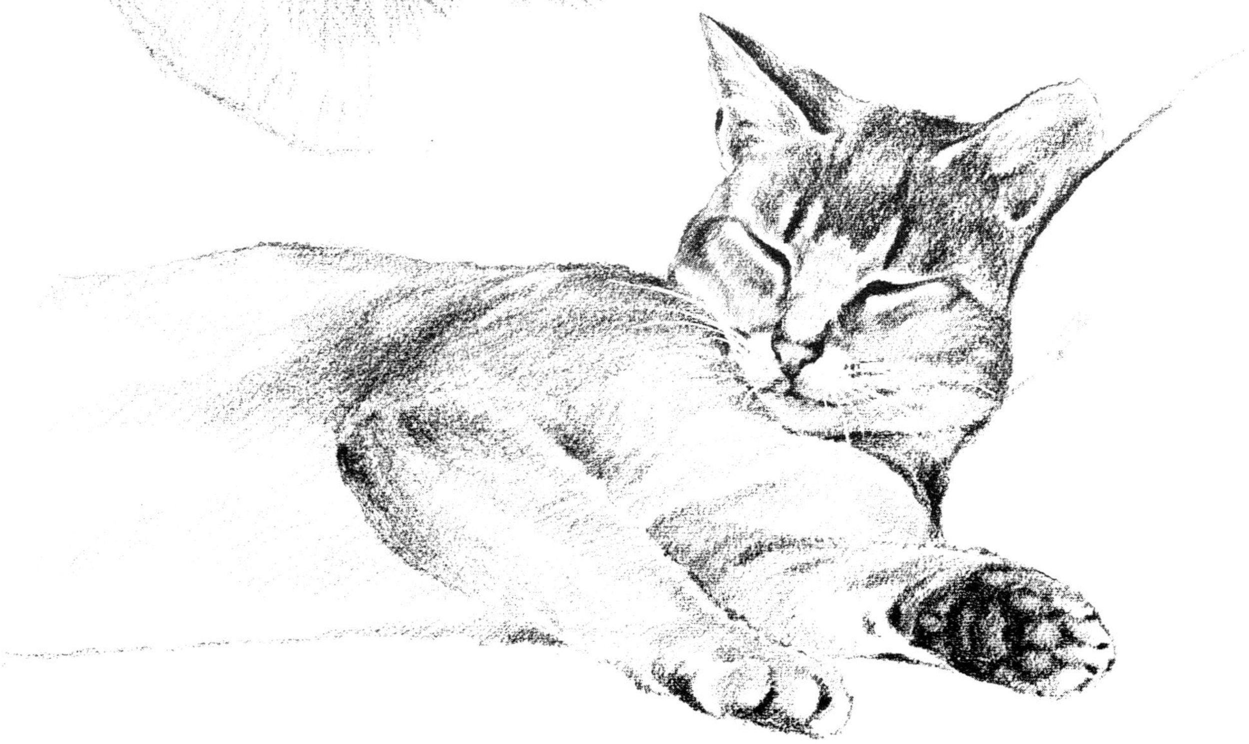

Action

Cats are more interesting to draw in action than when they are sitting still or asleep; but for a beginner, trying to draw a cat in movement can become frustrating. One way to bridge this gap and gain experience in capturing movement is to draw a cat doing something on the spot. For instance, you will have time to do some quick sketches while your cat drinks a saucer of milk. At first you may be able to produce only one sketch, but with practice you will be able to draw more quickly.

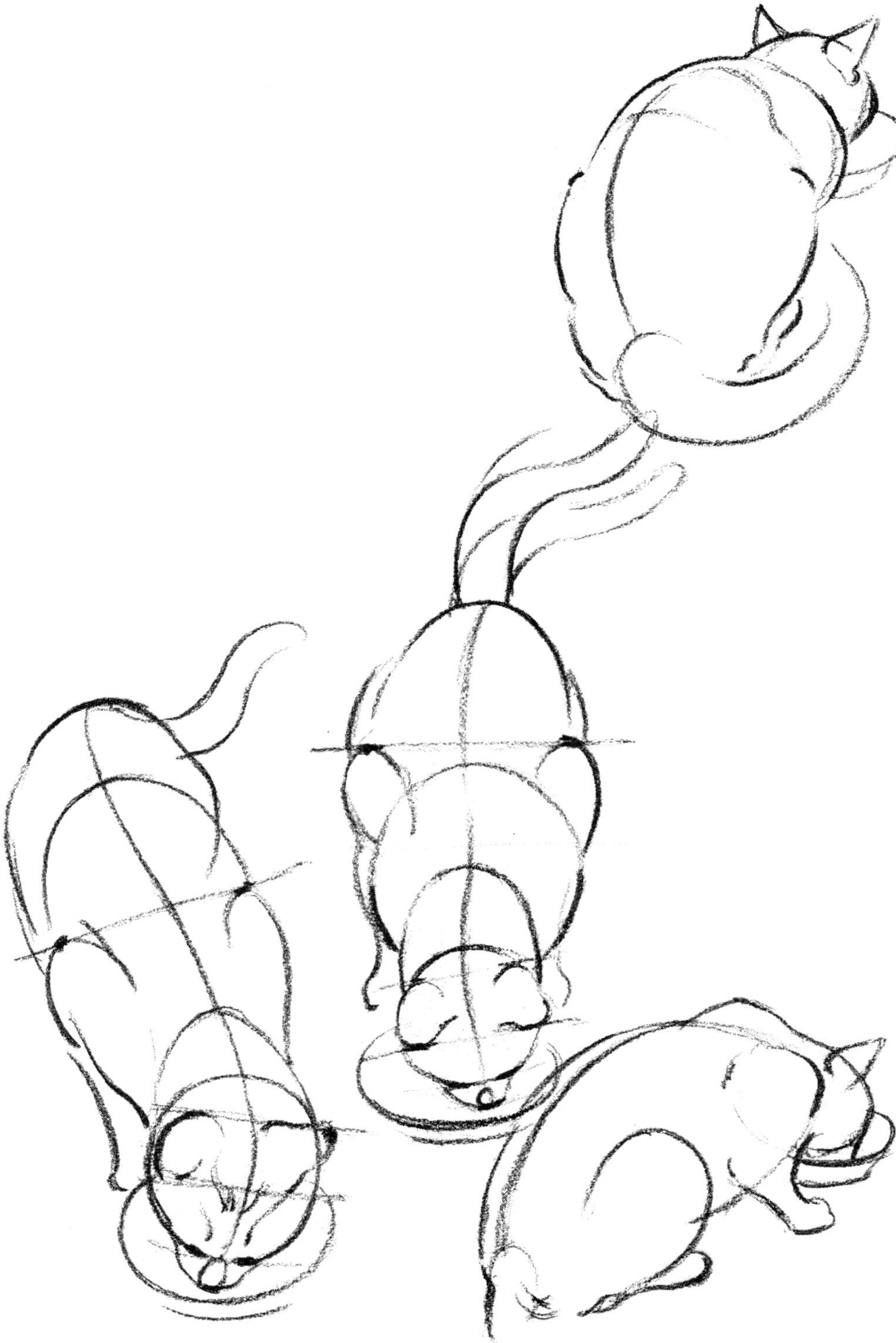

Another stationary 'action' is when your cat has a wash. You could encourage it by smearing a little food on its paw. Drawing in this way will help enormously to get movement into your lines.

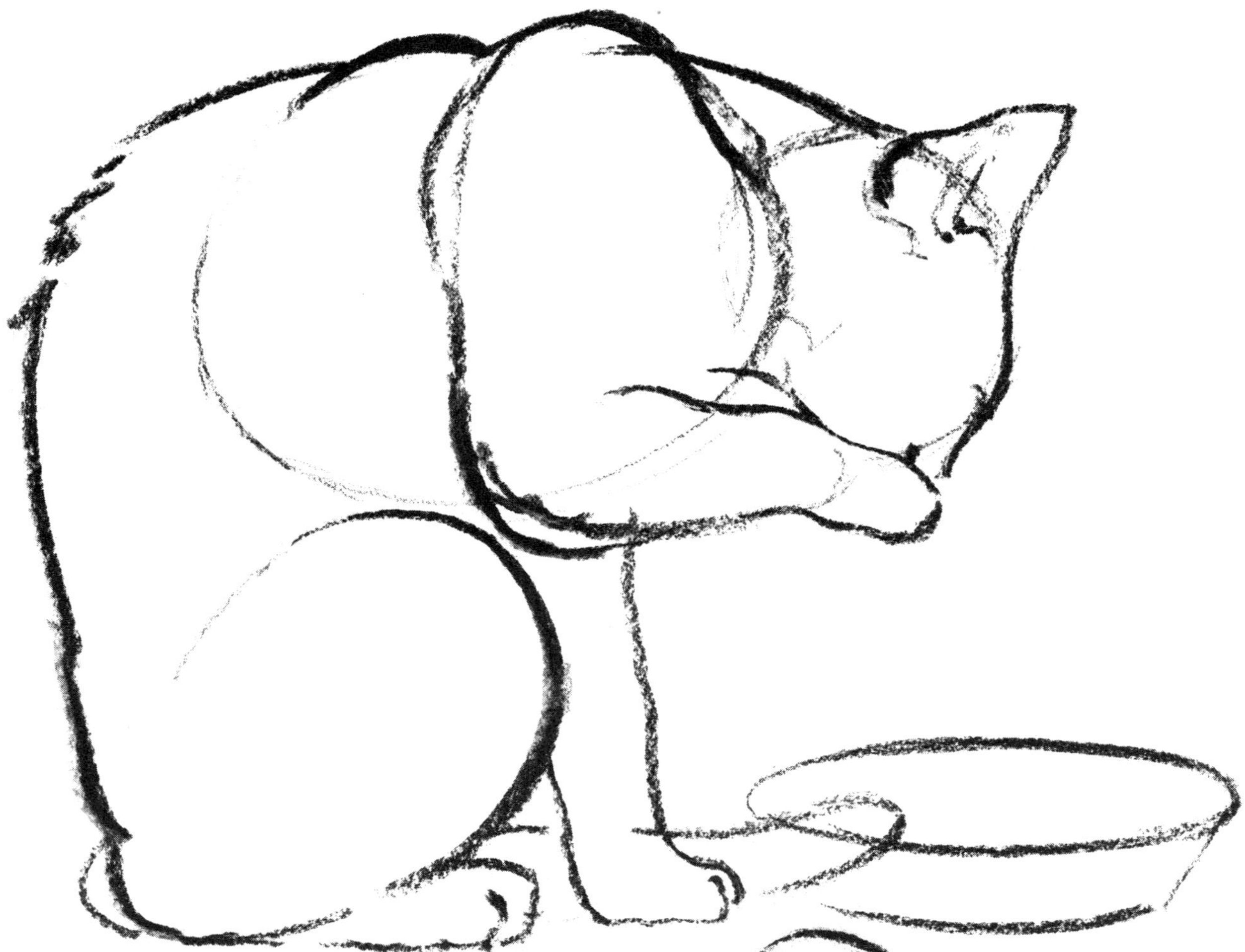

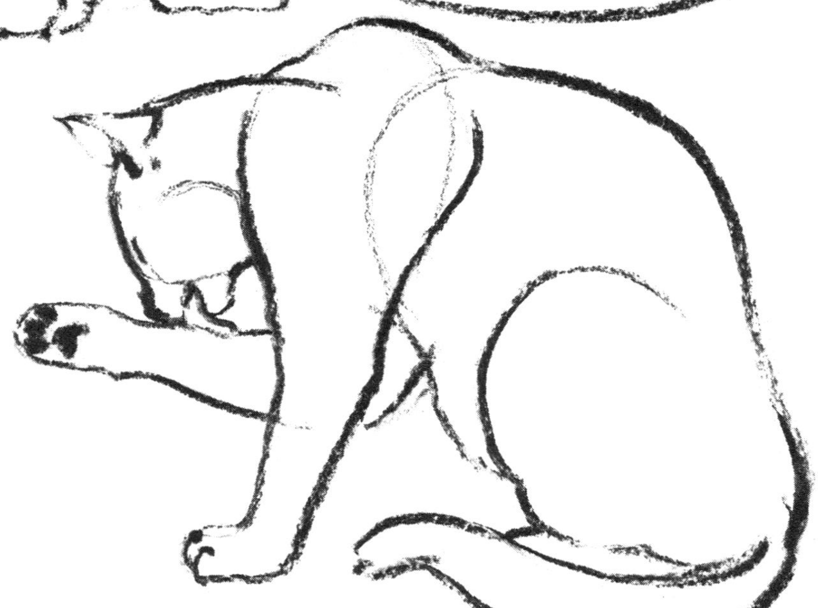

When drawing a moving cat, do not make a detailed drawing of one part of the body and expect the cat to be in the same position when you look up to draw the next part.

If possible, take the cat out of doors where you both have room to move around. Keep a close watch on its body movement. Then quickly draw as much of the cat as you can, from memory, concentrating on the basic form. Repeat the exercise, to develop or check your drawing. You probably won't get much down at your early attempts, but with practice your observation and memory will improve to such an extent that you will eventually find it possible to produce the basic lines of most of the body, finishing if off at the checking stage. Remember that facial details can be carried out when the cat is stationary.

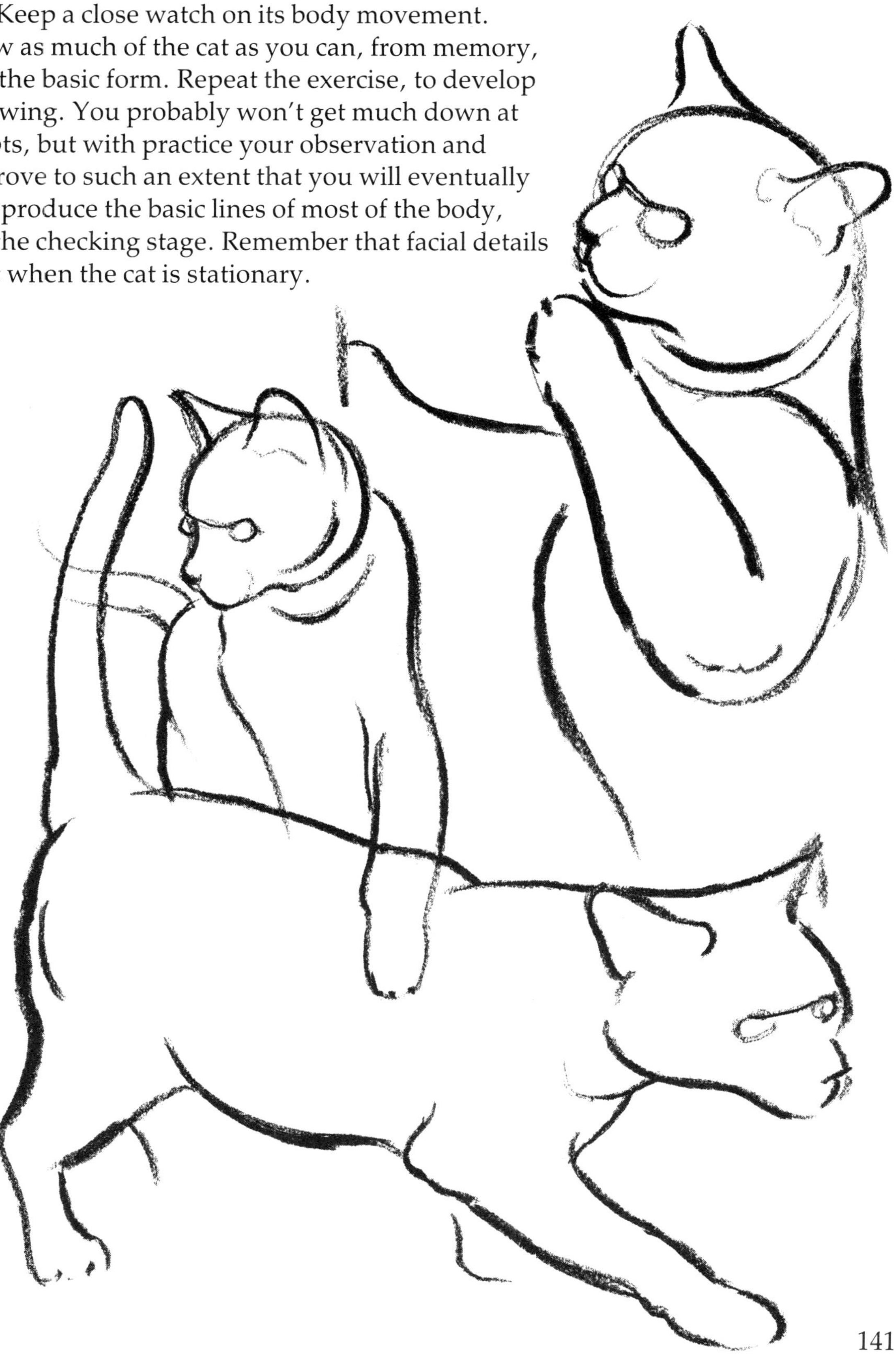

To draw from life you must draw quickly. This will produce lines full of movement. Draw your subject from as many different angles as possible to help you understand its anatomy.

If you don't feel confident enough for this, start by drawing from photographs. Remember that it is most important not just to draw the two-dimensional image but to see it as a living three-dimensional animal. Draw quickly. Draw a line along the backbone; draw in the bumps made by the shoulder blades—how do they relate?—is one lower than the other? See how the head fits on to the neck and the neck to the body. Construct your drawing, don't merely copy an image. When you have practised and feel more confident, move on to live cats.

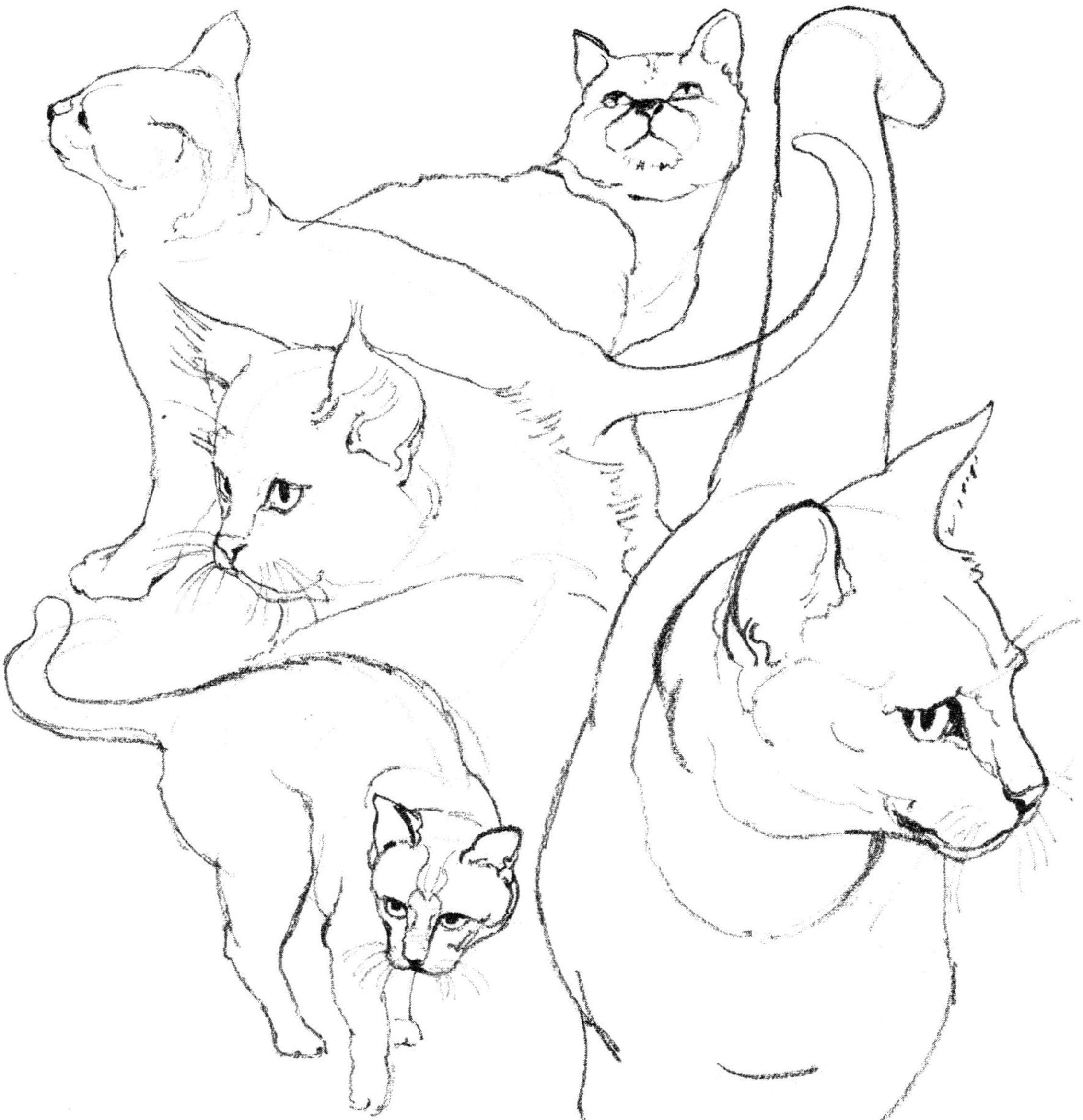

Tricks and techniques

This drawing was achieved by painting with masking fluid those areas which were to remain white. Using a stipple brush (A), the whole area was then stippled over with black designer's gouache. When this was thoroughly dry, the masking fluid was removed with a Cow Gum eraser. The stipple technique makes it possible to vary the density of the dark areas to give them added interest. Use a rough surface such as a 'NOT surface' cartridge or watercolour board. See also page 145.

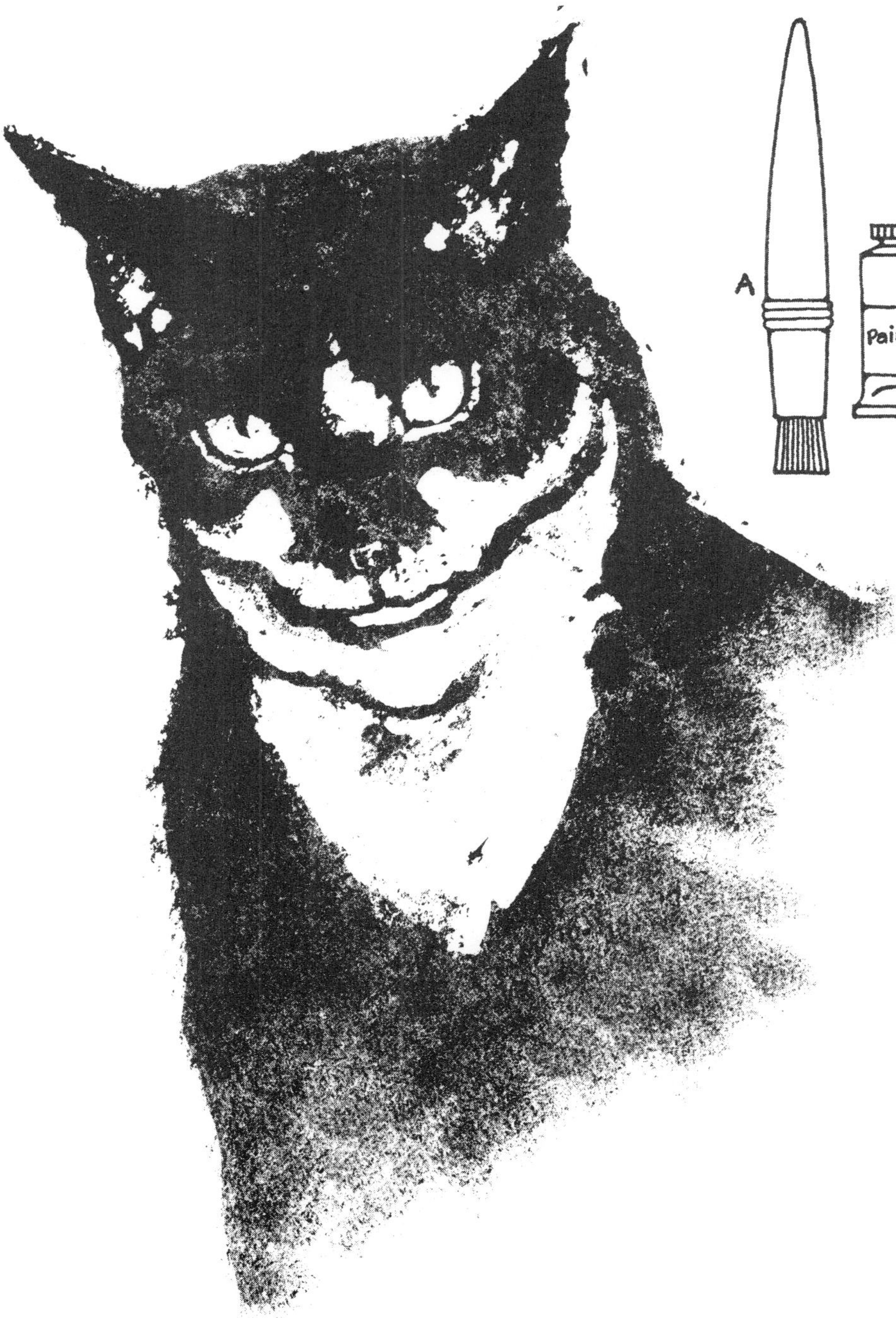

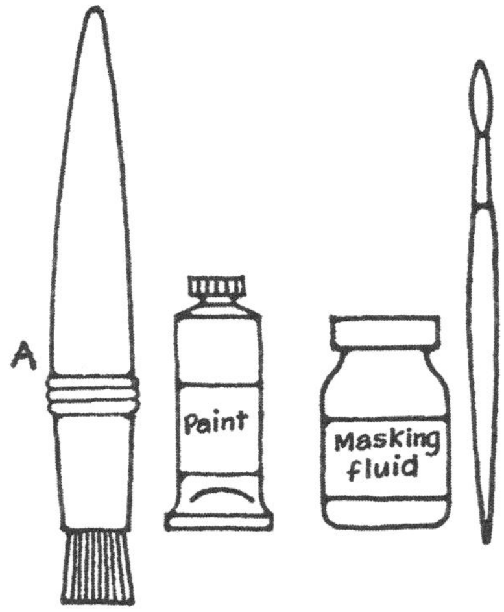

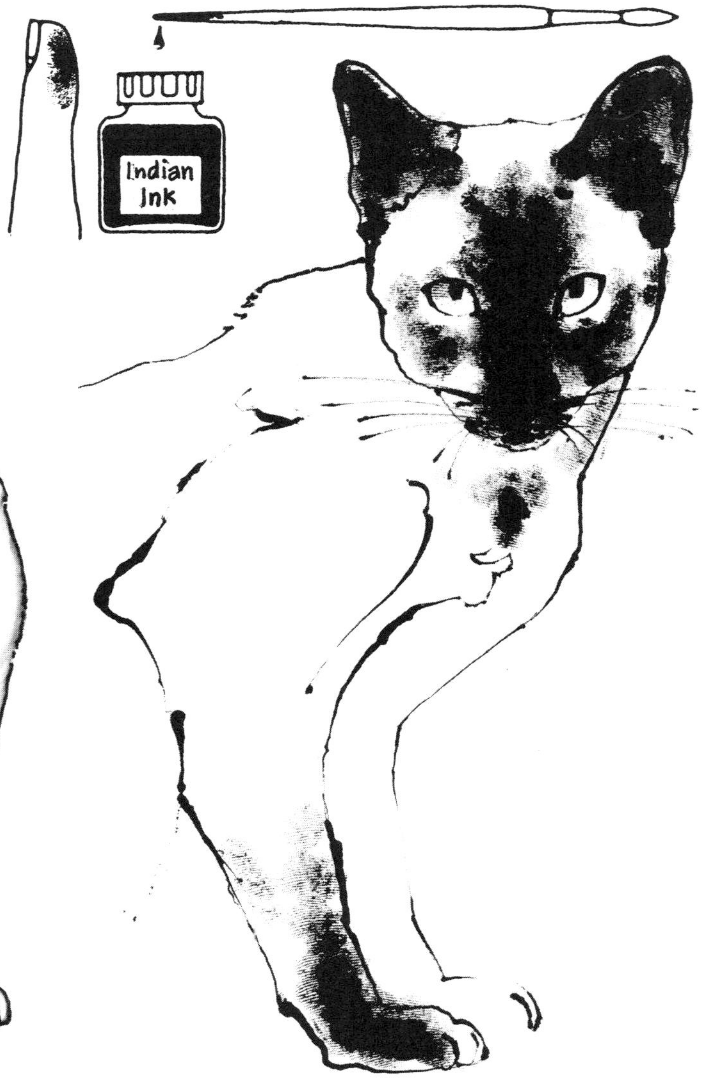

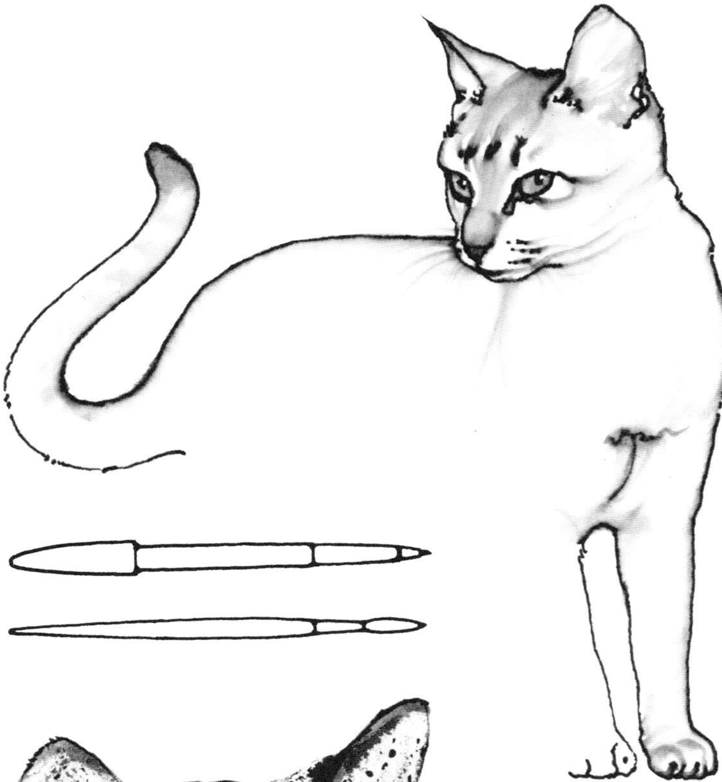

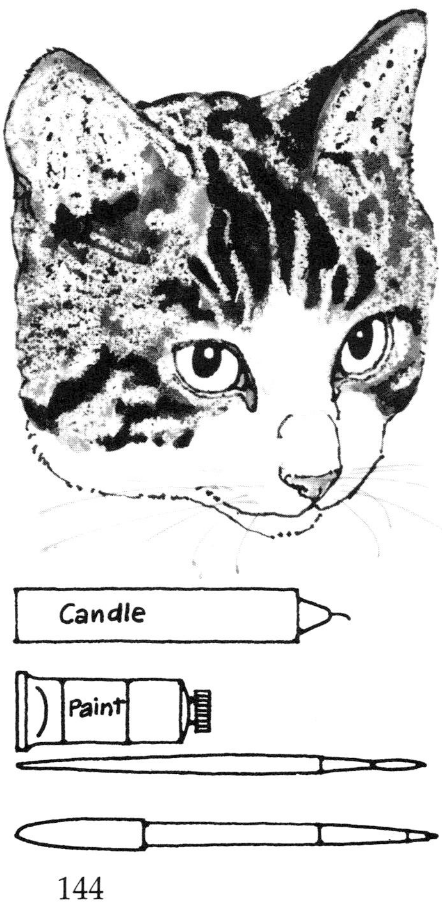

The Siamese (top right) was drawn with the handle of a paint brush dipped in ink. The dark areas were produced by placing a blob of ink on the appropriate spot, then spreading it while still wet by dabbing with the finger. Use a semi-rough surface. I suggest you try this first on a piece of scrap paper, until you have gained some control of the technique.

The Abyssinian (top left) was drawn with a fibre pen, then one edge of the line was lightly brushed with clean water. This technique can be difficult to control.

The head on the left was first drawn with a fibre pen. A candle was then used to draw the light areas (from around the eyes upwards, leaving the nose and lower area of the face untouched). The same area was then covered with a wash of watered-down black paint.

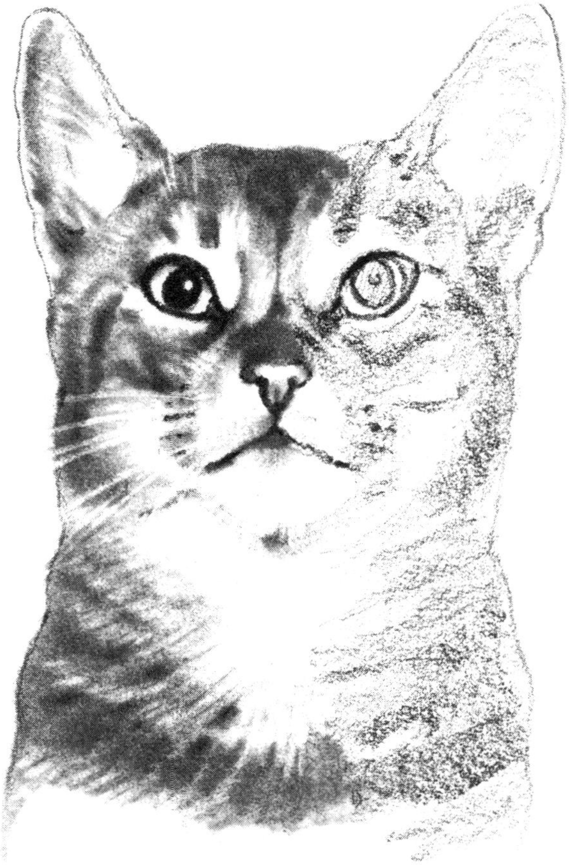

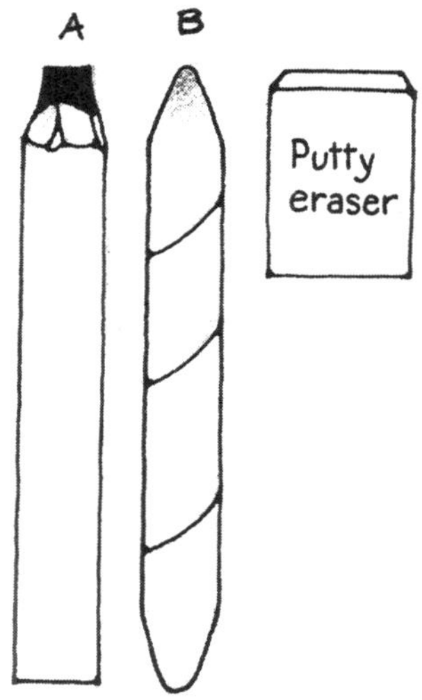

The Abyssinian on the left was first shaded with a chisel pencil (A)—see right hand side of drawing. This was then rubbed with a French stick (B)—see left hand side of drawing—and the highlights were brought out with a putty eraser. Use a smooth or semi-rough Ledger Bond (cartridge) paper.

The cat below was first lightly drawn in pencil. Masking fluid was then painted on each side of the pencil lines, i.e. all the areas that were to remain white. When dry the whole area was painted over with Indian ink, as on the right of the drawing. When the ink was absolutely dry an eraser was used to remove the masking fluid.

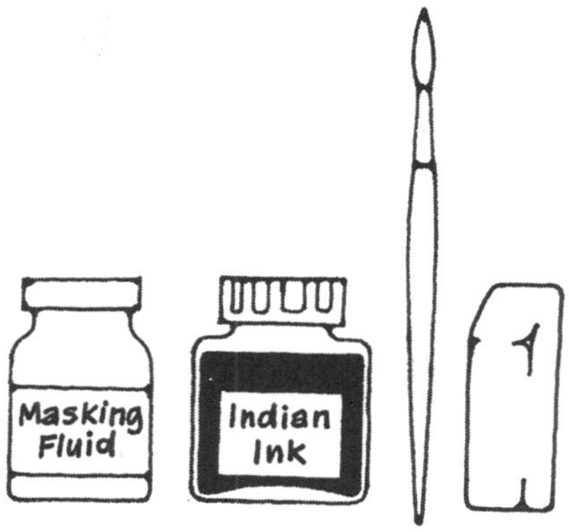

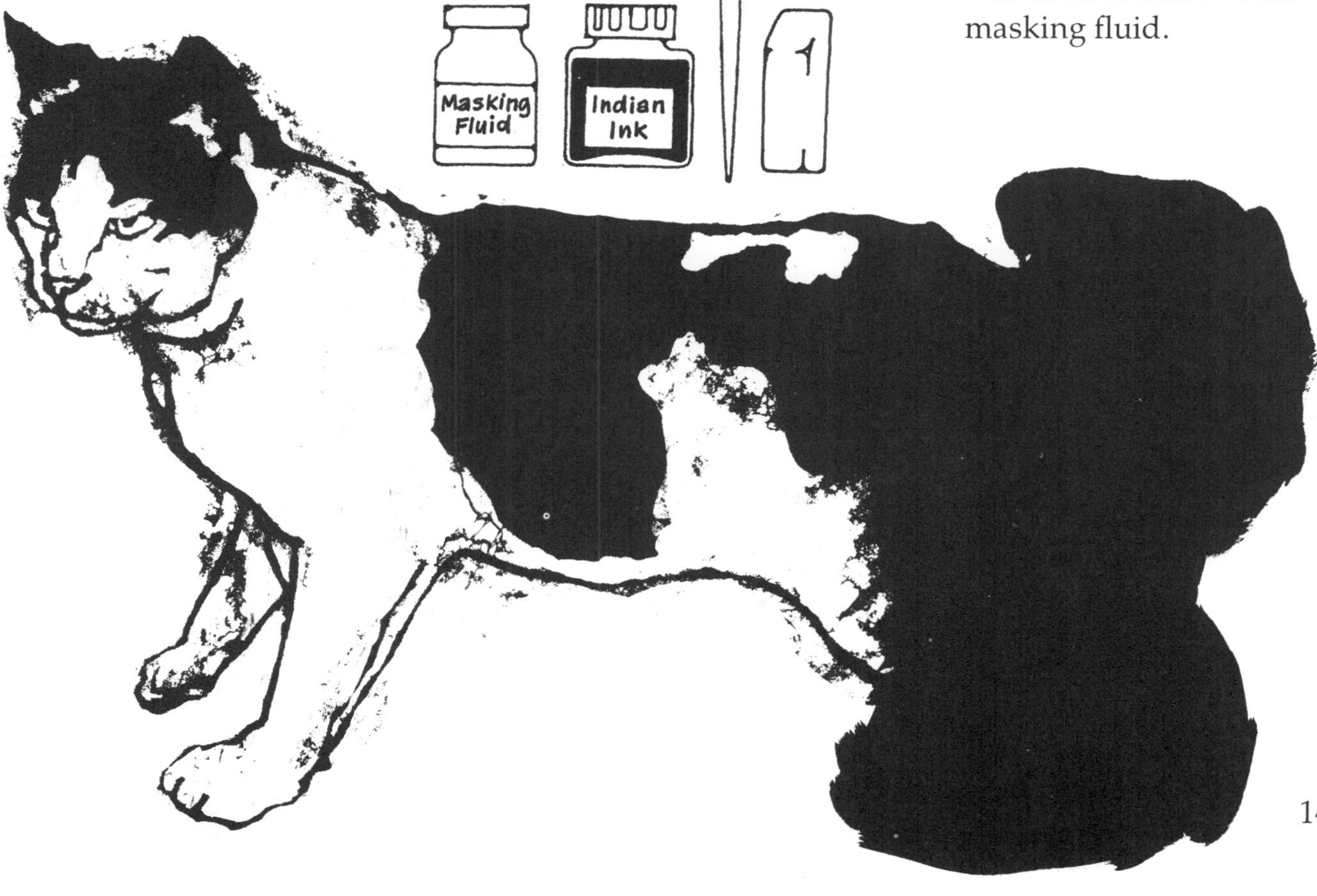

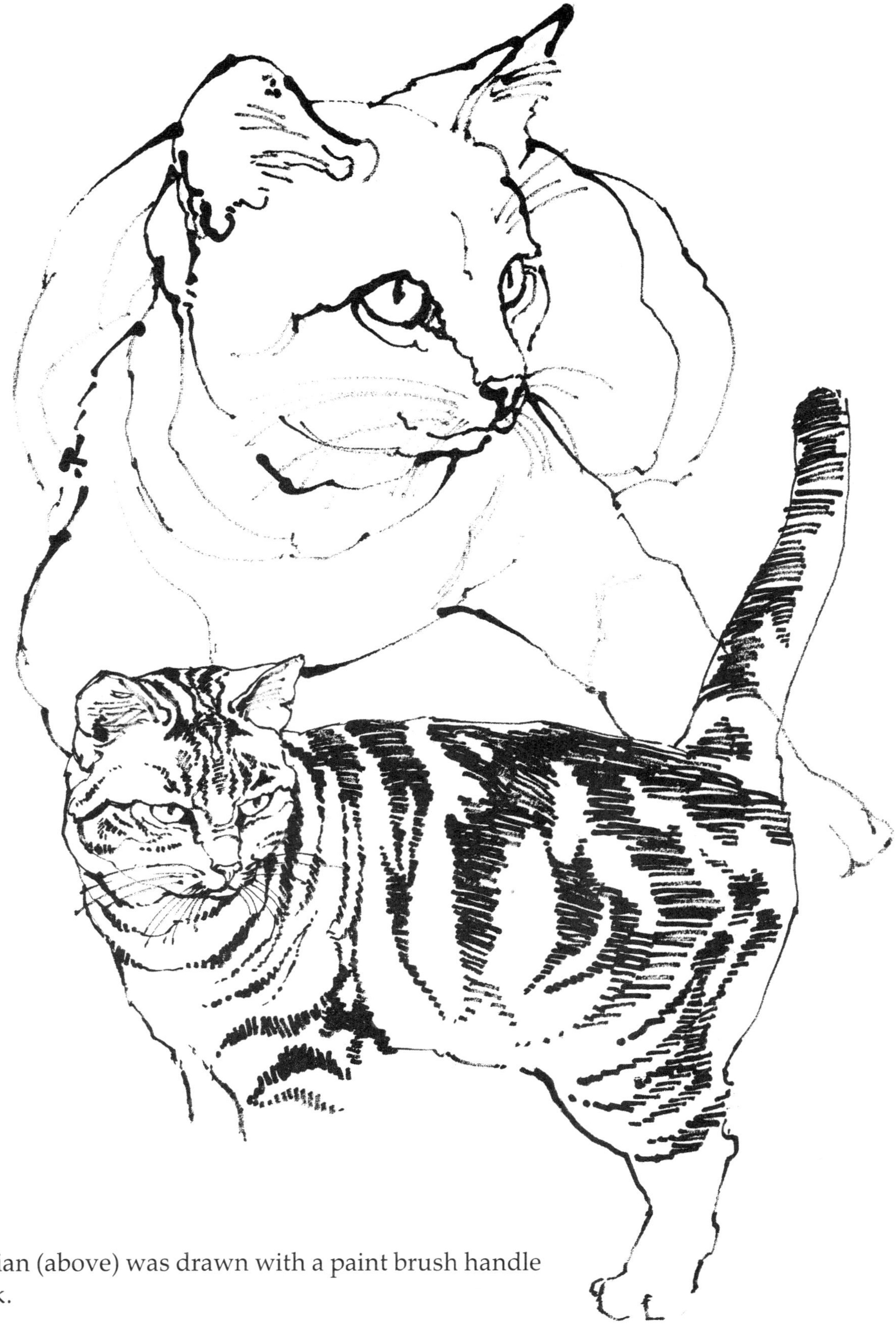

The Abyssinian (above) was drawn with a paint brush handle dipped in ink.

The Tabby was drawn in a similar way, but the brush handle was first sharpened to form a broad-tipped nib.

The Siamese with a menacing expression on the left was drawn with a wax crayon on a rough surfaced board, the head below with brush and ink, and the Siamese at the foot of the page in ink using a pen, brush and finger dabbing.

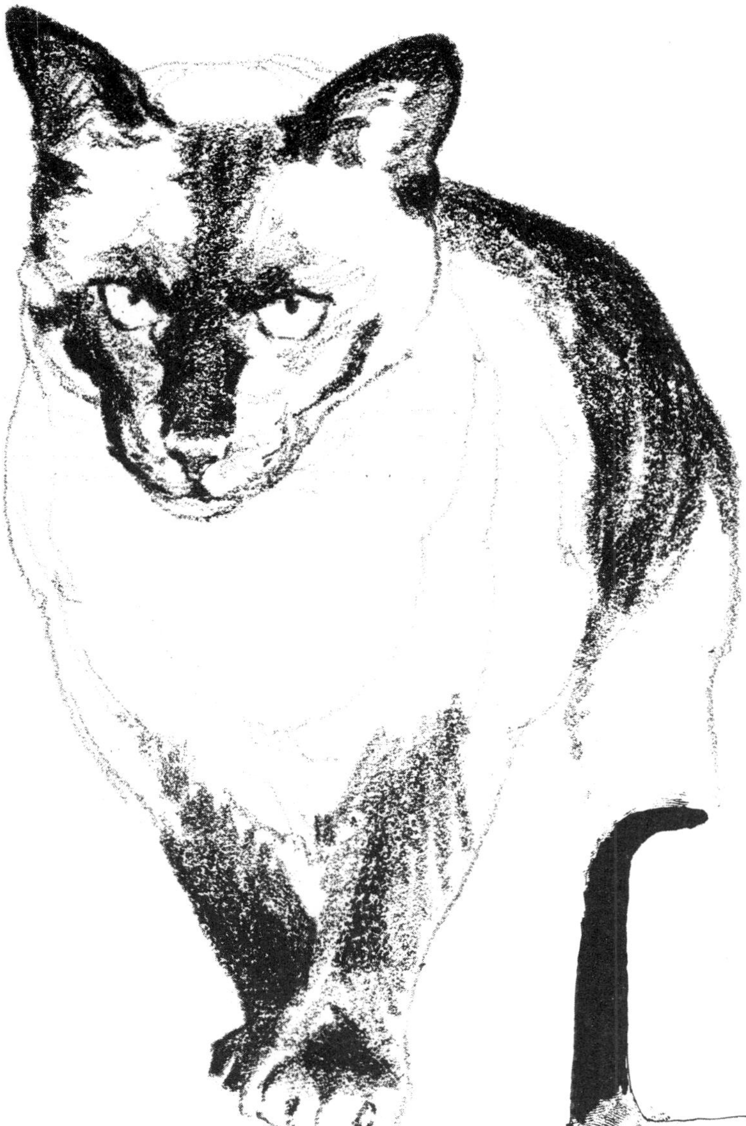

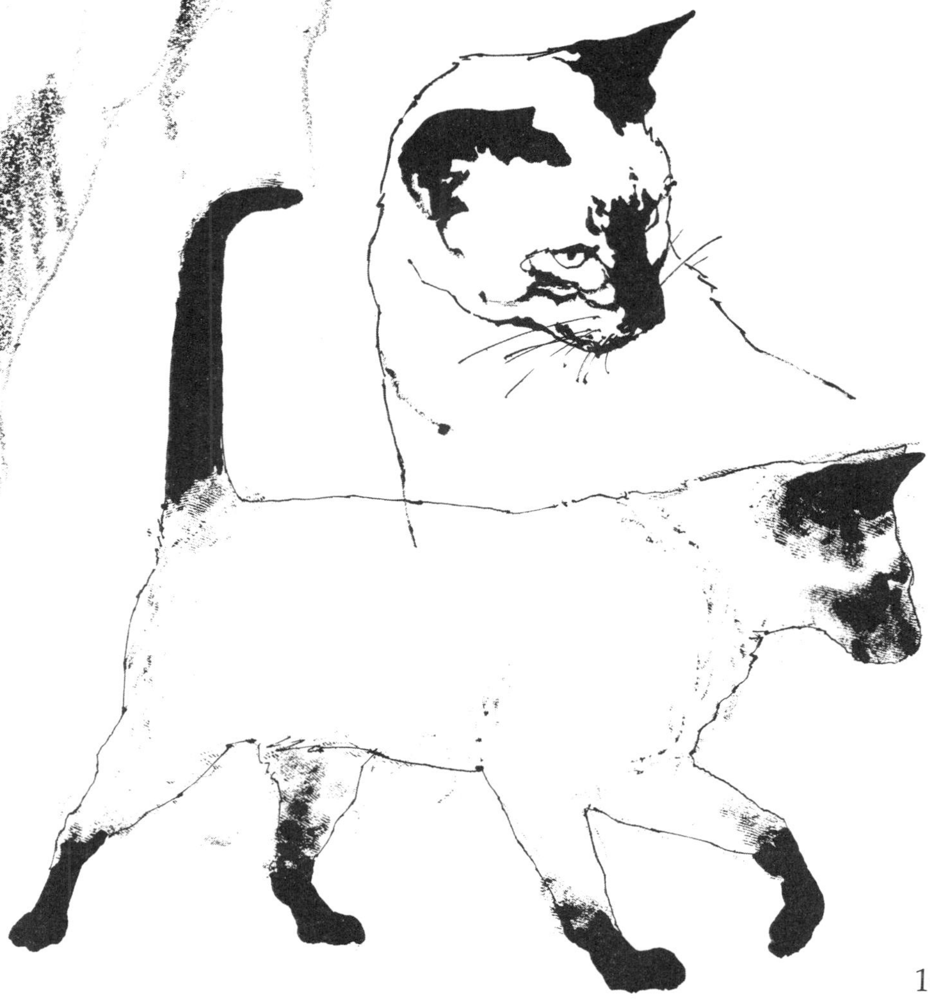

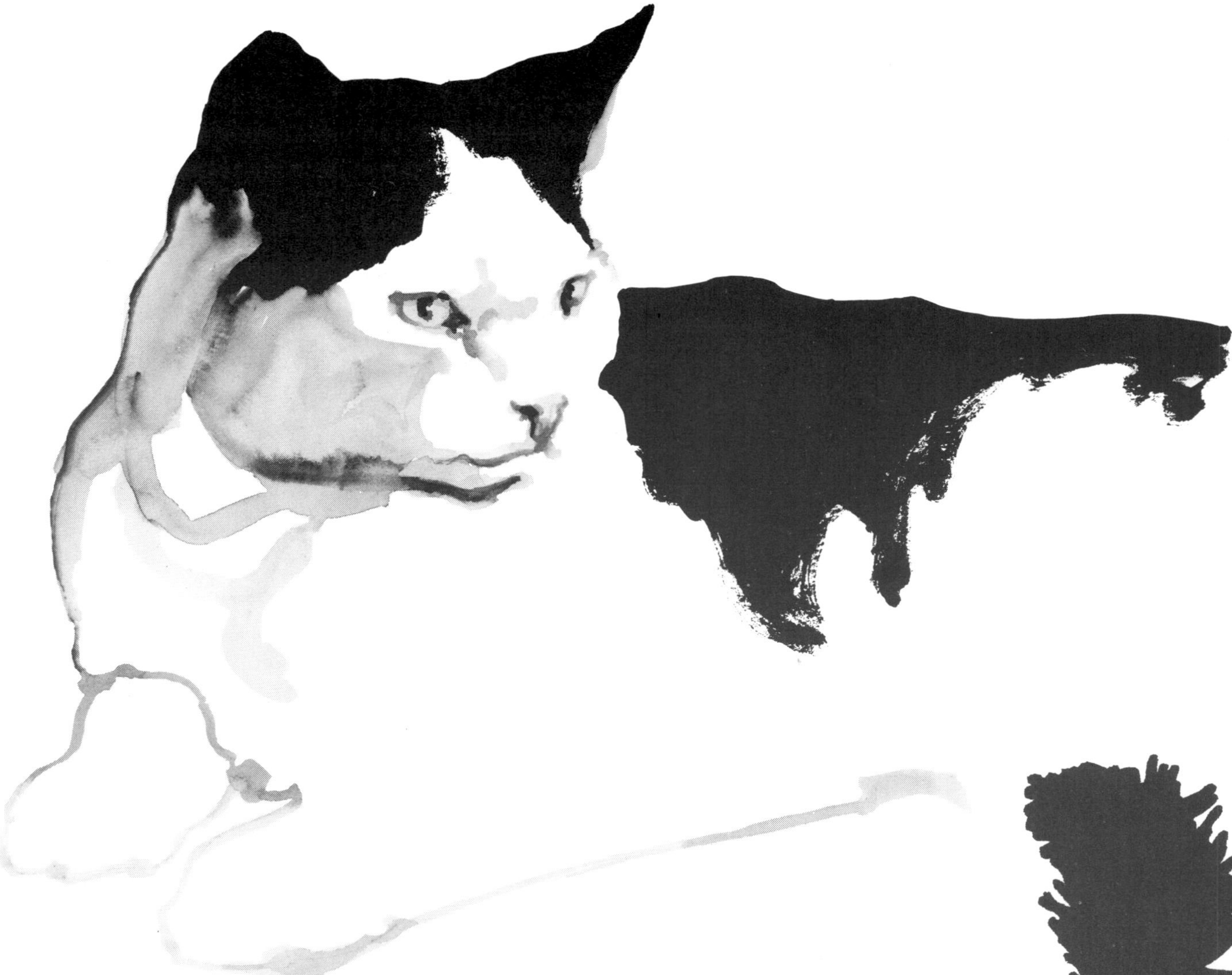

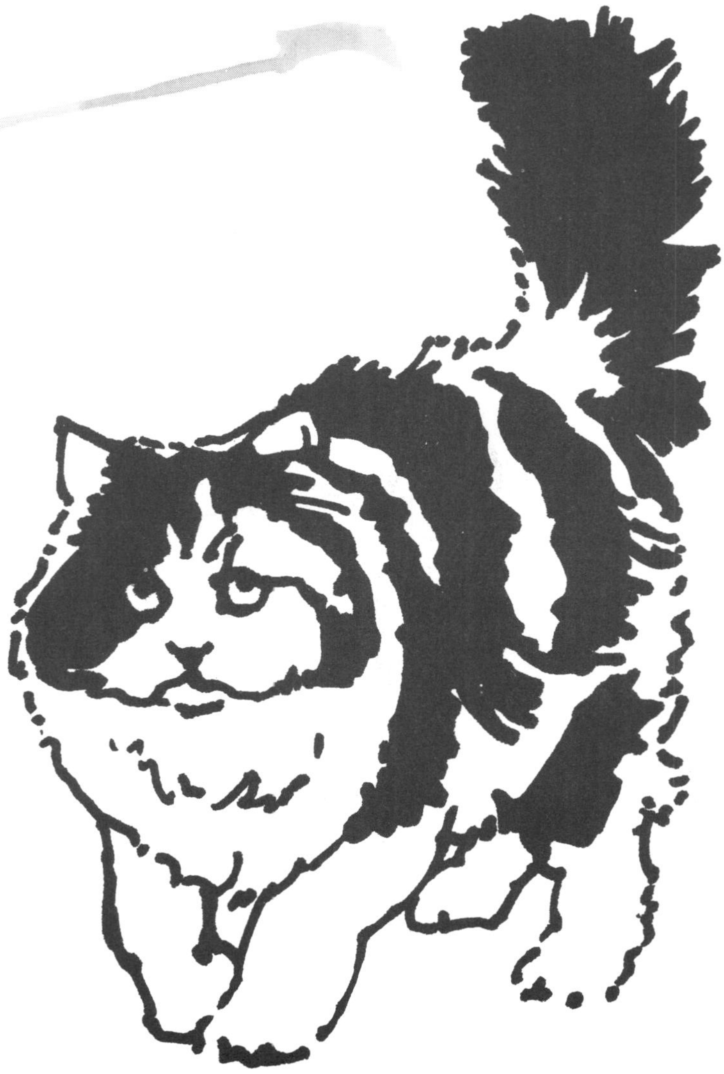

The drawing above was made with a brush and black paint, on watercolour board. This medium can produce subtle and interesting lines.

The Tortoiseshell and White, commonly known as a 'calico' cat, was drawn with a felt marker. The line produced is too thick for detailed work.

For this Shorthaired Tabby I used the masking fluid technique described on pages 143 and 145. Have fun trying various media to obtain a decorative effect as a change from realism.

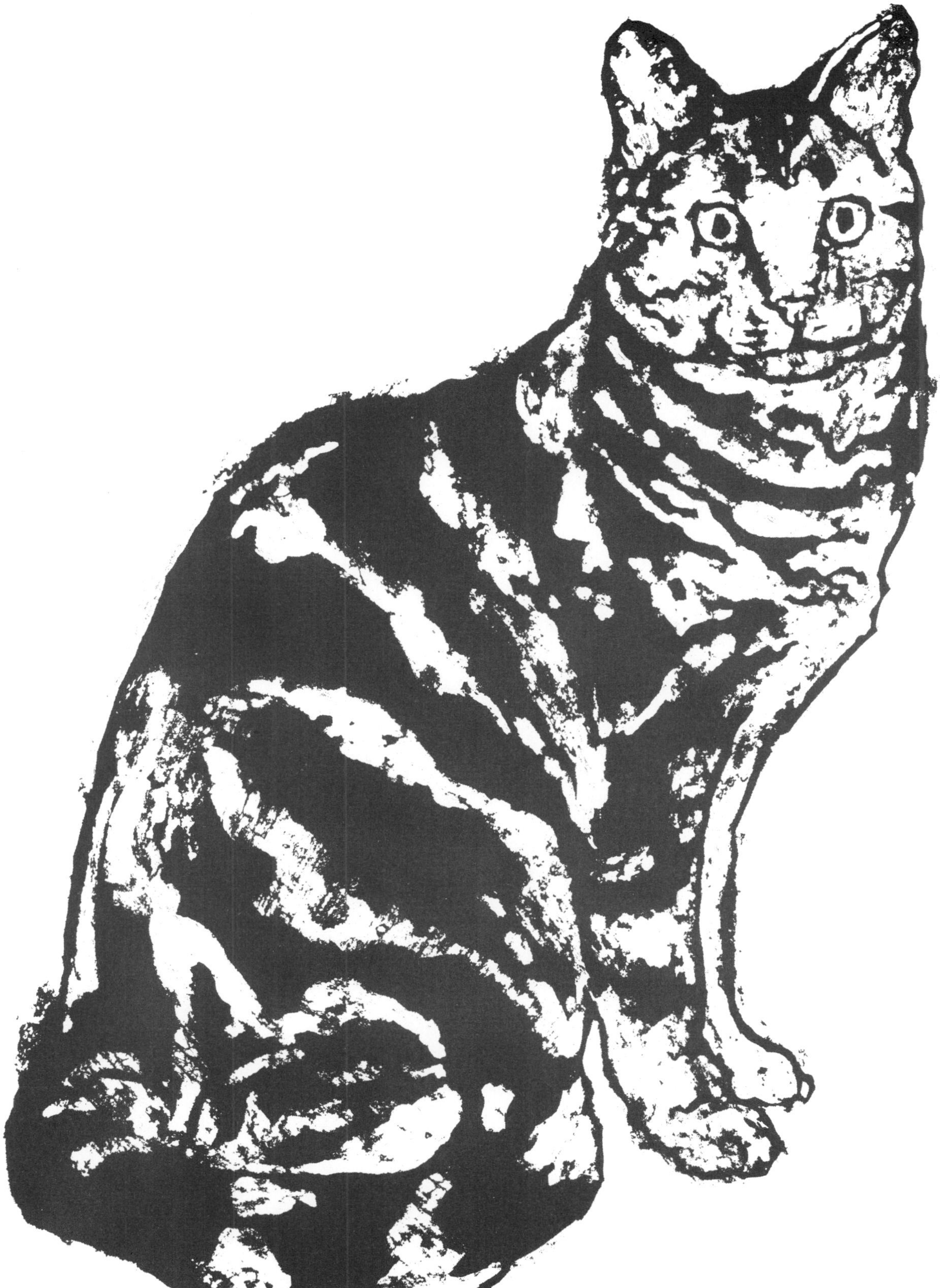

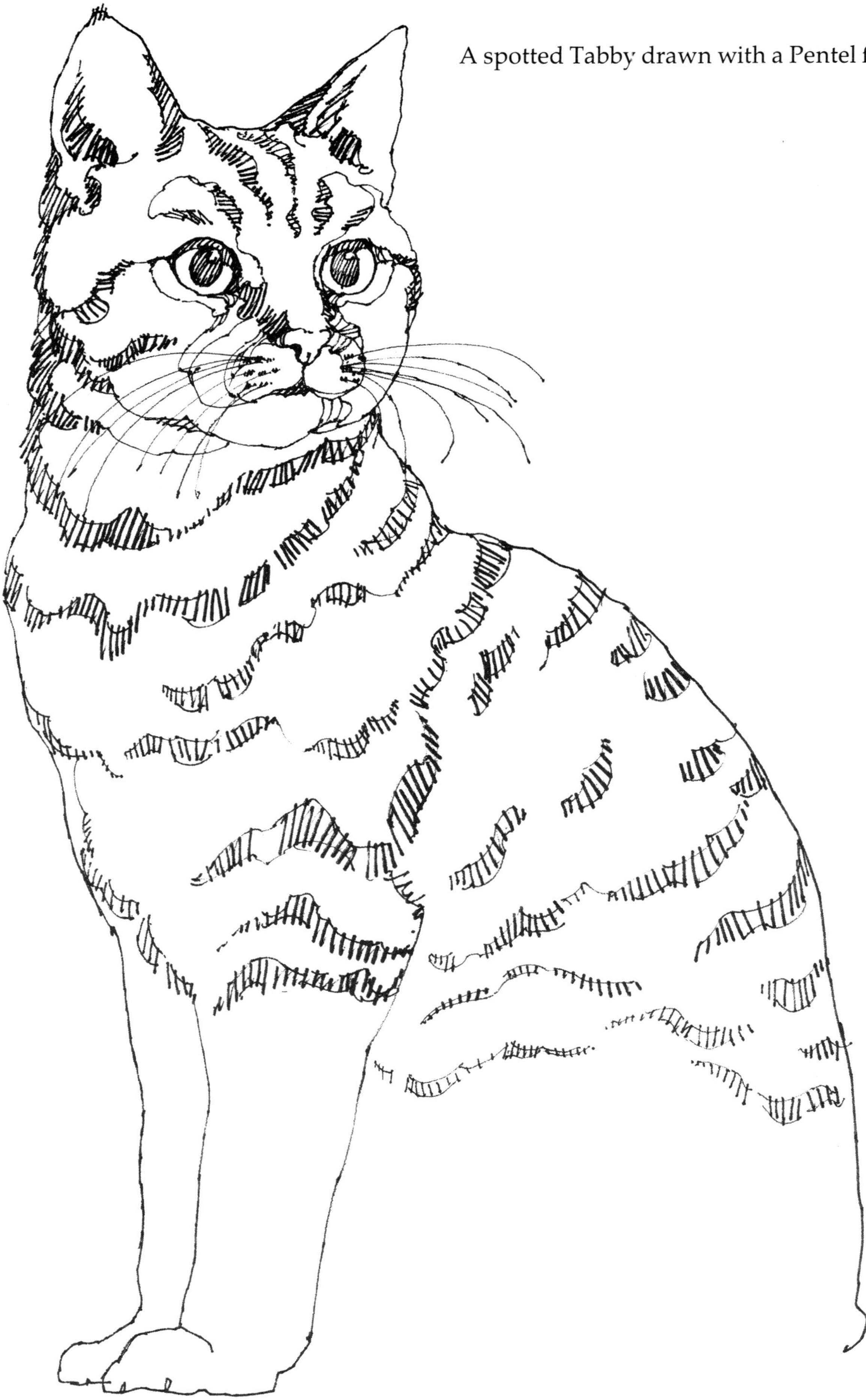

A spotted Tabby drawn with a Pentel fibre pen.

The soft woolly effect of this Chinchilla was produced with an HB pencil.

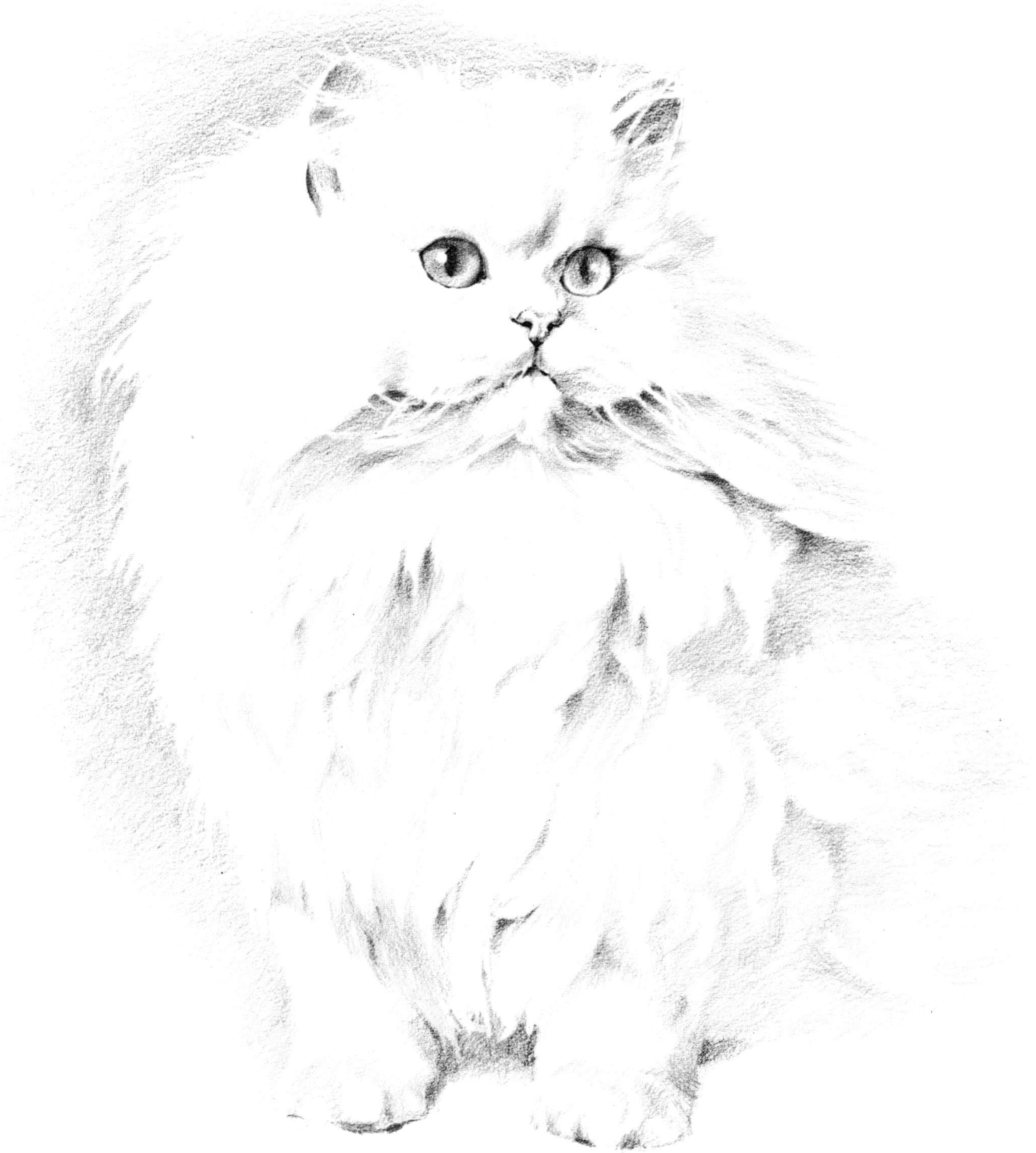

A Burmese drawn with medium thick willow charcoal. I broke off a small piece and used the side of the stick for the broad strokes on the back of the cat.

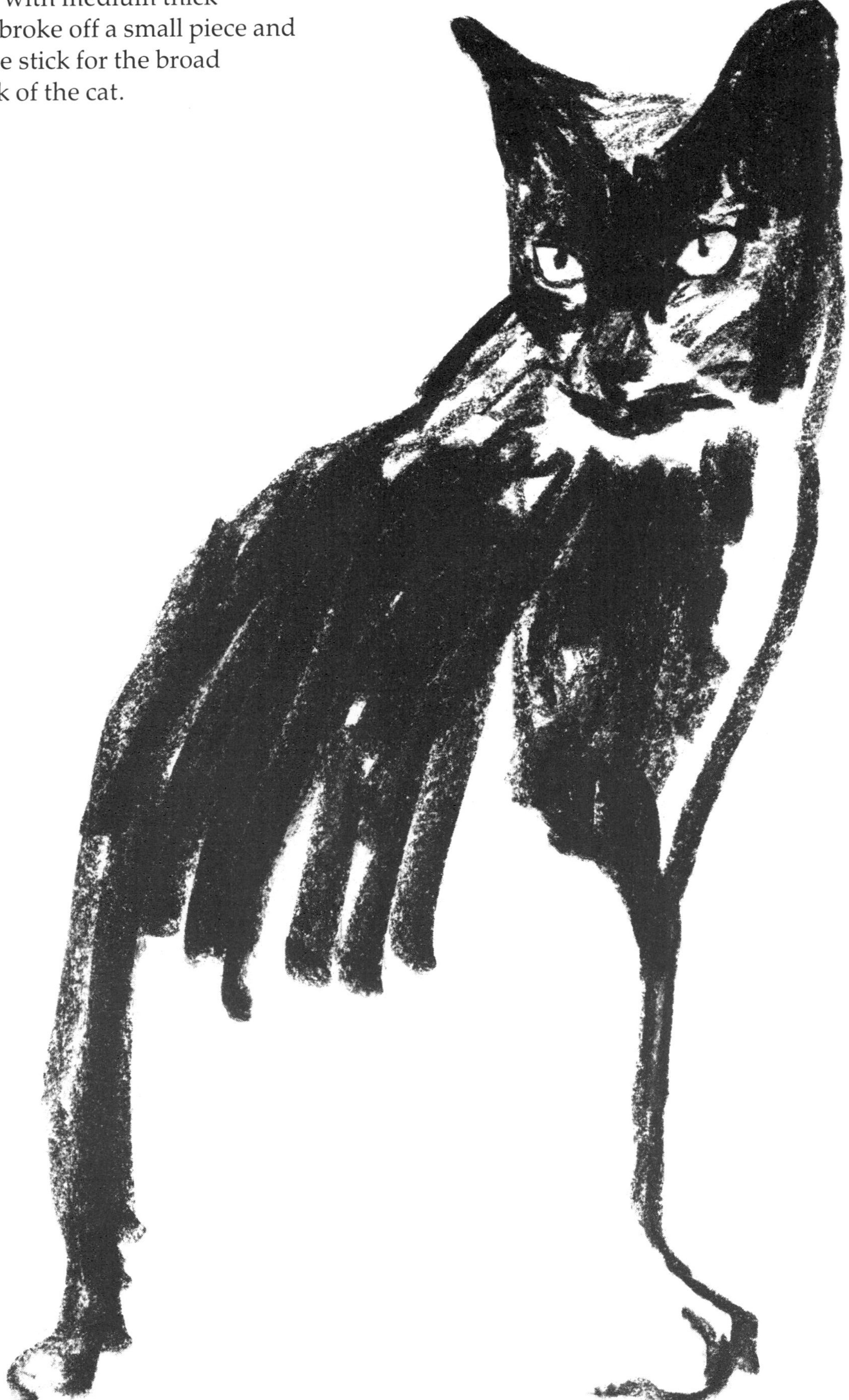

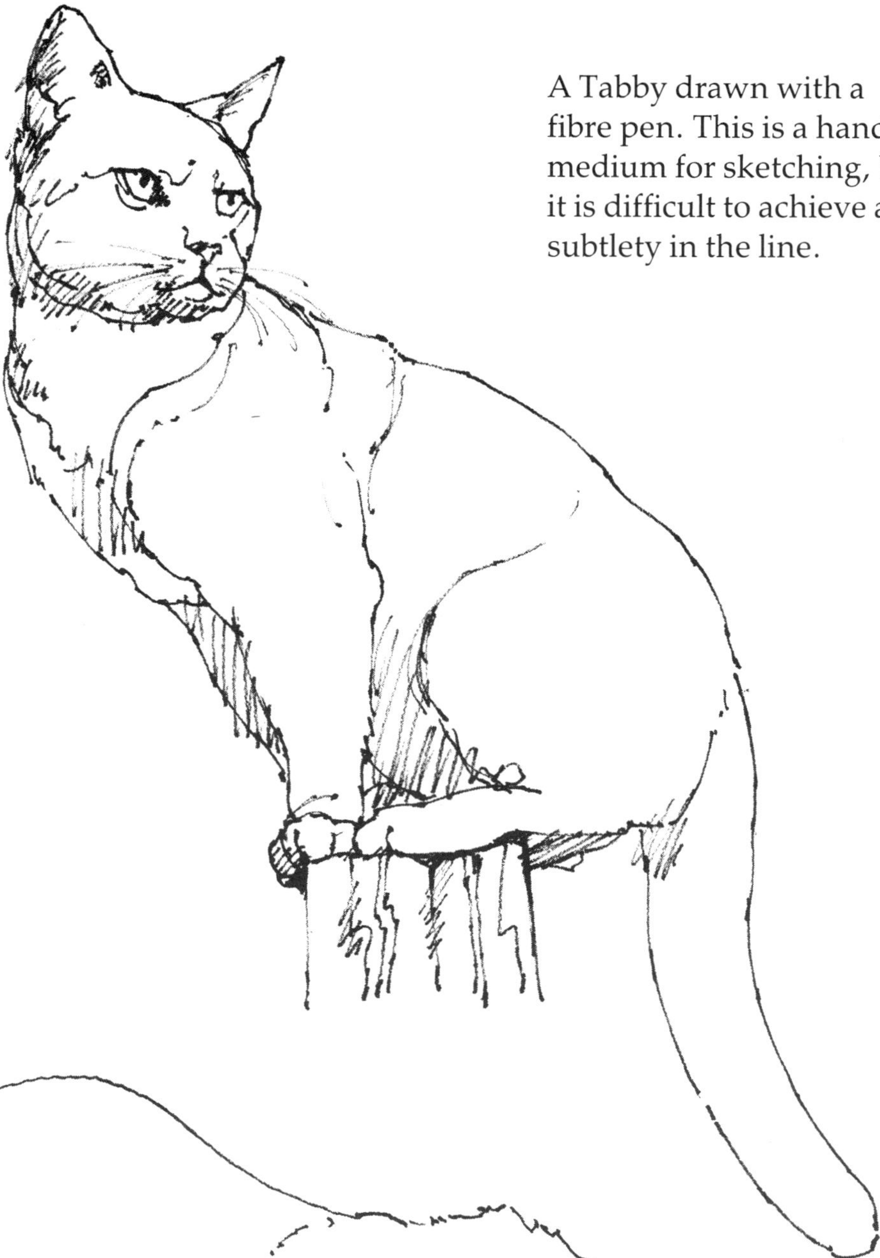

A Tabby drawn with a fibre pen. This is a handy medium for sketching, but it is difficult to achieve any subtlety in the line.

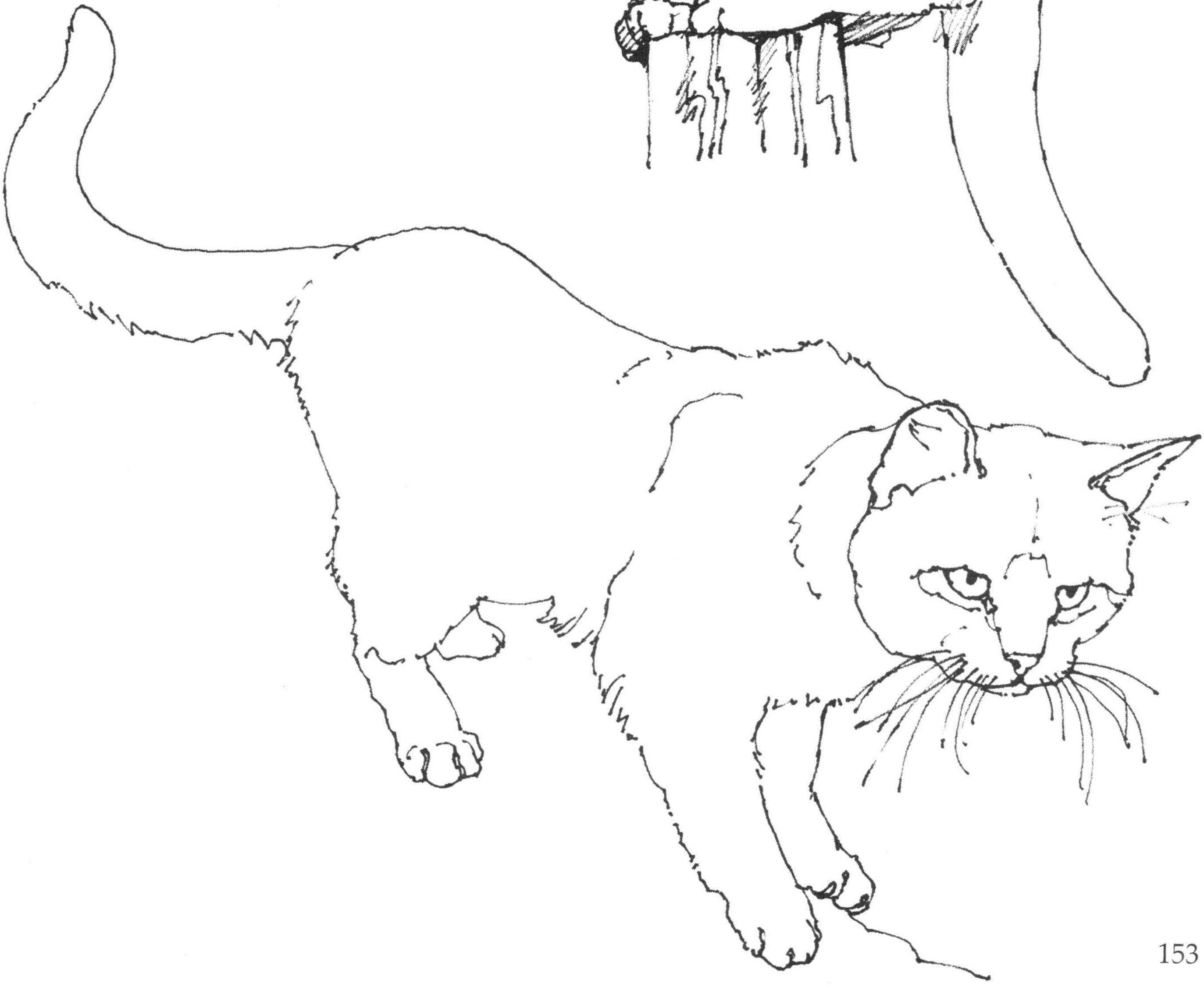

A startled Abyssinian; this drawing was done with a 6B pencil and then rubbed with a French stick.

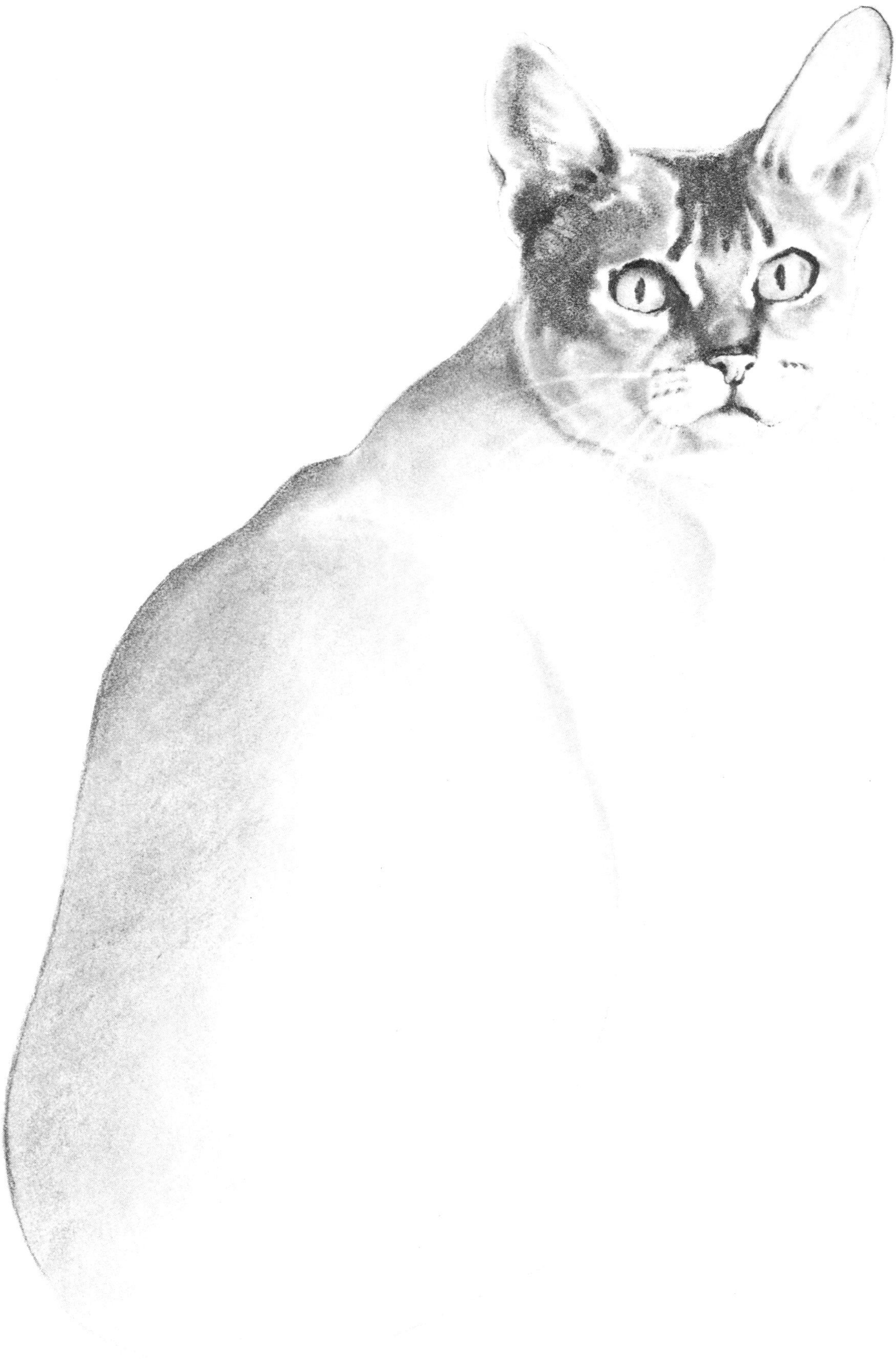

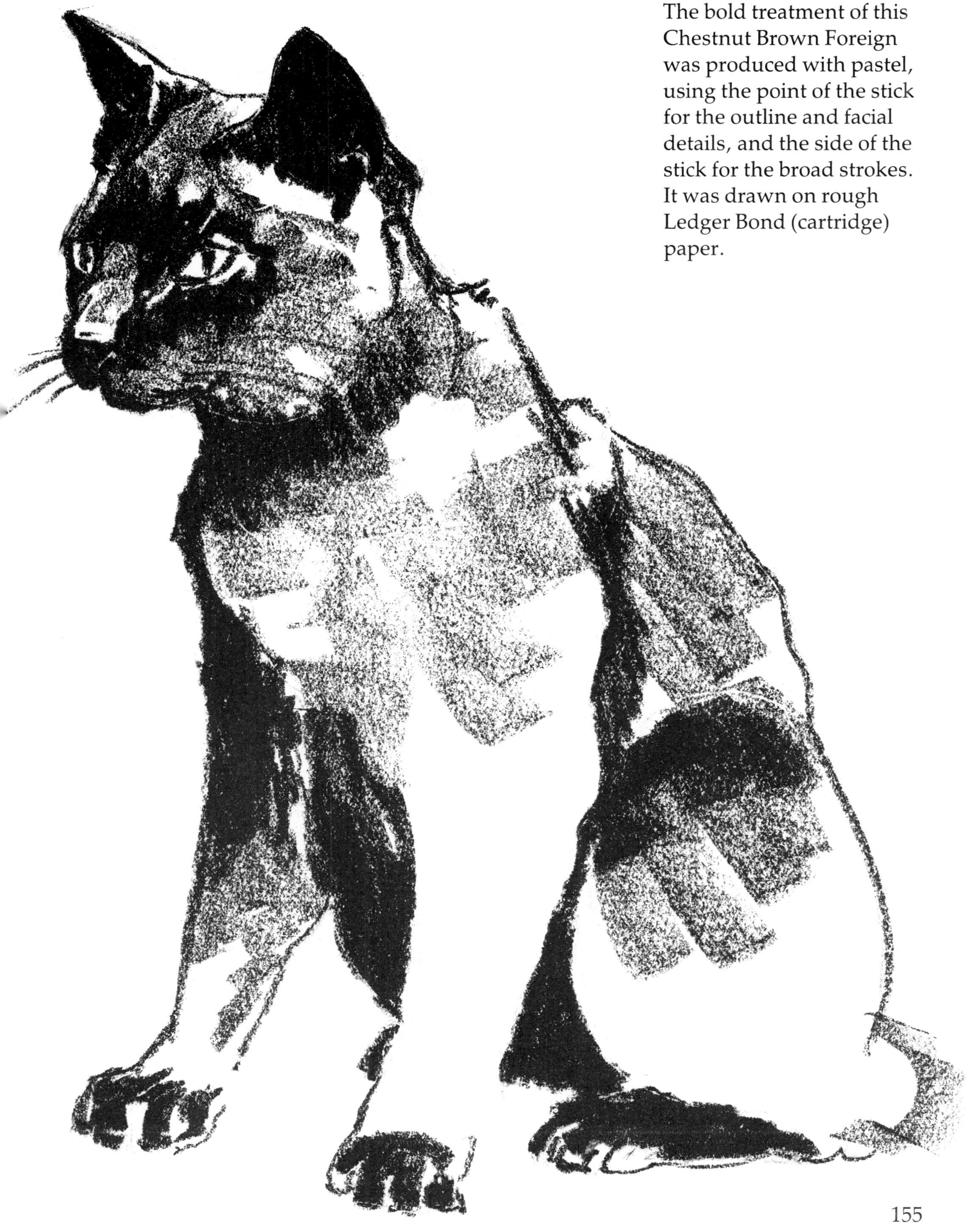

The bold treatment of this Chestnut Brown Foreign was produced with pastel, using the point of the stick for the outline and facial details, and the side of the stick for the broad strokes. It was drawn on rough Ledger Bond (cartridge) paper.

A 6B pencil on Kent cartridge (semi-rough) paper conveys the dark fluffy character of this Blue Persian's coat. A putty eraser was used to lighten certain areas.

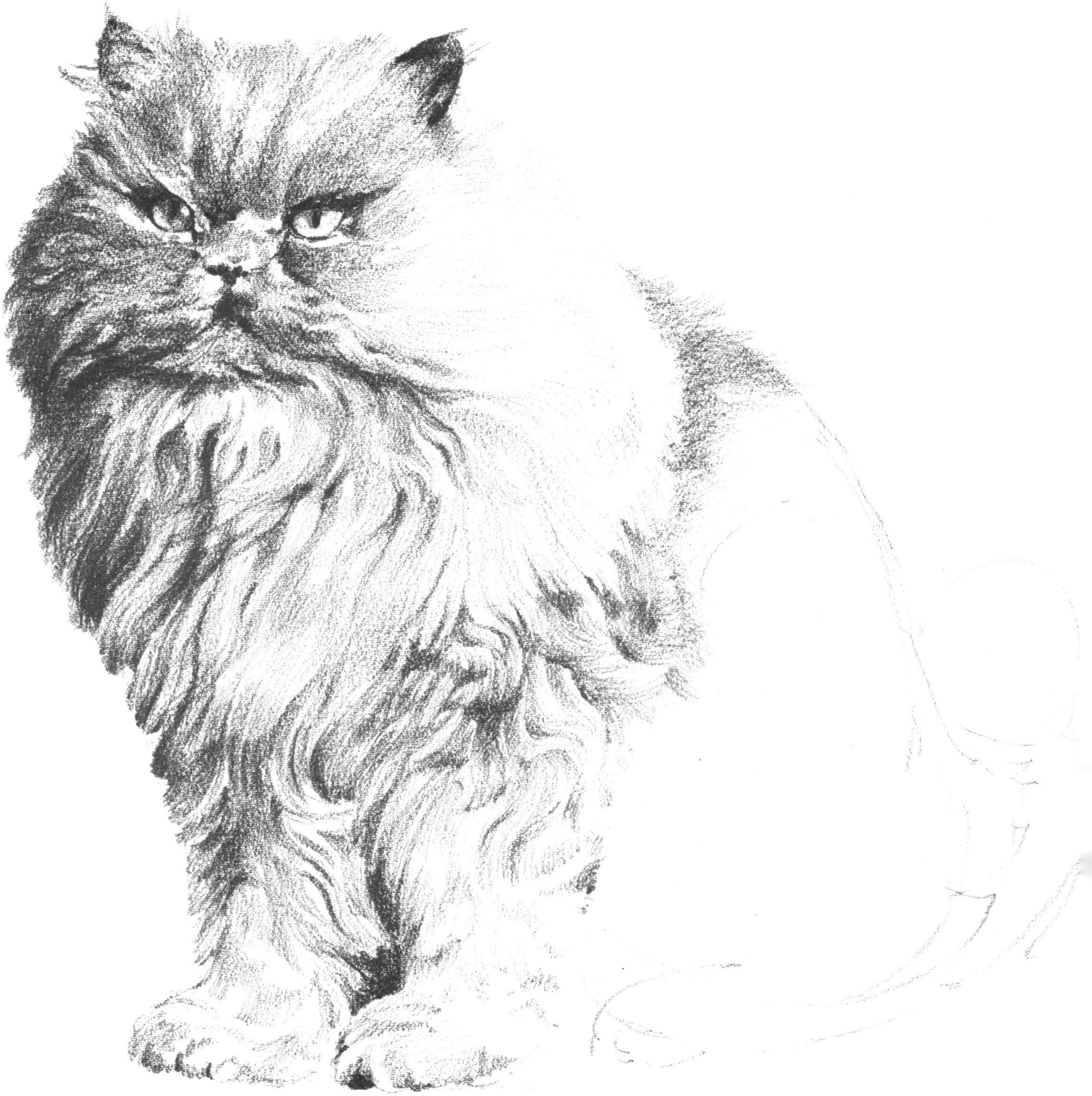

Pastel drawing on Ingres paper; only black and white pastels were used, the grey paper provided a middle tone.

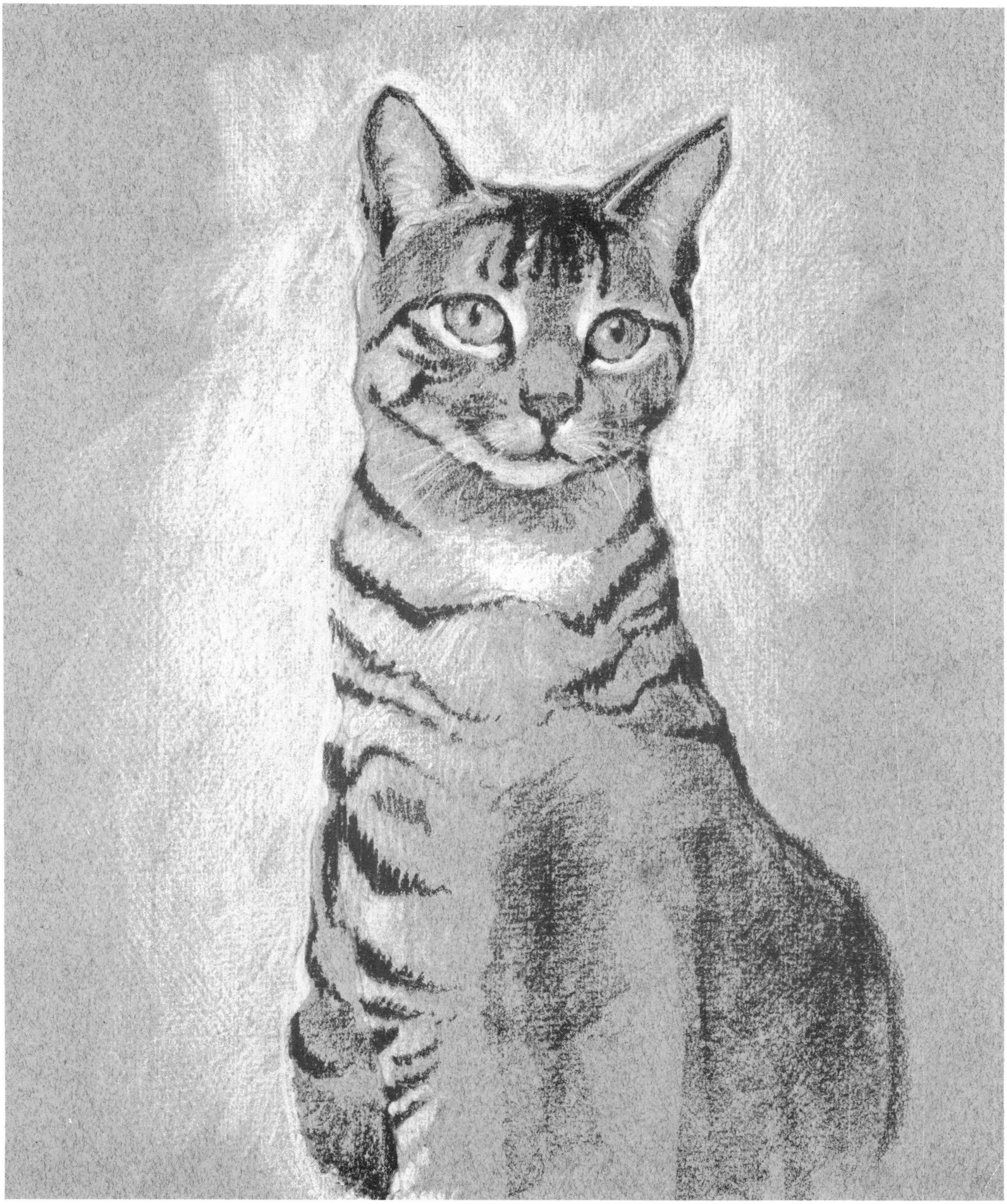

Birds

David Brown

This drawing shows a bird's bone structure. Take a close look at the next chicken you have for dinner, particularly if it is a fresh one, complete with head and claws. Study it before and after it is carved. Make detailed drawing notes—like these ones here, which show the varying shape of a claw brought about by the lifestyle of different birds.

Anatomy and shape

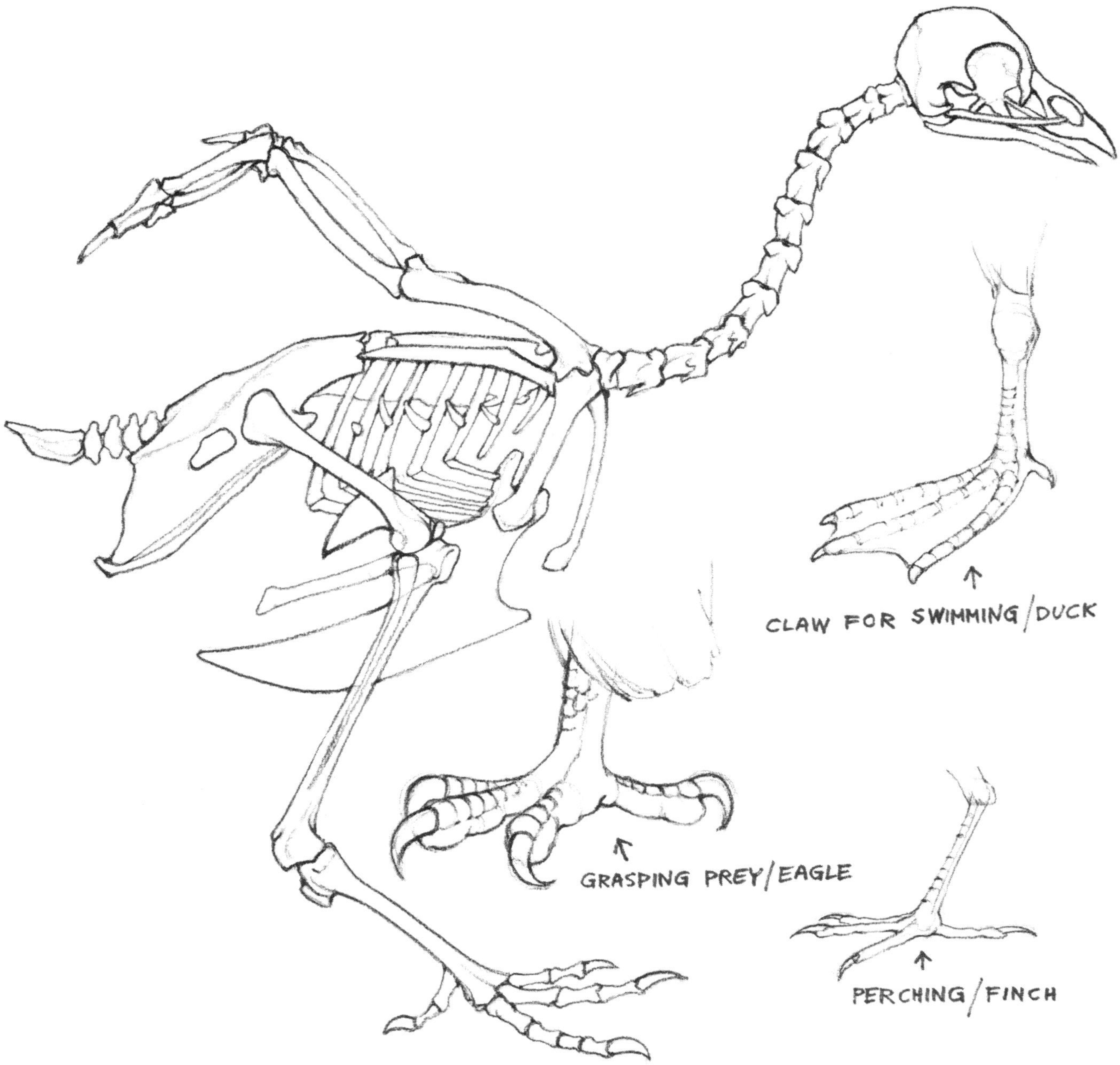

Study the various parts of the body, and again make detailed drawing notes and sketches. Notice how the wing of a swift (left) differs in shape from that of a thrush (right) although the construction is the same. Remember that tail feathers fold so that the centre ones are on top and the outside ones underneath, as in the diagram. The shape of each part of a bird's beak, eye, neck, wing, tail, leg, claw varies according to the needs of its environment and eating habits.

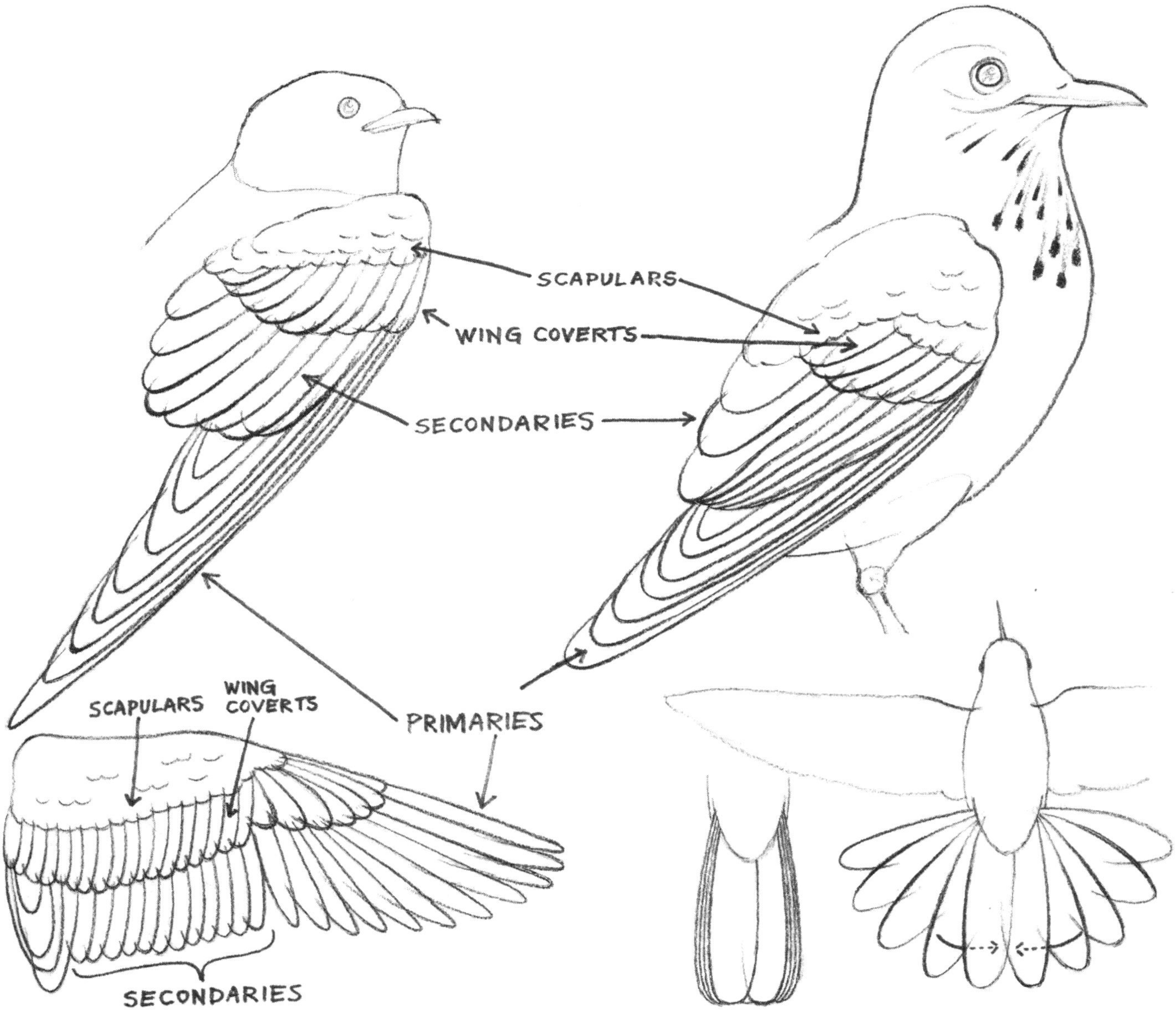

Heads come in many shapes. Notice the beak size of the hornbill compared with that of the birds or prey below—who need a small curved beak to tear the flesh of their victims. The long, streamlined beak of the kingfisher helps it to catch fish. Notice also the size of the eye in relation to the rest of the head. Flesh-eating birds need large, powerful eyes to see, from great distance, the small animals on which they live.

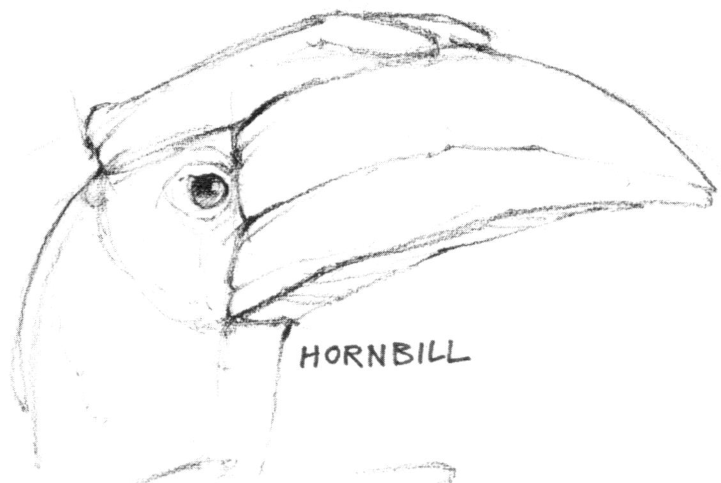

HORNBILL

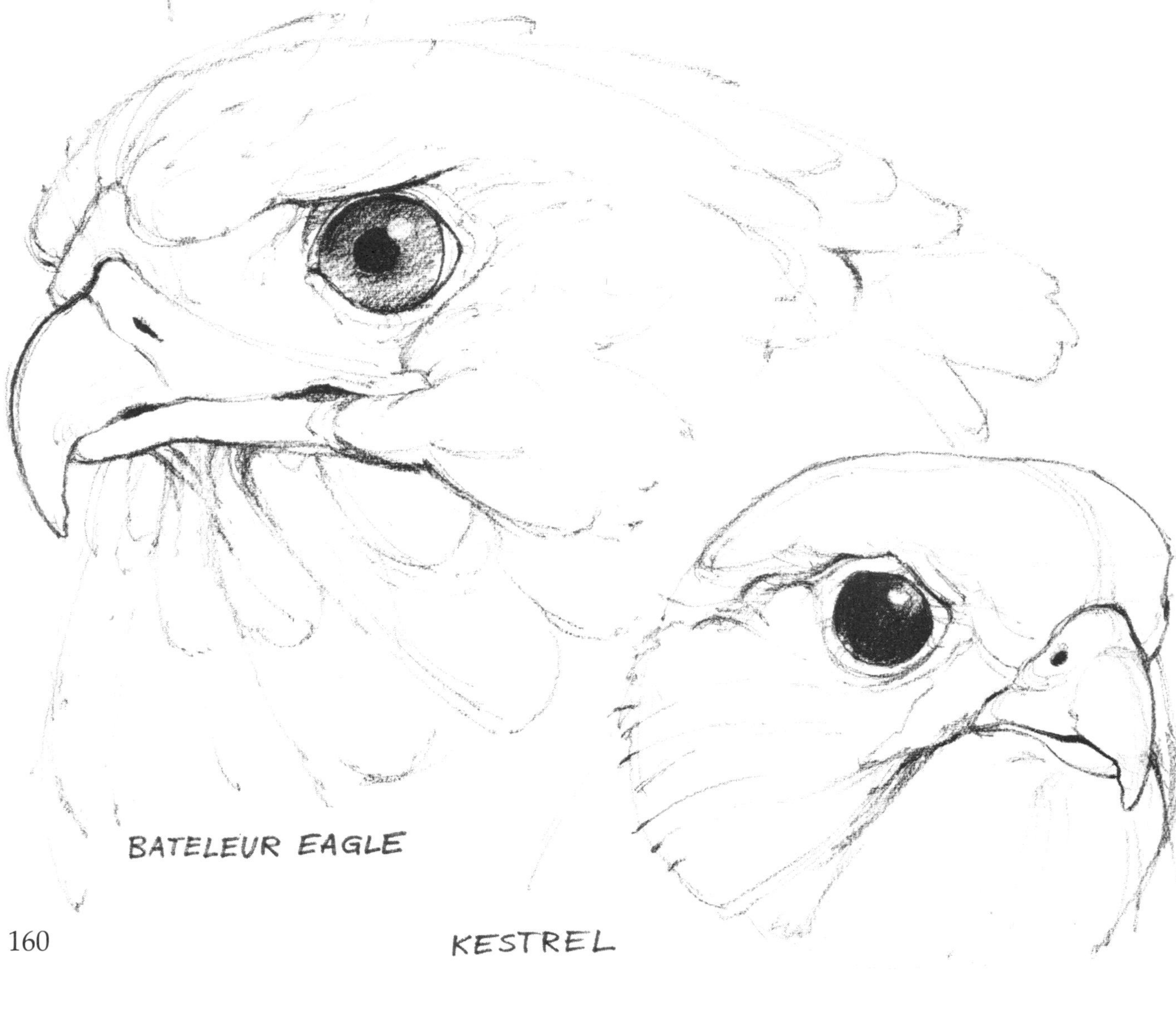

BATELEUR EAGLE

KESTREL

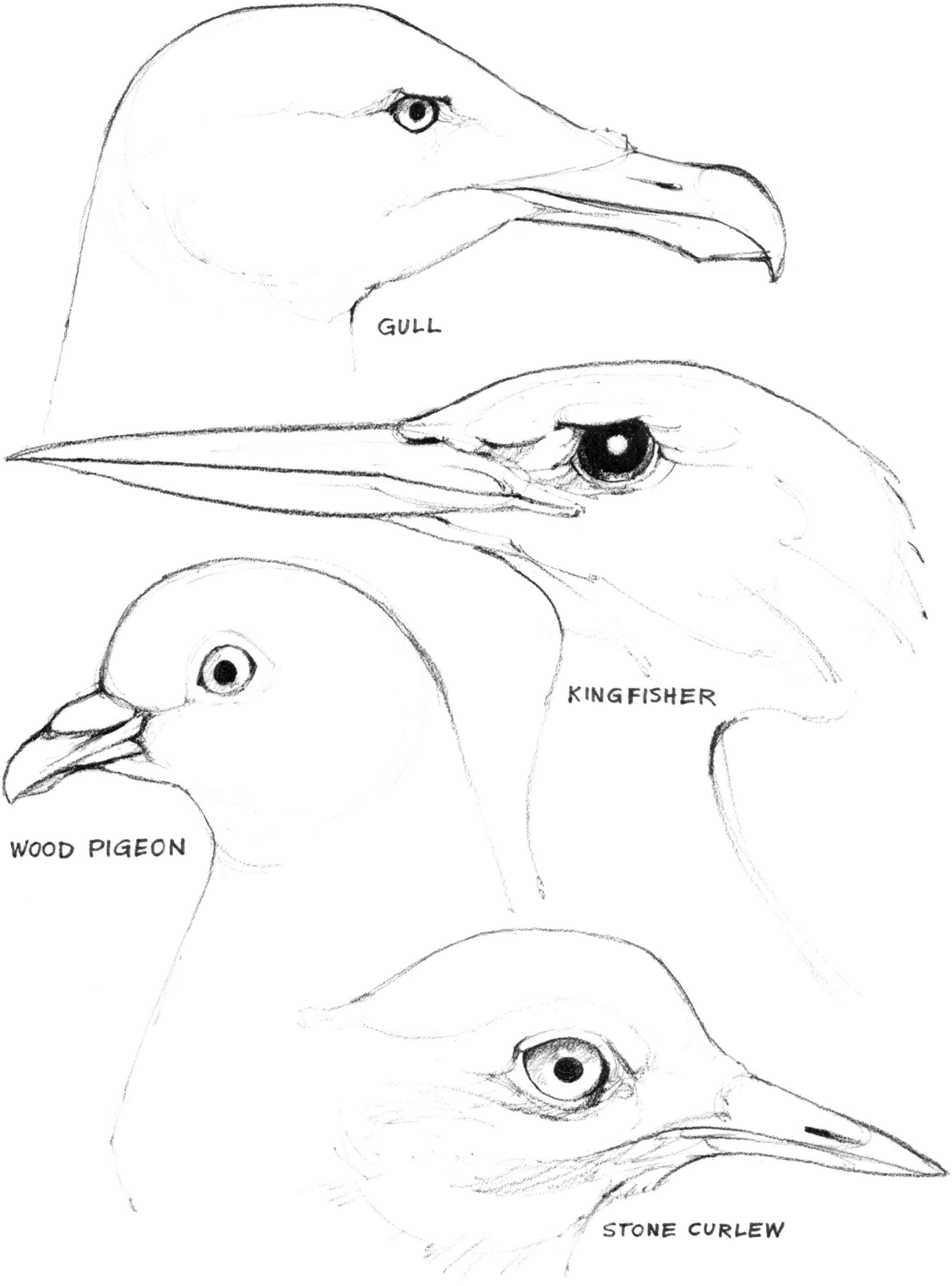
GULL
KINGFISHER
WOOD PIGEON
STONE CURLEW

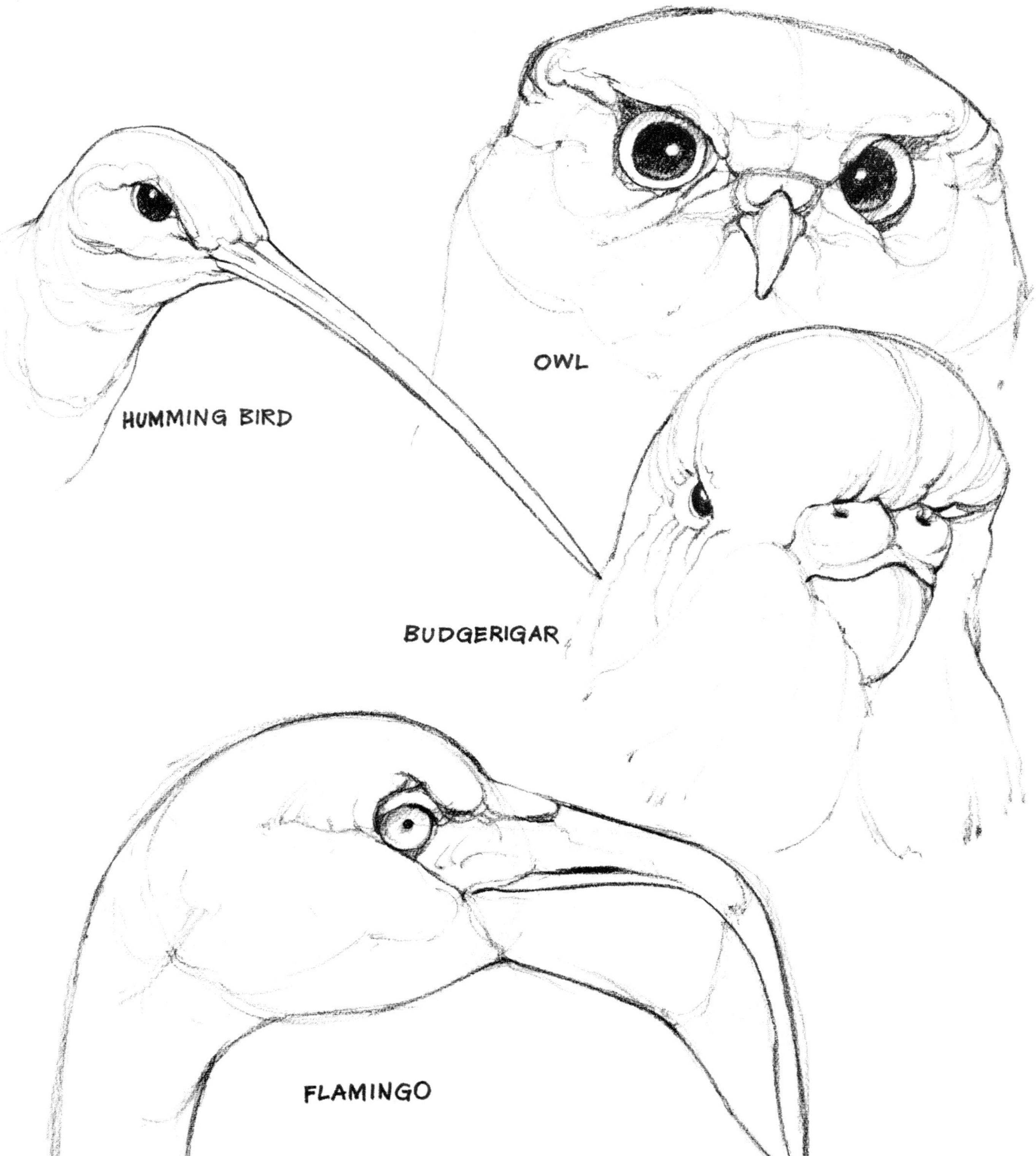
OWL
HUMMING BIRD
BUDGERIGAR
FLAMINGO

You can best capture the expression and mood of your subject by studying the eyes. Compare the penetrating gaze of an owl with the inquisitive wide eyes of a parrot.

While actually drawing, go on comparing the shapes and proportions of the various parts. Observe, for example, whether the distance between the base of the beak and the eye of a Blue Tit is equal to the width of his eye.

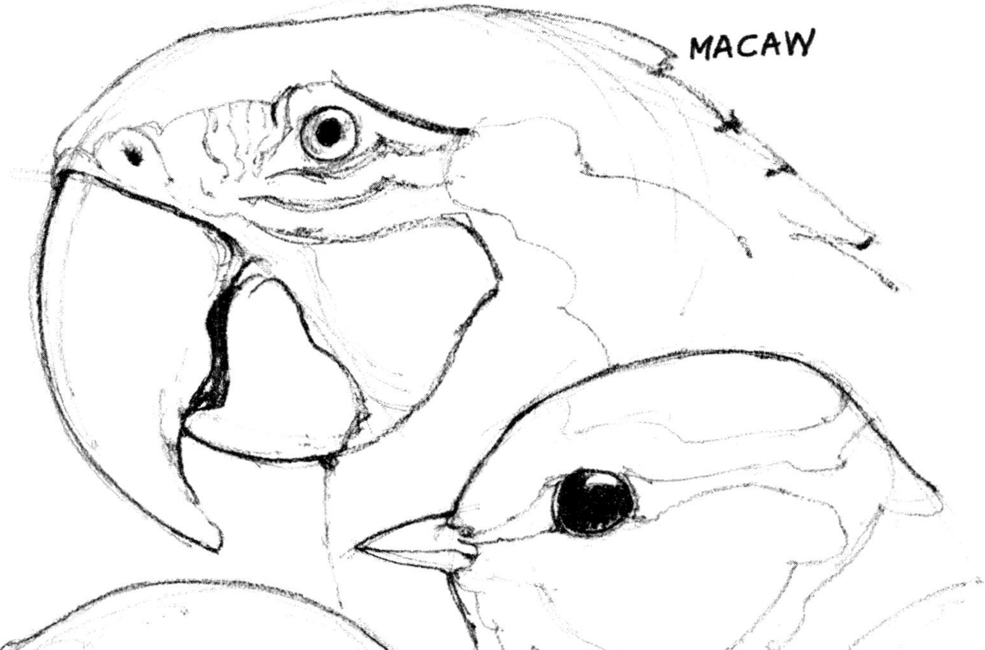

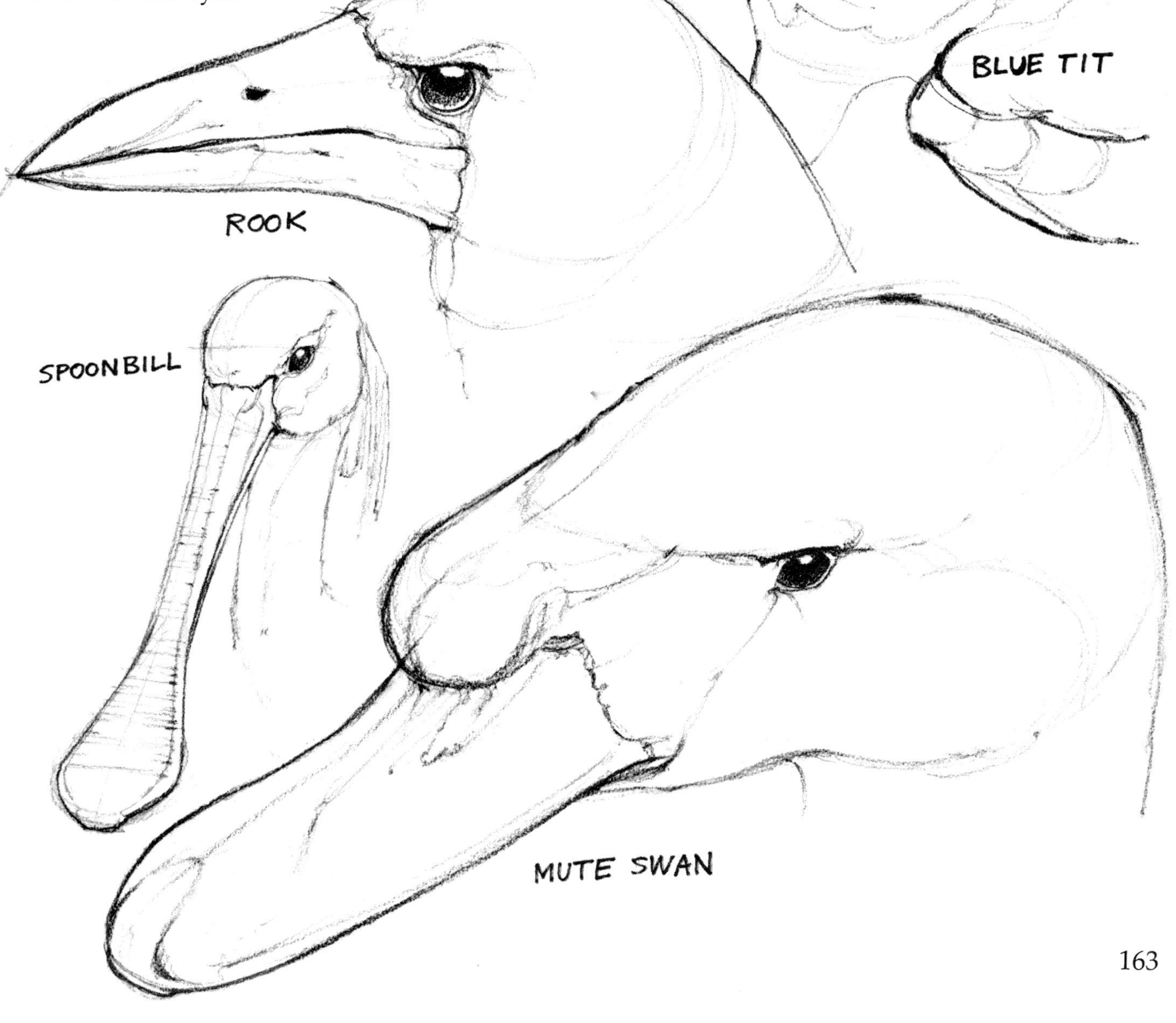

Proportion

Compare the drawings on these two pages with those on pages 52, 101 and 127. The advice given there will help you to get the proportions right in your drawings of birds and to get a feeling of movement into their poses.

Practice in measuring proportions will train your eye to *see* proportions correctly. You can use photographs to start with, or better still visit a museum which has cases of stuffed birds.

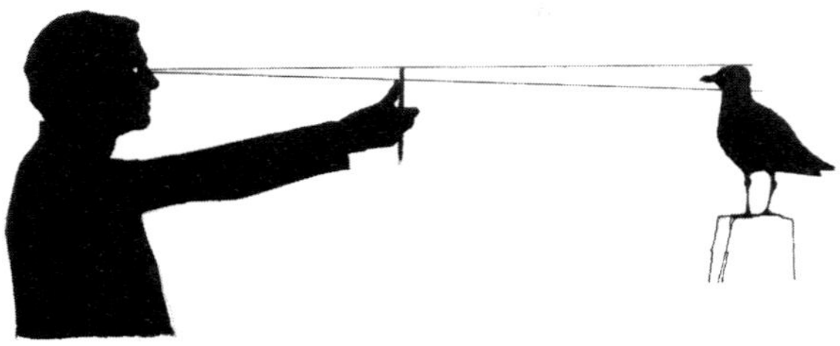

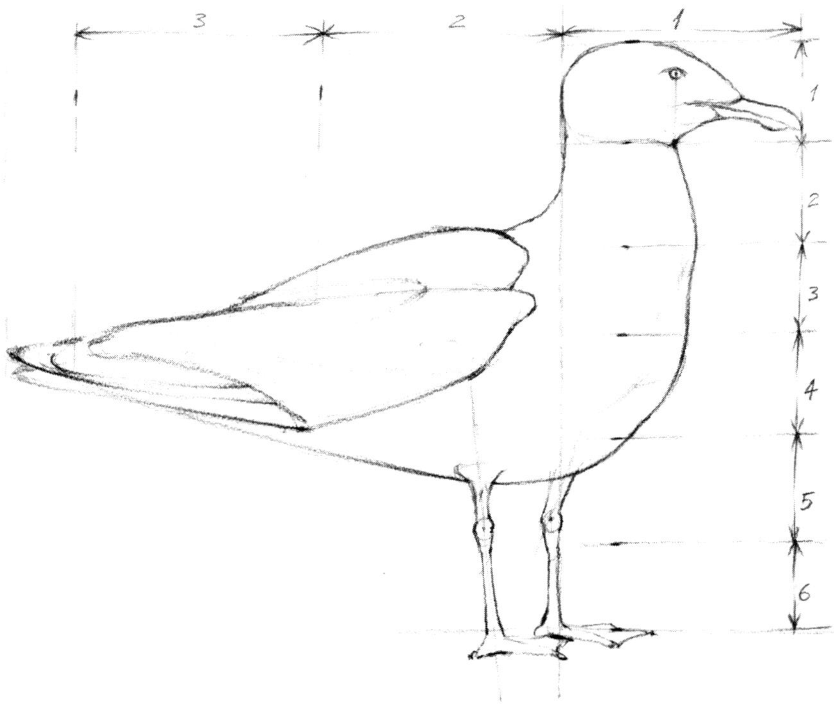

Study the shape of a bird carefully, noticing which parts of the body line up and what angles are produced by the shape of the body. Draw contour lines over various parts of the anatomy to show the whole form.

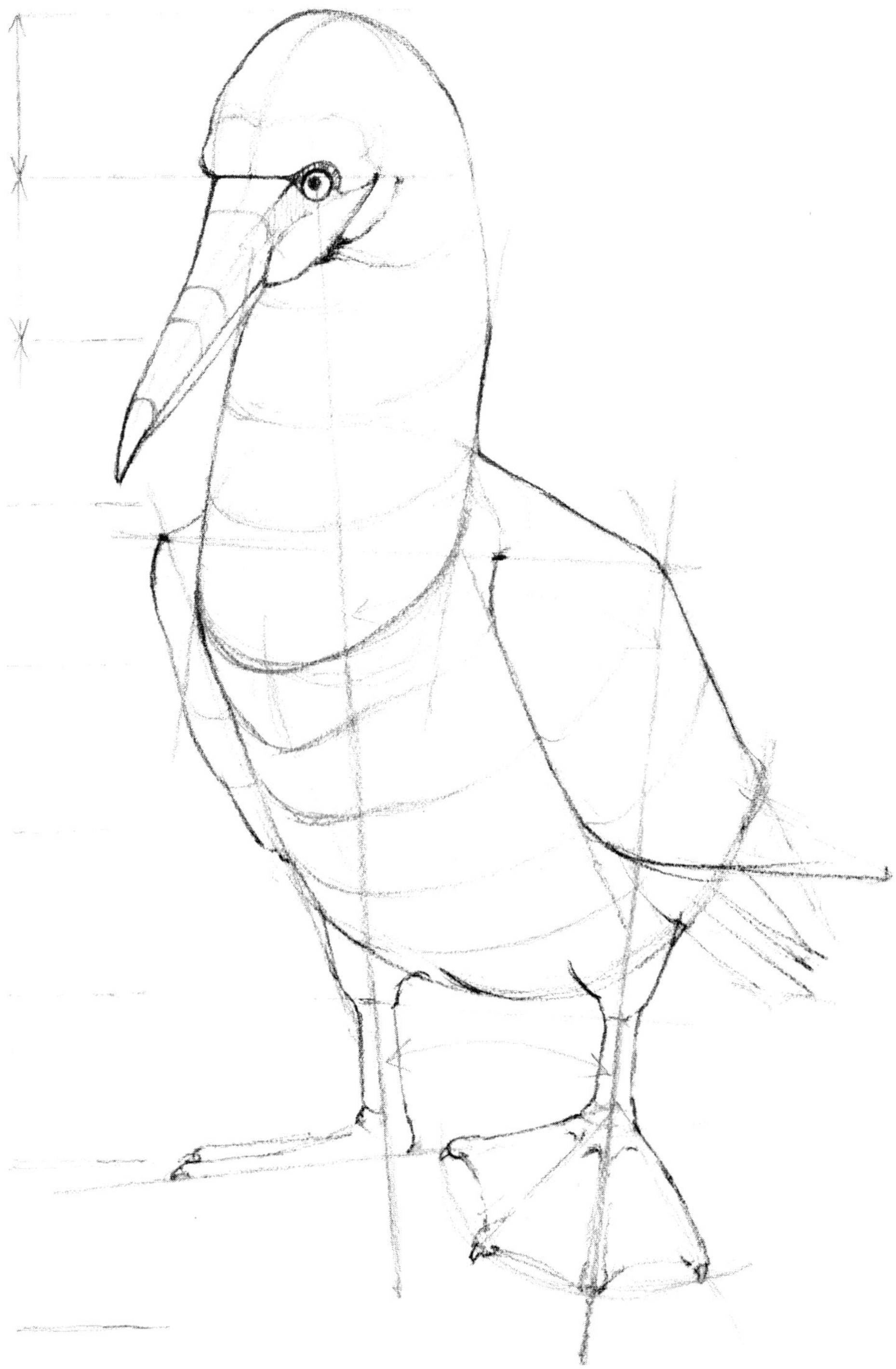

Basic shapes

As with other animals, when starting a drawing, try to see your subject in its simplest form. It helps to half-close your eyes. By doing so you shut out most of the detail, which allows you to concentrate on the basic shapes.

Notice how similar is the basic body shape of each of these long-legged birds.

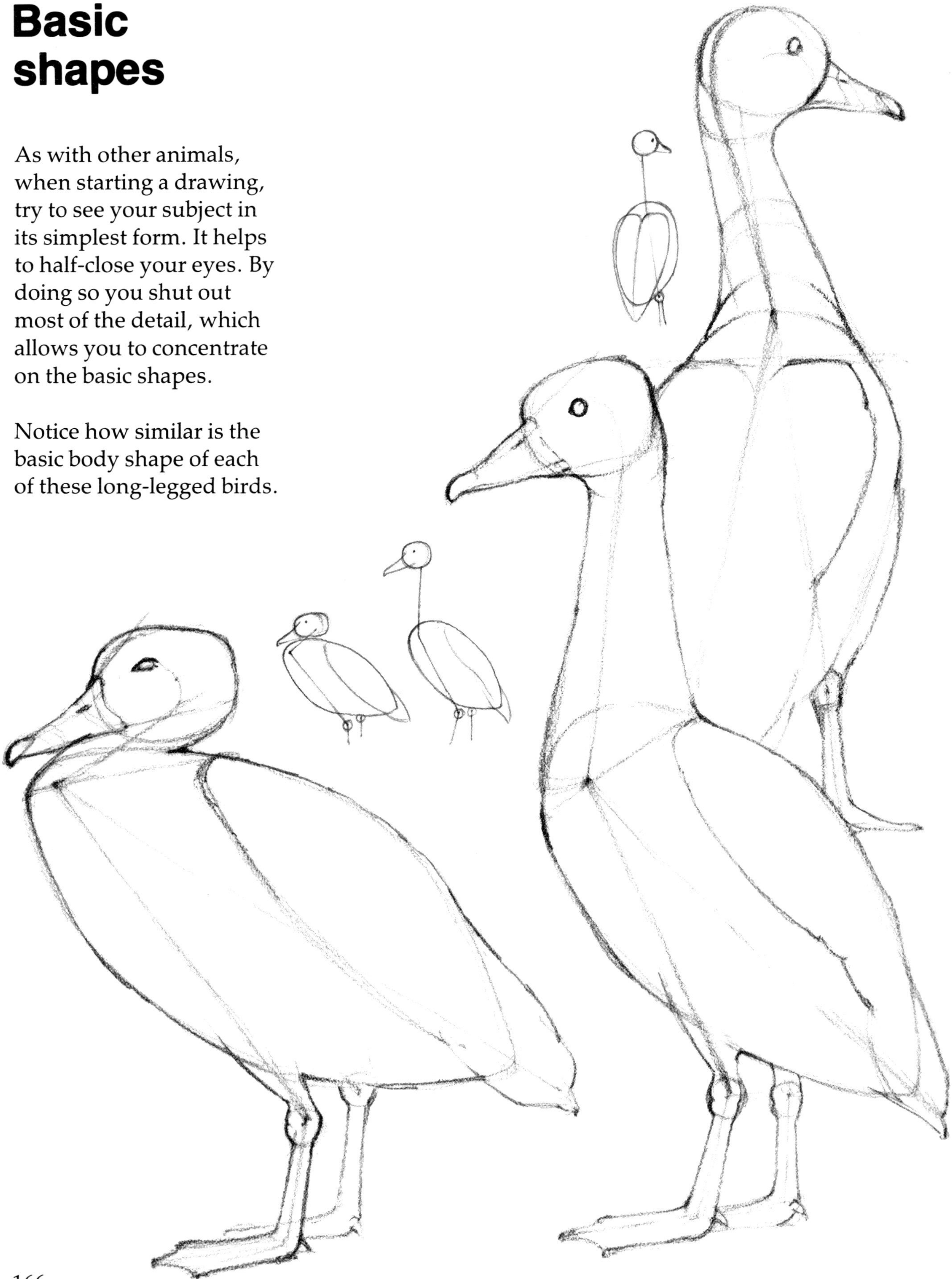

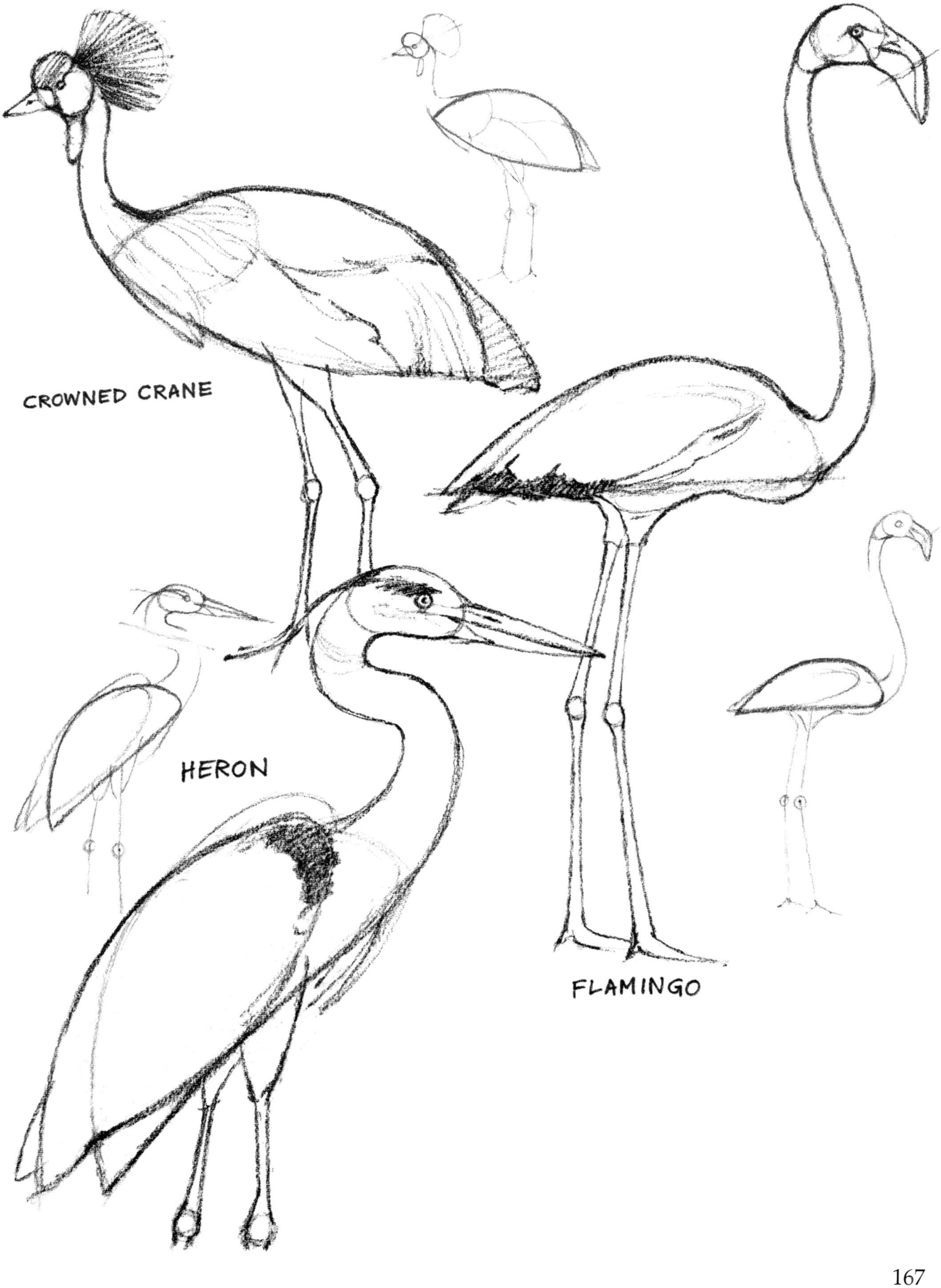
CROWNED CRANE
HERON
FLAMINGO

The penguin makes a good model, because he will often hold a pose for several minutes. Take a sketching pad with you the next time you visit a zoo.

Little birds are not so obliging. You need a lot of patience to draw them from life, though a bird-table near a window will help.

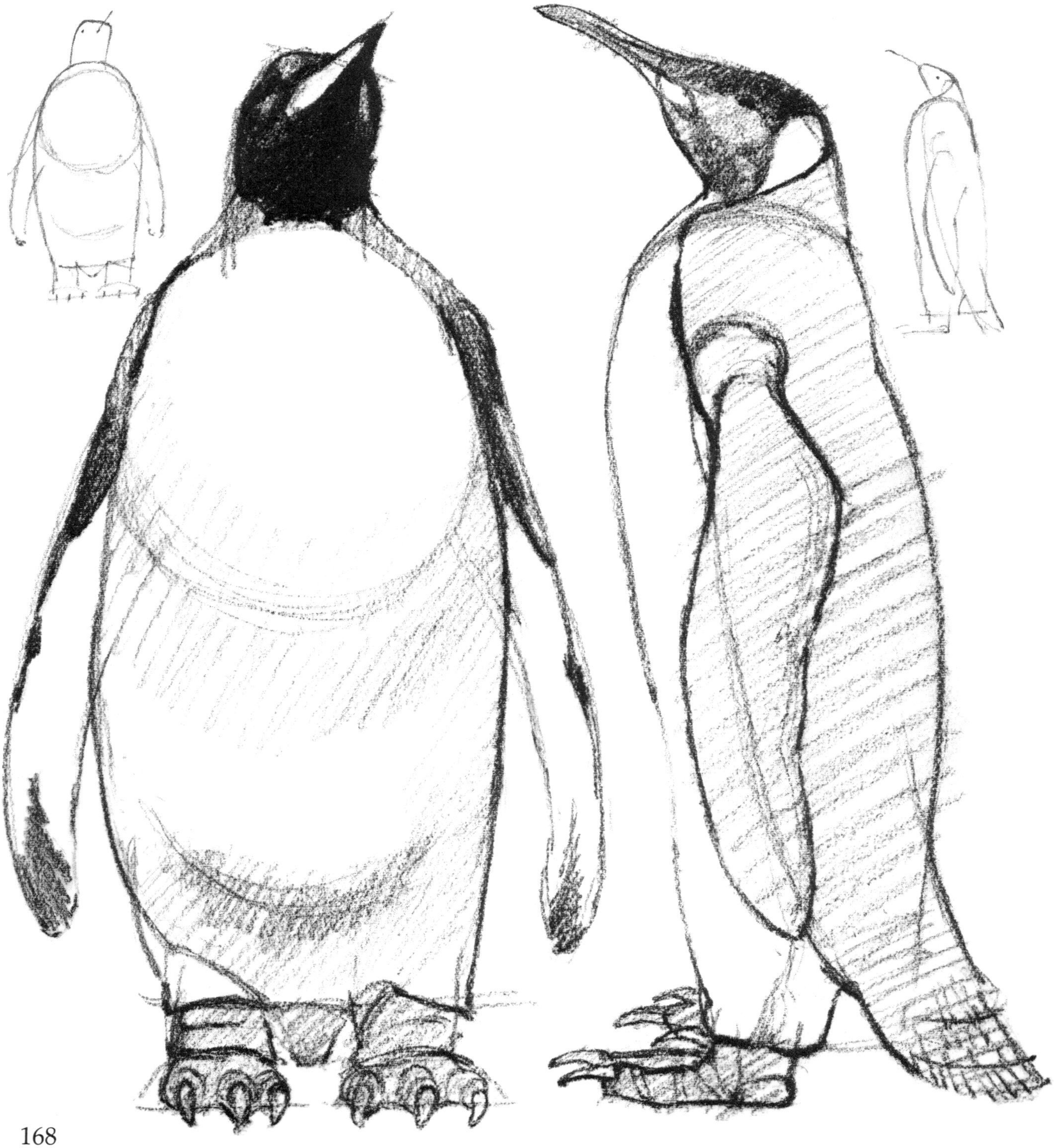

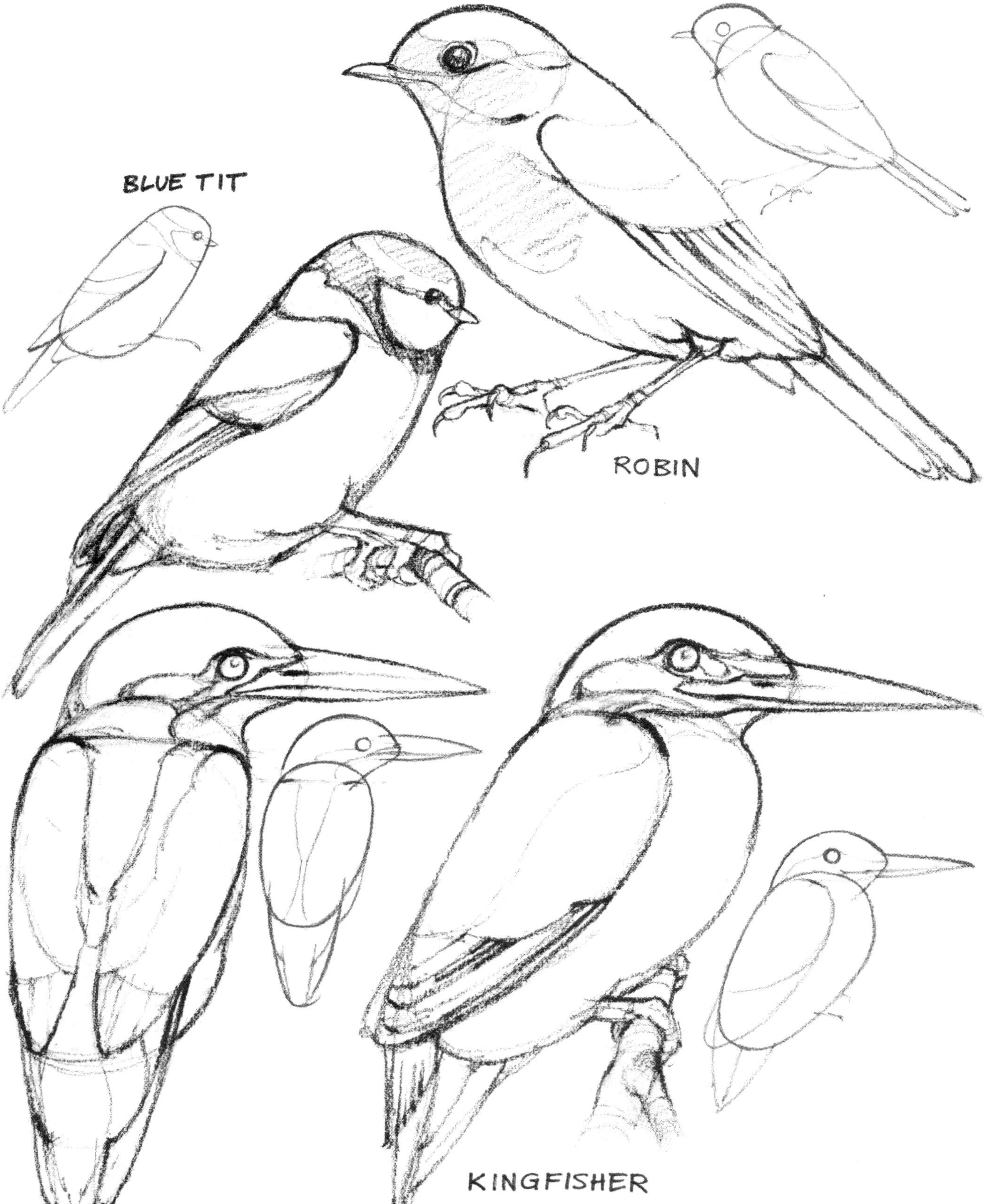
BLUE TIT
ROBIN
KINGFISHER

Construct your drawings; don't simply draw them in outline. Notice how one part of a bird fits into the next. Look at the size of its feet in relation to its head. Chickens need large, strong feet for scratching the ground.

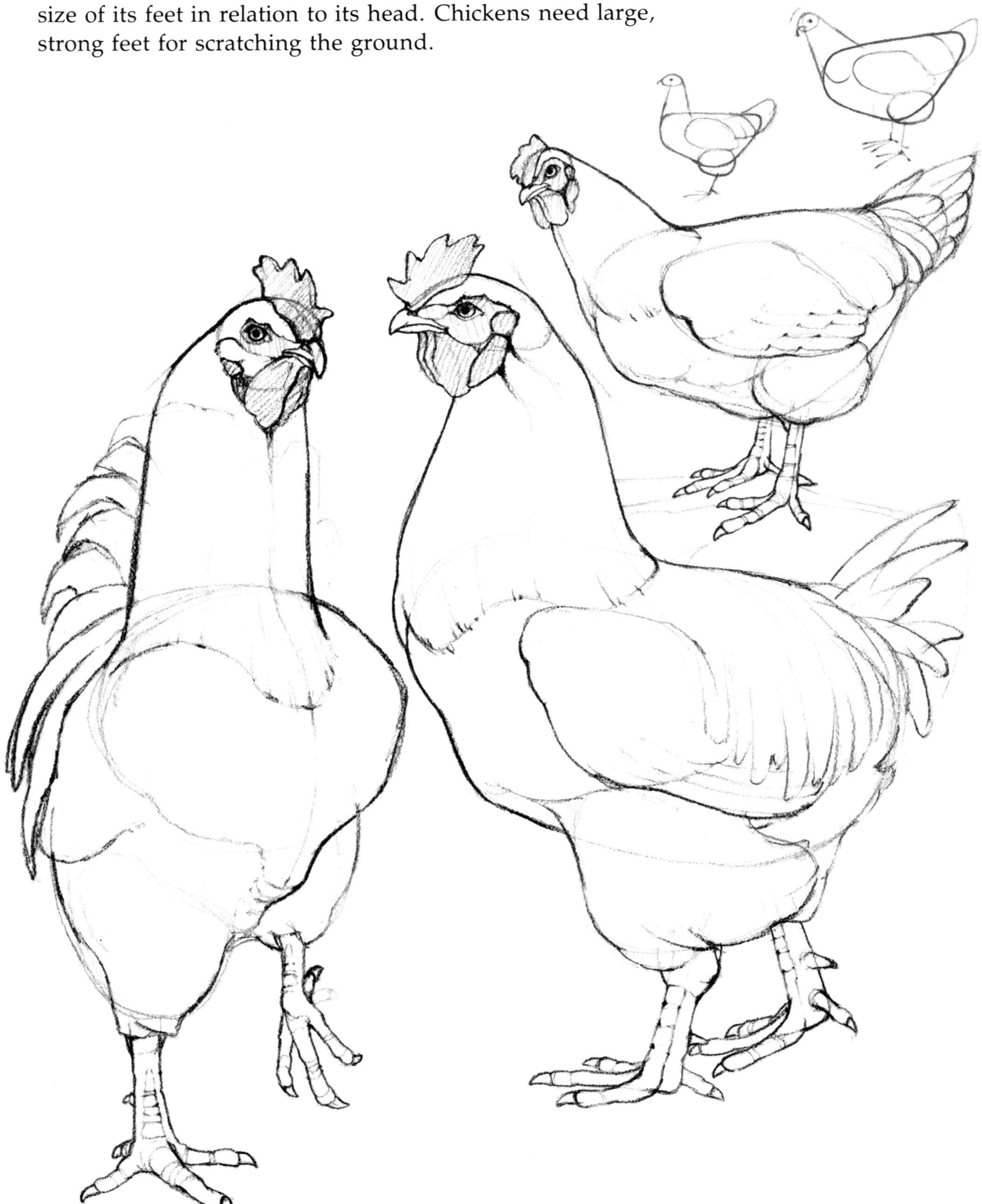

The basic shape of a puffin is a pointed egg. This is true for its head as well as its body. A goose's body-shape is more of a triangle.

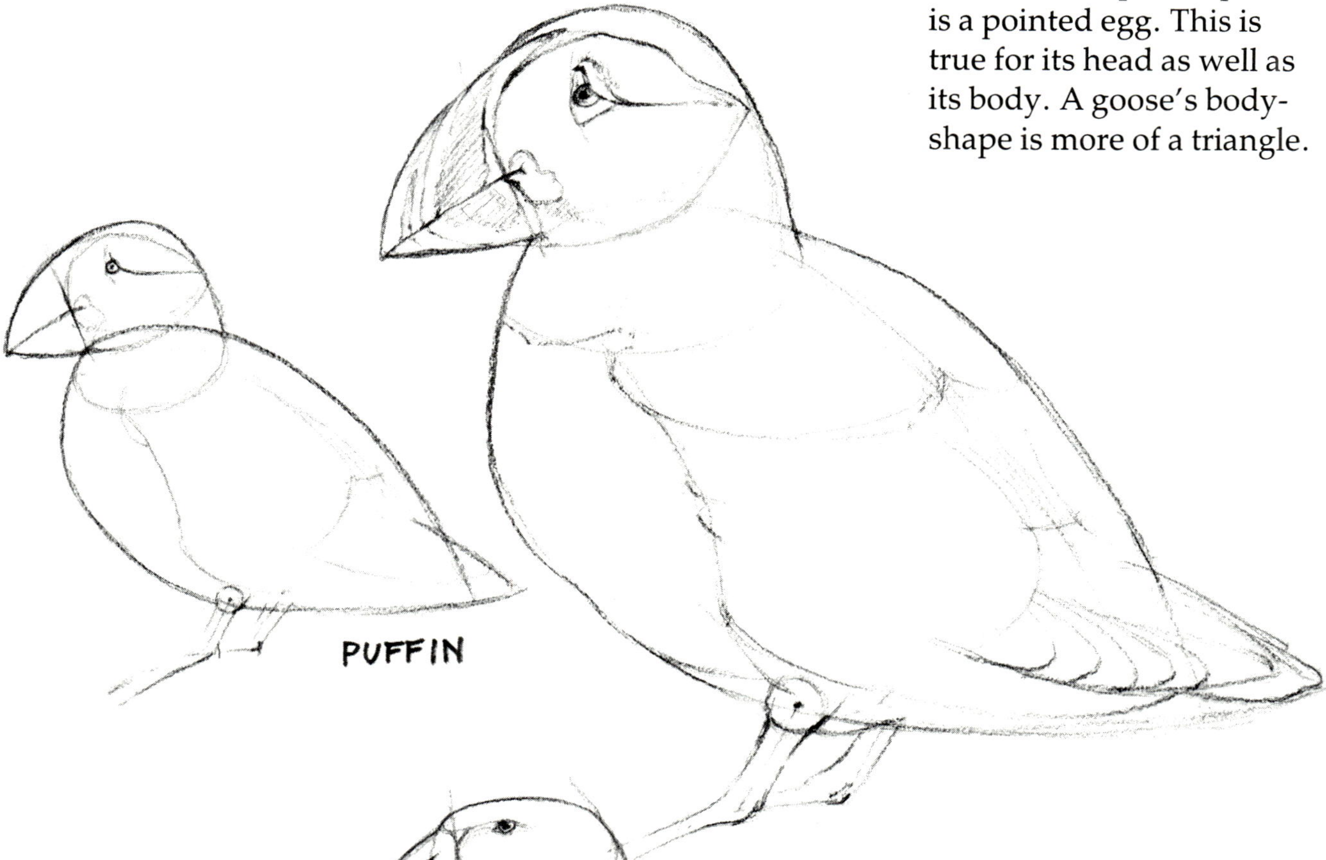

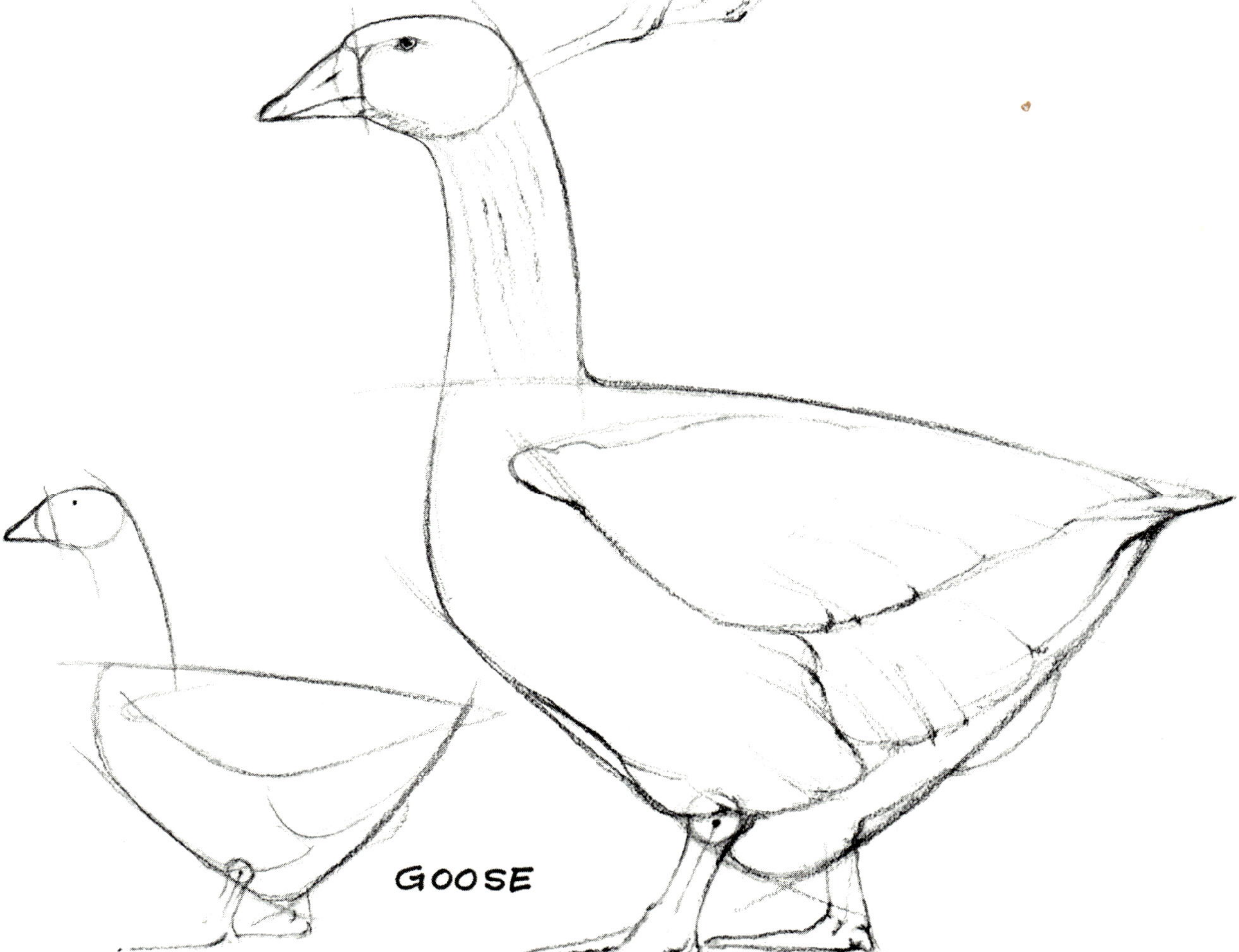

If you draw one particular bird from several viewpoints, you will get to understand its anatomy more quickly than if you always draw the same view.

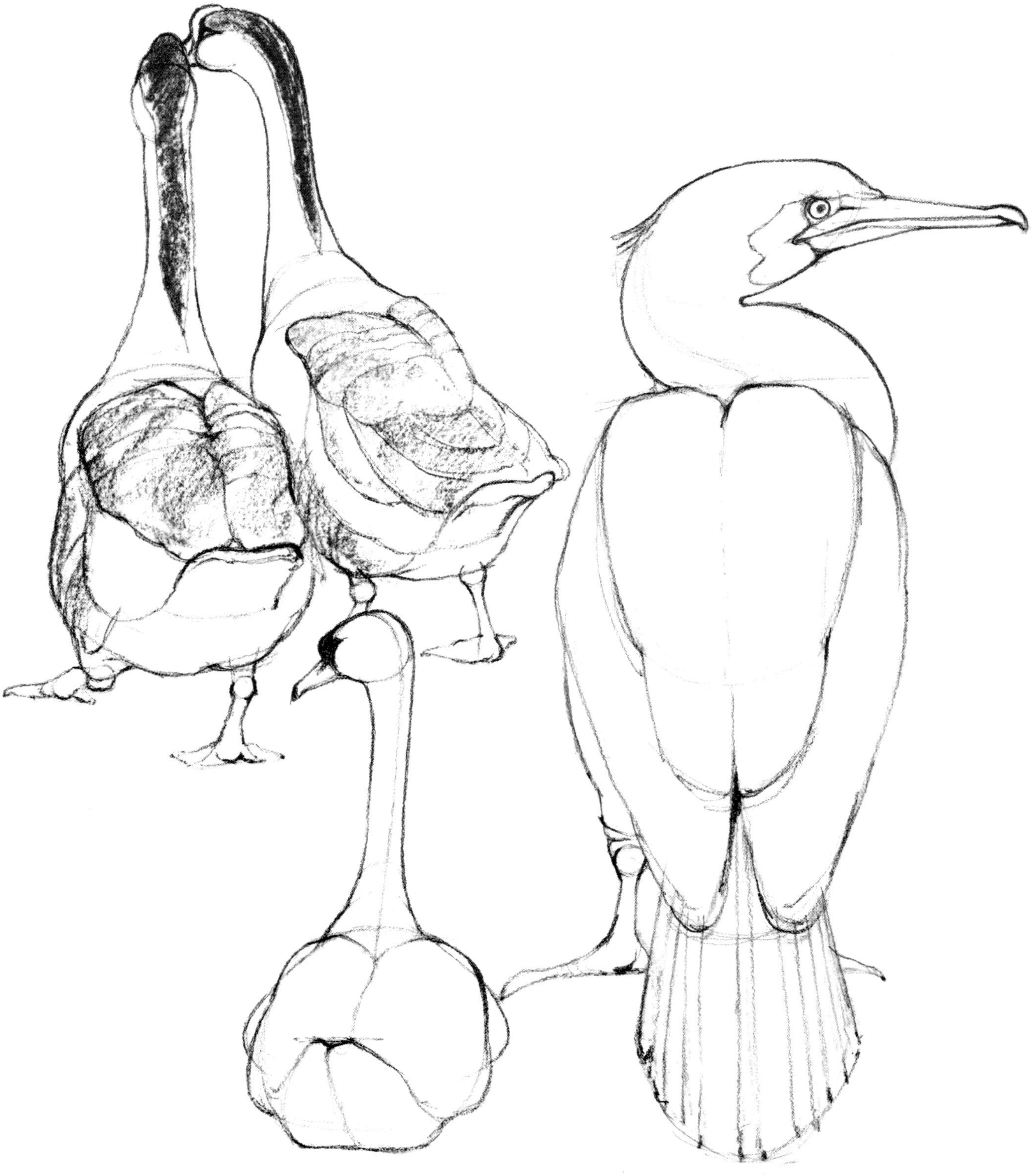

It is not easy to capture movement when drawing from photographs or stuffed birds. I find it helps to hold my pencil vertically (making sure it is at right-angles to the floor) and then run my eyes down it noting the position and angles of the various parts of the subject's body.

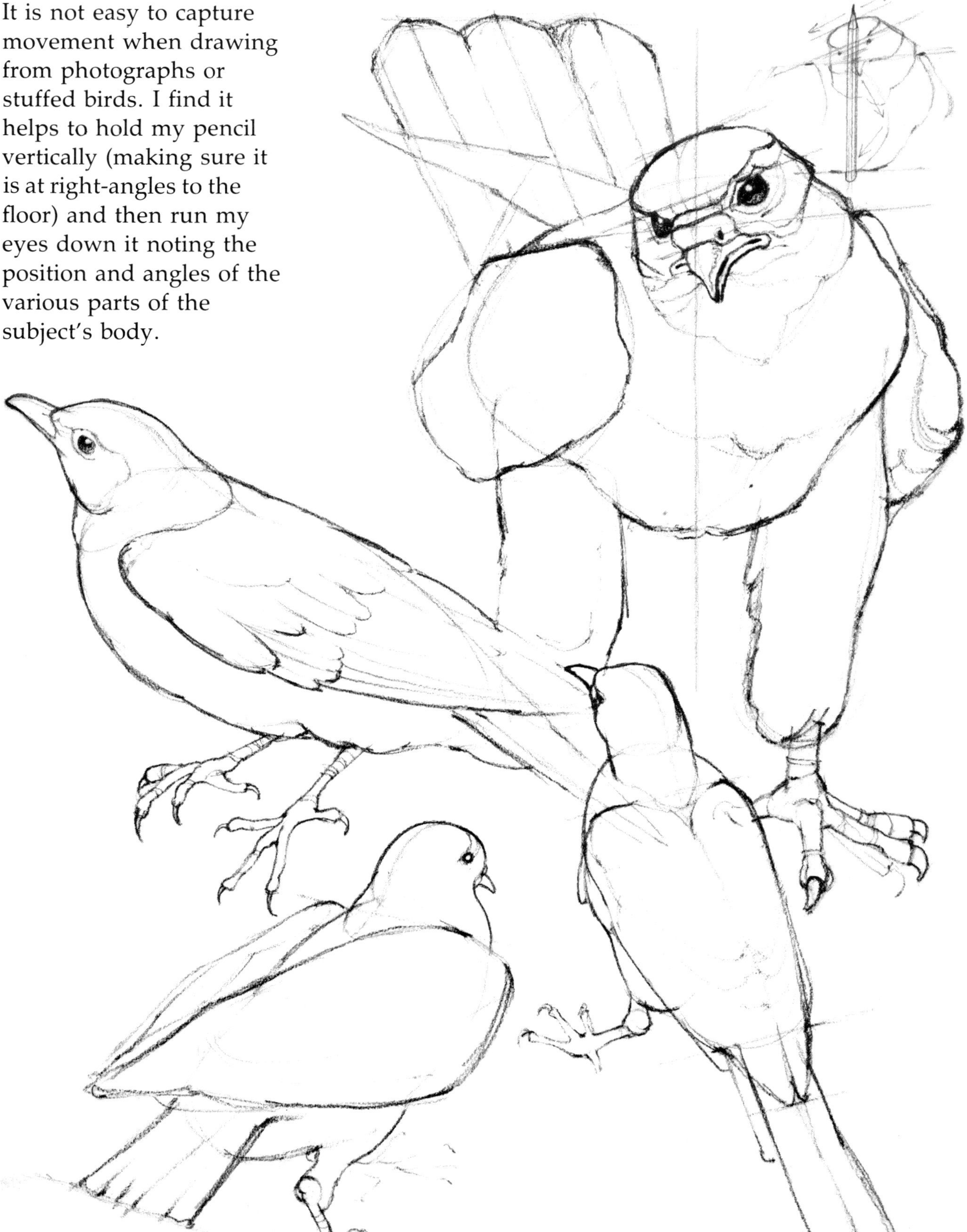

Step-by-step

The following pages show the development from first lines to the finished drawing. Draw the basic lines, and don't be timid about adding imaginary ones such as those marked 'A' to help you get the correct position of features in relation to one another. For instance, the lower vertical line on this page helps to establish correctly the curve of the neck in relation to the head. Remember, to get the proportions right, you must continually compare the length, width and shape of the various areas (see pages 162–4).

Note the direction from which light is coming and put in shaded areas. Vary line and shading by varying the pressure on your pencil. In the finished drawing opposite notice that the line is soft in light areas and heavy in dark ones.

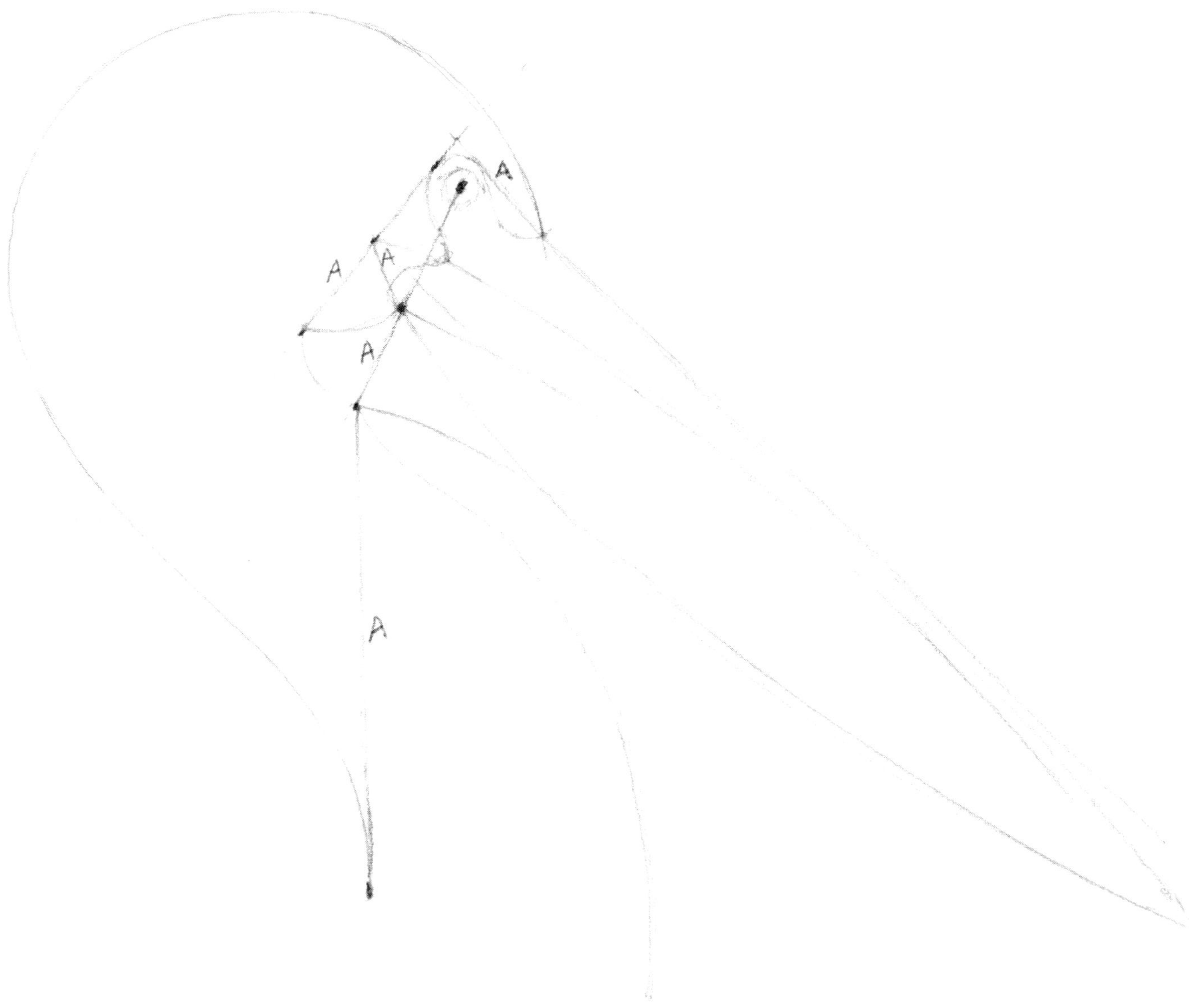

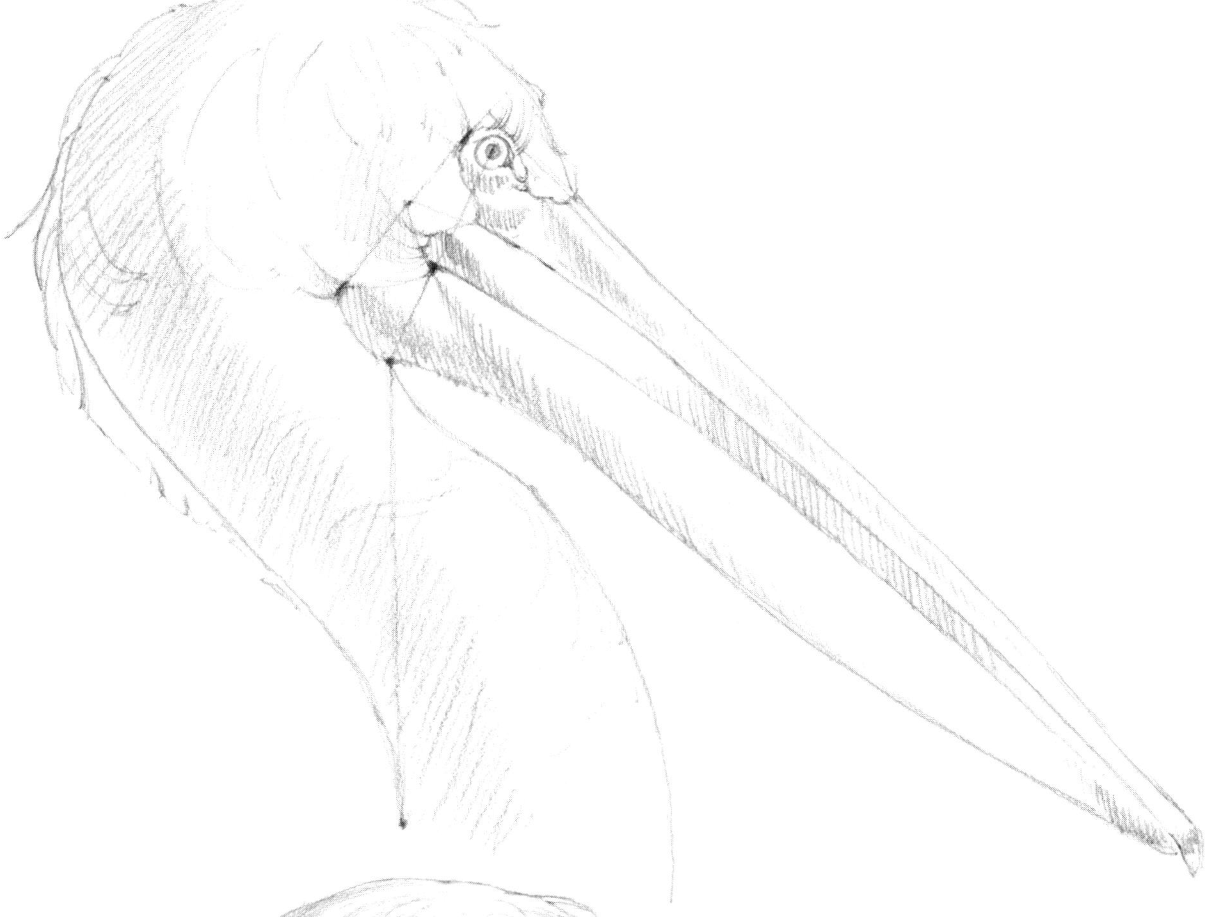

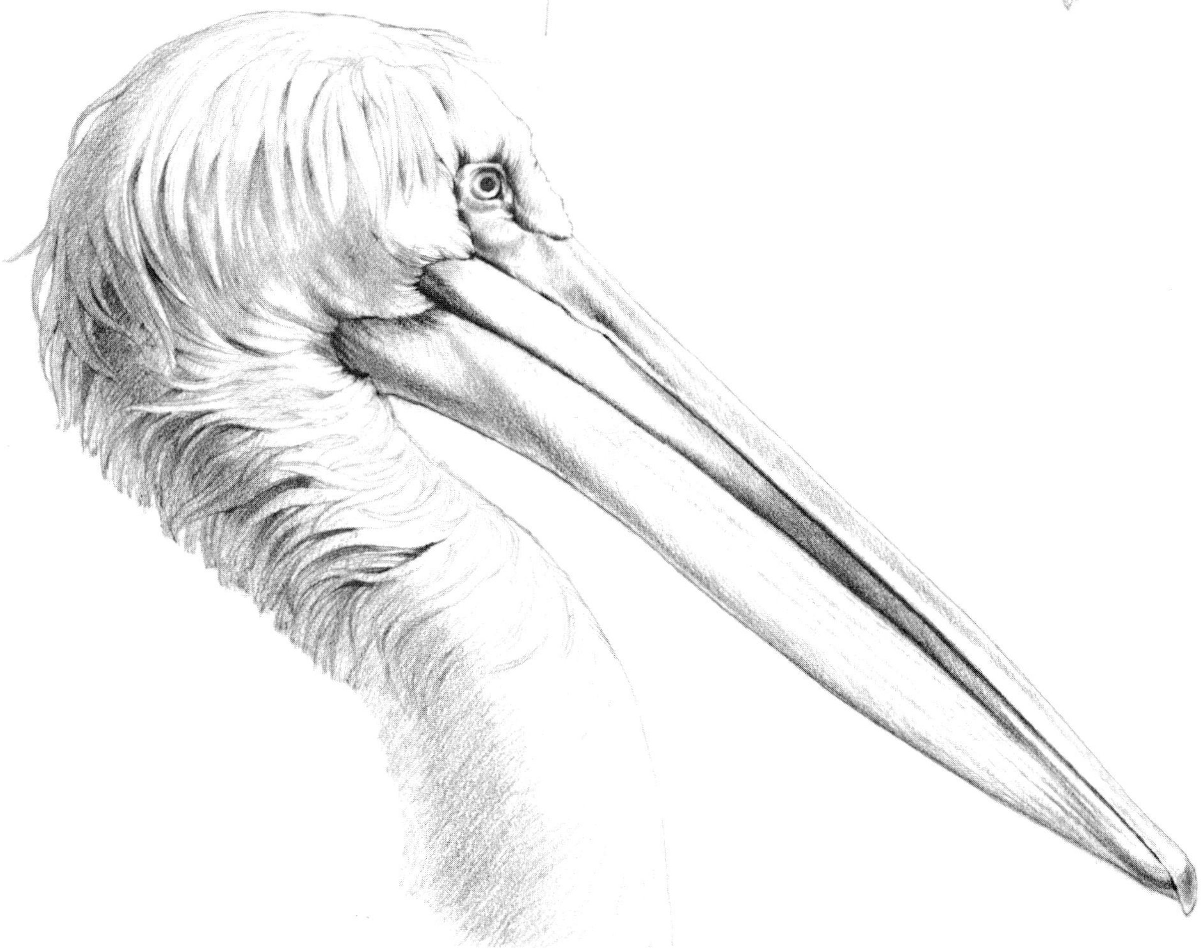

A lapwing. If you half-close your eyes, most of the detail will be shut out which helps you to see your subject in its simplest form.

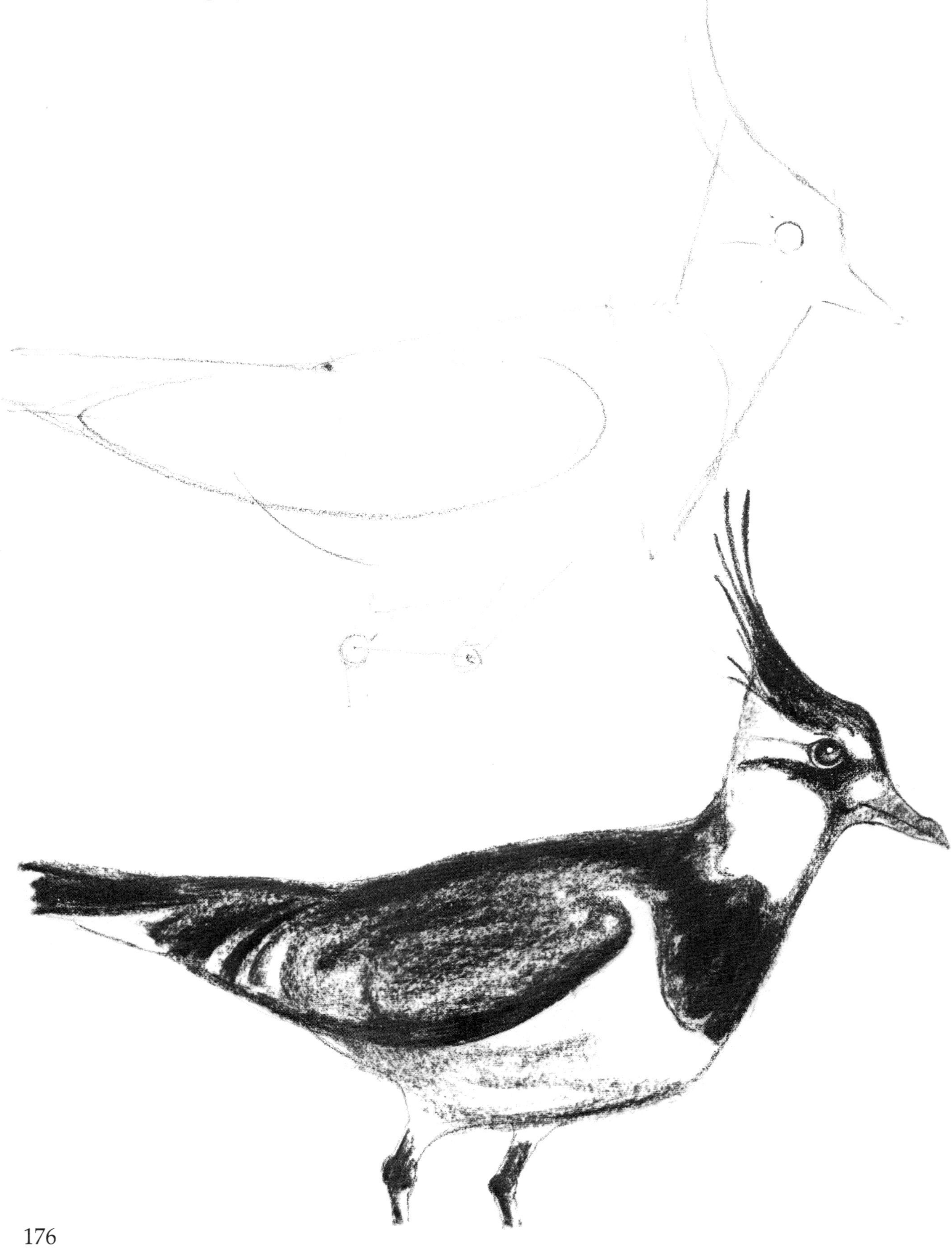

This pen and ink drawing of a little owl was finished with a wash of diluted ink.

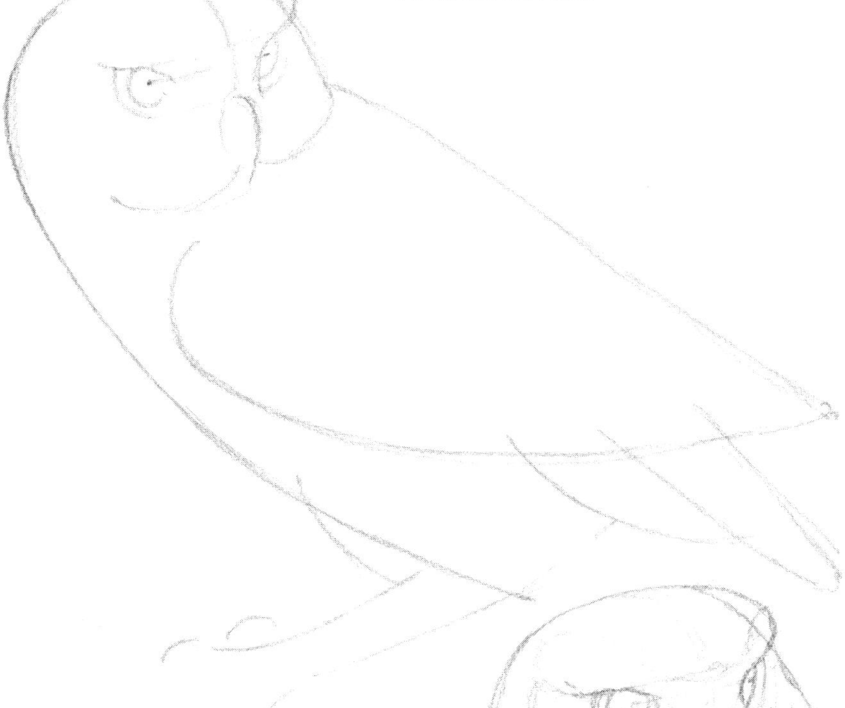

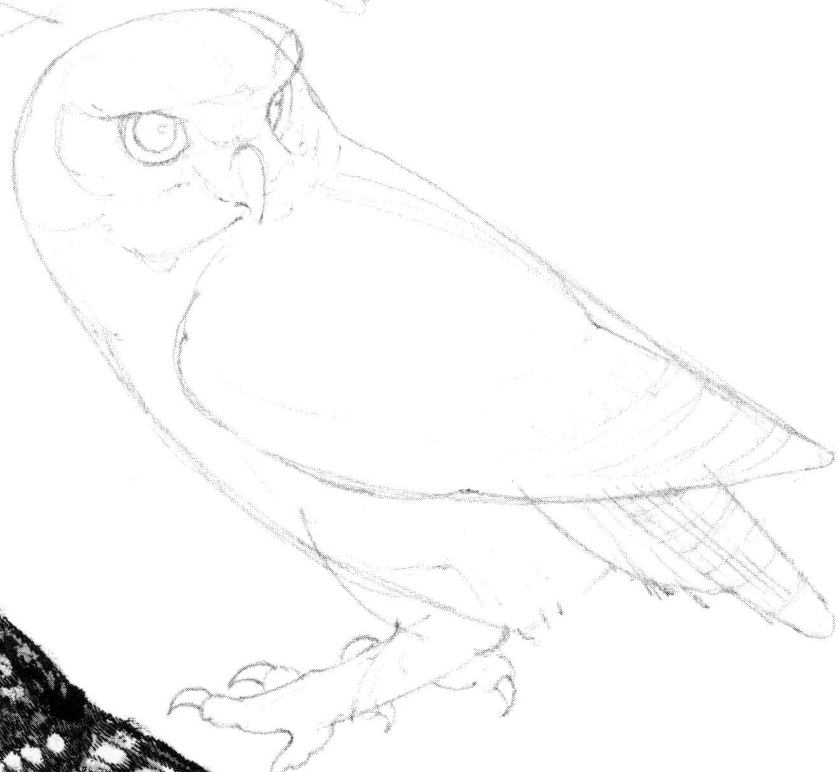

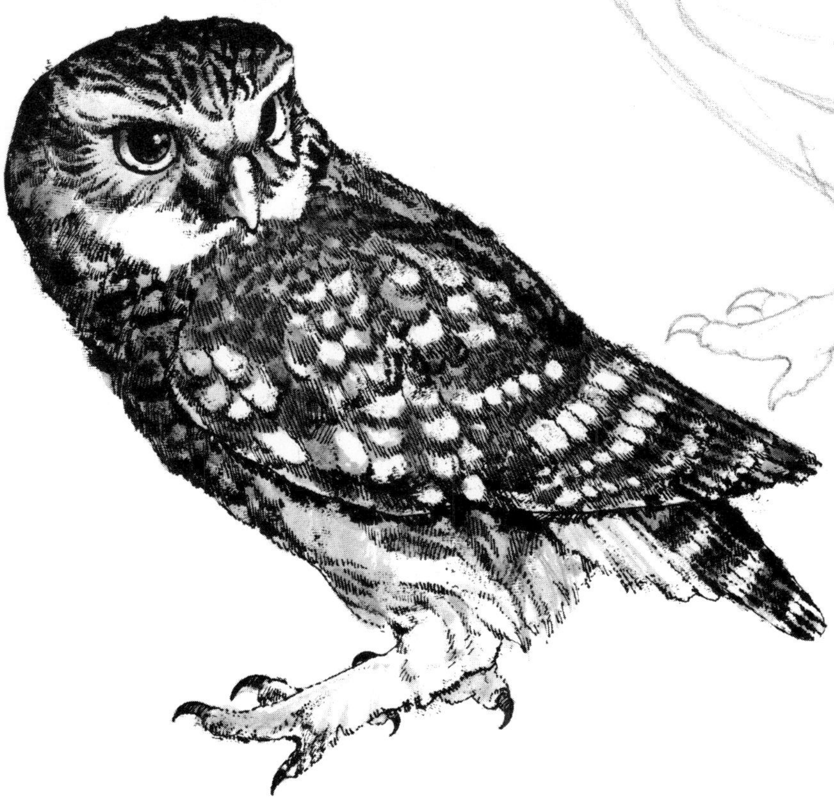

The basic drawing of this Crowned Crane was done in a soft pencil (2B). The details were put in with a fibre pen (in this case a fine Pentel) then lightly brushed with clean water. It is a technique that needs practice, but it can produce pleasant results.

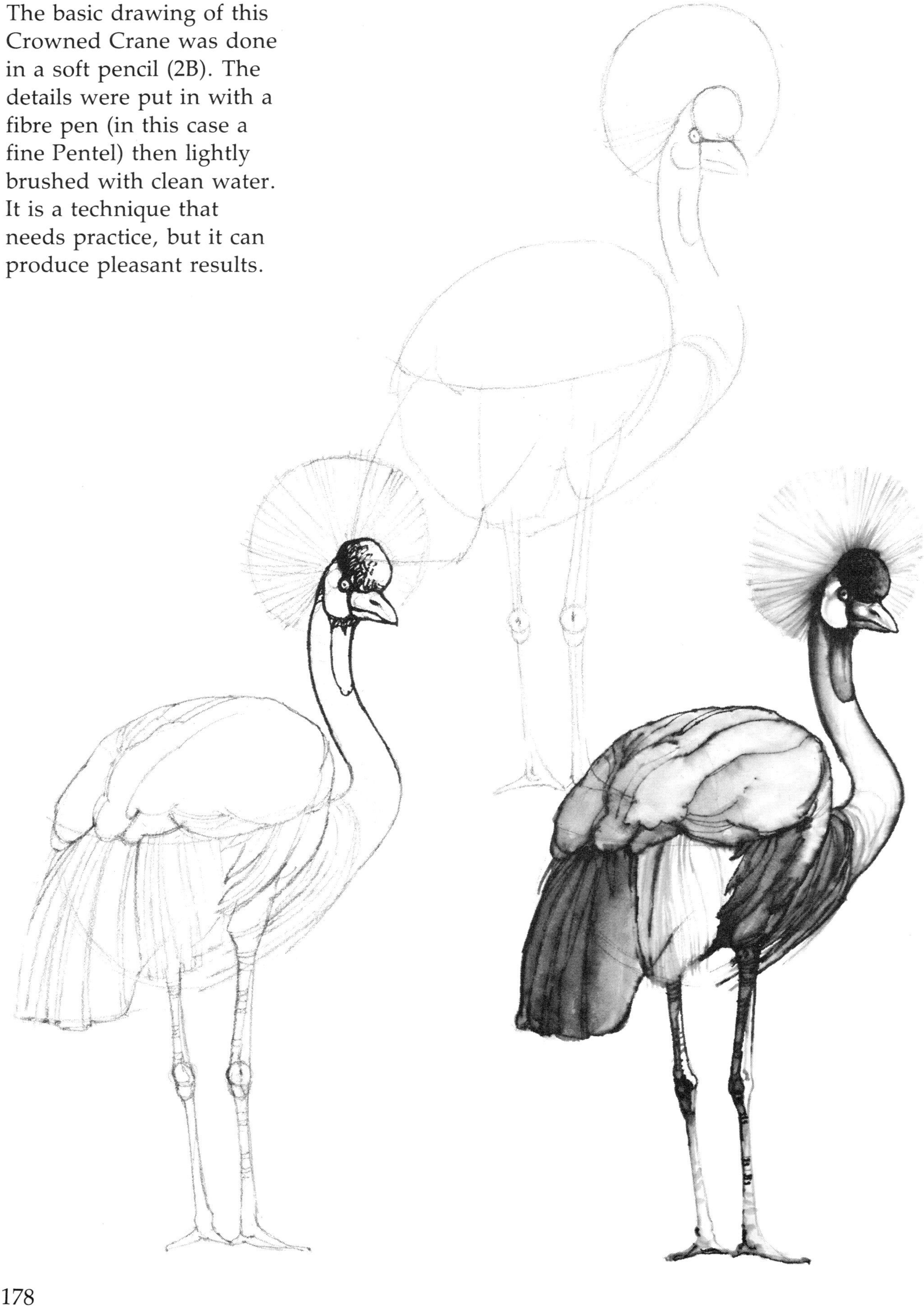

After drawing the basic shape of this ostrich, shading was added with the same HB pencil. The drawing was finished with a weak pale wash over the skin areas (using just a very small amount of black paint in a lot of water), and a stronger, darker wash over the body features.

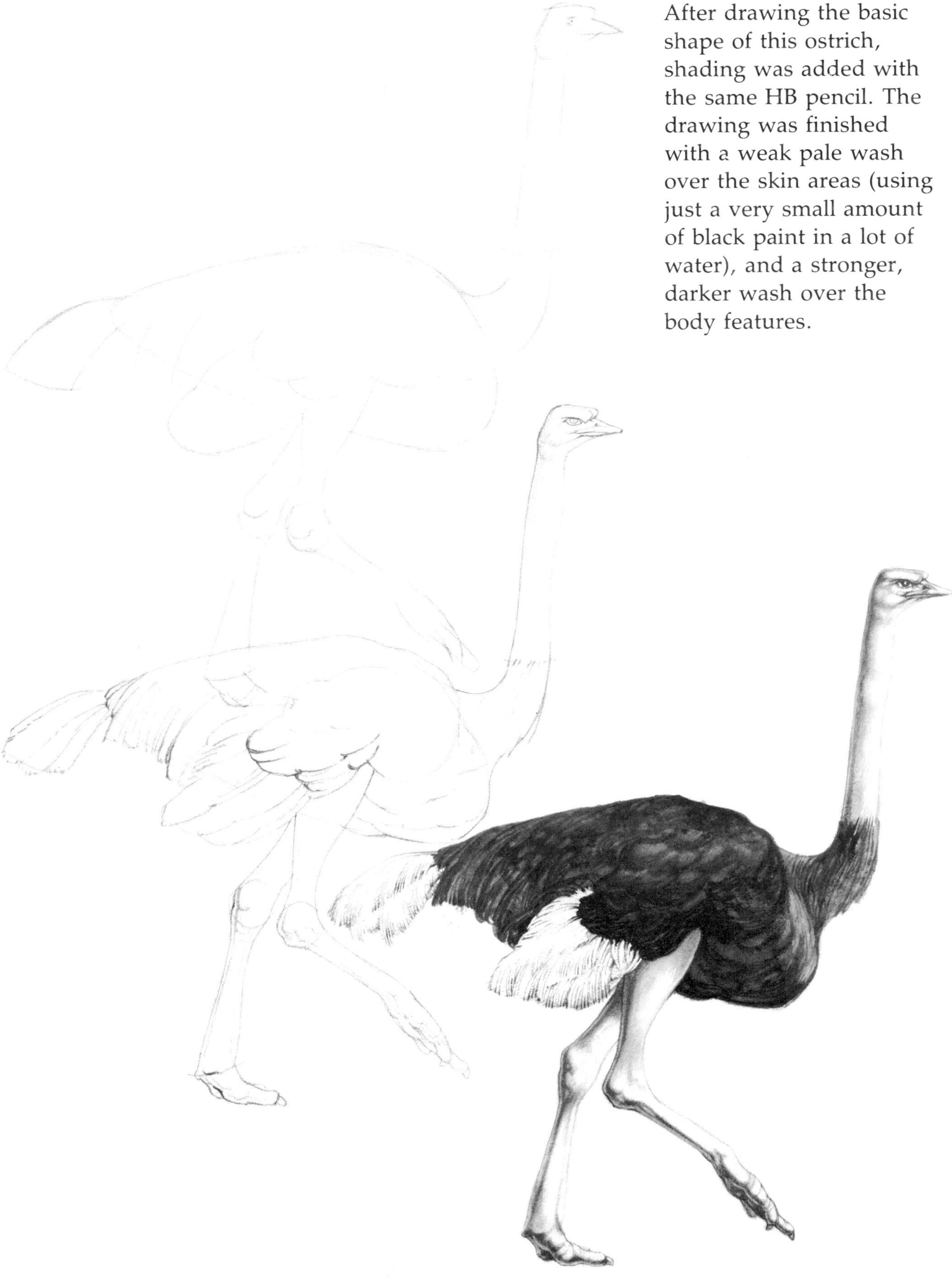

A hard charcoal pencil was used to capture the character of this raven. I used the pencil method described on page 173 to line up the various parts of the body.

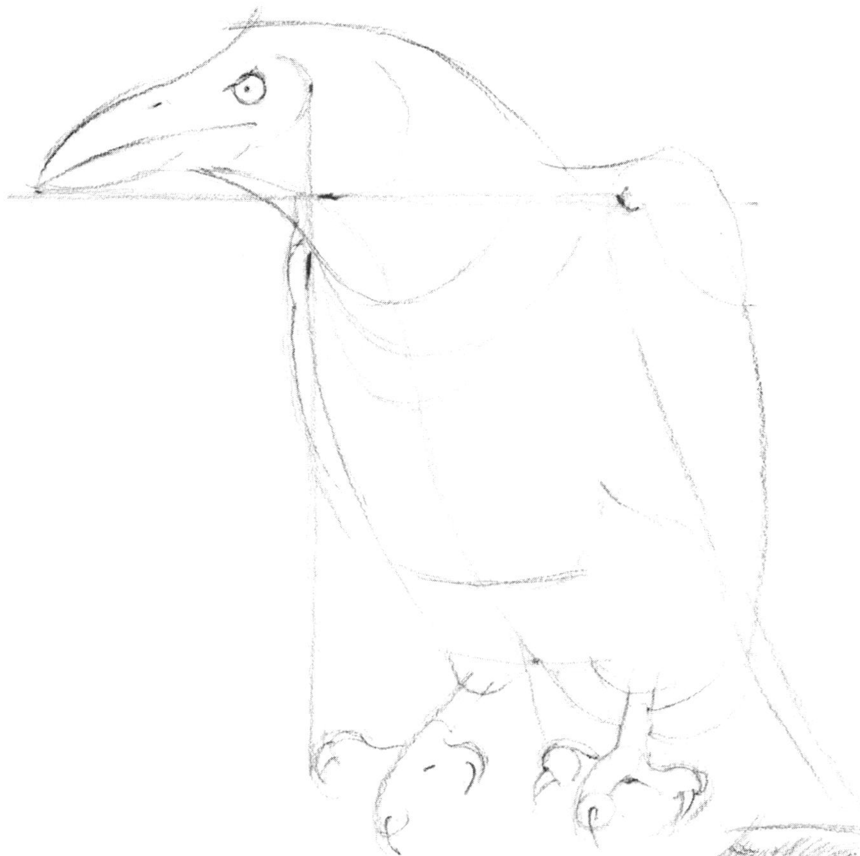

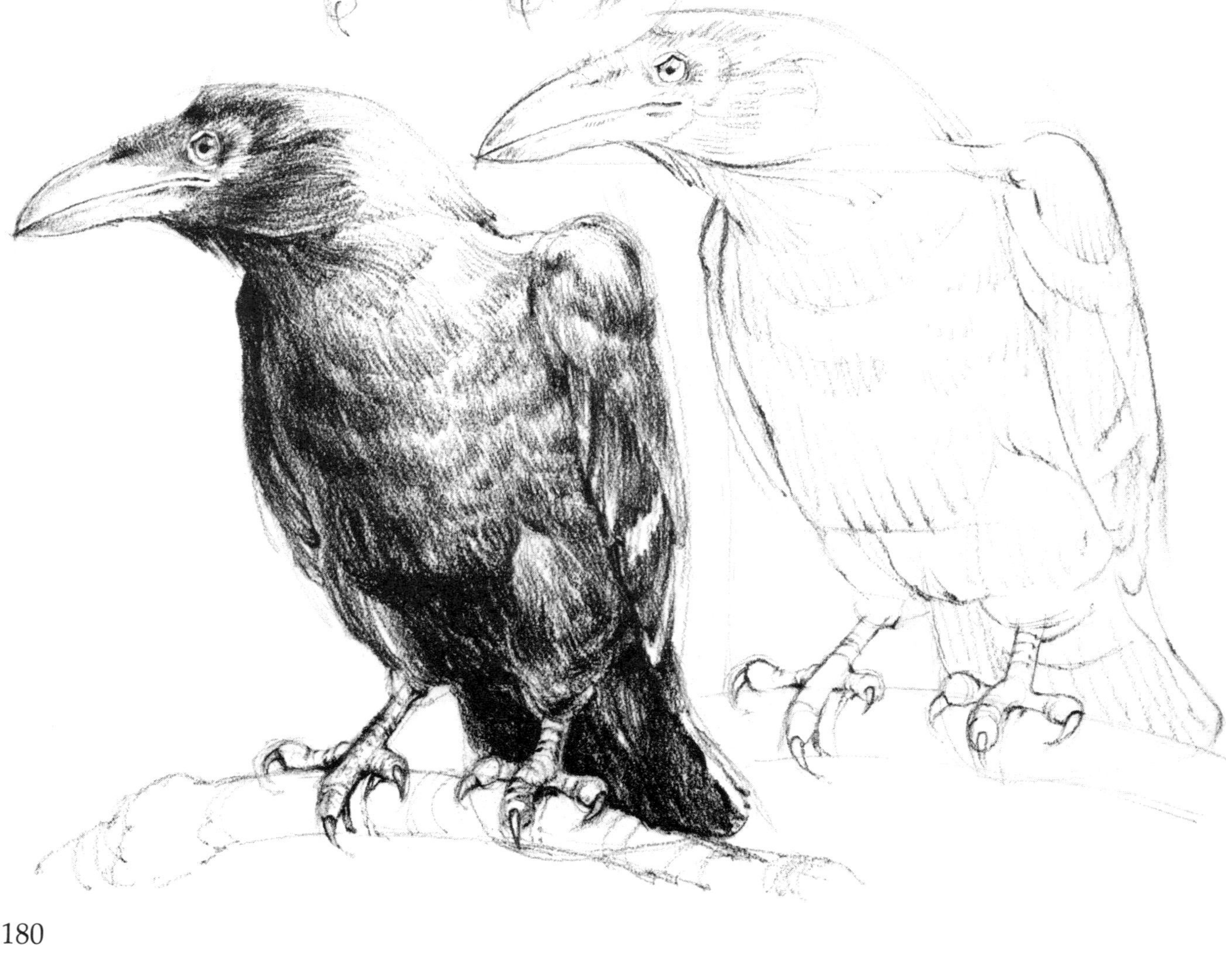

This magpie was drawn with a 6B pencil and rubbed over with a French stick (or smudge stick).

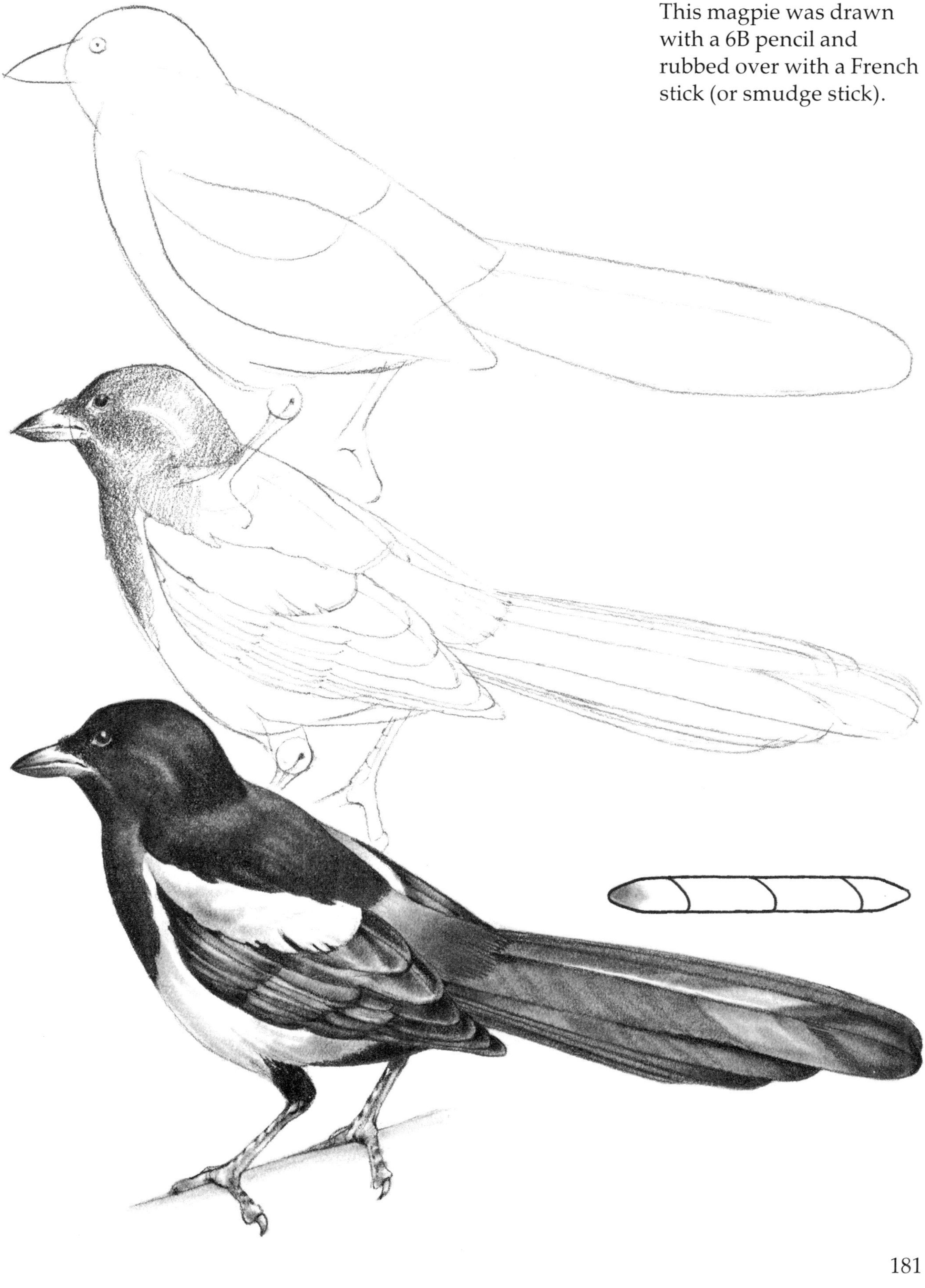

Action

When you first attempt to draw birds in action, choose the more simple and continuous actions, such as cleaning, eating and drinking.

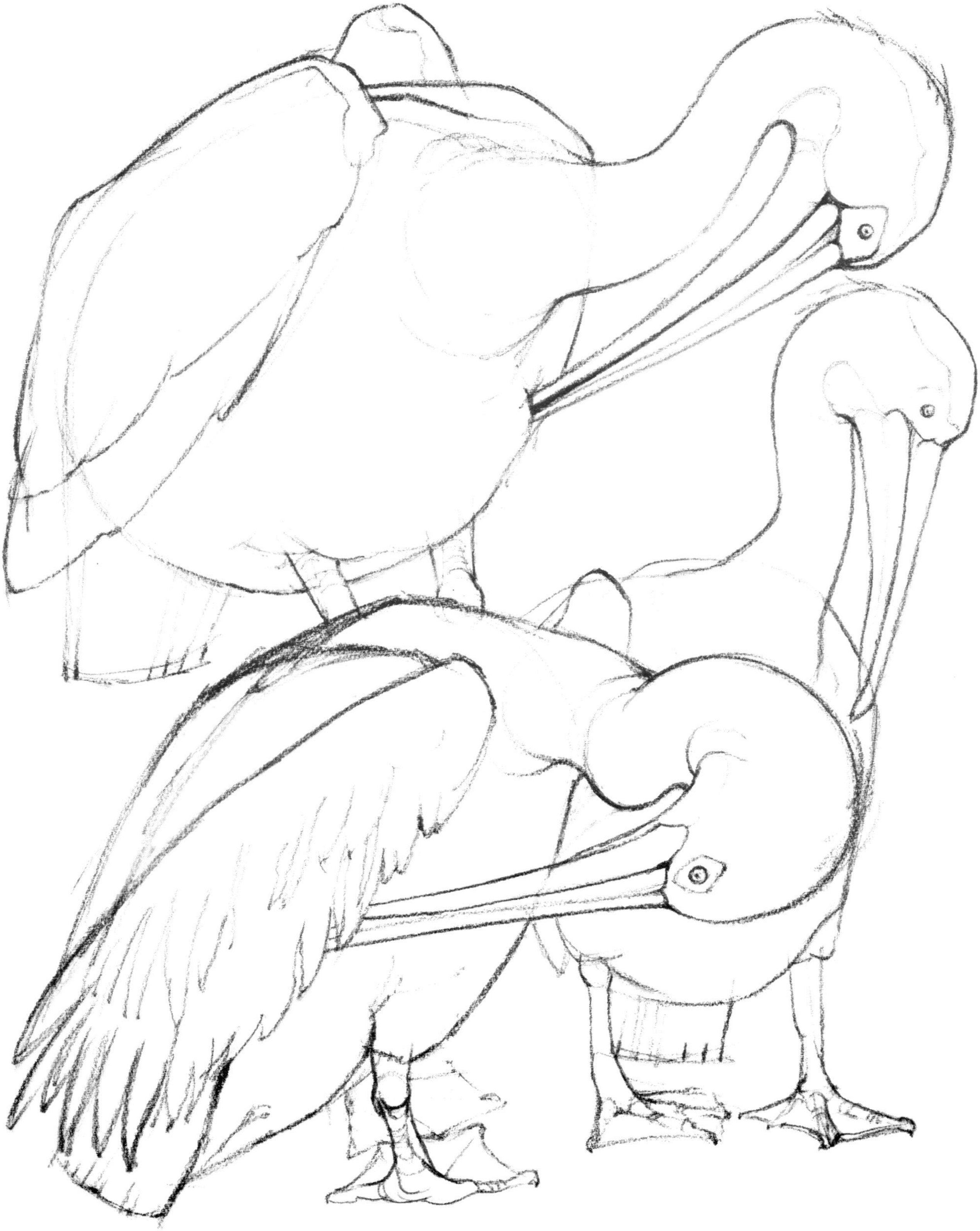

Draw quickly, ignoring details. Concentrate on capturing the basic shape (as in the small drawings here), and the movement in the pose. Facial and other details can be put in later.

Drawing live birds in flight is extremely difficult; but if you work from photographs (as you really must) make sure they are of good quality. Notice the wing and body movements of the various birds here and on pages 184–6.

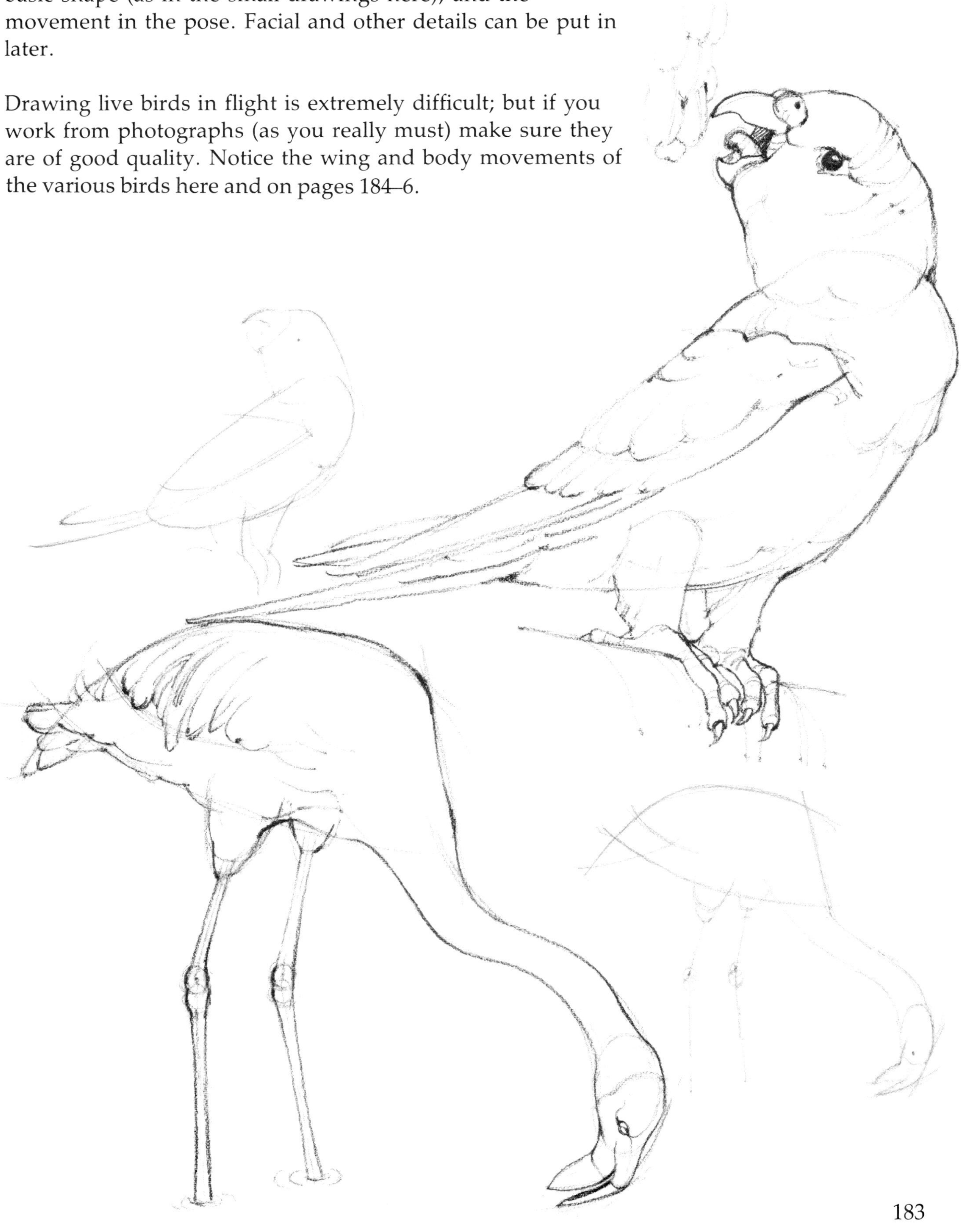

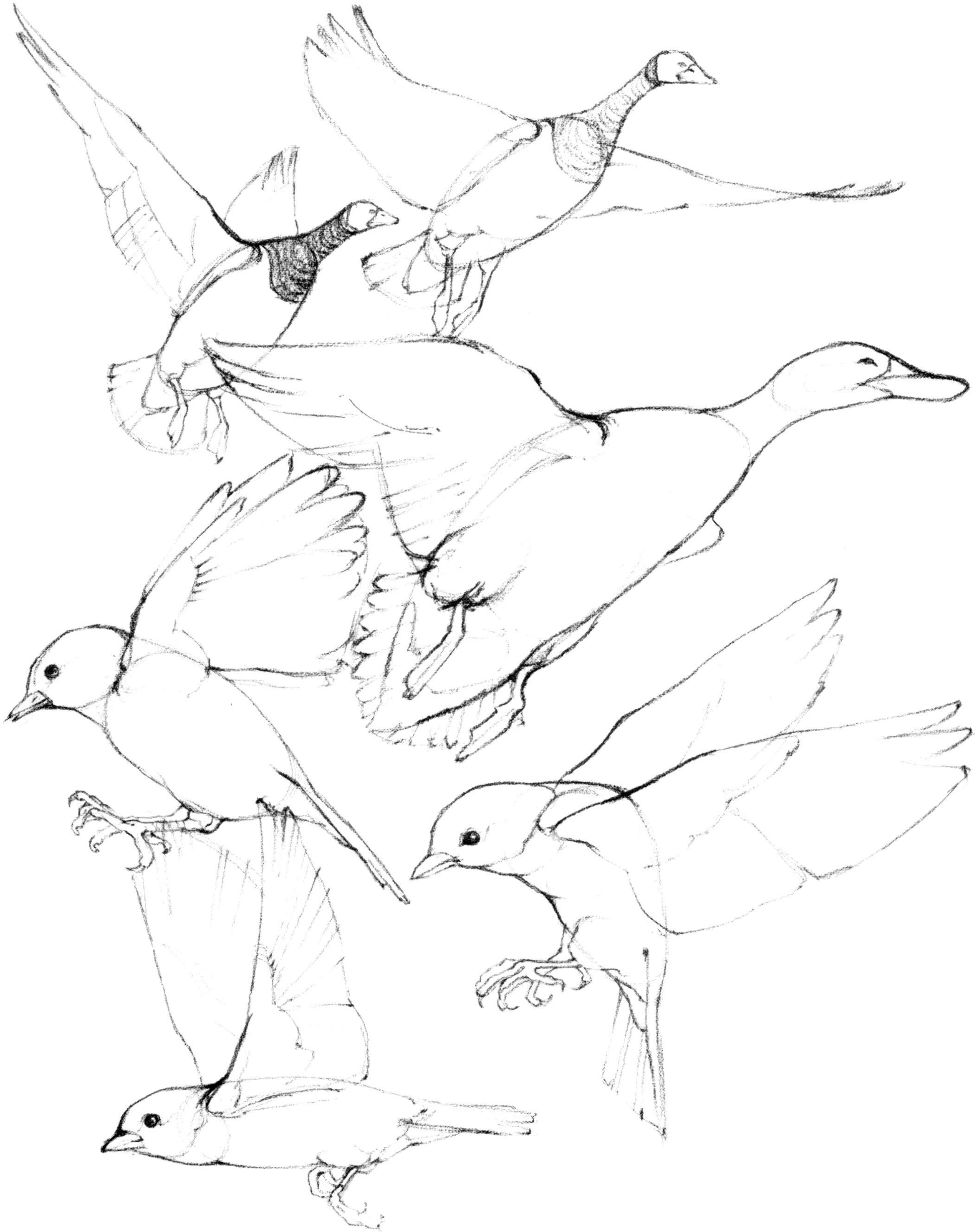

Be careful not to copy the two-dimensional image of a photograph; make yourself see the bird as living and three-dimensional. Construct your drawing.

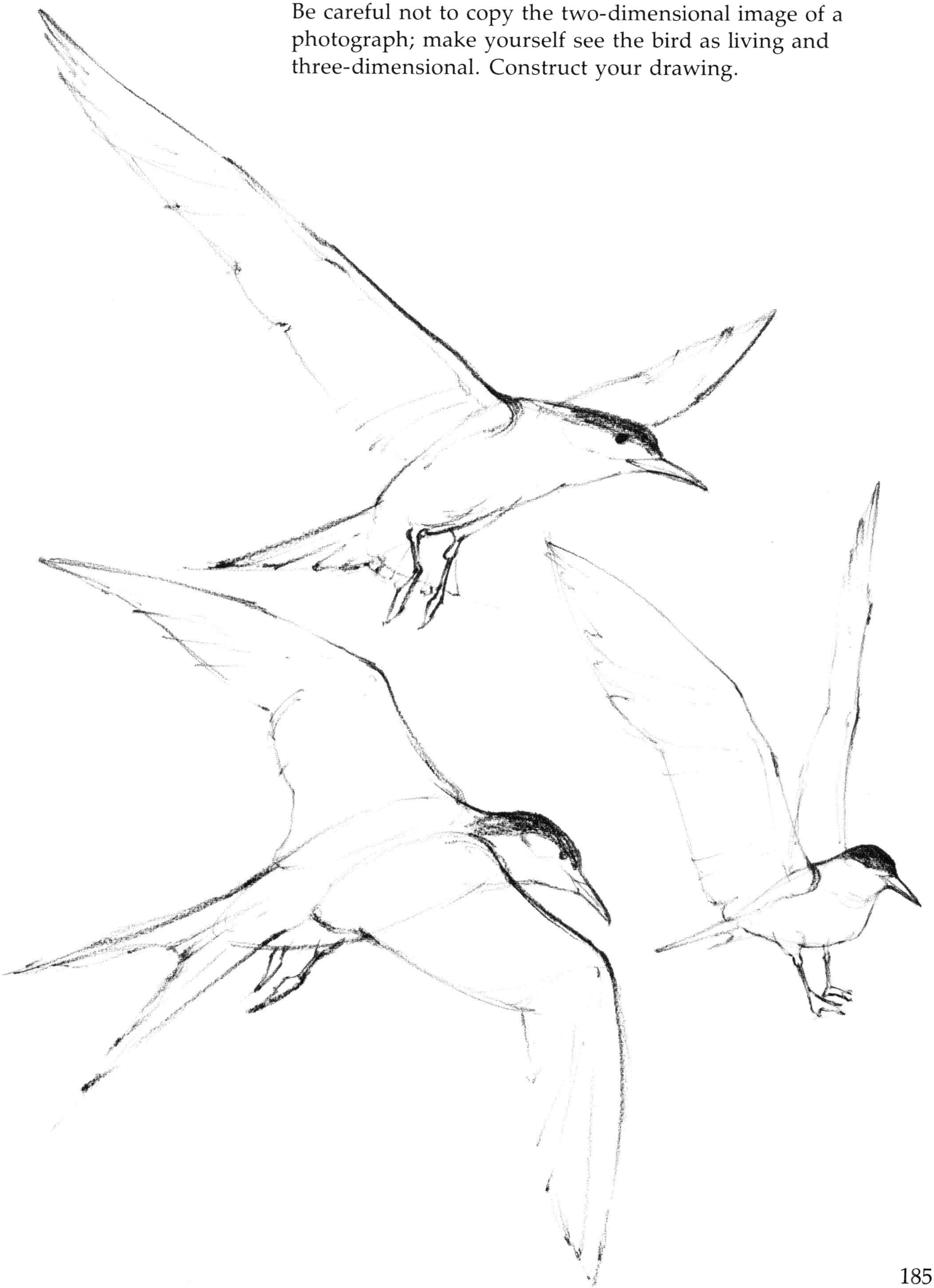

Notice how the head and wings fit into the body. Once again, draw quickly to produce lines full of movement.

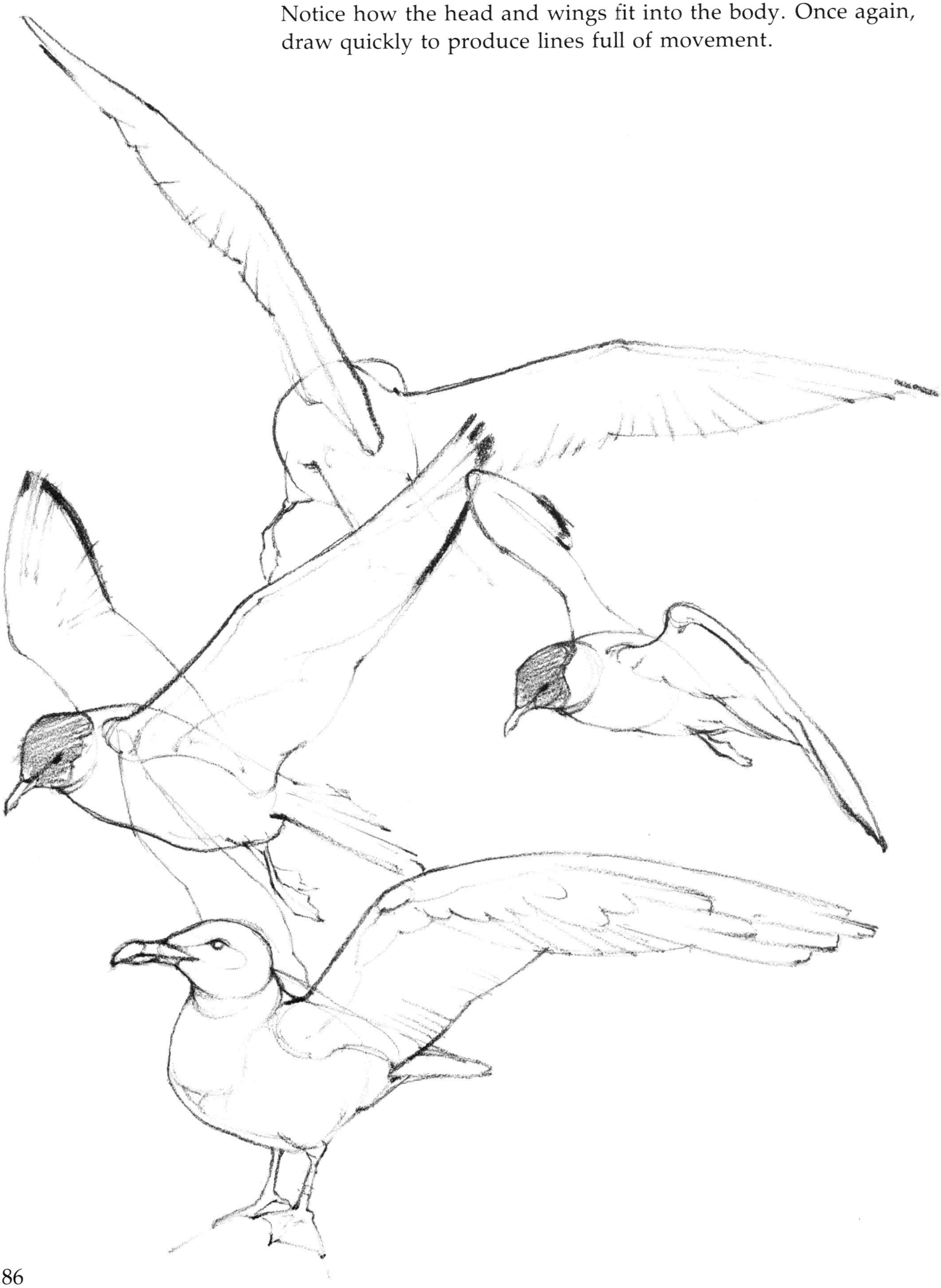

Tricks and techniques

This skylark was drawn with a fibre pen. I then used a candle for the light areas. Finally, I washed over the whole drawing (except the stomach area) with watered-down black paint. You can increase the darkness of a wash by mixing in more paint; use a watercolour board.

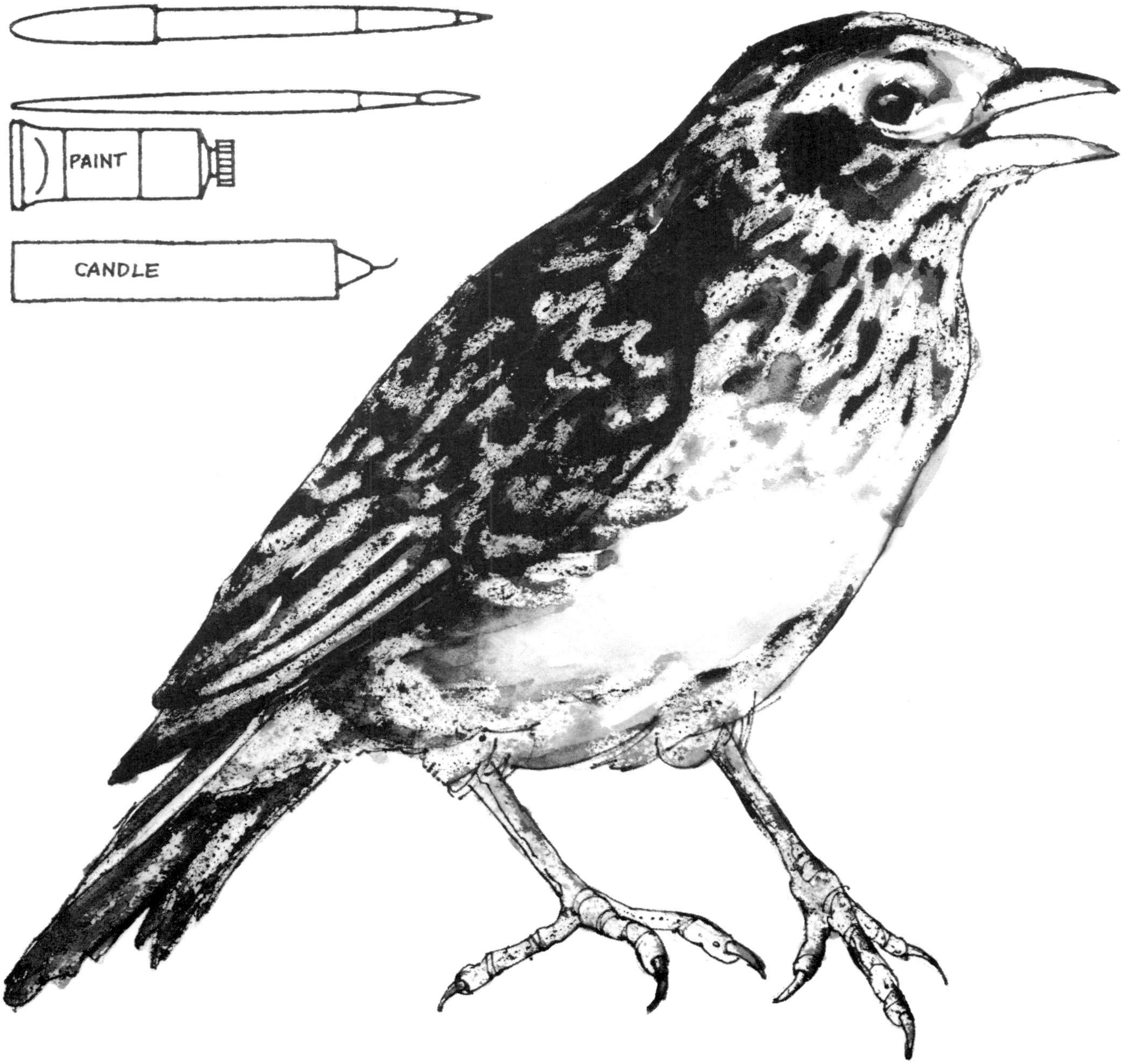

The Great Tit was drawn with pen and ink and dabbed with a finger when still wet. The thrush was drawn with a fibre pen and then some parts were lightly washed over with clean water. I used a rough cartridge paper.

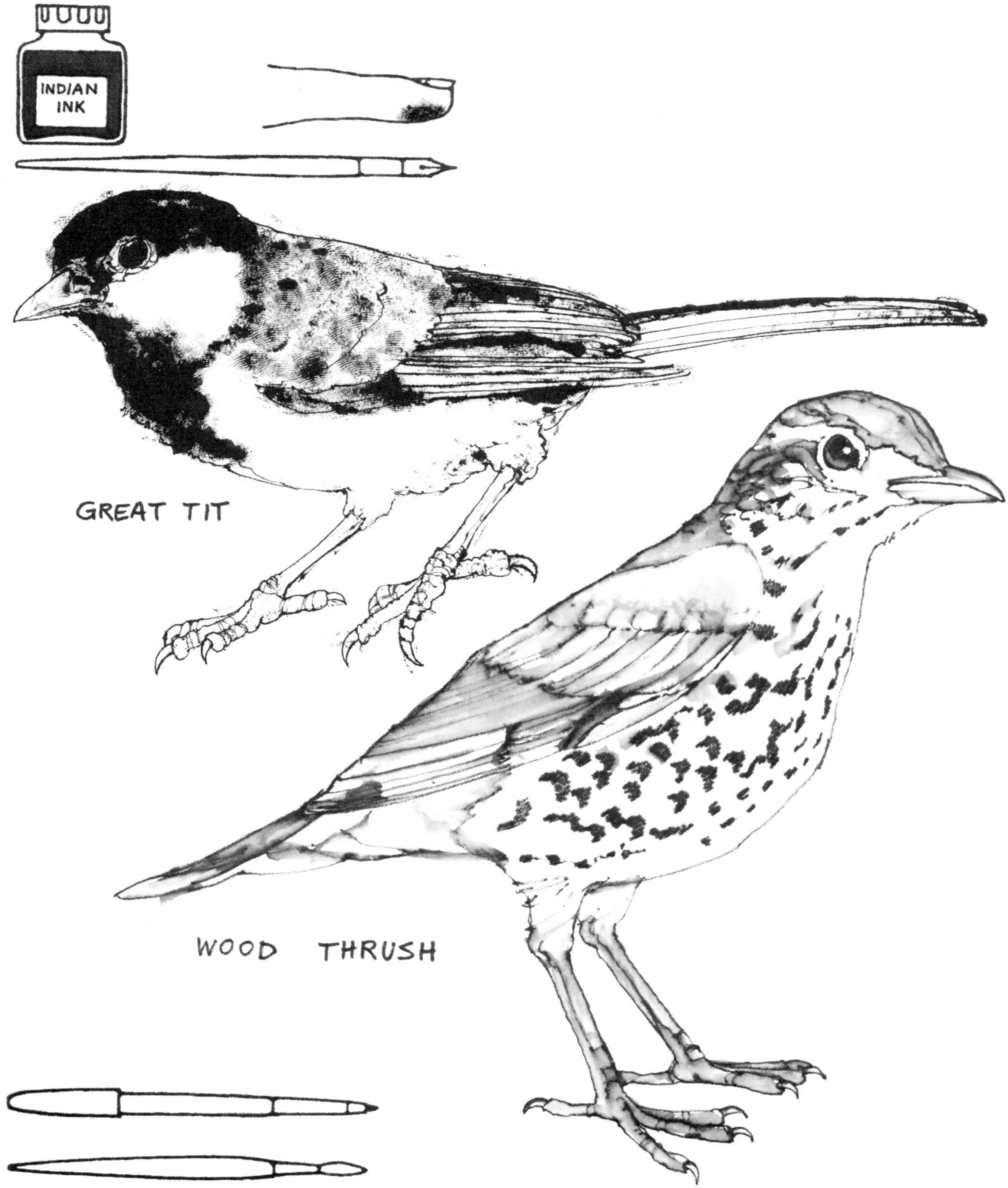

This macaw was drawn with a wax crayon on rough cartridge paper.

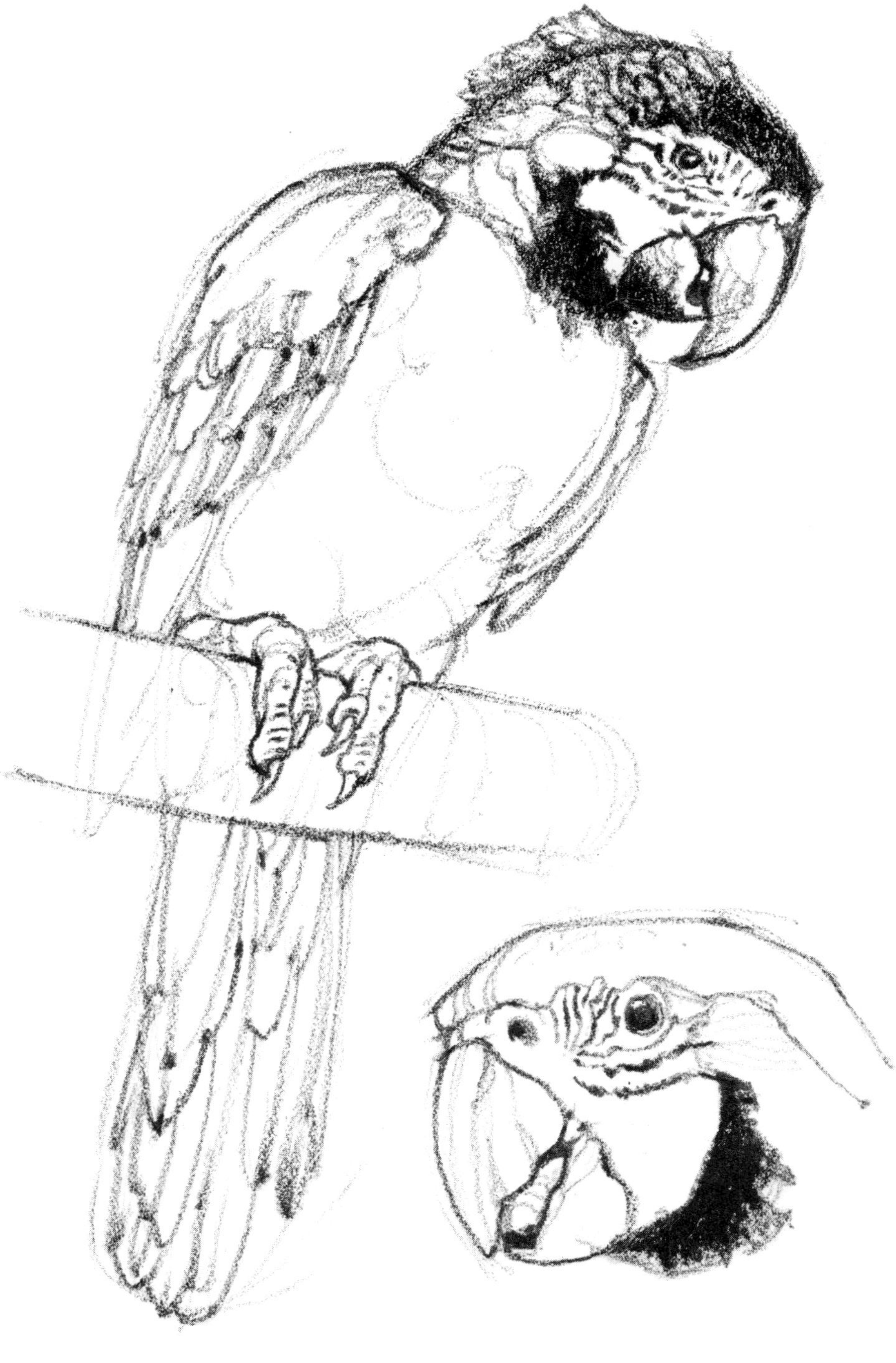

The magnificent Bald Eagle, emblem of the USA, was first drawn here with the *handle* of a brush dipped in ink and then painted with the brush's right end. I used a broad flat brush on rough board.

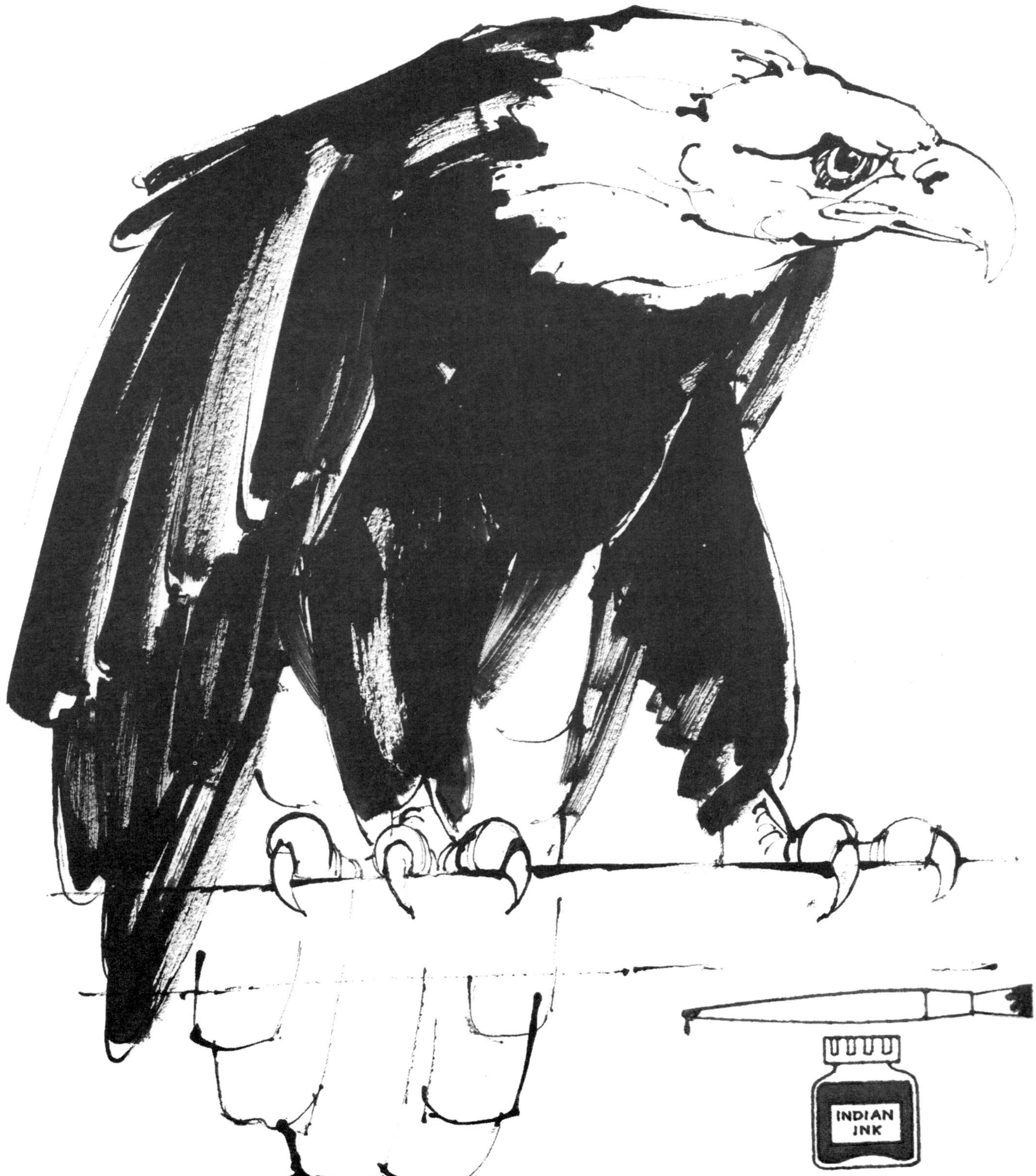

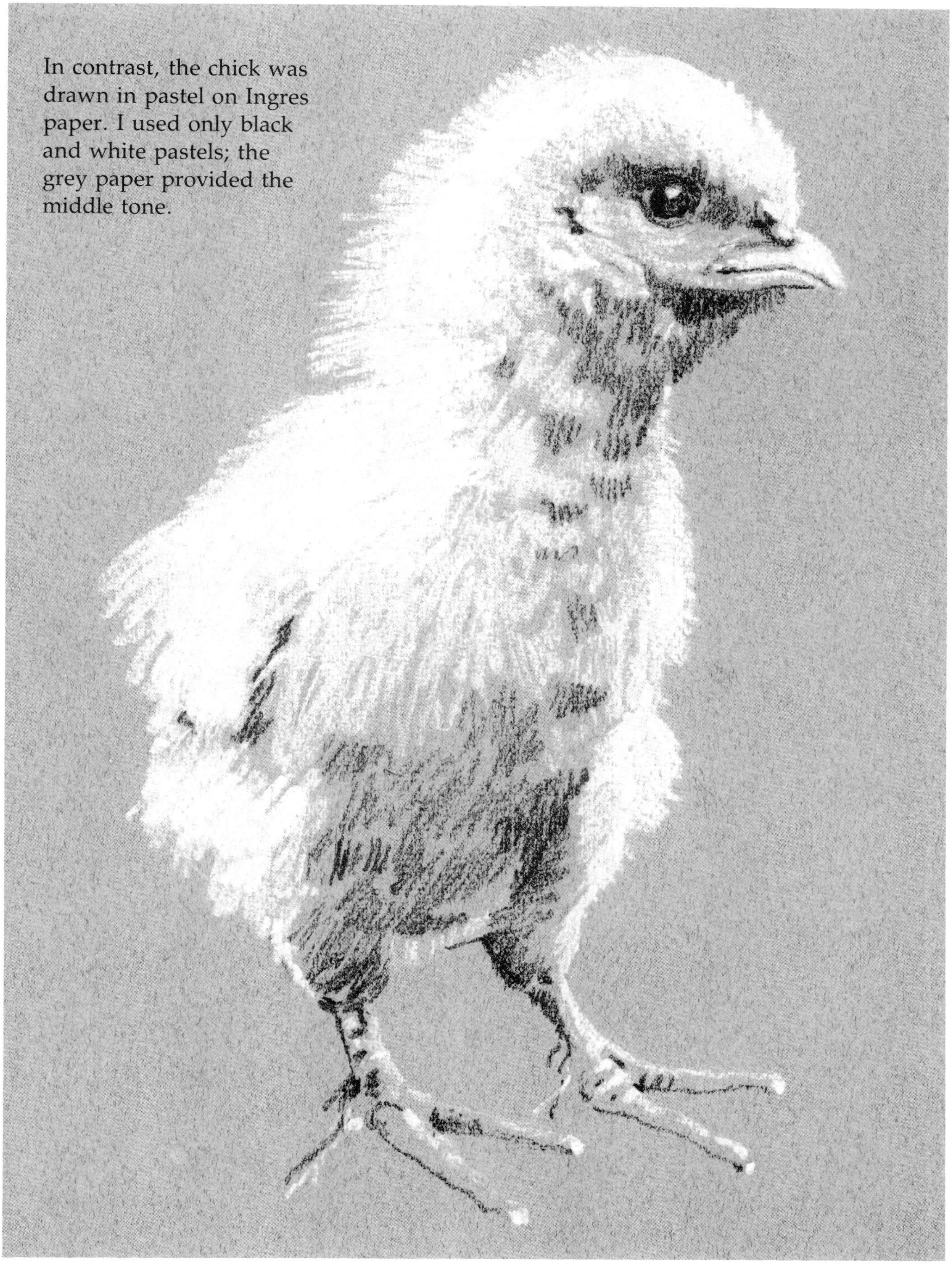

In contrast, the chick was drawn in pastel on Ingres paper. I used only black and white pastels; the grey paper provided the middle tone.

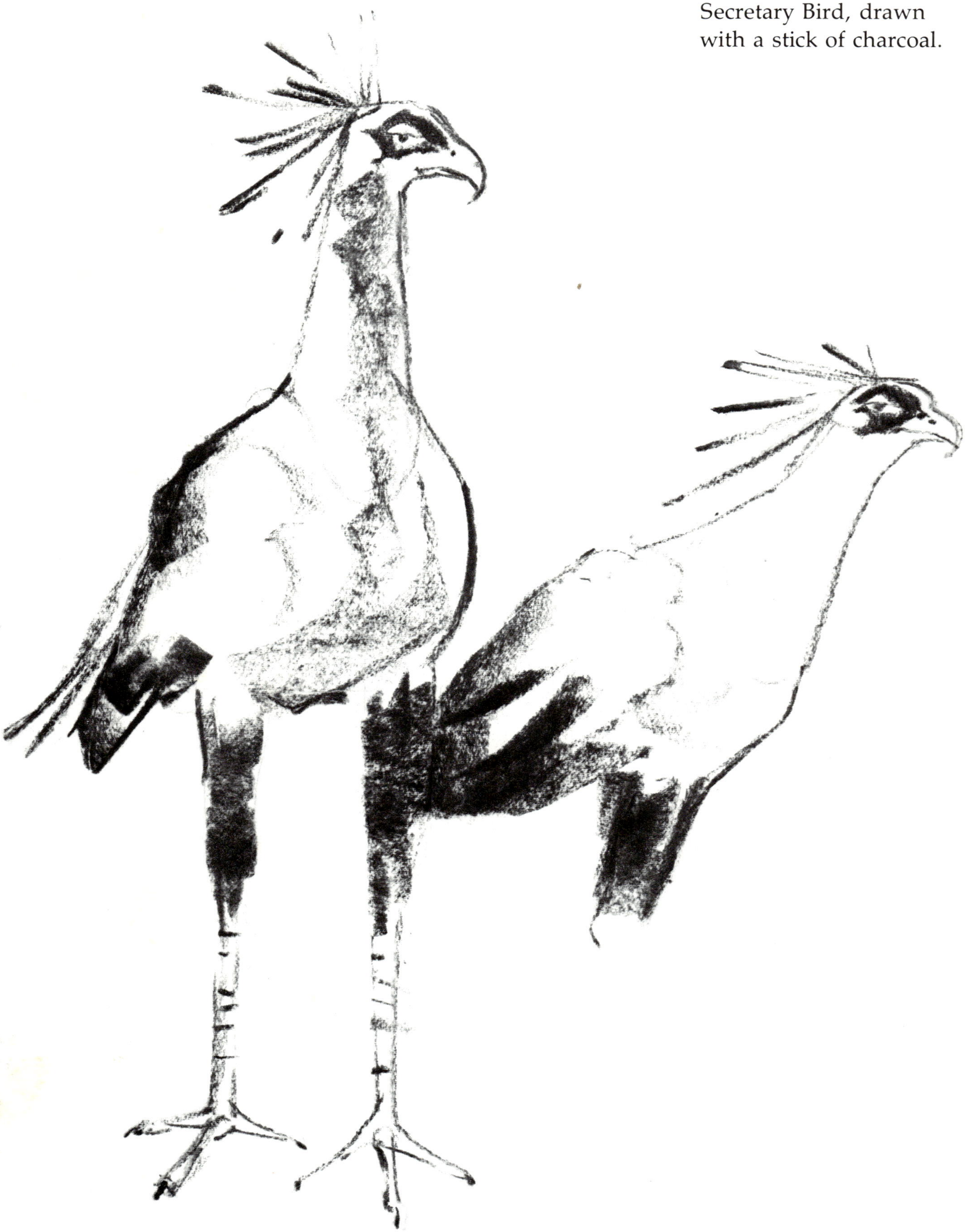

A snake-catching
Secretary Bird, drawn
with a stick of charcoal.